A CONCISE HISTORY
OF WARFARE

❖

Field-Marshal Viscount
Montgomery of Alamein

D1426128

WORDSWORTH EDITIONS

First published in Great Britain in 1968
by William Collins, Sons & Company Limited

Copyright © George Rainbird Limited 1968, 1972

This edition published 2000
by Wordsworth Editions Limited
Cumberland House, Crib Street, Ware,
Hertfordshire SG12 9ET

ISBN 1 84022 223 9

© Wordsworth Editions Limited 2000

Wordsworth® is a registered trade mark of
Wordsworth Editions Limited

Printed and bound in Great Britain
by Mackays of Chatham plc, Chatham, Kent.

CONTENTS

PREFACE

I HAVE NOT WRITTEN THIS BOOK TO GLORIFY WAR. I have sought to highlight the human endeavour of men and women which is brought out in wartime – on the home front as well as in battle. The need to understand this human factor and to avoid all unnecessary suffering and loss of life makes it vital that national leaders should be decisive regarding the political object of a war and should then give clear instructions to Service Chiefs on this and all other relevant matters. Two verses from the New Testament, Corinthians I 14, might well be their guide:

> 8. If the trumpet give an uncertain sound,
> who shall prepare himself to the battle?

> 9. Except ye utter by the tongue words easy to be
> understood, how shall it be known what is spoken?

The aim of the general must be not only to win wars but also to play his part in preventing them. Some years ago Winston Churchill said: 'Peace is the last prize I seek to win.' Nobody knows better than a soldier the overwhelming value of that prize, because nobody knows better than a soldier the monster called War.

In a full life I have seen much fighting in major conflicts, which have ended without the secure and lasting peace for which we fought. But I am not weighed down under despair in the world of politics and so-called peace in which we live in 1968; indeed, my gaze is hopefully directed forward and outward. It is in that sense that I offer this book to the public, dedicating it to my comrades-in-arms on the battlefields of Africa and Europe – many of whom gave their lives that we who remain might have that freedom in the West for which we all fought.

Thucydides, writing of the Peloponnesian War, is reputed to have said: 'If anybody shall pronounce what I have written to be useful, then I shall be satisfied.'

And that is exactly what I and my research team would like to say.

MONTGOMERY OF ALAMEIN
F.M.
ISLINGTON MILL,
ALTON, HAMPSHIRE

Author's Acknowledgements

THE LEADER OF MY RESEARCH TEAM, Alan Howarth, was a scholar at Rugby, then a major scholar at King's College, Cambridge, where he studied history. I could not have made a better choice. This very gifted, brilliant young graduate, only twenty-one when he joined me, brought to bear on our work the full power of his abilities, organizing the research and writing drafts of the historical chapters. He chose as his team-mate Anthony Wainwright who was at Rugby with him; he was at Loughborough College but agreed to leave before his time and join the team; he proved a splendid second to Alan Howarth. That was the research team – I the soldier and they the young historians. Some might wonder how it worked, the soldier being nearly eighty, and the historians only twenty-one! My answer is that it worked well; what they thought of me I have yet to learn; I thought the world of them and they helped to keep me young in my old age. There were no set office hours or trade union rules, it was solid work day in, day out, with no holidays; but we had a great deal of fun, and many happy days were spent together at my home in Hampshire.

Then I needed somebody who would help me by reading the chapters as they were produced, and comment freely. I looked for an experienced military historian; his further task would then be to draw battle sketchplans. I found exactly the right person I needed in Anthony Brett-James, Lecturer in Military History at the R.M.A. Sandhurst, and himself an author of military works. His knowledge and help were invaluable.

We had behind us the experience and willing help of the editorial staff of George Rainbird Ltd. I must also mention our typist, Miss Bunney. Finally, we received most valuable help from the Chief Librarian at the Ministry of Defence, Mr D. W. King, O.B.E., F.L.A., and his staff.

MONTGOMERY OF ALAMEIN
F.M.

A CONCISE HISTORY
OF WARFARE

1 The Nature of War

War is not the concern of soldiers only. Throughout history civil life has always been affected by warfare, and the history of warfare is worth studying by everybody. In this book my emphasis will be upon strategy and tactics, leadership and weapons. Where more general historical factors are discussed they will be those scientific, technological, social, economic or political factors which have affected the history of warfare. My hope is that the reader will feel he is absorbed in a momentous and engrossing story.

Man's progress in all fields has been basically affected for good and for ill by the impact of armed conflict – the process and verdict of war, time and again, shaping history. It is impossible to study the history of warfare as if war has existed in a vacuum. As just one example, some historians have suggested that the beginning of large-scale metal industries was due to a certain extent to the demand for cannon (though I must admit that others claim it was due to the need for church bells!).

Why do wars happen? Some will say that war is the child of civilization, others that war stems from raw human nature. But war has always been the arbiter when other methods of reaching agreement have failed.

With nomadic peoples, such as the Magyars, movements of population mainly determined by the locations of good grazing lands and the prospects of easy plunder were the cause of war. The Persian wars, on the other hand, were fought to save Greece, and therefore Europe, from Asiatic tyranny. The Roman empire was established by warfare, and warfare contributed to its destruction; the same is true of the German empire created by Bismarck. There was a time when religion was one of the great causes of international strife. Later, the possession of colonies brought wealth to the colonial powers of western Europe, wealth which was gained by armed strength; it was commercial rivalry that then pushed nations into conflict.

At this stage some definitions may be useful. War is any prolonged conflict between rival political groups by force of arms. It includes insurrection and civil war. It excludes riots and acts of individual violence. Grand strategy is the co-ordination and direction of all the resources of a nation, or group of nations, towards the attainment of the political object of the war – the goal defined by the fundamental policy. *The true objective of Grand Strategy must be a secure and lasting peace.* Strategy is the art of distributing and applying military means, such as armed forces and supplies, to fulfil the ends of policy. The strategical background to a campaign or battle is of great significance. What was the aim? What was the commander trying to achieve? An objective may be very desirable strategically; but that which is strategically desirable must be tactically possible with the forces and means available.

Tactics means the dispositions for, and control of, military forces and techniques in actual fighting.

Throughout history certain factors have been constant in warfare. Since the earliest days there have been the problems of movement and of firepower: how to be able to move one's own forces freely and to prevent the enemy from moving. The requirements of mobility, firepower and security have always to a certain extent conflicted. The development of the armoured fighting vehicle, dominating the land battle as it ranges over ever wider fronts, and the parallel development of wireless communications to maintain control over distances previously considered unthinkable – these are only recent forms of one of the fundamental exercises of war.

Seapower has had a decisive influence on warfare since very ancient times. In their wars against the Persians the Athenians realized that the enemy could not be beaten so long as the Persian fleet could transport men and supplies across the Aegean and land them at will along the Greek seaboard. Athens, by a supreme effort, built up her naval power and defeated the Persians in the sea battle of Salamis in 480 B.C. The Persian campaign ended a year later. Greece then dominated the eastern Mediterranean, enjoying an age of commercial prosperity and producing a great civilization. Similarly, Rome collided with the mercantile state of Carthage in North Africa, whose navy controlled the western Mediterranean, and found that it was necessary to become a naval power to defeat her.

It was because Britain had defeated the French and Spanish fleets at Trafalgar that the invasion of England was rendered impossible and in 1808 a British army was able to land in Portugal. Some years later Britain beat Napoleon, who wielded far greater military power but was confined to a land strategy. Seapower has been just as important in more recent history. Because the Allies were masters of the sea, Alamein was fought and won. If they had not been able to build up their forces and supplies faster than Rommel the issue would have been lost, and with it Egypt, the Suez Canal, and possibly the whole of the Middle East. The lesson is this: in all history the nation which has had control of the seas has, in the end, prevailed.

Air power, when developed to its full potential, made a profound impact on war at sea, as well as on land. In 1941 and 1942 the Japanese showed in south-east Asia and the Pacific what could be attempted with superior sea and air power. At Pearl Harbour on 7th December 1941 they revealed the tremendous offensive power of a carrier task force, launching over 300 aircraft which sank most of the battleships of the U.S. Pacific Fleet. In 1942 two naval battles were fought between American and Japanese naval forces which clearly demonstrated the dominant role of air power in modern naval warfare. The first was in the Coral Sea between 4th and 8th May, when the U.S. fleet foiled a Japanese amphibious attack on Port Moresby and removed the threat to Australia. The second was off Midway Island between 3rd and 6th June. These two naval battles marked the real turning point of the war against Japan. The action in the Coral Sea was remarkable as being the first naval battle in which the opposing warships never once sighted each other – not one direct shot was exchanged.

In war on land the advent of the aeroplane enabled commanders to see 'the other side of the hill'. As air power grew and developed it was able to prevent movement in daylight to any appreciable degree, so much so that it became necessary to gain mastery in the air before beginning a land battle. The mighty weapon of air power enabled armies to win victories more quickly than before and to win them with fewer casualties. Air bombing could also carry war deep into the heart of the opponent's homelands, causing heavy civilian casualties and tremendous damage to property on the home front, with a cumulative adverse effect on the war effort of the nation so attacked.

Generalship is a theme which will run like a golden thread throughout this book. 'Captaincy', or leadership in the higher sense, is of supreme importance in warfare. A leader must have the ability to make the right decisions and the courage to act on the decisions. The qualities that go to make a military leader are, of course, the qualities most prized in other fields, such as industry and politics.

A commander must know what he himself wants. He must see his objective clearly and then strive to attain it; he must let his subordinates know what he wants and what are the fundamentals of his policy. He must, in fact, give firm guidance and a clear lead. It is necessary for him to create what I would call 'atmosphere', and in that atmosphere his staff and subordinate commanders will live and work. Nelson's genius, for example, lay very much in the ability to create such atmosphere. He must have the 'drive' to get things done; he must have the character and ability which will inspire confidence in his subordinates. Above all, he must have that moral courage, that resolution, and that determination which will enable him to stand firm when the issue hangs in the balance. Only one thing is certain in battle, and that is that everything will be uncertain. Therefore one of the greatest assets a commander can have is the ability to radiate confidence in the plan and operations even (perhaps especially) when he is not too sure in his own mind about the outcome. To achieve this with all those under his command, a commander-in-chief must watch carefully his own morale. A battle is, in effect, a contest between two wills – his own and that of the enemy commander. If his heart begins to fail him when the issue hangs in the balance his opponent will probably win.

I believe that generals can be divided broadly into two classes. To make the distinction I will use two very expressive French definitions. *Le bon général ordinaire* is the general who is good so long as his superior will tell him in detail what to do, will stand by him and help him, and will see that he does what he is told. *Le grand chef* requires only a general directive covering the operations which are envisaged; he requires no detailed instructions, he knows what to do and can safely be left alone to do it; he is a very rare bird. As we study the commanders of history we shall have the opportunity to decide to which class each belongs.

But generals can be judged fairly only in the exercise of their own profession and on military grounds. Some campaigns have been undertaken, and some battles have been fought, for political reasons only; those have been the graveyard of the reputation of many soldiers.

Intelligence and Secret Service must never be underrated by a commander. Polybius wrote that a general must 'apply himself to learn the inclinations and character of his adversary'; about two thousand years later, Moltke, chief of the general staff of Prussia, said to his officers: 'You will usually find that the enemy has three courses open to him; of these, he will adopt the fourth.' A good military leader must dominate the events which encompass him; once events get the better of him he will lose the confidence of his men, and when that happens he ceases to be of value as a leader. He has therefore got to anticipate enemy reactions to his own moves, and to take quick steps to prevent enemy interference with his own plans. For these reasons a first class Intelligence organization is essential and the head of it must be an officer of brilliant intellectual qualities, who need not necessarily be a professional fighting man. He must be a very clear thinker, able to sort out the essentials from the mass of incidental factors which bear on every problem concerning the enemy. Service Intelligence organizations must be in the closest touch with the Secret Service.

In all Secret Service activities, the operations of spies, saboteurs and secret agents are regarded as outside the scope of law. Nevertheless history shows that no nation will shrink from such activities if they further its vital interests.

I always had in my caravans during Hitler's war a picture or photograph of my opponent. In the desert, and again in Normandy, my opponent was Rommel; I would study his face and see if I could fathom his likely reaction to any action I might set in motion; in some curious way this helped me. I must admit that I do not know of any other commander-in-chief – except Slim – who adopted the same practice! Yet it has always been a prime necessity for a commander to seek to understand the mind of his opponent. Any battle can very quickly go off the rails. If this should happen the initiative may well pass to the enemy. If there is one lesson which I have learnt in my long military career it is that without holding the initiative it is not possible to win.

While the factors of command and control play a large part in the winning of battles, the greatest single factor making for success is the spirit of the warrior. The best way to achieve a high morale in wartime is by success in battle.

The raw material with which the general has to deal is men. *Battles are won primarily in the hearts of men.* An army is not merely a collection of individuals with so many tanks and guns, and its strength is not just the total of all these added together. The real strength of an army is, and must be, far greater than the sum of its parts; that extra strength is provided by morale, by fighting spirit, by mutual confidence between the leaders and the led (and especially between field leaders and the high command), and by many other intangible spiritual qualities. Pent up in men are great emotional forces which have to be given an outlet in a way which is positive; which warms the heart and excites the imagination. If the approach to the human problem is cold and impersonal, a commander will achieve little; but if he can gain the trust and confidence of his men, and they feel their best interests are safe in his hands, then he has in his possession a priceless asset and the greatest achievements become possible.

Generals are meant to win battles, but the good general of today will do so with the least possible loss of life. Throughout the Middle Ages in the Western world the manpower of a nation was considered of small account; the serf was expendable in battle. Then came the series of epidemics in Europe in the fourteenth century known as the Black Death; manpower was scarce, the economic value of the serf increased, and his life had to be safeguarded. In modern times when a nation goes to war the ranks of its armed forces are filled with men from civil life who are not soldiers, sailors or airmen by profession – and who never wanted to be. Such men are very different from the serf or the mercenary of by-gone days; they are educated, they can think, they can appreciate and they are prepared to criticize. They want to know what is going on, and what the general wants them to do, and why, and when; they also want to know that in the doing of it their best interests will be absolutely secure in the general's hands. And, of course, they want to see him and decide in their own minds what sort of person he is.

Discipline and comradeship are also crucial. Why does the soldier leave the protection of his trench or hole in the ground and go forward in the face of shot and shell? It is because of the leader who is in front of him and his comrades who are around him. Comradeship makes a man feel warm and courageous when all his instincts tend to make him cold and afraid. The human side to warfare which, unfortunately, has often been neglected by historians. It will be referred to frequently throughout this book and for that I make no apology, because it is the crux of the whole matter. Tiredness, fear, appalling conditions, great privations, the virtual certainty of wounds and the probability of death – all will be faced by the fighting man if he has a stout heart, knows what he is fighting for, has confidence in his officers and his comrades, and if he knows he will never be required to do anything which is not possible.

Modern war is *total war* and over the centuries has become very complicated, embracing the life and activities of a nation to an ever increasing extent – so that the morale of the whole nation is involved. In the days of levies and mercenaries comparatively few men did the fighting or were engaged in the national war effort. But today the whole manpower of a nation, and womanpower too, together with its industrial strength, is mobilized to provide the necessary sinews of war. Furthermore today, whether a man is drafted to the fighting services or employed in industry, he is subject to dangers almost wherever he may be. Generalship is the science and art of command. It is a science in that it must be studied theoretically by officers, and an art because the theory must then be put to practical use. Above all, it involves an intimate knowledge of human nature. Mao Tse-tung, no mean commander, has written (*Selected Military Writings*):

All military laws and military theories which are in the nature of principles are the experience of past wars summed up by people in former days or in our own times. We should seriously study these lessons, paid for in blood, which are a heritage of past wars. That is one point. But there is another. We should put these conclusions to the test of our own experience, assimilating what is useful, rejecting what is useless, and adding what is specifically our own.

Both study and practice are necessary. The first is always possible and there is no excuse for its neglect; the opportunity for the second may not often come.

My own reading and study of military history has been extensive, but it has been confined mostly to books written by British historians during my own lifetime. I did make attempts to read the writings of Clausewitz and Jomini but I couldn't take them in. I decided that I would learn more if I turned to more recent historians, and particularly if I studied the lives of the great captains of the past to learn how they thought and acted, and how they used the military means at their disposal. A knowledge of the detailed dispositions of an army at any time was not what mattered to me; I wanted to know the essential problem which confronted the general at a certain moment in the battle, what were the factors which influenced his decision, what was his decision – and why. I wanted to discover what was in the great man's mind when he made a major decision. This, surely, was the way to study generalship.

Of the military historians of my own nation, language and times, I found Sir Basil Liddell Hart far and away the best; his military thinking has always appealed to me and it had a definite influence on my own conduct of war. Some historians are wise after the event; Liddell Hart was wise before the event – a prophet at last honoured in his own country. Where he stands supreme is that not only is he an historian, but he is also a theorist, and has produced from his vast knowledge a philosophy of war; and unlike many theorists he has generally proved to be right.

The great captains have always been serious students of military history; T. E. Lawrence rightly said that we of the twentieth century have two thousand years of experience behind us, and, if we still must fight, we have no excuse for not fighting well. My reading over the years has convinced me that nobody can become a supreme practitioner of war unless he has first studied and pondered its science. The conduct of war is a life study and if the study has been neglected a general can expect no success. Of course, certain natural gifts are also essential: the power of rapid decision, sound judgment, boldness at the right moment, toughness.

The general has to create the fighting machine and forge the weapon to his own liking. This involves a profound knowledge of the conduct of war, and of training. He also has to create an organization at headquarters which will enable the weapon to be wielded properly. I very soon learnt by hard experience that the administrative situation in rear must be commensurate with what I wanted to achieve in battle in the forward area. The fighting machine must be so set in motion, at the appropriate time, that it can develop its maximum power rapidly. The troops must be launched into battle in a way which promises the best prospect of success – and the troops must know this. The 'stage-management' of the battle must be first-class. A main responsibility of a general is to organize training, not only for the campaign which is to be opened up but also for any particular battle during the campaign. The fighting man must have confidence in his weapons and in his ability to use them effectively in all types of situation, of ground, and of climate. This confidence can be achieved only by intensive training – which, if successful, will raise morale.

The essence of tactical methods in battle lies in the following factors: surprise, concentration of effort, co-operation of all arms, control, simplicity, speed of action, the initiative.

A commander has got to be a very clear thinker: able to sort out the essentials from the mass of lesser factors which bear on every problem. Once he has grasped the essentials of the problem which faces him, he must never lose sight of them – he must never allow a mass of detail to submerge what is essential to success. The ability to simplify without falsification and to select from the mass of detail those things and only those things which are important, is not always so easy. The general must have this capacity for essential detail, without loss of vision. He is likely to fail unless he has an ice-clear brain at all times and a disciplined mind; this implies being abstemious, particularly in drinking.

The plan of operations must be made by the commander; it must not be forced on him by his staff, or by circumstances, and never by the enemy. Most opponents are at their best if they are allowed to dictate the battle; they are not so good when they are thrown off balance by manoeuvre and are forced to react to your own movements and thrusts. Surprise is essential. Strategical surprise may often be difficult, if not impossible, to obtain; but tactical surprise is always possible and must be given an essential place in planning. The enemy must be forced to dance to your tune all the time. This means that the commander must foresee his battle. He must decide in his own mind, and before the battle begins, how he wants operations to develop; he must then use the military effort at his disposal to force the battle to swing the way he wants. My own military doctrine was based on unbalancing the enemy by manoeuvre while keeping well balanced myself. I planned always to make the enemy commit his reserves on a wide front in order to plug holes in his defences. Having forced him to do this, I then committed my own reserves in a hard blow on a narrow front. Once I had committed my reserves, I always sought to create fresh reserves. As the battle develops, the enemy will try to throw you off your balance by counter-thrusts. This must never be allowed. Throughout the battle area the whole force must be so well balanced and poised, and the general layout of dispositions so good, that one will never be dictated to by enemy thrusts. Skill in grouping forces before the battle begins, and in regrouping to meet developing tactical situations, is one of the hallmarks of generalship. A general must understand the mind of his opponent, in order to be able to anticipate enemy reactions to his own moves and to take quick action to prevent enemy interference with his own plans. The initiative, once gained, must never be lost; only in this way will the enemy be made to dance to your tune. In a campaign a commander should think two battles ahead – the one he is planning to fight and the next one. He can then use success in the first as a springboard for the second.

While operational problems will tend to be the main preoccupation of a general, he must never forget that the raw material of his trade is men, and that generalship is, basically, a human problem. The soldier can feel intense loneliness during moments in battle. In the early stages of the 1914/18 war, as a young platoon commander on a patrol at night in no-man's-land, I was several times cut off from my men. I was alone in the neighbourhood of the enemy, and I was frightened; it was my first experience of war. In those days I came to realize the importance of the soldier knowing that behind him were commanders, in their several grades, who cared for him. The general who looks after his men and cares for their lives, and wins battles with the minimum loss of life, will have their confidence. All soldiers will follow a successful general. A general, therefore, has got to 'get himself over' to his troops. My own technique in the 1939/45 war was to speak to them whenever possible. Sometimes I spoke to large numbers from the bonnet of a jeep, sometimes I spoke just to a few men by the roadside or in a gun pit. I would also address them less directly by means of written messages at important phases in the campaign or before a battle. These talks and messages fostered the will to win and helped to weld the whole force into a fighting team which was certain of victory. In the 1914/18 war Sir Douglas Haig never seemed to me to get himself over to the soldiers. He would inspect troops in complete silence. There is a story told that one of his staff suggested it would create a good impression if he would occasionally stop and speak to one or two men. He took the advice and asked one man: 'Where did you start this war?' The astonished soldier replied: 'I didn't start this war, sir; I think the Kaiser did.' I understand that Haig gave it up after this encounter! Nevertheless, it is the spoken word above all which counts in the leadership of men.

A general must never be chary in allotting praise where it is due. People like to be praised when they have done well. Sir Winston Churchill once told me of the reply made by the Duke of Wellington, in his last years, when a friend asked him: 'If you had your life over again, is there any way in which you could have done better?' The old duke replied: 'Yes, I should have given more praise.'

I have learnt from my own experience that a commander has a need for robustness, the ability to stand up to the shocks of war – which will come as surely as the dawn follows the night. Perhaps *toughness* is a better word for this quality. I have mentioned my sense of loneliness as a young platoon commander. There is also a loneliness about high command. A C-in-C has immense responsibilities which he cannot pass on to his staff or to his subordinates; his are the decisions, and his the responsibility for success or failure and for the lives of his men. This aspect of generalship applies particularly in adversity, but it is of permanent relevance and is a severe test for a commander. When things are not going exactly as planned, all eyes look to the commander-in-chief for confidence, fortitude, for him to show the way. In such conditions of adversity, when things may not be going too well, a commander, besides commanding his armies, has got to learn to command *himself* – which is not always too easy. In the Civil War in America, Lee retained the devotion of his army even although he lost.

Until political leaders can find some sensible way of settling international disputes, war will remain with us. When a nation decides to resort to armed force to achieve its political ends, or is itself attacked, the ultimate responsibility for the direction of the war lies in political hands. Service chiefs will find it difficult, if not impossible, to give success to a government which vacillates and lacks courage and clear-sightedness. It is vital that the political aims and the strategy be clearly defined. The issue then passes to the generals – who must be backed to the utmost. Talleyrand is reported to have said: 'War is much too serious a thing to be left to military men.' This was quoted by Briand to Lloyd George during the 1914/18 war, and is of course very true. Equally it could be said that war is too serious a thing to be left to politicians. The truth is that in modern war the closest cooperation between the two is vital.

In a major war, resources may be relatively equal between the nations involved; in such a case victory will go to that side which is best trained, best led, and of higher morale. However skilful the general may be, there comes a stage in every battle against a determined enemy when victory hangs in the balance; the power then is out of the hands of the general and goes finally to the soldiers; victory will depend on their courage, their training, their discipline, their refusal to admit defeat, their steadiness and tenacity in battle. During the long march from Alamein to Berlin in the 1939/45 war, I had pinned in my caravan the following quotation from Shakespeare's *Henry V*: 'O God of battles! steel my soldiers' hearts.' As our study of war unfolds, I hope the reader will recognize the truth of what I have written. Many of the battles we shall examine were won, in the end, by the soldiers or sailors. When planning the battle, a general is faced with the fog of war; but provided he has a sound plan, the soldiers will disperse the fog.

A study of the history of warfare will illustrate not only the evolution of the art of war but also the uniformity of its basic conceptions. The same principles of war which were employed in the past appear again and again throughout history, only in different circumstances. Although weapons have become more powerful and the problems of the battlefield have grown more intricate and more complex, nonetheless the art of war is fundamentally the same today as it was in the ancient world.

I will finish these few thoughts on a note which will be clear as the historical chapters are read. Field-Marshal Wavell once told me that when the Spartans were at the height of their military fame they sent a deputation to the oracle at Delphi and demanded, arrogantly enough: 'Can anything harm Sparta?' The answer came quickly: 'Yes, luxury.'

I have visited the scene of this somewhat disturbing interview. How true was the answer! Throughout our study it will be seen that national history is a fight which goes on from age to age: each advance has to be won, each position gained has to be held. In war, the enemy is plain and clear. In peace, a nation is confronted with a more insidious foe: the weakness within, from which alone great nations fall. If an example from modern times is needed, it is France. In the years before the 1939/45 war the weakness within attacked her soul; and the crash came in 1940. She was given back her soul in 1958 by General de Gaulle, and has risen again phoenix-like.

Naturally I know best my own people, the British. For many years we have not known final defeat; freedom is in our blood and has given us a sturdy and unique strength. With such men as the Glasgow Scot, the lad from Lancashire, the London cockney all things are possible. But the danger from within is always present and must be kept in subjection. The oracle was right: if undue luxury gets a hold on the manhood of a nation, and martial qualities are neglected, that nation is likely to fall. Francis Bacon, long ago wrote the following: 'Walled towns, stored arsenals and armories, goodly races of horse, chariots of war, elephants, ordnance, artillery and the like; all this is but sheep in a lion's skin, except the breed and disposition of the people be stout and warlike.' A study of the history of warfare proves the absolute truth of this statement.

2   War in Earliest Times

War has been constant in human affairs since the earliest societies of which there is record. In 7000 B.C. Jericho was strongly fortified by a wall 21 feet high; out of 2,500 citizens 600 would have been fighting men armed with the bow and arrow. But the art of warfare had clearly been evolving for long before those days. How then did war first arise?

War is a basic part of history because it is concerned with the essentials of life. Food, and a secure place in which to live, were the two basic necessities for primeval man – just as they are for us. But these things which man needs, as well as many other things which he desires, such as mates, wealth, power and prestige, are often available only in short supply. The basic reason why individual men and societies have almost incessantly fought each other lies in this economic fact – they have always had to compete for the minimum conditions of existence. Animals fight each other for the same reason. The urges of rage, aggression and fear are natural only because in a competitive social situation each creature represents a frustration or a danger to his neighbour. Human beings of course, have been much less successful than animals in avoiding the resort to violence.

What traces we can discover of the primitive peoples of ancient times show that, from the first, men have had to organize themselves for defence. It was because their dwelling-places had to be refuges as well as shelters that they so frequently lived in cliff-side caves, on hill-tops or in houses built on piles in lakes and marshes so as to be moated. Among the palaeolithic instruments which could be used as weapons of war were stone cleavers and knives, and blades and lance-heads of bone, flint and horn. Since it is virtually impossible to discover the causes and modes of warfare among these earliest peoples, the most instructive approach for us is to look at the primitive peoples of other continents, some of whom in our twentieth century are passing through their stone ages.

Few generalizations can be made about the bellicosity of primitive peoples. Motives for war vary, and the degree of ferocity depends on circumstances. Some tribes slaughter all their prisoners, while others treat them leniently. The pygmies are extremely peaceable, but for that very reason, and because they are weak, they have been driven into the least habitable area of Africa by other more aggressive peoples. In many parts of the world there are tribes which, until very recently, regarded war as normal and acceptable – such as the Masai of East Africa and the Guaranis of Brazil. Tribes ruled by kings are usually more prone to war than those with more democratic forms of government. A hundred years ago tribal wars were much less frequent and ferocious in the Gaboon and Lower Niger, where the consent

War has existed in almost all primitive societies. An archer engaged in combat with a rival tribe is depicted in the rock paintings of Tassili, *c.* 3000 B.C.

of the elders was needed before a tribe could go to war, than in East Africa where the kings were absolute.

The most common and infallible cause of war among primitive peoples is overcrowding. Population has to be kept down, and this has generally been brought about by war or by disease. The history of the Red Indian tribes of North America illustrates well how territorial possessiveness can lead to war. From about A.D. 1600, when enough Europeans were established on the east coast with superior weapons, the Indians were driven westwards. There was more than a century of continuous war among the tribes as each was forced back to intrude into the territory of its westerly neighbour. A succession of great battles was fought between the Chippewa and the Sioux, at Mille Lacs in the seventeenth century, at Elk River in the eighteenth century, and at Cross Lake in 1800. In the nineteenth century the situation was aggravated by the disappearance of the buffalo, the main food of the Indians, and by the need to compete for horses and firearms. The chain of enforced migration continued, the defeated Sioux in their turn pushing the Cheyenne farther west and the Cheyenne eventually driving the Comanche back towards Mexico.

War can appeal because it is exciting, it can be amusing; it can also offer easy profit, colour and romance, discipline and ritual, self-sacrifice and comradeship, status, and the admiration of women. Among the Tahitians a sufficient reason for going to war was the custom that a youth might not marry unless he had the tattoo which signified that he had killed a man in battle.

But a more fundamental explanation of the frequent occurrence of war may be the deep-rooted desire of men to belong to groups. If loyalties and a sense of group identity and patriotism are to develop in a society, it must perhaps be positively antagonistic to its neighbours. It was actually a religious belief among the Mbaya of South America that they should live by assaulting all other tribes. When the Polynesians were prevented from warring by Europeans, they underwent a profound social and cultural crisis; their values had been related to conditions of constant war; when that had to stop they lost their energy, dignity and religion.

The factor which underlay all military and political developments in the history of the Near East during the four thousand years before Christ was overcrowding of population. The first civilizations arose in great river valleys, Babylonia and Sumeria on the lower reaches of the Euphrates and the Tigris, and Egypt astride the Nile. Warfare was inevitably continuous because of the competition to possess the small quantity of fertile land which there was in a densely populated and otherwise very arid area. Egypt had continually to thrust back from its frontiers aggressive and less civilized neighbours – the Nubians in the south, and Semitic nomads in Sinai. Similarly, Babylonian kings undertook continuous border police operations. Occasionally raids from the wilds developed into much bigger onslaughts, when great masses of migratory peoples were attracted to the river valleys. In ancient times there were three great eruptions of the Semites of Arabia. Some time in the fourth millennium the Median Wall was built from the Euphrates to the Tigris to keep out the nomadic invaders of the first great migration – in vain.

The second half of the fourth millennium, and the third millennium, the period of the clash between the Semites and the Sumerians, of the Akkadian empire and the Egyptian Old Kingdom (3500–2400 B.C.), was an age of great military activity. Two great commanders in this period were Sargon, a priest of Ishtar, goddess of battle, who first ruled all Mesopotamia, and Naram-Sin, who extended the Akkadian empire to the Mediterranean. The Mesopotamians were a great deal more advanced in military technique than the Egyptians, who did not use a chariot until twelve hundred years after them.

The basic instrument of war in Mesopotamia after 3500 B.C. was the chariot. It had a high and upright protective panel at the front, and was normally used for direct frontal assault. The crew consisted of a driver and a soldier armed with a javelin and a spear. The chief function of the chariot was to charge and panic the enemy, joining battle first at medium range with javelins, and then at short range with the spear. Later, between 2000 and 1500, improved mobility was achieved with the discovery of the spoked wheel and the means of making a lighter car. Asses were replaced by horses, which first appeared in Mesopotamia from the northern steppes about 2000. Improved firepower came with the introduction of the composite bow. The mace was a much used weapon, but when strong helmets were introduced its blunt head was less effective, and the axe became more important. In the third millennium axes with copper blades were developed for both piercing and cutting; they were used by infantry spearmen and charioteers. The sword appeared in Mesopotamia, where the technical ability to produce and fashion a long blade of hard metal was acquired. The first swords were like daggers: short, straight and double-edged. Later came curved, sickle swords for striking. But the knowledge spread slowly, and elsewhere iron swords were used regularly only from the fourteenth century B.C. Before that the standard weapon of the Mesopotamian phalanx was the metal-bladed spear, shoulder-sloped on the march and carried horizontally in assault.

The bow is depicted on many monuments from the end of the fourth millennium. In Egypt it was double-convex in shape, but in Mesopotamia single-arc. It is strange that it was not used by charioteers till after 2000 B.C. Arrowheads were made of flint. The victory monument of Naram-Sin (2800) portrays for the first time the composite bow. It was then that the bow emerged as a battle weapon of first importance. Hitherto the bow had always been made out of one material, but there was no single material of sufficient strength and elasticity to give it much range. The new composite bow was made of four materials – wood, animal horn, sinews and glue – so stuck or bound together that, before the string was attached, the arms of the body bent the other way. When it was strung it was thus very tense. It was now possible to make a light bow with an effective range of 300 to 400 yards. The impact of the composite bow was revolutionary: for the first time, enemies could be surprised and attacked from beyond their range of hearing, vision and retaliation. It was their chief weapon. In reaction to this bow, shields were made larger, and armour was introduced. The first mail coat was a cape worn by the Sumerians, studded with small circular pieces of metal.

In open country the functions of infantry and chariots were closely integrated. The phalanx probably went into action in the immediate wake of the chariot charge. The chariots would first confuse, scatter and trample the enemy by storming through their ranks. The phalanx would follow up the charge from the flanks or centre and finish off the enemy with piercing axes and spears. The organization of the Mesopotamian phalanx was methodical and disciplined. The unit would move forward as a column of six files, with eleven men in each file – then present itself for battle by a right or left wheel, which would offer a line six ranks deep. Archers were added to this battle formation by the Akkadians; but long-range archery units were possibly only fully integrated with chariots, and with infantry armed with spears and swords, by the Egyptians – when they fought the Hittites a thousand years later.

Advanced techniques of siege warfare did not appear until the time of the Assyrians. But in the third millennium cities were fortified. They were effectively defended by bowmen firing from square or semi-circular bastions. The monument of the siege of Deshashe in Egypt indicates clearly how a fortified city was attacked in this period. The assailants are climbing a scaling-ladder, which has wheels. They are covered by archery fire. Meanwhile a battering ram is being used to breach the wall, probably at the gate – which would be the weakest point.

The second great wave of Semitic migration began about 2500 and penetrated from Arabia first of all into Canaan on the Mediterranean coast. It was then that those tribes with sinister names, the Ammonites and the Moabites, first appeared in the history of Israel. The Canaanites swept on, into Mesopotamia; it was they who first made Babylon an important city; they refounded Ur, and united all southern Mesopotamia in the Chaldean kingdom. In Egypt the Middle Kingdom had begun about 2375 when the Theban rulers of the south conquered the Nile delta. But then Egypt entered a prolonged phase of peace and high civilization and military strength was neglected. This was the situation when in about 1800 Egypt was invaded and enslaved by the Hyksos, an offshoot of the second wave of Semitic migration. In about 1630 B.C. the Egyptian struggle for liberation was begun and eventually around 1580 Ahmose drove out the Hyksos.

What was the nature of the Egyptian army in the liberation struggle at the end of the Middle Kingdom? Its warriors continued to use piercing axes and spears, but the chief weapon was the bow. The Hyksos in fact introduced into Egypt the powerful double-convex composite bow as well as the horse and chariot. Shields tended to be smaller and lighter to give mobility. The fortress of Buhen, surrounded by a dry moat, has all the elements of solid defence. Battlements facilitated defensive fire, and balconies on the walls would make it possible to fire vertically downwards on assaulting troops.

It was quite common for tribes to settle small disputes by single combat, which was considered an honourable and binding way. Major campaigns were not, however, settled like this, and the Egyptians had developed a complex military organization. The king had his body of professional guards and every local ruler had to supply a contingent; then it became necessary to have a more professional army.

Efficient systems of communications, intelligence and administration were de-

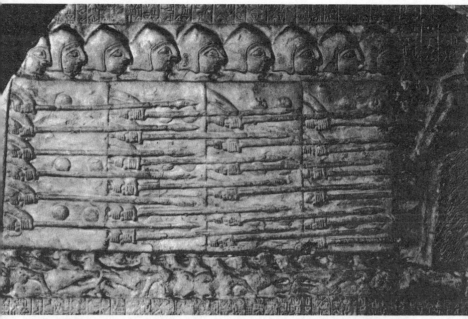

A Babylonian phalanx, armed with spears and large rectangular shields, followed behind the charge of the chariots

veloped. There was a code of torch signals; runners relayed messages and orders on the battlefield; sometimes semaphore and trumpet calls were used. With large bodies of troops campaigning in unfamiliar and difficult terrain it was necessary to have good intelligence services. The Egyptians used to send out reconnaissance units to spy and to capture prisoners for interrogation. Frequent reports from officers in the front line were rapidly relayed to headquarters to provide battle intelligence. It was a rule that the source of information must always be stated, and the form of report was probably very like that used in a modern army. The army had a medical service; there were companies of engineers to construct siege equipment; and there was a transport service of ships and wagons.

The expulsion of the Hyksos and the establishment of the New Kingdom gave the Egyptians an appetite for further conquest, and Amenhotep I, Thutmose I and Thutmose III extended the Egyptian empire in the Near East. Then the third great migration of Semites out of Arabia began in about 1350, and the military strength of the Egyptian empire was undermined by attacks from the Aramaeans and Hittites. However, in 1292 Ramses II, a young man of great ability and energy, became pharaoh. He was determined to recover the former extent of the Egyptian empire. The previous period of peace had given the Hittites time to become very strong in Syria, making Kadesh the bulwark of their southern frontier. It was at this point

that Ramses decided to attack. But before examining the battle of Kadesh, let us first consider the weapons and organization of the Egyptian armies of the New Kingdom.

In this period, after 1500 B.C., the axe was less prominent than the sword which, like other important weapons, was introduced to Egypt from Asia. The sword replaced the mace as the symbol of the pharaoh's power. The sword of Ramses III was long and wide; the short dagger-like sword of earlier times was also still in use, and these were the most effective weapons for the phalanx in hand-to-hand fighting. The spear was also a basic infantry weapon, and at last the stronger socket-type, leaf-shaped head, known for centuries in Mesopotamia, was adopted in Egypt. A phalanx would have consisted of spear, axe, and sword units. The spear was also used for defending ramparts, but not by charioteers – in contrast to Asiatic practice.

Egyptian charioteers used javelins. This difference arises from their different chariot tactics. The Asiatic chariot would charge into the enemy, with a crew consisting of a driver and two spearmen. If the fighting became too congested for the chariot to be able to manoeuvre, the driver would join in as a spearman. Egyptian chariots, on the other hand, operated more as a unit; the chariots would charge in a solid mass, driving the enemy before them, and never allowing themselves to be surrounded individually in the battle. Chariots, which constituted a large proportion of the Egyptian army, were divided into units of fifty, each unit under an officer. Cavalry was still not used. But as weapons had developed in power, and conversely armour had been developed to give better protection, the outcome of a battle was increasingly likely to be decided by troops of the maximum mobility, and it is for this reason that the chariot now became of prime importance. It was a light vehicle drawn by two horses; everything was designed to make it strong, yet fast and manoeuvrable. Later on the Egyptians also developed a special heavier chariot. Chariot maintenance was provided along regular campaign routes by repair workshops, which kept stores and spares and also saw to repairs of transport vehicles.

In all large armies of this period the bow was the decisive weapon. It was difficult and expensive to make, and it was largely because they had the money and specialized factories to produce good bows that the Egyptians could deal so easily with the smaller states of Palestine and Syria. The bow was supplied to both chariot and infantry troops. The arrows had reed shafts and bronze heads, and at a reasonably short distance could penetrate the armour of the time; the infantry archer would carry on a shoulder-strap a quiver of up to thirty arrows.

In the Middle Kingdom Egyptian soldiers had worn no armour but carried large shields. In the New Kingdom charioteers and bowmen, who needed to have both hands free, took to wearing coats of mail and helmets, and used only a small shield or none at all. As weapons developed more penetrating power, armour was correspondingly strengthened. The armour was made of metal scales, but was flexible and fairly light. Expense was a problem, and generally mail armour was worn only

Ramses II extended the Egyptian empire with campaigns against the Hittites and the Nubians. A relief showing the pharaoh with Libyan and Negro prisoners by those who had to have both hands free; others, such as spearmen and swordsmen, used shields. All troops wore helmets, which were often highly decorated.

The Egyptians were skilled at ambushing, but with their superior resources they preferred to fight with large formations in the open. We will now look at the battle of Kadesh between Ramses II and the Hittites in 1288, the first battle in history which we can reconstruct in any detail.

The Hittites under Mutallu had built up a more formidable army than the Egyptians had ever before had to face. But by 1288 Ramses had an equally large army. Late that spring he reached the valley of the upper Orontes, overlooking the plain in which lay Kadesh, a day's march away. He divided his army into four, and with himself at the head of the division of Amon set off to ford the river, leaving the others to follow. He crossed the river in the vicinity of Shabtuna, six miles or so south of Kadesh, and advanced northwards. He was anxious to begin the siege, and was completely confident about pushing on ahead of his main army because two Hittite deserters had told him that the bulk of the Hittite army was far to the north. But he had been deceived. The two 'deserters' had been sent by Mutallu to lure him northwards, and make him fall unsuspectingly into the trap laid by the Hittite army concealed north of Kadesh.

As Ramses approached and passed northwards to the west of Kadesh, the Hittite army first moved across to the east of the river, and then south, always keeping the city between themselves and the enemy – to avoid being seen. Finally they completed a brilliant manoeuvre by closing in on Ramses from the south-east. The Egyptian army was now completely cut in two. Ramses was isolated and faced by over-whelming numbers. His other divisions were straggled out so far to the south that it was doubtful if they would be able to join in the battle at all. Mutallu had his whole army based on Kadesh, which could give him concealment and shelter. The Egyptian king perceived his desperate plight only when he captured two Hittite spies – genuine, this time – who admitted that the Hittite army was behind Kadesh.

The Hittites first attacked the second division of the Egyptian army, called Re. Taken completely by surprise, Re was broken in two and cut to pieces. Part of the remnants fled towards the pharaoh's camp, followed closely by the chariot units and phalanxes of the Hittites, in all about 17,000 men. Ramses' division of Amon was at first bewildered and driven back in chaos. The rout seemed to be complete. But then Ramses launched a desperate counter-attack. He could not halt the Hittites in the centre, but he observed that their eastern flank by the river was thin, and it was here that he flung his chariots. The Hittites should still have won. They were victorious in the centre, and they needed only to concentrate their forces against the Egyptian king on the eastern flank to secure a complete victory. But instead their discipline broke, and they began looting the Egyptian camp. This was the crucial moment of the battle. While the Hittites in the centre were looting and off their guard, they were attacked and overwhelmed by the Na'arun troops. These were a crack Canaanite

Egyptian soldiers assaulted a fortified city by scaling the walls with ladders, protecting themselves
with their shields

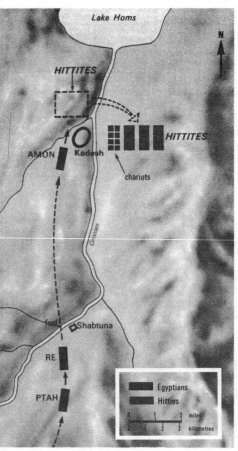 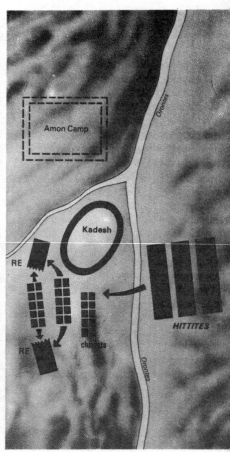

The battle of Kadesh

unit of phalanxes ten ranks deep, serving with the Egyptian forces; they only now arrived from the western flank where they had originally been deployed. At the same time that the situation in the centre was thus being salvaged, the Egyptians were pressing their attack relentlessly on the eastern flank. At this point the technical superiority of the Egyptian chariot, armed with the long-range composite bow, was decisive. The Hittite chariots were less mobile, and were armed only with a short-range spear.

Mutallu was driven back across the Orontes, and halted on the far side of the river with 6,000 men. He was now crippled, since he had already committed all his chariots in the first attack in the centre, and his infantry was powerless against the Egyptian

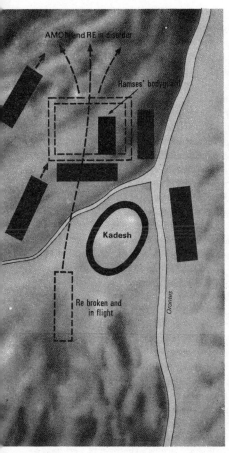

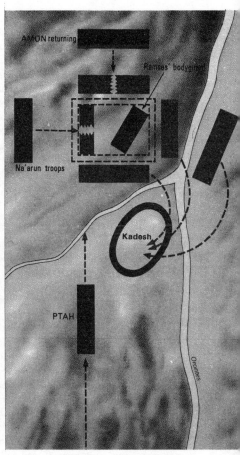

chariots. By this time it was evening, and the third division (Ptah) of the Egyptian army was arriving. The Hittites then retired into Kadesh, and there prepared for a siege. But the Egyptians also retired without attempting to take the city. The battle thus ended indecisively. Ramses had been outmanoeuvred strategically, but in the actual course of the battle he led his men so well that disaster was averted, although the Egyptian losses were severe. Mutallu, after a brilliant start, had lost his advantage because of faulty command and control; he also suffered from technical inferiority.

Both the Hittite and the Egyptian empires began to decay rapidly after this time. The Egyptians had exhausted their imperialistic drive, and the Hittites were already feeling the rising power of Assyria.

Assyria was situated in an infertile area of the upper Tigris, and thus had the
alternative of remaining small and poor or becoming rich by conquest. The power
vacuum left by the failure of the Egyptians and the Hittites gave the Assyrians that
chance. Assyrian expansion began under Tiglathpileser I (1115–02), and after him
many of her kings were very able soldiers; the greatest of Assyrian conquerors was
Tiglathpileser III (745–27). By the time upper Egypt was conquered in 671 the
Assyrians dominated the whole of the Near East.

The Assyrians never bothered to justify their empire, nor waited for any excuse
for an invasion. These ferocious people worshipped the stern god Ashur. The winged
disc, within which Ashur was shown leading his people, was always carried on the
king's chariot in battle and set up in every conquered place. Senior army officers
were also priests, and the word 'rebel' meant the same as 'sinner': a man to be
punished with the utmost severity. It was enough that the city of Arinna had
'despised the god Ashur' for it to be destroyed. After a victory prisoners were
slaughtered while religious rites were performed. The Assyrians brought no benefit
to their subject peoples. On the contrary, they pillaged every land, and cruelty and
mass deportations to swell the population of Assyria were regular policies. The
feelings of all their subjects were expressed in the cry of the Jewish prophet Nahum:
'Woe to the bloody city!' Tiglathpileser I boasted of his victims that 'their blood
in the valleys and on the high places of the mountains I caused to flow. Their heads
I cut off, and outside their cities, like heaps of grain, I piled them up. Their spoil
and their possessions in countless number I brought out.'

The Assyrians were the first great military power of the iron age, and their weapons
were stronger and sharper than any before. They were also the first people to use
cavalry, shortly before 1000 B.C. There were two branches of cavalry – bowmen and
spearmen – both of which were used in short- and long-range combat. In a battle
the mounted spearmen would open the charge, followed by infantry spearmen.
Mounted archers attacked mostly from the rear or the flanks, operating in pairs,
one horseman with a bow and the other holding both sets of reins and a large shield
big enough to protect two men. Chariots with bowmen were the main strength
of an army. The infantry consisted of spearmen, archers and slingmen. The
spearmen wore heavy coats of mail and helmets. Various experiments were made
with the size, shape and weight of shields, to achieve the right balance between
security and mobility, but no fixed pattern was settled. Spearmen were generally
shock troops who led the assault in hand-to-hand fighting, but they were also
very important in assaults on fortified cities. The main power of the Assyrian
infantry rested with its archers, who with their highly advanced composite bow
were used in all types of attack. In the earlier period they wore long coats of mail;
then, under Tiglathpileser III (745–27), who made radical changes in all arms,
they used a huge shield with a hood, taller than a man and carried by a special
bearer. Light archery units also existed. Tiglathpileser III was the first Assyrian king
to use slingmen. A relief shows them operating in pairs behind archers; their high-
angled fire was particularly effective in assaults up steep slopes on cities. All infantrymen were armed, in addition to their special weapon, with a long straight sword.

In centuries of almost incessant warfare the Assyrians were rarely beaten. Their armies were often outnumbered, and many of their enemies were as well armed as they were. Their success was partly due to the fact that most of the kings of Assyria were highly capable field commanders. But it was also to a great extent the result of sound organization. As the original oriental despots, the Assyrian kings had absolute power to direct all the resources of the state to military ends, and they were very efficient administrators. There was a regular army, and all adult males had to do a period of military service – although in practice the rich could, if they wished, commute service for a payment or send a slave in their place. Conquered peoples had to supply contingents. The troops and officers were probably well provided for by the central government and from exactions in the areas they occupied. At the close of a campaign a share of the spoil was divided among the troops. The army was backed by its own efficient intelligence system, and civil officials in the provinces regularly sent in information which could be of military use.

The formidable power of the Assyrian army meant that practically all other peoples stood little chance in open battle, and relied on defending fortified places. There are no detailed records of open battles, and it is impossible to be sure what the strategy and tactics of the Assyrians would have been in such operations. The key part was probably played by chariots charging from all directions and engaging in battle at all ranges; the other formations would mop up what was left by the chariots. The best evidence is a series of reliefs of c. 550, depicting the battle against the Elamites and Arabs on the river Ulai. The Elamite army of light archers, infantry and a few cavalry appears in a desperate plight. The Assyrian army, using units appropriate to the terrain, consists mainly of cavalry armed with bows and spears, and of infantry spearmen. Most of them are heavily armoured, but in addition lightly-clad auxiliary archers are moving through the field doing considerable damage. The scenes begin with the initial onslaught, and end with the retreat of the Elamites into the river and the decapitation of prisoners. It is clear that the cavalry and infantry are launched after the chariots have caused confusion among the enemy. The cavalry operates mainly on the flanks, to prevent any of the enemy escaping; they are all to be forced back into the river and slaughtered.

The Assyrians were good fighters in all kinds of country. There is a relief showing infantry advancing through wooded country. The unit of foot spearmen proceeds line abreast in separate ranks, while small scattered forces follow to secure the rear and flanks. In combat in partly wooded and hilly regions mounted archers and spearmen play the chief part, closely co-ordinated with infantry. They move forward in column, their flanks in the wooded areas protected by the infantry. The best example of the ability of Assyrian troops to deal with difficult terrain is the amphibious operations of Sennacherib (c. 690) in the marshland of the Tigris delta. The infantry appear as marines, charging into the swamps in light boats, manoeuvring among the reeds, seeking out the enemy and burning their refuges. The Assyrian army, capable of moving large formations over long distances in hilly country, reached a new level of ingenuity and technical skill in surmounting natural obstacles, particularly rivers. Another relief shows a chariot corps crossing a wide river with all its heavy gear. The vehicles are ferried across in large boats which are rowed and assisted on the far bank by an advance party hauling on ropes. The horses swim behind, tied to a rope held in the boat, while the troops swim across with the aid of inflated goatskins, and take great care to prevent their weapons getting wet. Assyrian sappers could build pontoon bridges across smaller streams.

The Assyrians were highly skilled in siege warfare. Their success here was due to the maximum co-ordination and exploitation of various techniques: storming of ramparts, battering and breaching of walls and gates, scaling, tunnelling, and psychological warfare. An example of the fortifications that the Assyrians might have had to deal with is the massive wall of Megiddo, built at the beginning of the nineteenth century B.C.: 7 feet thick at the base, it is constructed with 18-foot-wide salients and recesses, and crowned by a balcony with a crenellated parapet; a lower outer wall gives additional strength.

The fall of the Assyrian empire came at the end of the seventh century B.C., when there was a long and weakening dispute for the royal succession. Nabopolassar, king of Babylon, and Cyaxares of Media allied to destroy the Assyrians, whose manpower had been seriously depleted in the civil wars of the 620's. Sin-Shar-Ishkun, the last king of Nineveh, threw himself into the flames of his city in 612. So complete was the defeat and enslavement, and so extensive the slaughter and deportation of the victims, that the separate Assyrian nation ceased altogether to exist.

A relief of two two-wheeled Assyrian chariots

3   The Ancient Greeks

The 'heroic' age of Greek warfare began in about 1400 B.C. – it was in this age that the Trojan War took place. Battles in those days are recorded as trials of valour between mighty warriors: Ajax, Hector, Achilles. The warriors would ride on to the field in chariots, dismount, and engage in single combat, cheered on by their retainers. Lightly equipped for agility, each carried a round shield, two throwing spears, and a straight sword. The bow was despised as a cowardly weapon. If the spears did not settle the matter, a sword duel would follow.

Some time after 1100 Greece was invaded from the north by the Dorians. Four dark centuries followed, during which Greece entered the iron age. Finally, at the beginning of the sixth century Sparta entered upon 250 years of military pre-eminence in Greece. Sparta was a military state. Weakling babies were exposed to die on a mountainside, and Spartan boys from seven to thirty were trained to discipline and hardship in barracks. The whole male population constituted an intensely professional standing army, every man dedicated to the law that he must 'conquer or die'. Economic needs were supplied by slaves.

By 500 war between Greece and Persia was looming. In the second half of the sixth century the Persians, grasping the opportunity left by the disappearance of Assyria, had expanded their empire westwards, and in 500 the Greeks of the Ionian islands appealed to mainland Greece for help. Darius then decided that all Greece must be conquered. In the face of this peril for the first time the Greek cities united, under Spartan leadership. The first massive invasion by the Persians in 490 was repelled at Marathon, and the second in 480–79 at Salamis and Plataea. The Greeks won these victories against the vast and supposedly invincible Persian forces because they had perfected two highly effective instruments of war, the hoplite phalanx and the trireme.

Shortly after 700, battles at long range and in loose formations had given way to conflicts between close-order phalanxes of heavy infantry, or 'hoplites'. As smelting techniques improved and prosperity grew, more people could afford the panoply of the hoplite. This consisted of an 8-foot thrusting spear, a sword, helmet, breast-plate, greaves, and a round shield about 3 feet in diameter held on the left arm. The helmet was crested, and the shield often emblazoned with birds or wild beasts.

The tactic of the hoplite phalanx was to confront the enemy with a firm and solid line of alternate shields and spears. At the clash each man struck with his spear at his opponent's throat. The continuity of the line was vital, for every man depended on his neighbour. Personal distinction was to be sought not on the battlefield but in athletics. At Plataea there were eight ranks in the Spartan phalanx. The function of

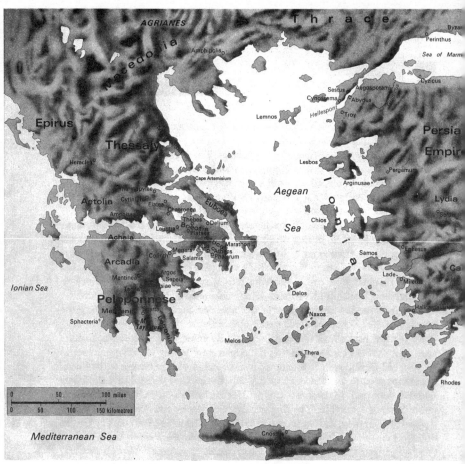

The ancient Greek world

the rear ranks was to fill the gaps as they appeared in front, to carry spare weapons, and to deal with the wounded – killing those of the enemy and tending their own. Discipline and tenacity were needed to maintain cohesion and to prevent dangerous gaps in the front rank. The battle was decided by steadiness and weight of numbers, and was usually short. Since it was important to be as powerful as possible in the initial charge, the whole strength of an army was committed straightaway. Once a line was broken the defeated hoplites turned and fled; with no reserves, a second assault was impossible. There was little pursuit, since the strenuous nature of the fighting was exhausting for heavy troops.

Tactics were thus extremely limited. But with their superior training and discipline the Spartans were supreme in this kind of war. They developed a simple refinement of the hoplite charge, which for almost three centuries brought them victory. Advancing troops had a natural tendency to edge towards their right, as each man sought the protection of his neighbour's shield. The right wing of the phalanx was therefore likely to some extent to outflank the enemy's left, and the Spartans exploited this tendency. After outflanking the enemy they would wheel and roll up his line. Their slow, steady charge to the music of flutes allowed them sufficient flexibility for the manoeuvre.

One short battle was generally enough to decide a campaign. In any case bad roads, mountainous country and rigid formations limited the scope for strategical or tactical conceptions. Wars were restricted to the summer months, since the only way to force the enemy to emerge from his walled city and fight was by ravaging his crops and herds. Sieges were rare. Hoplites hardly ever fought other arms. Cavalry would have been effective if the Greeks had had more and stronger horses; but Greece, with its poor pasture land, was not a suitable country for horse breeding; only the Thessalians regularly relied on cavalry. The Persians, who had conquered Asia with their archers and cavalry, confronted the Greeks with new methods of war. But they met their match in the Greek phalanx. After they had endured the rain of arrows at Plataea (479), Pausanias timed the charge of the Spartan hoplites perfectly, to hit the enemy while they were massed together.

The Greeks had no urge to develop further their organization for warfare. All except the Spartans resented discipline and disliked fighting. They could fight well enough when they had to, but they were interested in better things. 'The bravest spirits are those who, having the clearest sense both of the pains and of the pleasures of life, do not on that account shrink from danger.' When Pericles heard of the young men of Athens who were killed in Samos he felt 'it was as if the spring had been taken from the year'.

In the heroic age of Greece there had been no naval warfare; ships were used only as transports. But by the seventh century B.C. there were warships, with bows specially strengthened for ramming, and decks to carry marines who would bombard or board the enemy ship. From about 650 the emphasis in naval tactics was on ramming, and ships became longer, faster and lower in the water. Between 550 and 500 the Greeks developed the trireme, the prototype of the galley which was to dominate naval warfare until the battle of Lepanto in A.D. 1571. A trireme might be rowed by as many as 170 men, each pulling one oar; the oars were probably arranged in three superimposed tiers, with outriggers to support them and even-out the leverage. Fast and manoeuvrable, the trireme offered great scope to skilled navigators. The first battle involving fleets of triremes was fought at Lade in 494 when the Persians with greatly superior forces crushed the Ionian revolt.

In the spring of 480 the Persian forces under Xerxes, some 160,000 troops and, according to Herodotus, 1,207 warships and 3,000 transports, advanced into northern Greece. At a pan-Hellenic congress under the presidency of Sparta the Greeks concerted their plan of defence. To minimize the effect of Persian numerical superiority it was decided to meet them in the narrow pass of Thermopylae, some eighty miles to the north of Athens, and in the Euboean Channel to the east. Thermopylae was to be a holding operation to induce Xerxes to try to outflank the Greeks in a sea battle, on which everything was staked. A fleet of 324 triremes, under the Spartan Eurybiades, was sent to the north of the Euboean Channel. Its main force was the Athenian contingent under Themistocles.

The Persians aimed to force the Thermopylae Pass and bottle up the Greek fleet in the Euboean Channel. But as the Persian fleet was sailing down the east coast of Magnesia it was caught in a gale and severely damaged. Themistocles then persuaded the reluctant Greek admiral to attack immediately while the enemy fleet was in disorder. Two days of hard but indecisive fighting followed off Cape Artemisium. The Persians came off rather the better, and the Greeks were considering a retreat at the end of the second day. Then news reached them that Thermopylae had fallen. Leonidas, the Spartan king, and 7,000 hoplites (of whom only 300 were Spartans) had held out for three days against the whole Persian army. But in the end a traitor revealed to the Persians how the pass could be turned. The Spartans died to a man, and the Persian army having won the pass moved southwards towards Athens.

The Greek fleet sailed south down the channel and round Attica; now it alone could save Greece. The problem was to induce the Persian fleet to give battle in water that suited the Greeks. Themistocles decided that the place to fight was off the island of Salamis, which lies in the mouth of the bay of Eleusis. The bay can be approached from the west or from the east. The eastern approach is divided by the island of Psyttaleia into two very narrow channels, neither more than three-quarters of a mile wide. In these narrow waters the large Persian fleet would be cramped, and with their superior seamanship the Greeks should have a good fighting chance. The Persians, however, did not now need a sea battle. Would they choose to ignore the Greek fleet? The morale of the Greeks was low since Xerxes had now ravaged Attica and slaughtered the defenders of the Athenian Acropolis. Eurybiades was in a state of indecision. But Themistocles adopted a very bold scheme to induce the Persians to attempt to capture the Greek fleet. He left the channel between Salamis and Megara unguarded, and on 22nd September 480 sent a message to Xerxes telling him that 'fear has seized the Greeks and they are meditating a hasty flight'.

Xerxes fell into the trap. That night his fleet blocked the two straits of Salamis, and Persian troops landed on Psyttaleia. By dawn the bulk of the Persian fleet was deployed in a triple line from Cynosura across to the Piraeus. The Greeks rapidly deployed their fleet of 366 triremes. The Persians opened the battle. Because the channel was narrow their three lines had to break up into two columns, the Phoenicians on the right and the Ionians on the left. Almost immediately they fell into disorder, either because they were too congested or the sea was rough. The Greek ships charged at them, and a *mêlée* began. The tactic of the Greek triremes was to shear away the oars of the enemy ships, rendering them uncontrollable, and then ram them amidships, and sometimes board them. The decisive action was fought by the Athenians and Aeginetans on the left. Rowing close inshore, they turned the Persian right, and drove it in towards the centre. The Persians became more and

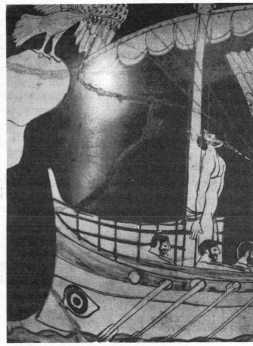

The battle of Salamis *left* was decided by the Greek tactics of ramming the enemy ships with specially strengthened bows *right*

more jammed up and confused. In the centre at first the fighting was evenly matched, and on the right the Greeks looked to be in trouble. But after seven or eight hours of hard fighting the wave of Greek victory spread across the battle area and the Athenians threatened to take the Persian left in the rear. The Ionians thereupon gave up and withdrew. Psyttaleia was cleared, and the Persians retired to Phalerum. Casualty figures are uncertain, but in any case the Greeks were not in a position to pursue and their fleet put in to Salamis.

The strategic value of the battle of Salamis was enormous. Without a fleet to provide transport and secure his communications, Xerxes dared leave only a small army in Greece, and this the Greeks were able to defeat at Plataea in 479. In the fifth century B.C. Athens continued to build up her naval power, but in the words of Thucydides, 'the growth of the power of Athens, and the alarm which this inspired in Sparta, made war inevitable'. In 431 the Peloponnesian War broke out. Almost every state in Greece was to be involved in it at some time during the next twenty-seven years. The period of the Peloponnesian War (431–04) marked the zenith of the Athenian navy. Yet Pericles laid too much emphasis on a purely naval strategy. He failed to realise that Athens could not win the war without a proper army, with

sea and land power balanced, and this negligence led to the final defeat of Athens in
404.

In its duration and scale of operations the Peloponnesian War was greater than
any previous war in Greece. During this period, and in the first half of the fourth
century while the struggle for supremacy in Greece was going on between Sparta,
Thebes and Athens, land warfare developed beyond the old Spartan methods.

There were several sieges during the Peloponnesian War. Delium, in 424, was the
first Greek town to be taken by assault; its hastily built palisades were burnt by fire
propelled through a gigantic blowpipe. The first Greek master of fortification and
siegecraft was Dionysius I of Syracuse (405–367). In his defence against the
Carthaginians he made the island of Ortygia impregnable, and built a magnificent
fortress on the heights of Epipolae. The introduction of siege-towers and torsion
catapults was revolutionary. There were two types of catapult. The small *katapeltes*
could project arrows, javelins, and an eight pound stone accurately up to 250 yards;
the bigger *petrobolos* could hurl stones of about 55 pounds weight. In each case the
motive power came from twisted skeins of sinew or women's hair. Towns were still,
however, more often taken by the old methods of starvation, fifth column and
treachery.

During this period arms began to be diversified, and more value became attached
to cavalry and lightly armed troops. In 415 Nikias took only thirty horses to Sicily;
but he soon found that he had to protect his foragers, and so he raised more cavalry.
But the old limitations on the use of cavalry still existed. Fodder and water were
scarce during the summer campaigning months, and the Greeks had no horseshoes
or stirrups – horseshoes were invented by the Celts in the fourth century B.C., and
the stirrup appeared in India in the first century B.C. The Greek horses were not
strong enough to support armour; hence they were vulnerable to spears, particularly
at the moment when cavalry wheeled away after a charge. But the obvious value of
cavalry in the broken countryside of Greece was increasingly recognized.

It was realized, similarly, that lightly armed troops were far more suited to Greek
terrain than hoplites; but in the past they had been despised as barbarian. The
Athenians learnt a sharp lesson in 426 when 120 hoplites under Demosthenes were
annihilated by Aetolian javelin-men who refused to close with them. Demosthenes
immediately raised a force of light troops and in 425, to the astonishment of Greece,
he used them to capture the Spartans on Sphacteria. Light foot soldiers were cheap,
and their development was furthered by the growth of the mercenary system. Many
Greeks who had fought in the Peloponnesian War had no other skill when it ended
in 404, so they became professional soldiers. In 401 Cyrus of Persia hired 10,000
Greeks to fight for him; Xenophon wrote a description of the 'Anabasis', their five-
month retreat to the Black Sea, and how they learnt much about light-armed warfare,
particularly archery, from the mountain tribes through which they fought their way.
Between 399 and 375, 25,000 Greeks took service as mercenaries abroad, and many
of them brought back the techniques they learned, such as those of the Rhodian
slingers and the Cretan archers. In Athens, shortly after 400, Iphicrates raised a
body of mercenary javelin-men, modelled on the Thracians and called 'peltasts'.

They wore leather jerkins, carried a sword and a small shield, and were trained to rapid manoeuvre. In all but big set battles they were the most effective infantry of the time; for example, in 390 near Corinth, they annihilated 600 Spartan hoplites.

As these new arms became organized, so tactics began to alter. Brasidas, the victor of Amphipolis in 422, was the last of the great Spartan hoplite generals in the old tradition. In 424 the Theban general Pagondas defeated the Athenian army at Delium by deepening the right flank of his phalanx and using cavalry as a mobile reserve. At long last there was some forward military thinking in Greece. Xenophon observed that 'wise generalship consists in attacking where the enemy is weakest'. and the army of Dionysius I of Syracuse consisted of integrated bodies of hoplites, light infantry and cavalry – a great advance.

Phalanx warfare was revolutionized at the battle of Leuctra in 371 by Epaminondas, the Theban general. His tactics were simple, though requiring skill to execute. His principle was to concentrate his strength at the crucial point of the battle, instead of applying it, as in the past, in such a way that he was weak everywhere and strong nowhere. Facing a Spartan army, he knew that the enemy would concentrate strength on their right, and aim to turn his left. Epaminondas therefore confronted the Spartan phalanx with an oblique line. He held back his right, and placed his striking force on his left in a column fifty ranks deep, guarded by a force of cavalry. He thus met the Spartan shock with counter shock, won the battle on the left, and had enough reserve force not to lose it in the centre and on his right. Leuctra, like Rocroi in A.D. 1643, destroyed a legend of invincibility. The way in which Epaminondas followed up his victory in the following year also showed new strategical vision. He marched from Thebes to Laconia, freed Messenia (the basis of Sparta's economic strength), and unified Arcadia – thus balancing what was left of the power of Sparta in the south.

In 359, shortly after the death of Epaminondas, Philip II became king in Macedonia. Ambitious and opportunistic, but also clear-sighted and a first class organizer, he reckoned that the city-states of Greece, having been perpetually at each other's throats for seventy years, would not unite to expel an intruder backed by a powerful army. 'Fraud before force, but force at the last' was Philip's method. In 338 he won a battle against Thebes and Athens at Chaeronea which finally brought him the mastery of Greece. After his victory, Philip proposed to the Greeks that they should unite under his leadership to invade the Persian empire. But before he could go further he was assassinated, in 336, and the project was left to his successor – Alexander. Philip's army, and his military conceptions, were the basis for Alexander's future achievement.

Geographical vision, mobility, and the co-ordination of arms were the principal features of the Macedonian art of war. The campaign before Chaeronea was a model of mobility. Long forced marches had been very rare in Greek warfare. Philip's path into Boeotia was barred both at the western and easterly routes. Concealing his intentions, he first placed himself at Elatea, and put the defenders of the western route off their guard. Then he marched rapidly by night to Amphissa, delivered a crushing attack on the 10,000 mercenaries there, and thus eliminated the

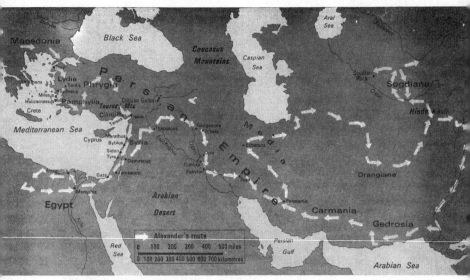

The route of Alexander's conquests

extreme left of an extended defensive line. He could now bring about the pitched battle with the Thebans and Athenians which he desired. But he did not at once advance due eastwards against the main enemy force, using a route which would have been more direct but which, by its terrain, favoured defence. Instead, he switched his army back to Elatea, and then descended rapidly through the pass of Parapotamii to come upon the enemy at Chaeronea.

There his conduct of the battle showed for the first time that a Greek army had learnt how to co-ordinate all arms successfully on the battlefield. The enemy presented a solid line, with the flanks protected by high ground and a river. Philip created a gap in their line by causing his highly trained phalanx on the right to conduct the difficult manoeuvre of a fighting withdrawal. The enemy left was then drawn into an advance, while their right clung to the protection it had on that flank. The moment a gap thus appeared, Philip launched the decisive charge of the cavalry from his left, led by his 18-year-old son, Alexander. At the same instant, with great speed and force, the phalanx went over to the attack.

The Macedonian army which Alexander commanded after the death of his father was the most superbly organized, equipped and trained that Greece ever produced. Philip had welded the old local levies of Macedonia together with his own royal retainers into an integrated force of all arms, in which the function of the 'Territorial Army' was to provide a tactical base for decisive action by the 'Royal Army'. The latter consisted of two *corps d'élite*, the Companion Cavalry and the 'hypaspists'. The Macedonian horsemen had always been good, and their role in battle was now

The hoplite phalanx advanced into battle to the music of flutes

to deliver the decisive shock, on the flanks or in a gap, when the enemy had been checked by the phalanx. There were eight squadrons of the Companions, each of two to three hundred horsemen under an officer. They were armed with a cuirass, and a short thrusting spear. The hypaspists were foot soldiers, probably armed in the same way as the hoplites, but distinguished as a professional *élite*. Their primary function was to form the tactical junction in battle between the cavalry and the remainder of the phalanx; but at different times they were also used for following up the cavalry, for rapid night marches, and for storming fortifications. They were divided into three battalions, each of 1,000 men. One squadron each of the hypaspists and the Companions formed the king's guard. Alexander himself usually led the Companions, but occasionally he led the hypaspists and the phalanx, and once even the archers.

The Territorial Army consisted of the main body of infantry, the phalanx. It was formed of six, later seven, battalions, each of 1,536 men, subdivided into units of 512 and ranged in files of 16 men. Each battalion had its commander, and Philip introduced the first officer hierarchies into Greek armies. He also armed his hoplites in a new way, making the shield smaller, and replacing the 8-foot spear with a 13-foot pike. The phalanx fulfilled the subordinate but vital function of holding the enemy while the cavalry dealt the decisive blow. Because they had this firm support, Alexander's Companions could beat the Persian cavalry, who were little inferior to them. Philip and Alexander also raised contingents from their subject and allied peoples, the most important of which were the Thessalian heavy cavalry, the Thracian lancers, the Cretan archers and the Agrianian javelin-men. Alexander was the first general to integrate fully his light troops with other arms; they proved devastating against the Persian chariots, and in mountain campaigns against tribesmen. He also relied increasingly on mercenaries to guard his communications, and in the last years of his wars raised a force of horsemen from the nomads of eastern Iran.

Alexander's siege equipment consisted of towers, rams, pent-houses and catapults, and it never failed him. He was the first general to use field artillery, which was organized in sections and carried on pack animals in all his campaigns. Unfortunately little is known about his system of supply. With the army travelled sappers, water and mining engineers, naval experts, surveyors and geographers, botanists, physicians, a secretarial department and an official historian.

The result was the best balanced and most powerful army of ancient times – an army equipped to fight in any type of country and against any enemy. The essence of the Macedonian technique of warfare under Alexander was the combination of the rock-like phalanx with light and heavy cavalry. The union of a dependable infantry base with the mobile shock supplied by cavalry was too much for the Persian masses, whose chief advantage lay in numbers. Numbers alone were of no avail against steadiness, missile fire, shock action and first class generalship.

Alexander spent the years 336 and 335 securing his home base. The barbarians were pushed back beyond the Danube, after his troops had crossed the river at night on rafts made of tent covers stuffed with straw. Then in the spring of 334 he invaded Asia Minor with 30,000 infantry, 5,000 cavalry, 160 ships, and almost no money. Within nine years he was to conquer the Persian empire from the Dardanelles to the Punjab. The feebleness of Darius III and the chaotic condition of his empire favoured an invader, yet the numbers and wealth of the Persians were prodigious.

Darius was not expecting an invasion, and Alexander was met only by a scratch force which he defeated overwhelmingly in a battle at the river Granicus – thereby gaining control of western Asia Minor. After this he proceeded round Asia Minor to take the defenders of the Cilician Gates unawares. His purpose was to secure his communications before striking farther east, and to eliminate the strong Persian fleet by depriving it of its bases. He won over most of the country by the mildness of his conquests. In addition, by supporting democratic movements in the cities, he induced many crews in the Persian navy to desert. In the winter of 334–3 he sent a large number of married soldiers home to Greece on leave – a gesture characteristic of the human touch which won the devotion of his soldiers.

Alexander's rapid advance ahead of his main troops through Cilicia to Tarsus was for once miscalculated. Darius, who was looking for battle, marched round him and severed his communications. But in November 333 at Issus, Alexander won another victory. The treasury at Damascus fell into his hands and his financial worries were over. At this point he did not immediately pursue Darius, but concentrated on destroying the other bases of the enemy's fleet in Phoenicia. Marathon, Byblos and Sidon quickly submitted. But Tyre proved difficult.

Alexander's siege of Tyre was the greatest siege of antiquity. Tyre had to be taken, for then the Aegean would be completely secured and the way into Egypt opened.

However, to capture the city posed formidable problems. Built on a rock half a mile off from the shore, it was surrounded by a wall at points 150 feet high. There were two harbours on the eastern side: the northern called the Sidonian harbour and the southern called the Egyptian.

The siege was opened in January 332. Alexander, and Diades, his chief engineer, started by building a mole out from the shore towards the rock, and progress at first was easy. But farther out the water was deep, and the workers began to be in trouble from gales as well as from missiles fired from the walls and from Tyrian warships. With some difficulty Alexander's men got two siege-towers out to the end of the mole. They were 150 feet high, and were covered with hides to protect them against blazing arrows. Catapults on the different storeys bombarded the defenders on the walls and the enemy galleys. The Tyrians dealt with this assault by sending against the mole two fire-ships filled with pitch, sulphur and shavings. When the towers had been burnt down, they sallied out in small boats and dismantled what was left of the mole. It was now clear to Alexander that he had to deal with tough opponents, so he ordered that a bigger mole should be built, and himself sailed northwards to gather a fleet.

The cities of Phoenicia had always been deadly rivals, and it did not take long to raise a fleet of 220 ships to fight the Tyrians. But when Alexander returned, King Azemilk of Tyre refused to give battle. Alexander therefore blockaded both the harbours – although without a proper anchorage this was difficult. By this time the new mole had been constructed, and another battery of siege-towers with rams and catapults was set up. Since only about 200 yards of the city wall could be bombarded from the mole, Alexander also mounted some battering-rams on ships, which could sail all round the rock. But once again the Tyrians were ready. By dropping rocks into the sea they made it impossible to approach the island closely, and their volleys of fire-arrows harried the assailants. When Alexander brought up ships to sweep the underwater obstacles, and warships to protect the sweeps, Tyrian divers cut their cables. So he moored them with chains – to which the defenders had no reply. Next thirteen Tyrian warships sailed out from the Sidonian harbour and surprised Alexander's fleet while the crews were having a meal on shore. Several of his ships were destroyed. But Alexander reacted quickly; he ordered a blockade of the Egyptian harbour, himself rowed round Tyre with a few ships, took the enemy in rear and beat them back. By now the battering-ships had found a weak point in the wall, just south of the Egyptian harbour, and a general assault was vigorously pressed. When a good breach had been made Alexander brought up two transports, carrying bridges and storming parties. He himself and Admetus led the royal guard of the hypaspists. Tyre thus fell after a siege of seven months. The Greeks, bitterly angered by the way the defenders had ostentatiously murdered their captives, retaliated by killing 8,000 Tyrians and selling 30,000 more into slavery.

The Greeks in his army imagined that with the conquest of Asia Minor the object of the war had been gained. But Alexander's vision was now wider. First he marched through Syria and Egypt. These submitted easily enough. Then he turned towards Persia.

In July 331 Alexander crossed the Euphrates, and pushed north-eastwards to the

Tigris. On 23rd September scouts told him that the enemy army was encamped on the plain near Gaugamela. The best policy for the Persians would have been to harry and exhaust the invading army rather than to give battle. However, Darius had decided that he would fight. Alexander was delighted.

In the twenty months since Issus the Persians had made an effort to build up a respectable army. But they had long before abandoned the methods of warfare by which the empire had been won in the sixth century. Apart from the small royal guard, their infantry now comprised only untrained levies and undisciplined tribesmen. The best part of the Persian army was the cavalry, equipped with link armour, a thrusting spear and a long sword. To supplement his cavalry, Darius had brought back into service the long disused scythed chariots, but there had not been time to train the drivers properly. The trouble with the Persian army was, in Fuller's words, that it had 'plenty of mobility, but little stability'. Besides, it was saddled with Darius as commander-in-chief. It included twenty-four nationalities, and decidedly outnumbered its opponents.

The Persian strategy was dictated by the composition of their army. The plain of Gaugamela was carefully levelled to make the terrain as suitable as possible for chariots. Darius took advantage of his numerical superiority and presented a long front with two powerful cavalry wings. He himself commanded in the centre, behind the 1,000 horse guards and the Indian and Carian cavalry. With him waited the only trained foot soldiers in the army, the guard of spearmen, and 2,000 Greek mercenary hoplites. On the left, under Bessus, were the cavalry detachments from the eastern provinces of the empire, including 1,000 heavily armoured cavalry from the Jaxartes known as the Saca 'cataphracts'. On the right, commanded by Mazaeus, were the western cavalry, including the Cappadocians. The infantry units were in rear of the cavalry. In the front were drawn up about two hundred chariots. In the centre of the Persian position were fifteen elephants. Horses dislike facing up to elephants, and if Darius had known what to do with his elephants they could have been very effective against Alexander's cavalry.

Alexander had the largest army he ever commanded. He had recruited a number of Greek mercenaries and been reinforced by three cavalry units, bringing the whole total up to 40,000 foot and 7,000 horse. It was certain that he would be outflanked and that the front line of Persian chariots and cavalry would attack all out early in the battle. He therefore assumed a defensive order of approach, his front consisting of a phalanx only about half the length of the enemy's line, supported by deep columns on the flanks. In the centre he put the six battalions of the phalanx and the hypaspists. On the left of the centre Parmenion commanded the Thessalian cavalry, half the allied horse, and some archers and mercenary infantry. On the right was the main strength, the Companion cavalry under Philotas, some other cavalry, and in front of them javelin-men and half the Macedonian archers. The left wing column was made up of more allied cavalry. The far right consisted of cavalry and the remaining archers and Agrianian javelin-men. A second line of mercenary hoplites would resist enveloping tactics by the Persian wings. Behind them were the baggage and prisoners guarded by the Thracian foot.

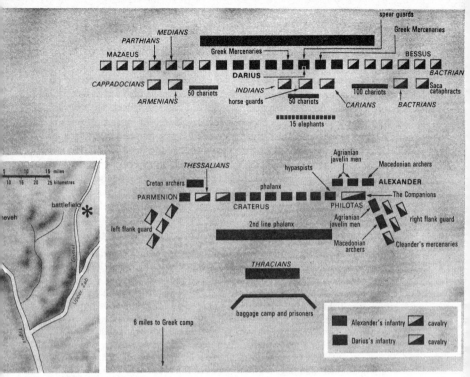

The battle of Gaugamela

Alexander's dispositions were perfectly planned to accord with Napoleon's battle principle of 'a well reasoned and extremely circumspect defensive followed by rapid and audacious attack'. It was a question of whether the instability of the Persians or the weakness of the Greek left would count first. The night before the battle Darius stood his men to arms all night – which merely tired them before the battle began.

Alexander, having made his dispositions in the early evening, slept well into the morning of 1st October 331. When he led his army out, he saw that the Companions were opposite the scythed chariots, so he inclined his advance to the right to bring the infantry opposite the chariots. This move brought the Companions almost to the edge of the levelled ground. Darius saw that he must stop the enemy moving to their right, or his chariots would be no use. So he launched the Saca cataphracts, followed by the Bactrian cavalry, against Alexander's extreme right. A hard fight took place, during which Alexander skilfully fed in new units one by one to produce the best results with fresh troops. But the Persians were only checked after some time by the Companions, and were then driven back by the lancers.

Meanwhile the charge of the Persian chariots had been launched. It proved a complete failure. Volleys of javelins threw the chariots into confusion, the horses panicked, and many of the drivers were killed; when what was left of them reached the phalanx, the hypaspists opened their ranks and let them run through – to be dealt with by the second line of infantry.

When Darius saw that Alexander had engaged his last mobile reserve on the Greek right, he thought that Bessus must be doing better than was in fact the case. Consequently he decided that the moment had come to launch the two decisive enveloping attacks. The whole Persian line of cavalry moved forward. Now came the crucial point of the battle. Instead of the Persian left concentrating their attack against the Companions, they headed towards the far right of the Greek army. This mistake may have been due to orders being misunderstood, or, as Fuller suggested, to the tendency of cavalry to follow the path of a previous charge – as happened to some of the French at Waterloo. It may also have been that the horses could not face the missiles in the centre. Anyway, the result was that a gap appeared in the Persian front.

Arrian describes how Alexander instantly seized the opportunity:

> When the Persians had made a break in the front line of their army, in consequence of the cavalry sallying forth to assist those who were surrounding the [Greek] right wing, Alexander wheeled round towards the gap, and forming a wedge of the Companion cavalry and of part of the phalanx which was posted here, he led them with a quick charge and a loud battle-cry straight towards Darius himself. For a short time there ensued a hand-to-hand fight; but when the Macedonian cavalry, commanded by Alexander himself, pressed on vigorously, thrusting themselves against the Persians and striking their faces with their spears, and when the Macedonian phalanx in dense array and bristling with long pikes had also made an attack upon them, all things together appeared full of terror to Darius . . . so that he was the first to turn and flee.

However, the battle was not yet won, since the advance of four battalions of the phalanx in the wake of the Companions had left a gap in the Greek line, and the Persian cavalry of the guard had flung themselves into it – cutting the phalanx in two. Most of them foolishly threw away the chance of helping Mazaeus destroy the Greek left, by riding on and looting the transport lines in the rear. But Parmenion's troops on the Greek left were surrounded and very hard pressed. Parmenion sent a desperate call for help to Alexander, which reached him as he was following up his victorious charge with an attack on the Persian left. It is an indication of Alexander's extraordinary control that he succeeded in turning the Companions immediately, and led them across to the other side of the battle area. There they encountered some of the Persian guard returning with the Parthian and Indian cavalry, and the fiercest cavalry engagement of the whole action then took place. But the Persian soldiery were now becoming aware that Darius had deserted them, and they lost heart. The Thessalians on the Greek left, who had been beaten back, made a second charge, this time successfully. The Persian right collapsed, while their left under Bessus made an orderly retreat.

Alexander ordered an immediate general pursuit; he was determined that the enemy should never reform as an army. His men chased the Persians for thirty-five miles as far as Arbela, pausing only to rest for a short time at midnight.

Gaugamela is one of the world's great battles, not only as the classic instance of Alexander's military genius, but in its historical consequences. It uncovered the heart of the Persian empire and made Alexander master of Asia, with all that this was to imply.

After Gaugamela Alexander marched on to take the great Persian centres of Babylon, Susa and Persepolis, all of which surrendered easily. In 330 he then set out to conquer the East. In the early summer of 326 he reached the Indus, after four years of fighting, he and his army having performed a number of remarkable military feats. In his pursuit of Darius towards the Caspian he covered 400 miles in eleven days, and then mounted 500 phalangists on horseback to ride another 50 miles at night. He defeated the nomads at the Oxus in 329 by bombarding them with catapults from boats, and then attacking with a force of heavy cavalry interspersed with javelin-men and archers. In the winter of 328 Alexander's men captured the stronghold of the Sogdian Rock, climbing 300 feet in the snow with the aid of ropes. In 327 he crossed the Hindu Kush with 27,000 men and, after very hard fighting reached the Hydaspes river in the following year. There he won the fourth of his great victories. He had first to cross the river while the enemy were massed on the other bank, and then fight against elephants which put his cavalry out of action.

But shortly after, at the river Beas, Alexander's army mutinied and would go no further. It was eight years since they had left Greece, and they had marched 17,000 miles. He led them back to Susa, which they reached in spring 324. That last phase of the war was the toughest of all. Alexander was wounded, and he died in June 323 at the early age of thirty-three.

It has never been disputed that Alexander belongs to the top flight of military captains. But Alexander had also a great civilizing imagination. Everywhere that he carried his wars he introduced new standards of humanity and tolerance. At Ephesus he supported the democrats; in Caria he respected the matriarchal system; he was always careful not to violate the religion of his subjects; for example, at Babylon he rebuilt the temple of Marduk which had been destroyed by Xerxes. He is said to have founded seventy new cities in his empire. He was responsible for the hellenization of the Near East. But Alexander's greatness lies above all in his departure from the traditional idea that civilized Greece must be apart from the barbarians of the rest of the world. He told the priest of Ammon in Egypt that God was 'father of all men' and at a great feast at Opis in 324 some nine thousand guests of every people in his empire sat down together. Alexander's dream of the brotherhood of man was not fulfilled; once his own personality and stature had been removed, the empire disintegrated. But his vision was one of the great milestones in the development of civilization.

After Alexander Greek armies became excessively complex and elephants were increasingly used. Elephants could be effective against cavalry and against troops who had not seen them before – as at the battle of Heraclea in 280 when Pyrrhus, king of Epirus, won a notoriously costly victory against the Romans. But on the whole elephants were not a success in battle, and the Hellenistic art of war did not develop beyond the high level attained by Alexander.

4   The Expansion of Rome

Rome was founded, according to the legend in 753 B.C.; five hundred years later she dominated the Italian peninsula, and seven hundred and fifty years later she ruled western Europe and the Mediterranean world.

Little is known about the Roman army before the fourth century B.C. But by the sixth century the Romans had become a nation in arms. In Roman history military development and social organization influenced each other profoundly. All male citizens between seventeen and forty-six were liable for military service, and those between forty-six and sixty were available as a reserve. The tactics of the Romans at this time were almost certainly the standard Greek hoplite tactics.

A severe defeat by the Gauls at the Allia in 391 necessitated a new start, and at the inspiration of Marcus Furius Camillus Rome was refortified and her army reorganized. The army remained a citizen levy, paid when on active service, but the phalanx was replaced by the legion. The main troops of the legion were heavy infantry; it also contained cavalry and *velites* (poorer men, who were less well equipped). The infantry was organized in three lines – the *hastati* in front, behind them the *principes*, and in the rear the *triarii*. Each of these lines was broken up into ten companies called 'maniples' (handfuls), the light infantry being interspersed among the maniples of the heavy infantry. The whole infantry force of the legion was drawn up in a chequered formation, the maniples of the second rank covering the intervals between those of the first, and the third those of the second. Each line was probably four files deep; the front two contained 1,200 men each, or 120 to a maniple, and the *triarii* 600. The cavalry was disposed on the wings, and numbered altogether 300 in ten squadrons. Later the numbers in the legion rose towards 6,000 and troops were increasingly recruited from the Italian allies.

The *hastati* and the *principes* were protected by a bronze helmet and a breast-plate, and a semi-cylindrical rectangular shield. Their weapons consisted of two javelins, a dagger, and a pointed double-edged sword 2 feet long. The *triarii* were similarly armed, except that instead of javelins they had a thrusting-spear. The *velites* were armed with a sword, two javelins and a round shield, and wore a head-dress of wolf's skin. The javelin could be thrown with the aid of a thong attached to the shaft behind the centre of gravity; when pulled this worked like rifling, causing the javelin to rotate in flight, thus increasing its range and accuracy. The legionary cavalry units were poorly armed, with a leather shield, a lance and a sword.

The virtue of the manipular formation was that it made possible both an elastic defence and a flexible attack. The legion's attack was begun by the *velites*, who as light skirmishers covered the advance of the heavy infantry. When the *hastati* got

The Roman soldier of the Republic

Roman infantry of the fourth century B.C.: a light foot soldier of the *velites* (far left); heavy foot soldiers of the *hastati* or *principes* (centre left and right)

within range they hurled their javelins, and immediately advanced to engage the enemy with their swords. During the struggle the rear ranks supplied support to those in front who fell or tired. The legionaries were thoroughly drilled to execute relay manoeuvres, by which one whole line replaced another and launched a new drive forward. If things went badly the *hastati* and the *principes* could form into one line, and retire through the intervals of the *triarii* – who would then fight as a phalanx. A third and final assault could well clinch a victory. The Romans applied this system with a high degree of discipline and training. The system of three lines was good for morale in that it kept two-thirds of the soldiers out of the danger area for as long as possible, and gave a defeated front line a good chance to retire safely. Cavalry was used for scouting and pursuit, but it had no part in the classical tactics of the legion, and troopers in fact often fought on foot.

It has been said that the Romans were 'the greatest entrenching army in history'. The legion was always backed by a fortified camp. The size and shape of the camp varied according to the terrain, but where possible it was built square and large enough to accommodate two legions. It was fortified by ramparts, palisades and ditches. The Romans took trouble to build these camps for two reasons. First, they recognized the value of security and comfort. They used much of the time spent in the camp in drill and physical training, in order to instil the qualities of steadiness and order which were necessary for the tactics of the legion. Secondly, the legions generally did not offer battle unless they had a fortified area near at hand to retire into if the fighting should go against them. As a result, the reverses they suffered were rarely disastrous.

Apart from their weapons, the Roman soldiers on the march had to carry a considerable load – including entrenching tools and cooking equipment. The men were not particularly well fed. They seldom ate meat, and the staple food in camp was unleavened bread made of wheat baked on hot stones or embers.

The army was commanded by two consuls, elected annually; these were generally politicians who had received no training in generalship. This peculiar dual command was designed to lessen the possibility of military tyranny, but it was a military nonsense. The ancient Romans did not have an aristocratic officer class. The maniples, the essential tactical units, were each led by two centurions, who were experienced soldiers of the same social background as the privates. The tactical functioning of the legion was thus in the control of tried professionals who understood their men. Polybius describes the centurions as 'not so much bold and adventurous as men with a faculty for command, steady and rather of a deep-rooted spirit . . . who, in the face of superior numbers or overwhelming pressure, would endure and die in the defence of their post'. They were steady and brave; they understood war and they treated it as a job which had to be done. It was largely because she could always produced first class N.C.O.'s and privates that Rome proved so successful in her campaigns.

For over seven hundred years after the middle of the fourth century B.C. the composition of the legion did not fundamentally change.

By the middle of the third century Rome, with her widening political and commercial interests, came up against the challenge of Carthage, the richest city of the west. The First Punic War (265–41) went in Rome's favour. But by 220 Carthaginian power was reviving in Spain and in 218 Hannibal, a 29-year-old Carthaginian general, crossed the Pyrenees to invade Italy. Rome and Carthage were evenly matched in the Second Punic War (218–01), and each knew that she must win or be for ever ruined.

Hannibal had made a wide study of Hellenistic and Roman warfare, and he had already commanded armies for three years. He crossed the Pyrenees with a motley

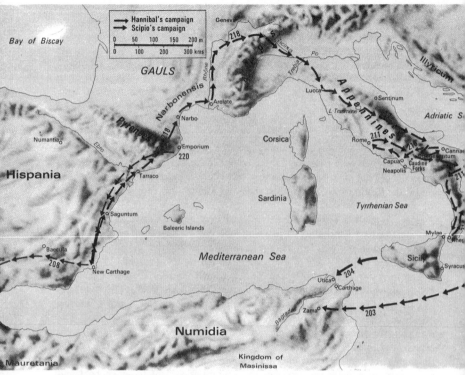

The campaigns of Hannibal and Scipio

army of about 40,000 men and 37 elephants. The army consisted mostly of mercenaries, recruited in Africa, Spain and Gaul, and it was held together only by Hannibal's leadership and the prospect of plunder. The main constituent was light infantry, armed with short sword, spear, shield, and little body armour. The best troops were the Numidian mounted javelin-men under a brilliant cavalry commander, Maharbal. Polybius says 'the army was not so much numerous as highly efficient, and in an extraordinary state of physical training'. All through the war the Carthaginians were to be heavily outnumbered by the Romans, who by 217 had raised their legions from five to eleven, and in the last stages of the war to over twenty – or 100,000 men. Hannibal's strategy in the war was not to destroy Rome, but by his victorious presence in Italy to break her hold over the Italian confederacy, and force her to agree to coexist with Carthage. He posed as a liberator, and proclaimed that 'I am not come to fight against Italians, but on behalf of Italians against Rome.'

Hannibal advanced rapidly round the Mediterranean. During his crossing of the Alps he was so beset by tribesmen and early snows that his army debouched into northern Italy reduced to 20,000 foot and 6,000 cavalry. But at the Trebia stream in December 218 he won the first of three great victories, destroying two-thirds of the Roman army. In 217 the Romans decided to meet the Carthaginians with their superior cavalry not in the plain, but further south in the Apennines. However, in April Hannibal caught his enemy between the hills and the northern shore of Lake Trasimene. The Romans had neglected their intelligence and reconnaissance. Screened by a mist, the Carthaginian forces launched a sudden attack from the foothills and in three hours destroyed or captured all the enemy. After this victory Hannibal marched down the Adriatic coast and in the spring of 216 he captured the Roman supply base at Cannae. There, in August, he brought the Romans to battle again.

Hannibal drew up his army in a convex crescent formation, with the infantry in the centre and on the wings powerful detachments of cavalry. The Roman infantry army was drawn up in conventional parallel formation; its commander that day was the consul Tarentius Varro, a business man whose turn it was to be general! Hannibal began the battle by routing the Roman cavalry. Then he let the Roman infantry advance and press the Carthaginian crescent back till it was concave. At that point he suddenly advanced his African infantry from left and right and turned them inwards on to the Roman flanks. The battle was completed when his cavalry returned from the pursuit and fell on the Roman rear. Assailed on all four sides, as Fuller put it, 'the Roman army was swallowed up as if by an earthquake'.

After Cannae most of southern Italy went over to the Carthaginians; but a large nucleus of Roman territory stood firm, and the Roman fleet was definitely in command of the seas. Maharbal urged Hannibal to march on Rome straightaway. He refused. As we have said, his strategy was not to prosecute a war to the death, but simply to bring Rome to terms; and in any case he lacked the resources to undertake a massive siege. A war of attrition followed, in which the Romans, chiefly led by Quintus Fabius Maximus, sought to avoid pitched battles; they took advantage of their fortresses and their greater numbers to wear Hannibal down, and contained him in the south of Italy. But they did not dare attack him. A naval victory in 208 gave Rome absolute supremacy at sea, making possible a future invasion of Africa.

This turn of fortune in Rome's favour in Italy in the ten years after Cannae coincided with success in the Spanish theatre. An army had been sent to Spain in 218 and at first had done well; but by 211 the Romans had been driven back north of the Ebro. In 210 the Spanish command was given to Publius Cornelius Scipio, aged twenty-five. Scipio Africanus was to become the greatest of all Roman generals.

Late in 210 Scipio landed in Spain at Emporium. He had with him 10,000 foot and 1,000 cavalry, with which to bring the shattered Roman army up to a strength of four legions. Scipio immediately set about organizing his army and raising the morale of his men, and then, by a daring and dramatic move, stamped his imprint on the war. Instead of engaging any of the three enemy armies in Spain he decided to make straight for New Carthage, their main base 300 miles down the coast to the south. The enemy armies were all a good ten days' march from New Carthage, and he reckoned he had time. He covered the 300 miles with his army and navy in about

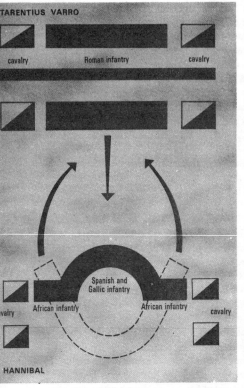

The battle of Cannae *left*. Hannibal's army included elephants *right*

a week. The fortress, built on a rocky promontary, was supposed to be strong, but Scipio took the defenders by surprise. Wading with his men through the lagoon, he had scaling-ladders placed at the weakest part of the wall, and New Carthage was quickly taken. Scipio thus captured the enemy's base, and established himself on their eastern flank and rear.

In 208 Scipio defeated a Carthaginian army at Baecula. Again in 206 at Ilipa, although outnumbered, he won a decisive victory. The Romans attacked with their thin centre held back, and the strongest legions on the wings thrown forward. The legions destroyed the Spanish levies on the Carthaginian wings before the armies had even met in the centre, and then turned inwards to decide the battle. Scipio pursued the enemy to the sea, where they surrendered. In 205, when the Carthaginians had been completely cleared out of Spain, he returned to Rome.

Carthage had now lost Spain, Sicily and Sardinia, and Hannibal was contained in lower Italy. The Roman Senate intended to strangle his army where it was. But

Scipio proposed a different strategy. He was in favour of keeping Hannibal contained in southern Italy while striking at Carthage in North Africa. The Senate was uncooperative, but Scipio set about recruiting, organizing and training his army. In 204 he landed in Africa. He had 25,000 men and the support of Masinissa, king of Numidia, who could supply him with first-class cavalry. He was opposed by a Carthaginian army of 20,000 foot, 6,000 cavalry and 140 elephants.

In the spring of 203, after a four day march, Scipio with one legion and some cavalry caught the enemy on the Bagradas plain, and defeated them by the very un-Roman tactics of launching two decisive cavalry charges from the wings. Carthage now sued for peace and recalled Hannibal; but when in the summer of 203 he landed in Africa with 15,000 men, the Carthaginians decided after all to go on fighting. In the following year Scipio ravaged the rich Bagradas valley, and in the autumn he was met by Hannibal's army at Zama, five days' march to the south-west of Carthage. At Zama in 202 B.C. was fought the final battle of the Second Punic War. Each army was about 40,000 strong. Hannibal's forces may have been slightly more numerous, but most of Scipio's infantry had received a longer training, and he had the advantage in cavalry, with more than 4,000 to Hannibal's 2,000.

For the first time in his career Hannibal was inferior in cavalry, and this meant that he could not use the enveloping tactics which had been so successful at Cannae. In front of his forces he placed 80 elephants. His infantry stood in three lines. The first consisted of Ligurian and Gallic heavy infantry interspersed with Moorish light infantry and Balearic slingers. In the second line he placed the troops in whom he had least trust – the newly-levied Carthaginians and Africans. The third line, consisting of his own veteran infantry from Italy, was held about 200 yards behind the second, so that it should not get involved before it could deliver the decisive blow. Hannibal posted 1,000 Carthaginian cavalry on the right wing and 1,000 Numidians on the left. His aim was simply to break the Roman front. Much would depend on the elephants.

Scipio adapted the normal dispositions of the legion to deal with the enemy's elephants and to exploit his own cavalry superiority. Instead of drawing up the maniples of the three lines chequer-wise he disposed them in columns, leaving gaps so that the elephants could pass through and be dealt with on the way by the *velites* in the lanes. The lines were also spaced farther apart than usual, with the *triarii* particularly far back, to give the *velites* room to retire between them if necessary. He put his main force of cavalry, Masinissa's Numidians, on the right wing, and the Italian cavalry under Laelius on the left.

The battle opened with a skirmish between the opposing forces of Numidian cavalry. Hannibal then launched the charge of his elephants. As they pounded towards the Roman army Scipio ordered a blast of trumpets and horns along the whole of his line. The sudden blare caused the elephants to panic. Those on the left turned and crashed back into Hannibal's Numidians. When Masinissa saw that the enemy's prize cavalry was in confusion he seized the opportunity to charge, and drove the Numidians from the field. In the centre Scipio's disposition of his maniples in lanes paid off, for although the elephants punished the *velites* severely, most of them passed straight through the Romans without touching the heavy infantry. Some were driven back from the lanes towards the Carthaginian right, pursued by javelins from the Roman cavalry. Laelius exploited the confusion thus caused among the enemy's cavalry in the same way as Masinissa had on the other wing, and hurled his cavalry at the Carthaginian right. Thus Hannibal's cavalry on both sides of the battle area were routed at the start, and his flanks exposed.

The Roman cavalry pursued the Carthaginians into the distance, and the second phase of the battle, the infantry engagement, now began. Hannibal's Gauls and Ligurians at first got the better of the struggle because of their mobility; but they could not actually break the Roman line which, with its superior weight, gradually began to press them back. When the Roman *principes* came into action the Carthaginian second line failed to support their front; and when it seemed to the Gauls that they had been let down they gave up the fight and melted away, leaving the second line to face the Romans. The ground was now encumbered with corpses and slippery with blood. For a while the Roman *hastati* were driven back by the new Carthaginian front. But then the Roman officers rallied the *principes*, and with their longer line the Romans forced back the Carthaginian second line and cut it to pieces. The survivors, as before, fled back towards the next line for refuge, and, as before, Hannibal refused to allow fresh and disciplined troops to get involved with defeated ones; his veteran *triarii* levelled their spears, and the remnants of the Carthaginian second line disappeared towards the flanks.

The third and toughest phase of the battle now opened. The Romans had routed two lines of the enemy already, and no doubt were elated at their success. On the other hand, except for the *triarii*, they had exerted themselves heavily and now had to face Hannibal's veteran infantry in perfect order and completely fresh. With extraordinary coolness, Scipio at this point checked his highly disciplined troops. He had the wounded carried to the rear, ordered the exhausted *hastati* to the flanks, and reformed the *principes* and *triarii* together, in close order and on a more extended front so as to concentrate the shock of the charge while at the same time overlapping the enemy. Polybius relates that, when this had been done, 'the two lines charged each other with the greatest fire and fury. Being nearly equal in numbers, spirit, courage and arms, the battle was for a long time undecided, the men in their obstinate valour falling dead without giving way a step.' The infantry struggle was for some time very evenly matched.

Then, finally, the Roman cavalry of Masinissa and Laelius returned from their pursuit of the Carthaginian cavalry and struck Hannibal's infantry in the rear. 'The greater part of his men were cut down in their ranks; while of those who attempted to fly very few escaped with their life.' The battle was over. Scipio's cavalry made thoroughly sure of the victory, and the outcome of the war, by scouring the whole countryside. Hannibal himself escaped. Scipio did not march on Carthage because he had not the means to conduct a siege, and he wished to impose moderate rather than vindictive peace terms.

The comparative merits of the two great generals who opposed each other at Zama cannot be evaluated simply. Hannibal was probably the better tactician; indeed his tactical genius at Cannae can compare with the conduct of any battle in the history of warfare. Hannibal's army at Zama was inferior in quality to Scipio's – a considerable proportion of his infantry was semi-trained and he was at a grave numerical disadvantage in cavalry. He had to take a chance with the elephants, and everything depended on their behaviour. In the event they let him down disastrously. And yet even after that, by holding his best infantry back till the end, and by letting the Roman infantry blunt its attack on his secondary troops, he almost pulled it off. Scipio made no mistakes at Zama, and his cool reorganization of his troops in mid-battle was masterly. Even so, it was the providential return of his cavalry in the nick of time, together with the fighting quality of the Roman infantry, which really won the battle. Hannibal did everything he could have done; but by 202, after sixteen years of continuous high command, he may well have been past his best.

Scipio was the most original of Roman tacticians. The legionary infantry was superior to any that the world had yet seen, but Scipio perceived that without a good cavalry arm Roman armies were gravely handicapped, and he temporarily repaired this deficiency. But here, both in his recognition of the need for cavalry and in his method of using it, Scipio acknowledged Hannibal's mastery. His use of cavalry was in the classic pattern set by Alexander and Hannibal, and his crescent formation at Ilipa was closely similar to Hannibal's at Cannae. Unfortunately Scipio relied for cavalry on allied or mercenary contingents, instead of training Romans. In the wars of the second century, when the Romans found themselves opposed by enemies who fought in an infantry phalanx, Scipio's tactical lessons were forgotten.

Both Hannibal and Scipio were outstandingly good at handling men. Hannibal invaded Italy with a motley army recruited from all parts of the western Mediterranean. He trained it and led it to win great victories. Altogether, as Polybius says, 'for sixteen continuous years Hannibal maintained the war with Rome in Italy, without once releasing his army from service in the field, but keeping the vast numbers under control without any sign of disaffection towards himself or towards each other'. Both generals were personally courageous and popular with their men. Before the battle of Zama Scipio rode up and down the ranks of his men personally inspiring them.

Maharbal was right when he told Hannibal after Cannae that he did not know how to use a victory. It is extraordinary that he never raised a proper siege-train, if not to attack Rome at least to reduce the fortresses upon which the Fabian strategy of the Romans depended. After Cannae, Hannibal lost the initiative, allowed Fabius to turn the tide of war against him, and eventually found himself trapped in southern Italy. Clearly he never understood fully the importance of seapower. By contrast, Scipio showed his military greatness in the originality and vision of his strategy. Whenever possible he struck direct at the enemy's base, each time with the most successful results. His plan of leaving Hannibal contained in lower Italy and striking straight at Africa, thus devastating the enemy at home and forcing them to abandon activities in Italy, was the strategy of a genius. The way in which Scipio brought Hannibal to the final battle at Zama was also brilliant. By marching up the rich valley of the Bagradas, ravaging it as he went, he threatened Carthage with the

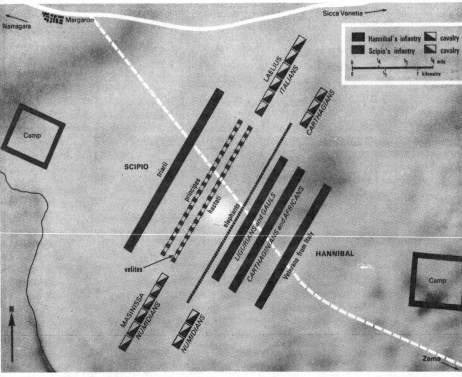

The battle of Zama

destruction of one of her chief sources of supply, drew Hannibal away from Carthage itself, and at the same time shortened the distance which Masinissa had to cover in order to reinforce him and thereby produce the superiority in cavalry which would be decisive. Where Scipio was undoubtedly superior to Hannibal was in strategy. It was this which in the end mattered most, and which marks out Scipio as one of the great captains of history.

Out of the Second Punic War emerged the beginning of the Roman empire, and during the second and first centuries Rome was continually at war to preserve and extend her power in the Mediterranean. Some of these campaigns, it must be admitted, were notable only for incompetent generalship and the indiscipline of the legions. But Rome lived off imperial tribute and slave labour, and such an economy necessitated endless conquest.

Although a major factor in the victory of Rome over Carthage had been her superiority at sea and although the Roman empire was to be Mediterranean-based the Romans were by inclination landlubbers. Episodes in Roman naval history worth noting are the victories of Duillius in the First Punic War and Pompey's systematic sweeping of the Mediterranean to clear it of pirates in 67. But the Romans introduced no significant developments in the art of war at sea.

Between 104 and 101 important reforms were introduced in the army by Gaius Marius. In order to give the legion more cohesion while retaining flexibility, he enlarged its basic tactical unit from the 120-man maniple to the 600-man 'cohort'. At the same time he fixed the total number in the legion at 6,000. There were thus ten cohorts in a legion. Each of these was divided into six 'centuries', under centurions. The thrusting-spear so far used by the *triarii* was abolished, and all three lines were armed with an improved javelin. The *velites* and the legionary cavalry disappeared, and from now on all cavalry and light troops were supplied by the allies. A more unified and formidable legion of heavy infantry emerged, which was to be the instrument of Julius Caesar's conquests. Marius also gave every legion an eagle standard; the new eagles became symbols of the legions, and their loss in battle came to be regarded as the worst of disgraces.

The most important change made by Marius was to widen the basis of recruitment; the army was thrown open to all who would volunteer to join. This change led to a rapid professionalization of the legions, and its effect on politics was revolutionary. Because the state did not undertake to provide pay the loyalty of the soldiers was given not to the state but to the general who recruited them. He equipped them, and they followed him for as long as he was successful and there were prospects of loot. It was this innovation which made possible the careers of a succession of soldier-politicians in the first century B.C. – Marius, Sulla, Pompey and Caesar.

At the end of 59 B.C. news reached Rome that the Helvetii were on the point of migrating from Switzerland across to the south-west of Gaul. As soon as he was free of his duties as consul for that year, Julius Caesar set off for Geneva at top speed. At this time Caesar was forty-one years old. His previous military experience had been very limited. In 81 B.C. he had served in Asia Minor, and at the storming of Mitylene he had won a civic crown for saving the life of a fellow soldier. But after that he had concentrated on a political career; he got his way as consul by a combination of rabble-rousing oratory and the threat of military force.

It is probable that when he hastened to Geneva in 58 Caesar had no definite schemes of conquest. But he was ambitious, and if he was to maintain himself at the top of Roman politics he had to have fame – and also an army. In the early summer of 58 he checked the Helvetii by building a 19-mile chain of fortifications along the valley of the Rhône, and then defeating them at Armécy. Posing to the Gauls as a saviour and not a conqueror, he then advanced north of the old Roman frontier to clear Alsace of the Germanic invaders who had recently settled there. Near Vesontio Caesar's six legions in triple line overwhelmed seven German tribes. In the winter of 58–7 Caesar left his legions quartered in that area.

The penetration of Roman arms into their country now aroused the hostility of the Belgae, the part-Germanic confederacy of tribes which inhabited northern Gaul. In the spring of 57 Caesar hurried northwards to meet the Belgic army of 300,000 men on the Aisne. The fighting methods of the Belgae were those of primitive barbarians; they fought as an undisciplined horde of infantry. Most of them were armed only with a long cutting-sword and a wooden or wattle shield, and fought half-naked, though their chiefs wore breast-plates of bronze and highly decorated helmets. Occasionally the shock of their savage onslaught prevailed, but generally when they fought the Romans, as Fuller put it, 'courage shattered itself on the rocks of discipline'. Dissensions among the Belgae allowed Caesar to deal with the different tribes separately. By the end of 56 all Gaul except for the Massif Central had been conquered.

In the autumn of 55 Caesar made his first expedition to Britain, on what was really nothing more than a reconnaissance trip. In July 54 possibly the biggest fleet ever seen in the Channel before the 1939/45 war sailed for Sandwich, carrying five legions and 2,000 Gallic cavalry. The Britons were too terrified to oppose the landing, and Caesar hurriedly pursued them inland. But within twenty-four hours he heard that his transports had been damaged by the weather. The Britons were encouraged, and under the leadership of Cassivellaunus conducted a vigorous guerrilla war. However, Caesar defeated them at a battle near Brentford, and captured the stronghold of Cassivellaunus on the other side of the Thames. It was now time for him to return to Gaul, so he imposed moderate terms and withdrew. The Romans did not again come to Britain for a hundred years, and the tribute was probably never paid. Caesar's own accounts of the two invasions of Britain should be read with some suspicion; they give the impression of trying to cover up failure.

It was more than time for Caesar to turn his attention to Gaul, for revolt was breaking out in many places. In 53 a rebel leader emerged in Ambiorix, chief of the Eburones. He annihilated a legion near Amiens, and then laid siege by Roman methods to a Roman camp. After a forced march Caesar relieved it, but he had to spend the rest of that year crushing the Eburones. Ambiorix was driven into the Ardennes, another chieftain was flogged to death, and the Eburones were systematically harried. Their crops and cattle were destroyed and, as Caesar tells us, 'every hamlet, every homestead that anyone could see was set on fire'. So far dissensions between rebel chieftains had enabled Caesar to get the better of them. But in 52 a new leader arose who was capable, principally by means of extraordinarily cruel discipline, of uniting the rebel Gauls. This was Vercingetorix, chief of the Arverni. At the beginning of the year Caesar threw the enemy into some confusion by a succession of lightning marches through snowy hills. Then he laid siege to the stronghold of Avaricum. Vercingetorix intended to fight a war of attrition, avoiding battle between his guerrillas and the legions. He attempted to relieve Avaricum by reducing the whole country around to a smoking wilderness, to deprive the Romans of food. But Caesar took the town, massacred its inhabitants and appropriated its corn stores. Caesar eventually caught Vercingetorix at his citadel of Alesia and there besieged him. Attacked by a powerful relieving army, so that he was both besieged and besieger at the same time, he held twenty-five miles of entrenchments and defeated two enemy armies. This remarkable victory broke the back of the Gallic revolt. A liberal peace was made, and thereafter Gaul caused no trouble to Rome.

Meanwhile the situation in Italy had altered completely, since in 53 Crassus, an important political figure with whom Caesar had been on terms, had been removed from the scene. With grandiose ideas of an eastern conquest Crassus had invaded the powerful Parthian empire. The Parthian army was composed entirely of cavalry. The nobles, mounted on large and strong armour-clad Nesaean horses, fought much like medieval knights, covered with armour and charging with a lance. The mass of their retainers were light horsemen, armed with a bow specially shortened below the grip for use in the saddle. They were trained to execute the famous Parthian shot, galloping away from the enemy in simulated flight and turning to fire low over the crupper. Crassus met the enemy force of 11,000 cavalry under Surenas at Carrhae. In typical tactics the Parthians drew on his advance guard, and then turned to encircle and annihilate it. The main body of the Roman infantry army formed a square and awaited their doom from the arrows of their more mobile enemy. Out of 36,000 Romans only about 10,000 eventually escaped.

When in the autumn of 50 Caesar returned to Italy, he and Pompey were thus left face to face, and civil war was inevitable. Caesar had a successful and devoted army of nine legions. Pompey had ten, seven of which were in Spain, and he also had command of the seas. Caesar was more likely to have popular support than Pompey. In January 49 Caesar committed himself to war by crossing the river Rubicon and pressing south. Pompey had not seen active service since 62 and with his poorly trained troops he had no wish to fight a battle against the conqueror of Gaul and his veterans, so at the end of March he shipped his army to Macedonia, with Caesar hard on his heels. Within ten weeks of crossing the Rubicon Caesar had mastered Italy. In April 49 Caesar departed for Spain, and there in seven months secured the submission of Pompey's seven legions without any bloodshed – by speed of marching he trapped the enemy in a defile near Ilerda. In January 48 he crossed with his army to Macedonia, slipping past Pompey's patrolling vessels to land seven legions. After being besieged for some time in Dyrrhachium, Pompey's army burst out. The crucial battle of the civil war was fought at Pharsalus in August. Pompey had still wished to avoid battle, but his officers were impatient. He was defeated; the remnants of his army surrendered, and he himself fled to Egypt, where he was murdered.

Caesar still had to mop up the Pompeians in various provinces. He first followed his enemy to Egypt; there he fell in love with Queen Cleopatra, and lingered for nine months. Then in July 47 he set out for Pontus, where at Zela he defeated the rebel Pharnaces and sent a dispatch to Rome telling the senators, '*Veni, vidi, vici.*' By now over a year had passed since Pharsalus and the Pompeians had rallied under Labienus in Africa. In December 47 Caesar landed in Africa with one legion and 600 cavalry. He was at first very hard pressed, but after receiving reinforcements the following spring he successfully concluded the African campaign with a victory at Thapsus. In 45 Caesar defeated the last of the Pompeians in Spain at Munda and thus became master of the world. He became life-dictator at Rome. Although his rule was not unpopular he was assassinated on the ides of March 44 B.C. by the republicans.

For a general who achieved such total overall success Caesar is extraordinarily open to criticism. He failed to make the changes in the organization of his army which were obviously necessary. Without proper light infantry it took him much longer to defeat the Gauls than it need have done. He did not train any proper cavalry, but relied on barbarian auxiliaries; again and again this deficiency handicapped him. His reconnaissance was often bad. He neglected his communications; through carelessness his fleet was twice almost lost off the British coast, and when this happened he had no proper repair equipment. His supply system broke down so completely at Ilerda and Dyrrhachium that his troops were almost starving.

As a strategist Caesar was, to say the least, erratic. He systematically overran Gaul, but then spent a summer in an island which was remote and unimportant, while massive revolt was brewing behind him. The swift, bloodless conquests of Italy and Spain contrast completely with his conduct of the later phases of the civil war. He threw away the advantage of his surprise crossing into Macedonia by informing Pompey of his presence, and by wasting time in Egypt and Pontus he allowed the Pompeians to rally and reorganize in Africa. He landed for the first time in Africa with absurdly few troops – one legion and 600 cavalry. As a tactician Caesar showed no originality. He neglected cavalry, and fought all his various enemies with a traditional three-line legion. He was, however, a very great leader of infantry. As in politics, so in tactics: when he saw his way he was swift in decision, rapid in action and bold to a degree. He was often too rash and hasty, but overall his reliance on mobility paid off – as against the Helvetii and Vercingetorix, in the descent to Brundisium, and before Ilerda and Thapsus.

As great a factor as any in bringing Caesar success was his own personality and character. His mere presence with his troops seems to have filled them with the same overwhelming certainty of victory that he had. His cheerfulness and wit, as well as his success, made his men devoted to him. He was a brilliant and popular politician with remarkable oratorical gifts, and it was above all because he was so popular with the masses that Italy fell to him immediately in the civil war. His only concern was power, and to secure it he was completely ruthless and amoral. No man ever made war so horrible as Caesar did in Gaul; yet when it suited him better, in the civil war and after, he was lenient and tolerant to his enemies.

As a man and as a soldier Caesar is perhaps the most disappointing of the great conquerors. Nonetheless, in his enlarging of the Roman empire he was one of the decisive makers of western history.

Egyptian soldiers. A company of Negro archers of the
period of the Middle Kingdom

Company of negro archers marching in fours from the tomb of an officer Masaḥti. The coffin on one side and the boat on the other, are from the same tomb.

"ne compagnie d'archers noirs formée de quarante hommes.

Company of light forty strong.

5

The Roman Defensive and the Barbarian Migration

The Roman empire, having been extended almost to its final bounds by Caesar, was, for over four hundred years, garrisoned by soldiers posted along the frontiers. The defensive was the order of the age, and this tended to react unfavourably on the fighting qualities of the Roman army. As the years passed barbarians were enlisted more and more into the army, mainly because of a manpower problem; this barbarizing of the Roman army gradually resulted in the disintegration of the old Roman military traditions, and decay from within, coupled with a series of migratory invasions from barbarian peoples, finally brought to an end the Roman empire in the west.

At the end of the first century B.C. Augustus (the first Roman emperor formally entitled as such) became aware that the condition of the army which he had inherited was far from satisfactory, consisting in the main of short-service private retinues. In order to garrison the long frontier, to police the conquered areas and to keep out raids and invasions, a disciplined long-service army was necessary – loyal to the state rather than to its various commanders. Augustus reduced the army to a standing force of 168,000 legionaries; he also kept 150,000 *auxilia*, which provided most of the cavalry and light infantry, and were organized in cohorts of infantry and squadrons of cavalry between 500 and 1,000 men strong. Seapower was no longer underestimated at Rome; Augustus founded two new naval bases in Italy, at Misenum and Ravenna; all provincial governors had ships at their disposal; and squadrons were maintained on the river frontiers. The equipment, strategy and tactics of the imperial army remained for three and a half centuries much as they had been under Scipio, Marius and Caesar. The fighting formation of the first century A.D. was normally a triple line of infantry cohorts, but a two-line formation was not uncommon; during the second century the army reverted to phalanx tactics. the *auxilia*, by this time much more professionalised, carried out the initial reconnaissance and probing, and the solid phalanx then bore the brunt of the heavy fighting. Another formation was the *testudo*, or 'tortoise', used when under heavy missile fire both in advance and retreat; the soldiers of the front rank held their shields up in front of them, and those in the ranks behind raised their shields horizontally above their heads; a shell of shields thus protected them all.

In the early period of the empire the northern frontier was not fixed. Augustus aimed to push forward to the Danube and the Elbe, and between 17 and 11 B.C. Tiberius, one of his stepsons, secured the line of the Danube. But the Germans were not a people to be cowed by a display of Roman power. Though their military organization was primitive they made up for it in fierce energy and independence.

An Asiatic nomad archer, *c.* 500 B.C.

The warfare between the Romans and the Germans was described by the great historian Tacitus, and it is clear from his account that German society at this early date was militarily orientated. 'Certain totems and emblems are carried into battle. The strongest incentive to courage lies in family and kinship. Some lost or losing battles have been restored by the women, by the incessance of their prayers and by the baring of their breasts.'

In A.D. 9 Arminius, a chieftain of the Cherusci, ambushed three Roman legions in the Teutoburger Forest. The Romans were marching through the thickets and swamps of the forest during a thunderstorm when the Germans hurled their volleys of javelins at them. The storm lasted all the next day and the attacks continued until the soldiers could beat them off no longer. The commanding officer, Publius Quintilius Varus, and the senior officers committed suicide; the soldiers who were not killed in the fighting were crucified, buried alive or sacrificed to the German gods.

The Romans eventually did slog and hack their way through to the Elbe, but it was clear that Germany would never submit passively to their rule, and after the semi-victorious campaigns of Germanicus between A.D. 14 and 17 they retired to the Rhine, where the frontier could more easily be held. This failure of Roman arms, and the fact that Roman civilization did not penetrate to Germany, was of profound significance for the whole development of German, and hence European, history.

Between 70 and 130, during the reigns of Vespasian, Domitian and Hadrian, the main work of consolidating the fortifications of the frontier was undertaken. On the German frontier a line of fortifications stretched for 300 miles between the Rhine and Danube. The occupation and fortification of Britain may be regarded as typical of Roman military policy in a frontier province. Hadrian's Wall, built between 122 and 125, stretches for seventy-three miles from Tyne to Solway. Built of stone with a concrete core, at most parts it is $7\frac{1}{2}$ feet thick, though at some points it is more. In Roman times the height to the wall-walk was about 15 feet. The wall follows a naturally defensible line; on lower ground, to give added strength, a ditch was dug. It was further strengthened by sixteen forts at intervals of approximately four miles. At every Roman mile there was a castle between the forts, and between the mile-castles the wall was again divided into three sections by turrets which served as signal stations. Hadrian's Wall was more a deterrent than a defence. It could not have checked a large-scale invasion, but it was a difficult obstacle to petty raids.

Britain had been conquered in the first century A.D. by four legions; after 85 she was garrisoned by three legions and 35–40,000 auxiliaries. The legions were each based on a fortress: Caerleon-on-Usk, Chester and York. To regulate and police the province there was also a whole network of small forts, in size between two and seven acres, each garrisoned by 500 to 1,000 auxiliaries. Most of these were in the north of England and Wales, sited along important roads or at strategic points about fifteen or twenty miles apart. The province had a network of roads, most of which had been built by the army for military purposes. The building of the famous Roman roads was one of the most important and enduring achievements of the Roman army; in this way, above all, the army contributed to unification in areas

Roman infantry cohorts often adopted a two-line formation

under Roman rule, and to the spread of civilization. Roman military camps, too, often became the original nucleus of towns and cities that have survived to this day.

In the first two centuries of the empire the total size of the imperial army fluctuated only slightly. The distribution of the army depended upon the general military and political situation in the Roman world: the legions being moved from point to point and concentrated where they were needed. Hadrian (117–35) made important changes in the workings of the Augustan system. After Hadrian a legion would consist almost entirely of soldiers recruited in its area of service, and during the second century the distinction between *auxilia* and legions died out.

It was in some way an advantage to defend vulnerable areas on the frontiers with troops familiar with the district, because it meant that they were defending their own homes. But there were two dangers in such a policy. First, the idea of imperial unity could be lost, as the troops on one frontier had no contact with those on another. The worst instance of this occurred in 69, when different armies rose up and struck down three candidates for the emperorship before a fourth, Vespasian, secured the position, backed by the armies of the east and the Danube. Secondly, the garrison forces were liable to degenerate into a local militia of idle and inefficient peasants, confident in the imperial peace and reckoning on an easy life. Quite often troops who were willing to serve in their own country were unwilling to be posted elsewhere. The legions of the eastern frontier were notoriously inefficient and indisciplined.

Corbulo, commander in the successful war against the Parthians of 56–63, restored discipline by severe measures. Stealing and physical unfitness were punished by flogging administered by a centurion, desertion was punished by death, and the army was toughened in a winter campaign in the Armenian highlands. The most severe punishment which could be inflicted was decimation of a unit; this was very rare, but in the year 20 Apronius, the governor of Africa, had every tenth man of a battalion which had run away in battle flogged to death. Units which had disgraced themselves might be disbanded altogether. Vespasian cashiered four legions which had lost their eagles or had joined in the revolt on the Rhine led by the Batavian chieftain Civilis in 69. At the other end of the disciplinary scale a centurion might lose his rank, or a soldier be required to parade all day outside the orderly room. Hadrian in particular fought against luxury and the lowering of standards in the army; but at the same time he reorganized the leisure of the soldiers to make life more pleasant, and improved their legal position and economic status.

The army offered a secure but dull life. The normal term of service was twenty years, during the last four of which a man served as a veteran in the reserve, being excused the more arduous camp duties. Good pay and pensions were provided from the military budget instituted by Augustus. A soldier had to buy his own food, weapons and uniform, and contribute to the funds of the annual camp dinner and the soldiers' burial fund; but there was little opportunity to spend the rest of his pay unless he dabbled illicitly in trade. He was encouraged to use the camp bank, where his savings were likely to be supplemented by occasional imperial bonuses. Soldiers of the rank of centurion and below were not supposed to marry, but many of them formed unions with women and these were tolerated.

There were various military awards and decorations. A victorious commander might be permitted to hold a triumphal procession in Rome. The Civic Crown was the coveted award for valour in the Roman army; Tiberius awarded it, for example, in 20 to Rufus Helvius, a private soldier who had saved a comrade's life in a battle in Africa. A *corona vallaris* might be awarded to the first man over the enemy's wall, and a *corona aurea* to a centurion for bravery on the field of battle. Other decorations included a silver spearhead or a miniature silver standard for officers, and bracelets, necklaces and embossed discs for the privates.

Vegetius, a military writer, describes the theoretical peace routine of a legion. Three times a month the infantry did a ten-mile route march, varying the rate of marching so as to give practice in rapid advances and retirements. During field training, open order fighting was given prominence, and tactics suitable for repelling sudden attacks and ambushes were practised. Considerable emphasis was laid on arms drill and barrack-square drill generally, as being an aid to discipline.

Although military activities at no time ceased, the second century saw the fulfilment of the ideal of Augustus. It was the period of the *Pax Romana*. Gibbon indeed considered that 'if a man were called to fix the period in the history of the world during which the condition of the human race was most happy and prosperous, he would, without hesitation, name that which elapsed from the death of Domitian to the accession of Commodus' (96–180). But by the end of the century things were altering. The death of Commodus in 192 was followed by a struggle for the throne. From the end of the second century the army was the chief and, indeed, the disastrous force in Roman politics. To maintain his power every emperor had to bribe and pamper the soldiers. Severus increased their pay by one third, allowed the soldiers to marry and to farm their own plots of land around the camps, and accorded the centurions certain new social privileges. His dying advice to his son Caracalla was to enrich the soldiers and disregard the rest, and that was exactly what Caracalla did. In the sixty years after 192 no less than twenty-one emperors rose and fell. It was a period of anarchy and misery, during which the army terrorized the civil life of the empire while becoming demoralized and inefficient, and the security of the frontiers was lost for ever. One of the main causes of a disastrous inflation was the continual increases in pay which the emperors had to give the army if they were to keep their thrones.

The troops in the frontier areas were by now enlisted mainly from the local farmers, who paid as little attention as possible to their military duties. Furthermore, the defensive strategy of armed forces strung out along the frontiers was unsuccessful; they were weak everywhere and strong nowhere; there was no defence in depth, and no reserves were kept for counter-attack. By 250 the fighting quality of the legions was deteriorating; imaginative tactics were needed to deal with new enemies who fought in ways strange to the Roman soldiery: and these were lacking. However, three emperors in the second half of the third century, Gallienus, Aurelian and Diocletian, overhauled the army and pulled the empire together again; their massive efforts enabled the empire to hold out against final ruin for almost another two centuries.

Stern measures were taken to restore order and discipline both in civil and military affairs, and under Diocletian civil government took on a stronger military character. Furthermore the Roman army began to assume a barbarian character; since plagues had caused a serious manpower problem, Aurelian took the momentous step of forming *auxilia* from among the Vandals and Alamanni, the Germanic tribes which were pressing most heavily on the northern frontier. The barbarians were to conquer the empire as much by infiltration as by force. The emperors had a bodyguard of German soldiers, and German troops were allowed to keep their native fighting dress and traditions. The eagle standards of Rome were replaced by barbarian dragons. As another method of maintaining numbers, sons were compelled to follow their fathers as soldiers – the army, in fact, became a hereditary caste – and the conscription laws were revived. Diocletian enormously increased the nominal size of the army – to sixty legions, although most of them soon fell below their theoretical strength of 6,000 men. Road buildings and fortifications were energetically kept up.

Gallienus realized the strategical mistake of the garrison policy of the previous 250 years. At the cost of permanently weakening the frontier forces, he created reserve armies based on northern Italy which provided defence in depth and could be used for counter-attack in an emergency. The long-established tactical traditions were discarded and reforms ordered which were more suited for dealing with new enemies, whose tactics were generally sudden cavalry attacks or long-range missile fire. Gallienus took the decisive step of relegating the legions to a subordinate position, and making cavalry the 'queen of the battlefield'. In 258 he formed corps of Dalmatian horsemen and Moorish mounted javelin-men who rode bareback. Further variety was added to Roman arms by an increasing reliance on oriental archers. There were also corps which used the long Iranian thrusting spear, barbarian infantry who fought in wedge formation, a camel corps, and heavy cavalry of the Parthian and Persian type. The throwing spear and short thrusting sword of the legionaries were replaced by the lance and long slashing swords of the barbarians.

This military overhaul came none too soon, for pressure on the frontiers was building up to an unprecedented intensity. The rise of the Sassanid Persian empire threatened to deprive Rome of all her eastern provinces. The low point of Roman imperial prestige came in 260 when Valerian was captured by the Persian ruler Shapur. Fortunately Odenathus, governor of Palmyra, succeeded in repelling the Persian forces. But the situation was even worse on the northern frontier, now pressed upon by migrant barbarian peoples. After Caesar's conquest of Gaul the old Celtic power in central and western Europe had crumbled, leaving a power vacuum both north and east of the Roman frontier. Into this area new peoples began to move, at first from Scandinavia, driven probably by climatic changes and over-population. But these people themselves were, by the third century, being driven further south and west by a new influx of migratory peoples from Asia.

It is arguable that the fall of the Roman empire was not, fundamentally, a military phenomenon. Economic weakness and the withering of the cities, the fall in population, the assimilation of provincial and barbarian culture, the adoption of Christianity, and the establishment of a new imperial capital at Constantinople (Byzantium):

all these were deeper causes and more significant symptoms of the passing of ancient Rome. But all the same, some of the most unmistakable landmarks in the process were military.

Militarily speaking the western barbarian peoples were all much alike. The same Celtic armourers on the Rhine and the Danube may indeed have made iron weapons for them all. Many of their swords were beautifully decorated with similar motifs: birds of prey, or snake-like creatures which seemed to devour themselves. The long slashing sword was their most valued weapon, but metal was costly; good weapons were passed on from generation to generation, and the most famous of them, such as Arthur's sword Excalibur, feature prominently in the sagas of the peoples. Mail armour was also highly prized. The great weapon of the Langobards was the broadsword, but they also used lances, some so strong that when the victim had been run through he could be held aloft, wriggling on the end. Another very popular weapon was the 'sax', a short, broad, slightly curved single-edged weapon, the ancestor of the sabre. The northern peoples also fought with spears up to 11 feet long. The shields of the chiefs were often highly decorated. The helmets were more or less skull caps made of bands of metal; some had neck and cheek guards, others a visor, and others again were adorned with beasts' heads.

Such equipment could not be afforded by every man of the tribe. The mass fought protected by leather caps and by round shields of wood or wicker covered with hide, and armed with a lance or club. Most of the migratory peoples preferred to fight on horseback, but the Franks fought as a horde of undisciplined and ill-armed infantry, the only mounted men being the king's guard. Their army was divided roughly into units: hundreds, thousands and clans. The most common battle formation was the V-shaped wedge. They fortified themselves with circular ramparts on the hills, and in the plains with leaguers of locked wagons. Physically they appeared formidable to the Mediterranean peoples; Sidonius wrote that the Burgundians were 7 feet high and greased their hair with rancid butter.

Some of these peoples were good seafarers; the pirate ships of the Saxons, with their leather sails, were the terror of the British coasts. Among the maritime tribes, boats evolved from dugouts holding thirty men to plank-built galleys of the Viking type which held over a hundred. The Vandals dominated the western Mediterranean with their piratical fleets, and in 455, led by Geiseric, they sailed up the Tiber with their galleys and fire-ships and sacked Rome. The Romans had long since lost their naval supremacy in the Mediterranean, and it was far too late when a law was passed at Constantinople forbidding the teaching of ship-building to the barbarians on pain of death. Between 253 and 267 the Goths had carried their raids by sea into Greece and Asia Minor, and already by then Rome could find ships only by borrowing them from the commercial ports of the eastern Mediterranean.

The Goths were the first of the migratory peoples to smite the empire; it was they who penetrated to its heart and who are of most significance in the history of the art of war. The emperor Valens met the Goths at Adrianople in 378. The imperial army came upon the Goths encamped in a vast wagon leaguer. Despite the changed character of the Roman army and all that should have been learnt from experience of fighting the barbarians, Valens drew up his forces in the historic Roman fashion, with the legions massed in the centre and the squadrons of auxiliary horse on the wings. When it was reported that all the enemy were in the leaguer Valens attacked. But he did not know that the bulk of the Gothic horsemen were away foraging; they were quickly recalled and formed together, and, as the battle raged, they charged down on the Roman left. The Roman cavalry on the left disintegrated instantly, and the Goths crashed on to roll up the infantry. The right fled, and the legions were crushed together in the centre by the cavalry of the Goths from the left and their infantry in front. The Roman infantry, thus left on the field to their fate, were cut down as they stood, so packed together that they could not move.

A total disaster for the Roman empire, the battle of Adrianople is also of great significance as the first victory of heavy cavalry over infantry; it was the Gothic horsemen who first crossed the threshold of medieval warfare. The heavily armoured knight with his lance, his retainers, and the characteristic features of his warfare (chivalry and heraldry), derived from the barbarians and was in opposition to the whole Roman infantry tradition.

The Gothic cavalry had developed into this formidable power for two reasons. First, in the long period of their migration they had become splendid horsemen. Secondly, they possessed a vital piece of equestrian equipment, the stirrup. Only with this support could the heavy cavalryman keep his seat in the saddle, bearing the weight of his armour and the shock of the lance's impact. The stirrup was brought to the west, together with a stronger type of horse, from Asia in the first century A.D. and adopted by the Goths. After Adrianople the Byzantines began to model their fighting methods on those of the Goths, and the emperors finally discarded the infantry legions. The emperor Maurice emphasized the value of the stirrup for cavalry in his treatise on 'The Art of War' in 590.

In the middle of the fifth century, the most terrible invasion of all fell on the Mediterranean world. Under a great khan, Attila, 'the scourge of God', the Huns were organized into a vast army, and the Asiatics made war against the Europeans. The Scandinavian and German barbarians at least invaded the Roman empire with the object of enjoying it; the sole object of the Huns, as with their descendants the Mongols, appeared to be to destroy. Ammianus Marcellinus, a contemporary soldier, described his impressions of them: 'The Huns surpass all other barbarians in wildness of life. They are of portentous ugliness and so crook-backed that you would take them for some sort of two-footed beasts. Wandering at large, they are trained to bear from their infancy all the extremes of cold, of hunger, and of thirst. On horseback every man of that nation lives night and day, on horseback he takes his meat and drink, and when night comes he leans forward upon the narrow neck of his horse and there falls into a deep sleep. When attacked, they will sometimes engage in regular battle. Then, going into the fight in order of columns, they fill the air with varied and disordered cries. More often, however, they fight in no regular order of battle, but being extremely swift and sudden in their movements, they disperse, and then rapidly come together again in loose array. It must be owned that they are the nimblest of warriors.'

The Hun horsemen overran the Roman empire and established the predominance of cavalry

The Huns were probably not, in fact, as numerous as they seemed. Their ferocity and ugliness were a valuable psychological weapon of war. Above all, their astounding mobility, both as a migrant nation on a continual war footing and as a tactical force, made them devastating. They had horses which could gallop twenty miles at a stretch and a hundred miles in a day. Superb horsemanship in rapid charges and retreats, and clouds of arrows, proved too much even for the Gothic cavalry. Their principal weapon was the bow, and they were wonderfully accurate marksmen. They also used iron swords, looted or bartered from European peoples. One of their techniques in close fighting was to entangle an enemy soldier with a lasso or a net while he was parrying another attack. They hardly bothered with armour.

In 451 the Huns crossed the Rhine. The Visigoths of Aquitaine joined with the Romans under Aëtius, and repelled the Huns and their subject-allies. Aëtius did not follow up his victory, for fear that if the Huns were destroyed the Visigoths would become too powerful. As a result, the following year, Attila invaded northern Italy. But he was checked by famine, disease, imperial reinforcements from the east, and the diplomacy of Pope Leo I. In 453 Attila took a new wife, and died as a result of a blood-vessel burst during his wedding night. As Chaucer later commented:

> Loke, Attila, the grete conquerour,
> Deyde in his sleep, with shame and dishonour,
> Bledinge ay at the nose in dronkenesse;
> A capitayn shoulde live in sobrenesse.

The defeat of the Huns did not save Rome, for in 476 Odovacar, the Herul commander of a 'Roman' army composed entirely of barbarians, finally threw off all pretences and deposed Romulus Augustulus, thus ending the Roman empire of the west. But shortly after, Justinian (527–65), the emperor at Constantinople, made a bid to restore the Roman empire in the west. In the pursuit of this chimerical objective the Danube and eastern frontiers were neglected, the eastern provinces were exhausted by taxation to finance the armies of the west, and Africa, Spain and Italy were subjected to twenty years of warfare. But the wars produced one outstanding general: Belisarius. The Byzantine army had for some time been adapting itself to be able to compete in the new era of Gothic warfare. It was formed almost entirely out of mercenaries from the various barbarian tribes, and consisted mostly of cavalry, with a few units of heavy infantry. In the 520's Belisarius set about training an *élite* corps of heavy cavalry armed with both bow and lance, trained to be skirmishers as well as shock troops. He also armed them with feathered darts which were thrown by hand at close quarters. Finally they carried a heavy broadsword. It required a lot of drill to become proficient with all four weapons and to be able to control the horse at the same time. Belisarius trained his men to support themselves in the saddle by the stirrups and to control the movements of the horse with their knees. The men had a small shield strapped to their left arm, and wore sleeveless mail shirts of thigh length. Archery methods were copied from the Huns, and tilting with the lance from the Goths. The training exercise to improve the skill of the knight was to gallop towards a stuffed dummy hanging from a gallows. The rider had to string his bow as he approached, fire three arrows at the swaying figure, and finish the charge with the lance or darts. Pay, rations and rank were awarded according to proficiency in this and other exercises.

Before the great wars of Justinian's reign, Belisarius had learnt his profession in operations on the Danube and in the east. Against the Hunnic mounted archers he had devised an original and successful tactic. The problem was to come to close quarters with them; his solution was to tempt them with live bait: a few men on swift horses, who would draw the eager Huns into a position where their retreat could be cut off. To deal with their wagon barricades, Belisarius ordered his men to ride to windward of them and set them alight with fire arrows.

In 532 Belisarius was given the command in the war against the Vandals. He set out from Byzantium with a multi-national army of 10,000 infantry and 5,000 cavalry. Most of these were mercenaries, but many were the general's own retainers and in a sense this was already a feudal army. The infantry soldiers were mostly of good quality: Isaurian mountaineers trained by Belisarius himself. Among the cavalry were 600 Huns and 400 Heruls, as well as Belisarius' own Household Regiment of 1,500 cuirassiers. His chief of staff was an Armenian eunuch called Solomon, and with his headquarters was the historian Procopius. As usual on his campaigns, Belisarius was accompanied by his wife, Antonina – a woman of sure courage but doubtful morals. The Vandals could muster many more fighting men, but their army was far less experienced than that of Belisarius, and not so well trained. Belisarius' victories of Ad Decimum and Tricamaron ensured the conquest of the Vandals in Africa.

The war was next carried into Italy. Between 535 and 540, with a force of only about 7,500 and hampered by the schemings of his enemies at the Byzantine court and by the indecision and jealousy of his emperor Justinian, Belisarius conquered the Ostrogoths. The most spectacular episode of this war was his defence of Rome: twelve miles of walls were held by 5,000 men for a year. Belisarius, and a new commander, the 80-year-old eunuch Narses, fought the Goths for another fourteen years. When peace came it was a peace of exhaustion, and an empty victory: for Italy was too devastated to be able to defend itself against the Lombards when they swept over the north in 565. Belisarius had done all that he could. He is the classic example of a loyal and capable soldier compelled by a second rate political chief to pursue an unrealistic strategical objective.

Justinian's reach had far exceeded his grasp. In 540 Antioch was sacked by the Persians. The drain of troops from the east hopelessly weakened that frontier despite the massive building programme which he undertook in order to fortify the whole of the east and north-east. However, the 700 or more fortifications built by Justinian marked an enormous stride forward in military architecture. The curtain walls, baileys, dungeons, battlements and keeps of Justinian's castles were a direct inspiration to the engineers and architects of the middle ages.

The failure of Justinian's scheme of reconquest in the west finally rang down the curtain on the western Roman empire. Militarily, ethnically and culturally it had long since disappeared; now the last political illusions were dispelled. In warfare the new medieval era, characterized by the heavy-armed knight and his retainers, was already two centuries old.

ET SYRIAM SOBAL · ET CONVERTIT
IOAB · ET PERCVSSIT EDOM INVAL
LE SALINARVM · XII MILIA

6   Early Medieval Warfare

When the western Roman empire disintegrated, its eastern counterpart at Byzantium lived on, and its struggle for survival, with the Arabs and then with the Turks and Bulgars, is a fascinating story. In 622 Mohammed led his followers from Mecca to Medina, and began the expansion of Arabianism and Islam. The Prophet himself won the first military victory, but the great leaders of Islam on the march were to be Khalid ibn-al-Walid and Amr ibn-al-As. Within a hundred years the Islamic empire extended from the Aral Sea to the upper Nile, and from the confines of China to the Bay of Biscay. Only one power in that century was able to resist the Arabs, Byzantium – and even she lost the south-eastern part of her empire. Then, as the Arab drive exhausted itself in southern France, the Franks came back into prominence. Finally, in the eighth century, the Vikings began raiding down from Scandinavia into Britain and western Europe. The feature to observe in the history of western European warfare between the seventh and eleventh centuries is the continued rise of cavalry.

The Arabs made their conquests by intelligent use of camelry and cavalry in suitable terrain, the open lands of North Africa and western Asia. But their organization and battle tactics were primitive, and their armour was poor. They usually fought in one, but sometimes two or three, closely packed lines, units being formed of different tribes. It was the numbers and appearance of the Arabs which made them so formidable. As a Byzantine commander observed, 'they are very bold when they expect to win: they keep firm in their ranks, and stand up gallantly against the most impetuous attacks. When they think that the enemy's vigour is relaxing, they all charge together in a desperate effort.' The infantry were mostly inefficient and ill-armed; their strength lay in cavalry. In the early part of the seventh century their cavalry was very lightly equipped and highly mobile; but in succeeding centuries the Arabs learnt much from their most stubborn enemies, the Byzantines, and relied increasingly on mounted archers and lancers, protected by chain-mail shirts, helmets, shields and greaves.

The best qualities of the armies of Islam lay not in equipment or organization but in morale, created by religion, mobility due to camel transport, and endurance bred of hard living in the desert. The crusading idea of the *jihad*, the holy war, was very real to the close followers of Mohammed. There was also an economic cause of Arab aggression, the old story of overcrowding in the Arabian peninsula. For some centuries southern Arabia had been becoming more arid, and the inhabitants had been drifting northwards. The Arab explosion of the seventh century was the fourth, last, and greatest of the Semitic migrations. In the traditional and natural pattern,

Under the feudal system the mounted knight developed as the chief figure on the battlefields of western Europe. A detachment of Carolingian cavalry preceded by a standard bearer

 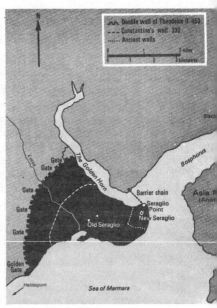

Cavalrymen *left* were the main strength of the Byzantine armies. Constantinople in 717 *right*; the line of fortifications was substantially the same in 1453 when the city fell to the Turks

the migrants went first for the Fertile Crescent, before overspilling towards and beyond the valleys of the Euphrates and the Nile. They conquered much farther afield than they had in ancient times, not only because they were now more numerous, but also because practically everywhere they went they were welcomed as the deliverers of subject peoples. Their tolerance, humanity and impressive civilization, as well as their inevitability, converted almost as many people as it defeated. Except for Spain, the areas which they conquered in the seventh century have remained Islamic in religion and culture to this day.

The first check to the Arabs came from the Byzantines. The Byzantine army and navy between the eighth and the eleventh centuries were, in fact, the most efficiently organized of any in Europe and the Mediterranean world. In 668, and again every year from 672 to 677, the Arabs attacked the Byzantine empire at various points; inroads were made but eventually the invaders were frustrated each time by the Byzantine fleet. The galleys of the Arabs and the Byzantines were more or less identical. The large fighting 'dromon' was rowed by 100 men in two banks; the upper bank of oarsmen were armed, and there was a complement of marines. But the ships and equipment of the Byzantians were better made, and they had the weapon of 'Greek fire', an incendiary mixture which could be shot out of a tube in the bows of a ship or thrown in pots by *ballistae*.

The culmination and the turn of fortune in the struggle between the Arabs and the Byzantines came with the siege of Constantinople in 717–18. When the Arabs invaded Asia Minor, the emperor Theodosius III retired to a monastery; but a professional soldier, Leo the Isaurian, grasped the leadership in this moment of crisis. He quickly repaired and stocked the massive fortifications of Constantinople – before the age of gunpowder such walls were impregnable to assault and the only way the city could be taken was by blockade. Since Constantinople was surrounded on three sides by water, all seemed to depend on the relative strength of the opposing fleets, and the Arabs had a vast superiority in numbers. Leo, however, led the twelve-month defence of Constantinople with courage and brilliant resource, and when the siege was raised the Byzantine fleet pursued the enemy down the Hellespont; there it ran into a storm and only a small proportion of the Arab forces survived. It was a great disaster for the Arabs, which they did not forget. By his further victory at Acroinon in 739, Leo forced the Arabs finally to evacuate western Asia Minor.

The means for Leo the Isaurian's great achievement were an army and navy built up over a long period in a tradition of military efficiency. From the time of Belisarius heavy cavalry provided the main strength of the Byzantine armies. The trooper was protected by a long shirt of mail reaching down from the neck to the thighs, a round shield of medium size, a steel cap, gauntlets and steel shoes. The horses of the front line were also protected by a steel poitrel. All horses were equipped with large comfortable saddles with iron stirrups. Offensive armour consisted of a broadsword, a dagger, a short bow and quiver, and a long lance. Sometimes an axe was also strapped to the saddle. Like its Roman predecessors, and unlike any other western army before the sixteenth century, the Byzantine army wore uniform; the surcoat, the lance-pennon, and the tuft of the helmet were of a particular colour for each unit. The cavalryman had to be well off to afford this equipment. All the officers, and every four or five troopers, had soldier servants; this also was expensive, but it was considered worthwhile if the soldiers could concentrate on their purely military tasks and keep in good physical condition by being well fed. The history of the rich Byzantine empire illustrates that a little comfort does not have a harmful effect on military standards.

The functions of infantry were limited to the defence of defiles and mountainous country, and the garrisoning of fortresses and important cities. Most of the light infantry were archers; the heavy infantryman carried a lance, a sword, and an axe. For every unit of sixteen men, two carts carried ammunition and food, cooking utensils and entrenching tools. The Byzantines maintained the classical Roman practice of regularly building fortified camps and a corps of engineers always marched with the vanguard of the army. Every unit of 400 men had its medical officer and six or eight stretcher bearers. The bearers were paid a bonus for every casualty brought in from the battlefield – less perhaps for humanitarian reasons than because the state was interested in restoring the wounded to battle fitness as early as possible.

The keystone of the Byzantine military system was tactical organization: they fought cunningly and efficiently. The Byzantines rightly considered that the methods to be employed in battle must be varied according to the tactics of their enemy, and they studied carefully the methods of probable opponents. Their most important military writings are the *Strategicon* of Maurice, *c.* 580, the *Tactica* of Leo the Wise, *c.* 900, and a manual on frontier warfare by Nicephorus Phocas (conqueror of Crete and Cilicia from the Arabs, and emperor 963–9).

The structure and recruitment of the army was reorganized by Maurice. He developed a hierarchy of units from the basic file of 16 men to the *meros*, a division of 6,000 to 8,000 men. There was a corresponding officer hierarchy and the appointment of all officers above the rank of centurion rested in the hands of the central government. The number of Teutonic mercenaries in the Byzantine army greatly decreased after Justinian's wars. There was no universal male conscription in the empire, but a system called on every region to send a certain number of men for training and active service when required. The frontier areas were divided into districts called 'clissuras', one of which might consist for example, of a mountain pass and a fortress; the command of a clissura was frequently the road to a successful military career. The tenth-century poem, *Digenes Acritas*, describes life on the Cappadocian frontier, with warlike barons dominating the country from their castles, and making endless forays into the Arab territories of Cilicia and Mesopotamia.

Byzantine tactical theory was based upon delivering a series of heavy cavalry charges. According to Leo the Wise, a cavalry force should be divided into a front fighting line, a second supporting line, a small reserve behind the second line, and a detachment thrown well forward on each wing with the role of turning the enemy flank, or, alternatively, of protecting its own. Up to about one-half of the available strength was in the front line, with the balance distributed in depth as the tactical situation demanded, and on the flanks.

There were, naturally, many variations in tactical dispositions. Infantry and cavalry would often act together against Slavs or Franks, whose armies were mostly foot-soldiers, or against large-scale Arab invasions. On such occasions the infantry would be placed in the centre, and the cavalry on the wings and in reserve. If the enemy was expected to open the battle with a cavalry charge, the light troops would retire behind the heavy infantry 'just as', Oman remarks, 'a thousand years later the musketeers of the sixteenth and seventeenth centuries used to take cover behind their pikemen'. In hilly country and in passes the infantry were disposed in a crescent formation, the heavy infantry blocking the enemy in the centre, and the light troops showering missiles down from above on the enemy flanks.

The Byzantines were the best soldiers of early medieval Europe, but the least spectacular; this was because their strategy was mostly defensive, and they preferred to rely on brain rather than brawn. They never fought a battle until as many circumstances as possible had been turned to their advantage and they often used ruses and stratagems such as spreading false intelligence or formenting treason among the enemy. They had constantly to operate defensively, either in keeping the Arabs out of Asia Minor or in holding back the Lombards and the Franks from the Italian provinces, and the Slavs, Bulgars, Avars, Magyars and Patzinaks from Greece and the Balkans. By their constant efficiency and vigilance they were highly successful in defending the frontiers; that was their main task, and only very rarely did Byzantium become an aggressive power.

The Arabs were the most formidable enemy Byzantium had to face. But the Arabs never appreciated the real merits of organization and discipline. Although to be feared because of their numbers and mobility, their forces remained basically just masses of aggressive and energetic tribesmen, and in battle the successive shocks of the disciplined Byzantine lines were too much for them. The Byzantine commanders of the provinces also developed an effective system of frontier vigilance. They would assemble their forces the moment it was reported that the Arabs were on the move. The infantry were then to block the passes while the cavalry, having collected at a central point, must maintain contact with the raiders and attack them. If a commander found himself outnumbered he was to avoid open battle, but must obstruct the enemy in every way possible – tapping in on the raiders at every opportunity, defending fords and defiles, blocking up wells and barricading roads. More troops would then be raised from distant provinces, until the Arabs could in due course be opposed with a trained army of some 30,000 cavalry. From the time of their defeat at Acroinon in 739 the Arabs were a nuisance rather than a real threat to the security of the Byzantine empire.

In the period after 950 the Byzantine emperors Nicephorus Phocas and Basil II took the offensive against the Arabs and the Bulgars. In 1014, at Belasitza, Basil annihilated the Bulgarian army, earning the title of 'Bulgar-Slayer'. He blinded 1,5000 prisoners, leaving every hundred with a one-eyed man to lead them back to their tsar.

In 1045 Armenia was annexed. But in the middle of the eleventh century a new enemy, the Seljuk Turks, began to press on the eastern frontier. The Turks were the perennial light horsemen of western Asia. They fought in numerous small bands, armed principally with the bow but also with the javelin and scimitar, in attack they would dash up and down the enemy front, showering it with volleys of arrows and delivering short, stinging charges. In the spring of 1071 the emperor Romanus Diogenes marched to Armenia with 60,000 men to meet 100,000 of the Turks under Alp Arslan. Romanus rashly threw aside all the traditional Byzantine principles of circumspection and efficiency. At Manzikert the flower of the Byzantine army was annihilated, and the emperor himself was taken prisoner. The Turks flooded into Asia Minor and within ten years had reduced it to a waste.

In western Europe the history of the Franks had followed a pattern not dissimilar to that of Byzantium. With an army in which cavalry played an increasingly important part, they had succeeded in checking the Arab advance; and then, after a period of military and cultural supremacy, they had weakened before the attacks of a different barbaric people: the Vikings.

For two centuries after the victory of Clovis at Vouglé in 507, which established their dominance in Gaul, the Franks did not change their military organization. Agathias describes the warfare of the Franks in the Merovingian period (*c.* 450–750):

The arms of the Franks are very rude; they wear neither mail-shirt nor greaves, and their legs are only protected by strips of linen or leather. They have hardly any horsemen, but their foot-soldiery are bold and well practised in war. They bear swords and shields, but never use the bow. Their missiles are axes and barbed javelins. These last are not very long; they can be used either to cast or to stab.

The Frankish throwing-axe, like the Red Indian tomahawk, was carefully weighted so that it could be thrown with great accuracy as well as being used in close combat. Frankish armies in these two centuries fought thus armed, in massive disorderly columns of infantry. Most of their fighting in this period was among themselves. However, as they clashed more frequently with different types of armies their methods began to develop. In the late sixth century wealthy men began to use protective armour of metal.

In 732 Abd-al-Rahman led an Arab army as far north as Tours. Charles Martel collected the Frankish forces, and advanced against the Arabs, who were retiring with their plunder. When Abd-al-Rahman attacked 'the men of the North stood as motionless as a wall; they were like a belt of ice frozen together, and not to be dissolved, as they slew the Arabs with the sword. The Austrasians, vast of limb, and iron of hand, hewed on bravely in the thick of the fight; it was they who found and cut down the Saracen king.'

It was a defensive victory won by infantry, and there was no pursuit. It cannot be said that the Franks had checked the Arabs in the same way as the Byzantines had done; the Arabs had merely travelled as far as their resources allowed.

In 768 Charles Martel's grandson, known as Charlemagne, succeeded to the throne as king of the Franks. There was much disorder and danger to his kingdom at first, and if aggressive neighbours would not respond to mild treatment the only policy was thorough conquest. Charlemagne regarded himself as a universal ruler and God's regent to command on earth in temporal matters. His missionaries advanced with his armies, often in a real sense as psychological shock-troops. As he wrote to the Pope: 'Our task is, with the aid of divine piety, to defend the Holy Church of Christ with arms. Your task, most holy father, is to lift up your hands to God, like Moses, so as to aid our troops.' The efficiency of Charlemagne's military system and his ceaseless activity created a peace and security which western Europe had not known since the age of the Antonines; the military achievement was the prerequisite of the economic, judicial and cultural achievements.

Many of Charlemagne's methods were, however, crude, such as the massacre in 782 at Verden of 4,500 insubordinate pagan Saxons in a single day. Between 768 and 814, Charlemagne fought almost annual campaigns. His Holy Roman Empire eventually included the areas which are now France, Belgium, Holland, Switzerland, West Germany, most of Italy, northern Spain and Corsica.

The army of Charlemagne was very different in character from that of his grandfather, the essential difference being in its striking force of heavy cavalry. Cavalry was essential for his far-flung campaigns against such enemies as the mounted bowmen of the Avars and the heavy Lombard lancers. The value of cavalry had long been recognized, but the expense of raising it had hitherto been an insuperable problem for the Franks. Apart from the cost of the armour, the knight had to maintain a suitable horse, strong enough to carry him when fully armed, sufficiently trained not to bolt or panic in a battle, and fast enough to take part in a charge at full gallop. Such a horse had to be specially bred and trained. Even the expense of stabling and providing winter fodder was considerable, and a knight had to have at least two attendants, one to deal with his armour and the other as groom for the horse; furthermore, he himself had to be able to give much time to training and active service. In the Merovingian period no ruler of the Franks was rich enough to pay an army of heavy cavalry.

This problem and others were solved by the development of feudalism. The system was that the 'lord', the king or a great man, granted some land and his protection to the 'vassal', in exchange for a sworn undertaking to furnish specific services, often military in character. Charlemagne feudalized his kingdom to a very great extent. The system appealed both to those who were rich and to those who desired protection in troubled times. In the disorder of the ninth century following the death of Charlemagne in 814, when his empire was divided and Europe was beset by the attacks of the Magyars and the Vikings, society became honeycombed with this pattern of mutual obligation: protection and service. The effect of feudalism on warfare was twofold. On the one hand, vassals with considerable lands could afford, and were required, to furnish knightly service; on the other hand, the bonds of loyalty and mutual interest improved the discipline of armies.

The heavy cavalry were the core of the Frankish army. Although not particularly numerous, they were of high quality. The knights were all equipped with a mailshirt, helmet, shield, lance and axe. The old Frankish *levée en masse* of infantry did not entirely disappear, but the infantry was reduced, and the quality improved by better armament; no man was allowed to appear at the 'March Field', the annual assembly of the Frankish army, armed only with a club – he must also have a bow. Charlemagne achieved a degree of training, discipline and general organisation unknown in the west since the barbarisation of the Roman legions. An interesting document survives, in which Charlemagne summons an important vassal to the royal army in 806:

> You shall come to Stasfurt on the Boda, by May 20th, with your men prepared to go on warlike service to any part of our realm that we may point out; that is, you shall come with arms and gear and all warlike equipment of clothing and victuals. Every horseman shall have shield, lance, sword, dagger, a bow and a quiver. On your carts you shall have ready spades, axes, picks and iron-pointed stakes, and all other things needed for the host. The rations shall be for three months. On your way you shall do no damage to our subjects, and touch nothing but water, wood, and grass. See that there be no neglect, as you prize our good grace.

The tactical dispositions of the Franks in battle are not known for sure; probably the infantry archers did some preliminary probing and skirmishing, and then the cavalry delivered the decisive charge *en masse*. Superior organization, the quality of the highly trained and well armed soldiery, and the strategical vision of Charlemagne were perhaps more responsible for his success than any tactical brilliance.

The thoroughness of his conquests was due above all to his policy of building a system of fortified posts along the frontiers and in disturbed areas, usually on hills near rivers.

In the ninth century, without any able kings, the quality of the Frankish army declines. Leo the Wise notes some of the characteristics and failings of the Franks:

> The Franks and Lombards are bold and daring to excess. They regard the smallest movement to the rear as a disgrace, and they will fight whenever you offer them battle. When their knights are hard put to it in a cavalry fight, they will dismount, and stand back to back against very superior numbers rather than fly. So formidable is the charge of the cavalry that it is best to decline a pitched battle with them till you have put all the chances on your own side. You should take advantage of their indiscipline and disorder; whether fighting on foot or on horseback, they charge in dense, unwieldy masses, which cannot manoeuvre, because they have neither organization nor drill. They readily fall into confusion if suddenly attacked in flank and rear – a thing easy to accomplish, as they are utterly careless and neglect the use of pickets and the proper surveying of the countryside. They encamp, too, confusedly and without fortifying themselves, so that they can be easily cut up by a night attack. They are impatient of hunger and thirst, and after a few days of privation desert their standards. They are destitute of respect for their commanders, nor are their chiefs above the temptation of taking bribes. On the whole, therefore, it is easier and less costly to wear out a Frankish army by skirmishes, protracted operations in desolate districts, and the cutting off of its supplies, than to attempt to destroy it at a single blow.

Charlemagne's empire began to fall apart very soon after his death, due to weak government and the pressure of simultaneous raids from three directions during the ninth and tenth centuries – by the Arabs, the Magyars and the Vikings. The most serious danger to Europe came from the Vikings of Scandinavia.

The eruption of the Vikings, or Norsemen, began at the end of the eighth century. The purpose of the raids which they conducted all over Europe seems at first to have been chiefly plunder rather than colonization, but later many of them settled in the lands which they overran. In 911 the area that was to be called Normandy was ceded to them by the Frankish king, and eventually the whole of England became part of the Scandinavian empire of the Danish king Canute (995–1035). Meanwhile the Vikings also penetrated to Iceland, Greenland and America, Spain, Morocco and Italy, Novgorod, Kiev and Byzantium.

The strength of the Vikings lay in their seamanship. Their ships were their supreme technical achievement and their great pride, and they themselves were sailors of outstanding skill and hardiness. The Gokstad ship, which has been excavated, is about 70 feet long and 16 feet in beam; it is built of oak and weighs over 20 tons. In its construction it is highly advanced. For voyages sail was used, but when fighting the ship was rowed. The shields were hung along the rail, painted alternately yellow and black. By the tenth century the ships were much larger, some

A Viking ship, designed to sail under square sails; oars were used for sea battles

of them holding as many as 200 men, and these could sail 150 miles in a day. Food
on board was preserved with ice and salt.

The sea battles of the Vikings were always fought close inshore, and usually
developed in three stages. First the commander reconnoitred the enemy and selected
the best position from which to attack, then he would begin to close, manoeuvring
for a favourable approach. The captain of the ship always steered it in battle. As the
fleets closed together, a missile bombardment would begin, usually volleys of arrows
but sometimes just lumps of iron and stone. Finally the Vikings would grapple,
and decide the issue by hand-to-hand fighting.

The fleet then remained the base of operations for inland raids. Generally, Viking
strategy was to work their way up an important waterway, living off the country and
plundering the abbeys and towns on either bank. When they got so far up the stream
that it was no longer navigable, or if they found further progress blocked by
fortifications, they would moor their ships or run them ashore – leaving them
protected by a stockade and a garrison, while they raided the surrounding country.
In the early days they would return to their ships on the appearance of a hostile
force, and drop back downstream. Later they grew bolder. But since they were not
numerous and their main object was plunder, they avoided heavy fighting. Eventually

they took to building strongholds to which they would often return. These water-girt camps, strengthened by stakes and a ditch, and defended by the Viking axemen, were extremely difficult to take.

When the Vikings began their offensives they were probably poorly armed; one of their chief aims in plundering was to secure weapons and armour, and by the middle of the ninth century they had captured plenty and had themselves learnt the techniques of manufacture. Practically all Viking warriors had a long shirt of chain-mail, and in other respects their body armour resembled that of the Franks. At first the wooden shield was round, but later it was kite-shaped, and was often painted in bright colours. Their great offensive weapon was the axe. This was not the light tomahawk of the Franks, but a massive weapon with a single broad iron blade welded on to a handle five feet long. Sometimes the blade was marked with runes. They also fought with short and long swords, spears, and long bows and arrows.

The Vikings were, basically, infantry – preferring to wield their great axes on foot. They achieved mobility when on land by rounding up horses from the neighbourhood for use as transport animals. The fighting formation they liked best was a shield-wall, and of necessity their tactics were defensive since they were infantry opposed to cavalry. They usually chose to fight at their camp, or behind a stream or on a steep hillside. Being professional soldiers, man for man they could almost always get the better of the hurriedly raised levies of farmers who opposed them; and they had the advantage of being exceptionally large and strong in physique. They had two particularly formidable classes of warrior. The first of these was the 'berserks' who, astonishingly enough, were probably a specially organized corps of madmen, selected for their exceptional strength and ferocity. The other, equally astonishingly, was the 'shield-maidens'; among these was Vebjorg, who 'attacked the champion Soknarsoti; she dealt the champion heavy blows and with a blow at his cheek cut through his jaw. He put his beard into his mouth and bit it, thus holding up his chin. She performed many great feats [but] finally she fell, covered with wounds.'

Towards the end of the ninth century the Franks and the English began to get the measure of the Vikings. In the preceding years of chaos feudalism had grown apace, and the Franks could now raise a large force of efficient cavalry. Paris successfully resisted the great Viking siege of 885–6. In England, Alfred the Great (died 899) similarly used a system of strong fortifications to check the Viking Danes. Instead of cavalry, however, he relied on an *élite* force of heavy infantry, which proved its worth by the victories of Ashdown and Edington. He also took the step, which the Franks had neglected to do, of building up a strong fleet modelled on the ships of his Viking enemies. From the time of Alfred until the mid-twentieth century England always had a strong navy in which to put her trust.

The annexation of England by Canute in 1016 was a political and not a military affair. Already by this time western Europe was breathing more easily, freed at last from the incessant barbarian raids which had lasted for seven hundred and fifty years without respite.

7

The Norman Conquests and the Crusades

The Vikings had been infantry soldiers; their descendants, the Normans, became Europe's greatest exponents of heavy cavalry and strategic fortification. The great period of Norman expansion was the eleventh century, followed by consolidation in the twelfth. Two separate areas of their rule were established by conquest – southern Italy and north-western Europe. The Normans imparted energy to Europe, and played a leading part in the movement which expressed Europe's revived vitality – the crusades. As it seemed to William of Malmesbury, 'they are a race inured to war, and can hardly live without it'.

To me, this part of our story is full of interest since my family has its origins in Normandy. Falaise, of which city I am a Freeman, has many Montgomery memorials; Roger Montgoméry, a cousin of the Conqueror, fought on the right wing of the army at Hastings; and, curiously enough, my old enemy Rommel received the wound which removed him from the battle of Normandy (1944) in the village of Ste Foy de Montgoméry near Lisieux – when I myself was commanding an army operating in the opposite direction to the one which Duke William had commanded.

Balanced armies like those of the eastern Roman empire, composed of all arms, were not compatible with feudal society. From the time of the defeat of the Anglo-Saxon axemen at Hastings in the eleventh century to the rise of the Swiss and English infantry in the fourteenth, the mounted knight was regarded as the ideal soldier and the real backbone of an army. We shall find that the armies of the crusades differed from a feudal array in that they contained more volunteers; they were also more incoherent because of the mixture of races, and the jealousy and friction between the leaders. I have found it difficult to raise any great enthusiasm over the operations of the crusaders.

The exploits of the Norman adventurers in the Mediterranean were daring and brilliant, but short-lived and there is no space here to deal with them. The other great conquest by the Normans in the eleventh century was England. In 1066, the year of his invasion and victory at Hastings, Duke William of Normandy had already ruled for thirty-one years. In the suppression of baronial revolts and in his conquest of Maine he had already acquired a reputation as an able general, as a good tactician but even more resourceful in strategy and ruses, and as a far-sighted, patient and masterful ruler of men. William's expedition against England was not a raid on the spur of the moment, but a drive of expansion – long prepared and well practised.

In 1066 Harold, earl of Wessex, was chosen as king by the national council. But Harold was in no real sense a national leader, and William had as strong a

Norman heavy cavalry carried all before them as they imparted a new energy to Europe

theoretical claim to the throne as he did. William crossed the Channel in September, after eight months of careful propaganda and preparation. The Norman threat was not the only one which Harold had to face that year; there was also danger in the north. Harold's brother Tostig had allied himself with the king of Norway, Harold Hardrada, and a Norse invasion was possible. Harold reckoned that William's threat was by far the more serious of the two, so he called out the limited naval strength of his realm, and all through June, July and August he maintained patrols in the channel between Dover and the Isle of Wight. At the same time the earls and sheriffs were ordered to keep the militia of the realm, the *fyrd*, ready for instant mobilization.

The *fyrd* was the main strength of the English army and was recruited on the basis of one man for every 600 acres, but it could be called out only for two months at a time. There was another class of fighting men called 'thegns', who were above ordinary freemen in status but below the aristocracy, and owed military service directly to the king. The English army fought on foot, the soldiers being armed with spear, javelin, two-edged sword, and the massive Danish axe. The shields were round or kite-shaped. All who were rich enough wore a metal helmet and coat of mail. The king had a personal force of professionals, the 'housecarls', and these waited with him in Sussex during the summer of 1066.

The crisis in the north came at the worst moment for Harold. On 8th September the English fleet ran out of supplies and was forced to return to London for revictualling and repairs. A week after he had thus been forced to abandon his watch in the Channel, Harold heard that 300 Norse ships had appeared off the Yorkshire coast, and that Cleveland and Scarborough had fallen to the invaders. He decided to leave the south coast undefended and marched his troops north at all speed. On his way he heard that the northern earls Edwin and Morkar had been defeated in a pitched battle at Fulford, outside York, and that the city was on the point of surrendering. He reached York in time to prevent that disaster, and on the afternoon of 25th September he brought the Norsemen to battle at Stamford Bridge. Here the English thegns won their greatest victory, Hardrada and Tostig being killed and their forces decisively defeated – only a small number escaping by sea.

On 28th September William of Normandy and his army landed on the south coast, unopposed. On that day Harold and his army were resting at York, 250 miles away, celebrating the victory over the Norsemen.

William had been hard at work since January preparing for the invasion of England. First he had to raise an army and, secondly, acquire a fleet of at least 450 transport vessels. In the strong Norman state the obligations of feudalism were clearly laid down. Every baron and bishop held his land from the duke on condition that he maintained for the duke's service a given number of knights, or heavily armoured cavalrymen. The knight was protected by a long mail-shirt, a peaked or conical helmet with a nose-guard, and a shield which was usually kite-shaped and 3 to 4 feet high. The principal weapon of the knight was a lance between 8 and 9 feet long. The medieval sword was to remain essentially unchanged for 400 years – two-edged, tapering to a point, some 44 inches from pommel to tip. The knight also carried on his saddle a broad-bladed battle-axe or an iron-headed mace.

Feudal custom had decreed that knightly service should be limited to forty days within the bounds of the duchy, and on this principle William's feudal resources would not be sufficient for the conquest of a foreign country. However, most of the barons were willing to go with him. Condoned by the Pope, the conquest of the large and reputedly wealthy country of England was tempting, especially to an energetic people already feeling the economic pressure of a rising population. And so William secured volunteers and mercenaries not only from Normandy but also from all parts of France and elsewhere. He raised altogether between 2,000 and 3,000 knights, of whom at least 1,200 were Normans.

To supplement his knights William enlisted between 3,000 and 4,000 infantry, consisting of bowmen and possibly crossbowmen, with foot soldiers armed with pike and sword. The Norman infantry soldiers, unlike most of the English *fyrd*, were protected by mail-shirts. The Norman bow was some 5 feet long. The crossbow may have come into use shortly after the beginning of the eleventh century; it is supposed to have been used by some of William's forces in 1066, though it is not shown in the Bayeux tapestry, the chief historical source for our knowledge of the conquest. (In 1804 Napoleon had the Bayeux tapestry exhibited at Paris to arouse enthusiasm among Frenchmen for his projected invasion of England.) The crossbow was a great deal more powerful than any previous bow; it derived from both the *ballista* and the ordinary bow.

At the end of August 1066 William had assembled his army on the French coast. Strong northerly winds prevented the sailing for six weeks, and the duke had to exercise all his qualities as a disciplinarian to keep his mixed army in order during that time. At last on the 27th September, when the wind had changed, the army embarked and the fleet crossed the Channel that night. Early the next morning William landed on an empty beach in Pevensey Bay, a few miles west of Hastings. On the 29th the Normans marched to Hastings; the countryside was then systematically ravaged.

Harold meanwhile was still at York, allowing his men to recover from their recent battle at Stamford Bridge. He heard the news of the Norman landing on 1st October and the next day started for the south with his housecarls, reaching London about one week after the Norman landing. There he had to wait while his army assembled after the long march, and it was not until the evening of 13th October that Harold reached the appointed rallying place of his forces, the landmark of the 'hoary apple tree', on a spur of the South Downs about six miles north of Hastings – near the present town of Battle.

William desired to fight a decisive battle as early as possible. He was indeed on English soil with his army; but behind him was the English Channel, now again patrolled by the English fleet. The longer the battle was put off, the more the Norman forces were likely to be depleted and their morale to sink, and the more troops would Harold be able to raise. William had gambled heavily. So far he had been lucky in that the Norse invasion and the unpredictable English weather had, together, enabled him to gain an easy footing on the south coast of England. But now he was to prove his generalship by cool and skilful calculation. William knew Harold personally, and estimated that he was likely to adopt an impetuous course. The devastation of Sussex was one of the duke's most characteristically intelligent and unscrupulous acts – that country being part of Harold's own earldom of Wessex, it was unlikely that he would quietly watch it suffering. Harold's best strategy would have been to wait in some suitable area to the south of London, collect a strong army, and order his fleet to attack the Norman ships in Hastings harbour. Then, if he could bring the Normans to battle in the Weald, the forest between Hastings and London, he might gain a major victory. This is what the English planned to do three centuries later, when in 1386 the French were threatening an

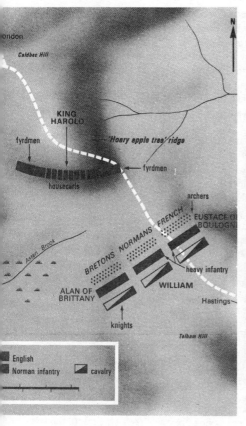

Norman soldiers before a battle *right*. The battle of Hastings *left*

invasion which, like that of 1803–5, never came. William had to fight Harold quickly, or risk a major disaster, and this Harold should have realized.

In the event Harold did none of these things, but acted impetuously as William reckoned he would. He left London and marched direct on Hastings before a third of his army was in fighting order. And he did not achieve the surprise which he desired, since William's scouts reported his approach. The Normans spent the night of 13th October in prayer and preparation for battle. Then, striking camp before sunrise the next morning, they marched the six miles to Telham Hill, opposite the hoary apple tree ridge. It was the English who were surprised; many of those who had arrived during the night were still asleep, and many more of the *fyrd* were still only just coming in. To maintain his fiction of legality, William sent an embassy to Harold to seek an eleventh-hour peaceful settlement, and he took advantage of the opportunity to unnerve at any rate some of his enemy by telling them, plausibly if untruly, that they had been excommunicated.

William had the advantage of surprise; but Harold's position, on ground of his own choosing which he had probably reconnoitred earlier in the summer, had great natural strength and was well suited to defensive tactics. The English army occupied a ridge some 700 yards long, with the ground sloping away gently to the west and east, and rising steeply to the north. To the south and south-east the ground sloped down at a gradient of about 1 in 13 to a boggy valley, and then rose up to the Norman positions on Telham Hill – about a mile and a half from the hoary apple tree. Harold extended his line of battle, the shieldwall, the whole length of the ridge, making it difficult for the Normans to take him in rear or flank. He set his two standards, his own Fighting Man and the Dragon of Wessex, in the centre, and drew up the housecarls on either side of them. The formation was ten or twelve ranks deep. The English force totalled 6,000 to 7,000 men, about the same as the Normans.

Many of Harold's men were tired after the forced march from London the day before, and some had not been properly re-equipped since Stamford Bridge. He lacked the archers who had served him well at Stamford Bridge, and who might have caused havoc among the Norman horse, and some of the hurriedly raised troops of the southern *fyrd* had little to fight with except clubs, picks and staffs. But all wanted to expel the harsh invader and the housecarls had the reputation of being the finest infantry in Europe – if depleted in numbers they still had confidence in their fighting ability. When the line of battle had been drawn up, Harold rode along it, reminding his men that nothing could go wrong so long as the solidity of the shield-wall was maintained.

The Normans were drawn up in three divisions: on the left the Bretons; on the right the French and other mercenaries; and in the centre the Normans, under William's personal command. There were three lines in each division: in front, the bowmen; next, the heavy infantry; and lastly, the knights. Before battle was joined the knights put on their heavy armour, having preserved their strength to the last moment. Finally, William hung round his neck the bones which were the holy relics of Bayeux. William's half-brother, Odo, Bishop of Bayeux, was armed with a mace rather than a sword – since as a priest he ought not to shed blood. When the Norman advance began their ranks deployed outwards so as to cover the full line of the English; they were led by the minstrel Taillefer, riding ahead of the army, twirling his lance and singing the *Song of Roland* – until he was cut down.

The first serious attack began at about nine o'clock. As the Normans closed, their archers began to fire; but since they had to shoot uphill most of their arrows passed over the heads of the English or were caught on their shields. The heavy infantry immediately took up the attack. But the English put up a very tough and successful resistance, taking advantage of their strong position and maintaining their front intact. At length the Norman foot soldiers and the Breton knights, panic-stricken, broke in flight. Soon, apparently, 'the whole army of the duke was in danger of retreat'.

So long as the shield-wall was unbroken and stood firm in its strong positions, the English army had nothing to fear. But some of the raw levies of Harold's army moved out in pursuit of the Breton knights retreating down the slope; for infantry to pursue mounted men was to court disaster, and it is unlikely that Harold would have ordered such a counter-attack so early in the battle. Actually, at that time William had been unhorsed and a shout went up that he had been killed. But he quickly mounted another horse, showed himself to his troops, and took a firm grip on the battle. Although some of the English right wing had broken out in pursuit, the rest of the line stood firm; on the soft ground of the valley the pursuing infantry soon wavered, and the Normans rallied under William's leadership.

William himself now led a renewed attack of the knights, and for several hours confused mass assaults continued. In the eleventh century, knights did not charge in one cohesive mass, but rode up to the line in groups or individually, hurling their lances rather than thrusting with them, and then hacking at close quarters with their

The Normans were Europe's greatest castle builders. Château Gaillard, plan *left* aerial view *right*, occupied an apparently impregnable position

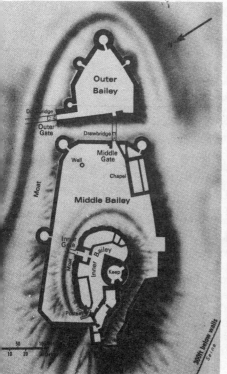

swords, maces and axes. William himself took an outstanding part in this fighting –
according to William of Poitiers, 'he dominated this battle, checking his own men in
flight, strengthening their spirit, and sharing their dangers'. On the other hand,
'the English fought confidently with all their strength, striving in particular to
prevent the attackers from penetrating within their ranks, which indeed were so
closely massed together that even the dead had not space in which to fall.'

In the early afternoon William tried a ruse. Remembering how the retreat of his
left in the morning had led the English right to break forward and lose cohesion, he
decided to carry out a feigned retreat on the other flank. The device worked admirably. Most of the English left, certainly without orders from Harold and possibly
against them, chased down the slope to the valley. When they were at the bottom the
Norman horsemen turned and savagely attacked them with great effect.

But the housecarls in the centre and part of the left stood rock-like, and as the sun
began to set in the later afternoon the Norman knights became tired and more than
ever apprehensive of the English axes. Once again William showed himself a
resourceful general. His archers, who had been unsuccessful in the morning, were
at any rate now fresh. Let them try a different attack! Drawing up the archers in a
long, loose line, with gaps through which the knights could ride, he sent them up
the hill at a run, with the horsemen trotting behind. A hundred yards short of the
English line the archers halted, and loosed their arrows almost vertically into the
sky. The arrows rained down on to the English, and, Wace says, 'all feared to open
their eyes or leave their faces unguarded'. At the same moment the knights charged
together, hitting the English a few seconds after the arrows had caused sudden
confusion and terror. Even then, for a while the fighting was hard. But the English
left cracked and finally the whole shield-wall began to disintegrate. The housecarls
retreated in good order, until William rode in pursuit and scattered them. He
returned to the field of battle after dark, to find Harold's body stripped and hacked
almost beyond recognition.

The Conqueror had still much work to do even after he was crowned in West-
minster Abbey, and some of it cruel work. Norman warriors, administrators,
churchmen and merchants completed the conquest enthusiastically, and the history
and civilization of England became intimately connected with that of France.

European society in the central Middle Ages was divided into three classes:
those who fought, those who prayed, and those who laboured. The foundation of
the strength of the military class and of all defence policy was the castle; and between
1000 and 1300 military architecture developed strongly. On the other hand there
was no comparable advance in the offensive weapons and techniques of siegecraft.
It thus came about that during this period men preferred to be secure inside strong
fortifications rather than accept risks in operations in the open country. The so-called
battles of this period may have had political importance, but they are much less
interesting to the military historian than the fortifications.

By the middle of the eleventh century the Normans had developed a new type of
fortification – the motte and bailey castle. The motte was a mound surrounded by a

ditch. Surmounting it was a stockade and a keep which was the residence and stronghold of the baron, his family and retainers. The bailey was a forecourt protected by another ditch and stockade, its original purpose being to protect the domestic animals. The outer entrance to the castle was by way of a drawbridge. Stone became increasingly used in building and from the end of the eleventh century castles became more massive and elaborate. Dover Castle has walls 83 feet high, corner turrets rising another 12 feet, buttresses about 20 feet thick, and three towers strengthening the forebuilding. A refinement of fortification was to pierce arrowslits in the walls and towers; these were more effective than battlements, since the defenders could shoot at the enemy outside while themselves remaining unseen and protected. Later they were cut in the form of a cross – to allow the archer a wide lateral sweep.

Towards the end of the twelfth century, bows and stone-throwing engines became more powerful. The reply of military architects was to build greater curtain walls and multiple baileys. The motte and keep shrank in size and importance. The

The backbone of the crusader armies was the mounted cavalry

powerful fortress of Château Gaillard, completed by Richard I of England in 1198, included the features most characteristic of the best fortification of that time. The site selected was a precipitous cliff 300 feet above the Seine. The castle consisted of three baileys in line downhill, as advance fortifications astride the only possible direction of approach. The inner bailey and the keep were on the edge of the cliff. The side of the keep which faced into the courtyard – the only side which could be attacked – was thickened and V-shaped like the prow of a ship, so that missiles would be deflected by the oblique alignment of the walls. It was protected against sapping by a deep plinth, and against battering attacks by 'machicolations', or openings beneath the battlements through which pitch and missiles could be dropped on to the heads of assailants below. It had two tiers of battlements. The baileys were each separated from the next by a moat and a curtain wall. While the curtains of the middle and outer baileys were strengthened by circular projecting towers, the inner curtain was given a continuous series of corrugations to enable the defenders to cover with missile fire the outside of the wall at all points.

Only a small proportion of the numerous sieges of the Middle Ages were success-ful. The weapons, tools and techniques of siegecraft had still not significantly changed since the time of the fall of the Roman empire. They consisted for the most part of battering-rams, siege-towers, scaling-ladders, pent-houses and mantlets, and projectile-throwing engines. The projectiles might be stones, darts, poles, fire, or even carrion. The engines ranged in size from the *trébuchet*, with its beam made of a whole tree trunk, to the crossbow. The best means of taking a castle were still mining, starvation and treachery.

In 1071, following the disastrous defeat of the Byzantines at Manzikert, the emperor Alexius Comnenus had appealed to the Pope for help from the West. But it was not until 1095 that Urban II preached his call for a European crusade: 'All Christendom is disgraced by the triumphs and supremacy of the Moslems in the East. The Holy Land . . . is profaned. Christian kings should therefore turn their weapons against these enemies of God, in place of warring with one another.'

The Christian army was to be commanded by the Bishop of Le Puy. There were no detailed plans; God would provide. The response to the Pope's appeal was tremendous. By the late spring of 1097 between 25,000 and 30,000 crusaders had crossed the Bosphorus.

There were many reasons for the appeal of the crusading movement. For a hundred years or more the population of western Europe had been increasing, and agricultural output had not kept pace. Many of the younger sons of the nobility contributed to the general restlessness, wanting to find new lands for themselves, as well as adventure. Peasants enrolled in the hope of thereby gaining freedom from serfdom. The merchants of Venice and Genoa saw an opportunity for com-mercial profit. But the prime motive of the first generations of crusaders was undoubtedly religious; in the words of a song of the second Crusade: 'God has fixed a day for you to be at Edessa: there the sinners will be saved who hit hard and who serve Him in His need.'

The Norman conquest of England. A detail from the Bayeux tapestry

Ever since the time of Charlemagne, European warfare had become increasingly affected by religion. The 'Truce of God' was a long-sustained attempt by the Church to regulate and restrict the depredations of private war, and to protect innocent people as well as agriculture and buildings. It is first heard of in southern France in 990, supported by the influential monastic order of Cluny. A Synod at Elne in 1027 prohibited all warfare at weekends and the Normans thereafter carried the Truce to many parts of Europe. The papacy took up the idea and reaffirmed increasingly elaborate regulations. For example, the Lateran Council of 1139 forbade the use of the crossbow – except against infidels – as being a weapon too murderous for 'Christian warfare'. However, except where the temporal authority intervened to enforce the Church's pronouncements, the Truce of God was not on the whole effective.

The first Crusade was a success. The crusaders marched across Asia Minor, suffering with immense fortitude the discomforts of hunger and thirst – the result of the inefficiency of their commissariat. They captured Antioch in June 1098, where they were smitten by dysentery and were themselves besieged by the Turks. In this critical position the crusading leaders abandoned their rivalries and appointed Bohemund commander-in-chief. Having discovered a holy lance they sallied out, and, aided by St George and other saints mounted on white horses, they defeated the Turks. At the beginning of January 1099 the crusaders continued on their way to Jerusalem and in July, after a five weeks' siege, captured the city – massacring its inhabitants. The crusaders had met practically no Moslem resistance, since, luckily for them, their enemies were divided.

The defence of the Holy Land thereafter was not so easy. Several of the leaders broke off with their followers to set up their own kingdoms, and the bulk of the crusading contingents returned home having completed their pilgrimage. But at an early stage the support of the Genoese and Venetian fleets was purchased to hold the coastal towns and keep the crusaders supplied. Numbers also increased to some extent after the foundation of the orders of warrior monks – the Knights Hospitaller (1113) and the Knights Templar (1119), who undertook to protect pilgrims and 'fight with a pure mind.' After the second Crusade the armies were supplemented by mercenaries.

The crusaders were obliged to formulate a strategy appropriate to their shortage of manpower. Their policy was to avoid open battles as far as possible, and to rely, even more than in the West, on castles. Good relations were cultivated with the local inhabitants. Many of the castles of the crusaders were built on sites chosen for administrative, economic and social purposes rather than for strategical reasons. But the crusaders eventually did build a large number of frontier castles such as Kerak of Moab, Krak des Chevaliers and Montferrand. These were visible one from the next in a chain across the country, visual signals being used for intercommunication.

The early success of the crusaders was due at least as much to the disunity of the Saracens as to their own courage and faith. The beginning of failure came in 1127 when Imad ed-Din Zangi set out to extend his power in Syria, capturing Edessa in 1144. The gravity of this disaster was recognized in the West, but the second

Medieval warfare. A miniature from a fifteenth-century French manuscript

Crusade was a total failure. In 1174 Saladin became king of both Egypt and Syria. Saladin systematically built up military strength, and by able preaching prepared his subjects for the *jihad* – the holy war against the Christians. The crusaders were now more seriously threatened than ever before: their enemies in the north and south were working to a common plan, and their supply lines were put in danger by Saladin's Egyptian fleet. But instead of uniting in this crisis the leaders wrangled ever more bitterly.

In 1187 Saladin laid siege to Tiberias. Some Christians urged that the crusaders should march to relieve the fortress. Some, on the other hand, argued that such an advance would be to fall into Saladin's trap; the crusaders would be greatly outnumbered, and, as it was the hottest time of year, they would suffer greatly from lack of water; it would be best to remain on the defensive. The upshot was that in July 1187 Guy de Lusignan led out the crusading forces to meet their greatest disaster – at the battle of Hattin, in the hills west of the Sea of Galilee.

The chief striking power of the crusader forces lay in the impact of the charge by heavily armoured mounted lancers – although this was still a combination of individual assaults rather than a mass charge. Foot soldiers normally carried out camp and siege duties. The most important infantry were mercenary bowmen. An organized and disciplined defensive order was the best hope against the Saracens. The main strength of the Saracen armies lay with their horse archers; these were more lightly equipped than the cavalry of the crusaders, the horses being faster and handier. Besides his bow, the mounted archer carried a small round shield, a short lance, a sword and a club. The Saracens usually took the tactical offensive – exploiting the superior mobility of their light cavalry, harassing the crusaders on the march, and in battle encircling them. To avoid having to withstand the shock of the crusader cavalry and also to break the cohesion of their enemy, the Saracens used tactics of evasion, adopting loose formations and keeping at a distance from the enemy until they could launch a sudden attack at the right moment. Sometimes they retreated for days on end, in order to draw the crusaders into difficult country and wear them out. Using such methods at Hattin Saladin all but destroyed the forces of the crusaders, and Jerusalem itself fell again into Saracen hands. Further crusades followed; but their history on the whole shows a degeneration of idealism and military competence. The military developments which should interest us were now happening in the West.

8 The High Middle Ages

Between the battles of Bouvines (1214) and Morat (1476), warfare was the rule in Europe. The disintegration of the Holy Roman Empire was furthered by the struggle between the Papacy and the Hohenstaufen imperial family, by the Swiss wars of independence, and by the wars of the Bohemian Hussites. The power of the English state was consolidated by Edward I's conquest of Wales (1277–95), although the English attempt to conquer Scotland (1296–1328) was a failure. Then came the clash between England and France, the series of English invasions between 1337 and 1453, together known as the Hundred Years' War.

From the military point of view these wars are immensely important. The knight, the castle and feudalism gave way to the infantryman, to firearms, and to professionalism. Strategically, it became clear that the defensive with the weapons available could win battles provided the enemy could be induced to attack; but to win campaigns offensive action was necessary. Tactically, superiority passed to new missile weapons, and these, rather than shock action, became the decisive factor in battle. Eventually the gun was to prove the most powerful instrument of war during the next six hundred years. But although artillery was effective by the beginning of the fifteenth century, the full impact of firearms was not felt for a long time after their first appearance. Interest in this period focuses rather on the revolutionary achievement of infantry, both spearmen and archers, who wrested from heavy cavalry its thousand-year mastery of the battlefield.

The battle of Hastings confirmed the supremacy of heavy cavalry inaugurated by the battle of Adrianople in 378. No commander in western Europe before the mid-thirteenth century grasped the lesson of the crusades: that the tactical sum of infantry and cavalry when carefully co-ordinated was far greater than the sum of the two parts when acting separately. Infantry became for the most part despised, though it is true that mercenary Flemish pikemen and Genoese crossbowmen were proficient and useful fighters in the twelfth and thirteenth centuries. The crossbow continued to evolve till the end of the fifteenth century. It was basically a miniature *ballista*, a small stiff bow set crosswise at the end of a stock. Eventually the bow was made of steel, being drawn by a cord-and-pulley or a rack-and-pinion, and discharging a short iron-headed bolt. The weapon was heavy, slow to operate, and did not work in wet weather. But it had advantages: it was accurate up to a range of about 100 yards, could be handled by relatively untrained men who were not strong enough to draw a longbow, and was a particularly good weapon for defensive loop-hole shooting.

Armour was in a continual process of development. By 1200 the conical helmet was giving way to the pot-helm, an iron cylinder covering the whole head, with slits to enable the wearer to see and breathe. The long mail tunic was supplemented by the surcoat and quilted protections called *gambesons*. Poorer men might wear the *gambeson* alone, without metal armour. Chain-mail was made finer, more supple and close fitting. Plate armour was a development of the fourteenth century, but by 1250 men began to improve their mail armour by the addition of metal plate caps for the knees, elbows and shins. Then the cuirass appeared; this provided a tougher protection against sword blows, but was heavy and left gaps. At Benevento in 1266 there were 1,200 German cavalry armed with breast-plates, whose advance was irresistible until the French noticed that they could stab them in the armpits with rapiers.

Light cavalry, such as the German *panzerati*, was used only for skirmishing and reconnoitring, and never had an integral part in the tactical systems of the Middle Ages. In the thirteenth century an army still often relied for victory on weight and main force alone. Groups of horsemen would hurl themselves against the enemy, hacking with sword or battle-axe. Some commanders adopted a different tactic, dividing their men-at-arms into three 'battles' or divisions – success depending on the timing of each successive mass charge. It was, for example, because Simon de Montfort chose his gound well, surprised the enemy, and used his reserve line at the right time and place, that he won the battle of Lewes against Henry III in 1264.

By the thirteenth century the feudal recruiting system was generally breaking down, although in principle the armies of the king of France continued to be raised in this way even in the Hundred Years' War. Obligations had become confused, and the feudal system was irregular and unreliable. The contingents tended to obey only their particular lord, and would serve no longer than forty days. A great disadvantage was that feudal levies consisted of amateurs, most of whom were not fully proficient in the use of their weapons. It is true that many knights had little to occupy themselves with except fighting; but their followers were farmers, who had other occupations and little time to spare for training.

Everywhere an increasing dependence was placed on mercenaries. In England the king allowed his tenants to commute their feudal service for payment of a tax called 'scutage'. With these funds he could hire mercenary adventurers and their troops – landless younger sons, adventurers, refugees from serfdom. These professionals would serve their paymaster for as long as required. Sometimes, however, they could be a great nuisance – in time of peace mercenary armies might turn into gangs of bandits, living off the countryside. One of the causes of John's unpopularity was that he brought over to England the mercenary crossbowmen of Fawkes de Bréauté; these ruffians were still around in the next reign. Roger de Flor's 'Great Company', more than a thousand strong, was made up from mercenary bands discharged at the end of the Sicilian wars.

The best training in arms was to be had in tournaments. In the thirteenth century these were more like war than sport, for knights armed themselves and fought exactly as they would in actual battle. The 'joust' was a combat of individual knights, who charged each other full tilt with their lances three times; then, if neither had been unhorsed, they dismounted and each dealt the other three blows with sword, mace or axe. The 'tourney' was much the same exercise, but performed by a group of knights. William the Marshal – pilgrim to Jerusalem, and regent of England for Henry III – as a young man was a star of the tournament circuit. For several years he fought about once a fortnight, winning renown all over northern France, and making considerable profit – in one tournament he captured ten horses, and twelve knights whom he held to ransom. Commoners also had their war-games; these might be bouts with the quarter-staff or sword and buckler, and tilting at a dummy with a bucket of water on it. The crusades were sometimes described as a 'tournament between heaven and hell'. With time, as life became more comfortable and tournaments produced too many serious injuries, elaborate rules were made. By the fifteenth century they were more popular than ever and far less dangerous. Even so, in a tournament in 1559 King Henry II of France was accidentally killed by a Norman ancestor of mine – who had to flee the country quickly.

By about 1200 knighthood had become associated with the concept of chivalry. Hitherto the knight had merely been the man who did military service on horseback in exchange for a grant of land. But the crusades, and the institution of orders such as the Templars, produced a new outlook. The theory came to be held that a knight was a man of particular virtue and valour who had been formally initiated into his caste. The old method of bestowing the status of knighthood, the accolade, still survived for the battlefield. The candidate knelt before another knight, who touched him with the flat of his sword on either shoulder, and pronounced a short formula of creation and exhortation. But a more elaborate initiation, later described by Selden, was now normal: 'The ceremonies and circumstances at the giving this dignity were of two kinds, which we may call courtly and sacred. The courtly were the feasts held at the creation, giving of robes, arms, spurs and the like. The sacred were the holy devotions in the church before the receiving of the dignity.' John of Salisbury wrote: 'For what purpose is knighthood ordained? To protect the Church, to attack infidelity, to protect the poor, to keep the peace, to shed one's blood for one's brethren.'

Another expression of the qualities that were idealised is the *Song of Roland*. It is a good story of heroism and treachery, and it emphasizes the virtues of personal valour, loyalty to one's comrades, and confidence in the aid of the saints. This was perhaps the best expression of the chivalrous spirit, reflecting a just pride in the achievement of knightly arms in Europe by the thirteenth century: the stabilization of the borders, the recovery of political order, and the possibility of economic progress which resulted from a measure of security. Otherwise, it can be said that chivalry was a force for good in reminding the upper classes of a standard of decency worthy of their privileges and in restraining brutality in a necessarily violent society. But the later literature of chivalry, the romances of Chrétien de Troyes and Thomas Malory, in which the knight is portrayed as engaged in a mysterious quest for virtue were of course sentimental. In reality the manners of the medieval gentleman were lacking in discipline and refinement: he relied on serf labour; and, whether or not he had reverence for the Virgin Mary, there is not much evidence that he often had it for other women. Courtesy was shown only to captives who were worth a ransom – other victims were usually slaughtered.

Another development of the thirteenth century was heraldry. This developed with the pot-helm, which by concealing the wearer's face made it necessary, for marshalling among other reasons, that he should carry some identifying mark. Individuals assumed more or less elaborate emblems, which were painted on the shield and embroidered on the surcoat, and crests were worn on top of helmets.

Possibly the most momentous invention in the history of warfare has been gunpowder. The first man in the western world to record the formula for gunpowder was Roger Bacon, an English monk, in 1260. His formula was seven parts of saltpetre, five of charcoal, and five of sulphur. 'With such a mixture you will produce a bright flash and a thundering noise, if you know the trick . . .'

Fifty years then passed before the first gun appeared. The earliest type of cannon was known as a *pot-de-fer*, because it was shaped like a vase. In an English MS. it is shown mounted on a bench, and loaded with a large crossbow-type arrow. The gunner fired it by thrusting a red-hot rod into the touch hole. From the same year a Florentine document survives, ordering the Council to see to the production of cannon and iron bullets. The first definite instance when a gun was fired in anger was in 1324 at Metz. In the next fifteen years they are heard of increasingly. Certainly

By the fifteenth century heavy cavalrymen were completely encased in suits of plate armour

the French used *canons et bombardes* to fire arrows at the English at Quesnoi in 1340, and Edward used artillery in his siege of Calais in 1346. There was also the *ribauldequin*, built of several metal tubes mounted on a sort of chariot and fired simultaneously – a sort of primitive rocket battery. Edward ordered a hundred of these to be made in 1345. By this time firearms were coming into regular use; but for some years they were not to make any real impact on the conduct of war.

Eventually guns were to break the impregnability of castles, but between 1260 and 1320 some of the most efficient fortifications of any age were built. The principle was to build a series of concentric powerful curtain walls. The moat was often a lake. Gatehouses were strong and square, of three or four storeys and surmounted by twin towers. Approaches could be defended by one or more drawbridges, and then the gate by machicolations, portcullises and loop-holes. The central bailey enclosed by the walls frequently included a town, as at Flint, Conway and Caernarvon. These castles, built in Edward I's Welsh wars (1277–95), served a strategic purpose comparable to the chain of forts built by the Teutonic Knights to hold down the barbarians of Prussia. By the fourteenth century, however, the demands of comfort were increasingly outweighing the requirements of security.

In the second half of the thirteenth century tactical conceptions altered dramatically – with the ideas of Edward I of England and of the Swiss leader, Rudolph of Erlach. In the years after 1282 infantry won an outstanding but logical series of victories, until finally the battle of Crécy (1346) announced to Europe the downfall of the heavy cavalry arm after its thousand-year supremacy. That battle showed beyond doubt that cavalry could not win against archers supported by men-at-arms and drawn up in a strong position. Meanwhile in central Europe the Swiss pikemen, using a different method, had also been winning victories. A little later in eastern Europe the Bohemian Hussites, using guns, demonstrated at Sudomer (1419) a third method by which foot soldiers could get the better of cavalry.

Infantry defeated cavalry on the Continent at Courtrai (1302) and Morgarten (1315) but it was possible to explain away these episodes by attributing them to unfavourable terrain and poor command. But the Swiss victory over their feudal lords at Laupen in 1339 decisively upset old assumptions. Rudolph of Erlach, the Swiss commander, being outnumbered, adopted a defensive plan. He stationed his few cavalry on the right where the slope was steeper, and the bulk of his infantry on the left where the severest attack was expected. His plan was to wait for the enemy to begin the ascent towards him, and then charge down in a dense mass. The Bernese, on the right, were immediately successful. But on the left the men of the Forest Cantons, clashing with the baronial cavalry, soon found themselves in trouble. Their charge downhill was halted, they were surrounded and forced to make a stand back to back with their halberds bristling – in the 'hedgehog' formation which was to become famous. The fighting was close and ferocious, but the mountaineers held firm until the Bernese came to their relief, charging the enemy cavalry in flank and rear to win the battle. It had been a fair fight. The Swiss peasants captured 27 feudal banners and 70 crested helms.

At Laupen the Swiss were still using the 8-foot halberd; but already they were changing over to the weapon which they were to keep, the 18-foot pike: an ash shaft with a 10-inch steel head, held level at shoulder height, and totally effective against cavalry. Thus formed, with the pikes of the first four ranks projecting together in front, they presented an impenetrable bristling hedge – equally effective in a defensive wall or in a mass advance. The tactical system of the Swiss was so efficient and simple, like that of the Spartans, that it was hardly ever varied. Their light armour (due originally to poverty, but then found to be an advantage) gave them great mobility, and they usually took the offensive. They were the first modern troops to march in step to music. Their usual method of attack was to advance in an *échelon* of three parallel columns, one slightly behind the next. This gave flank protection and a reserve to the attacking column in the lead.

For two centuries the Swiss pikemen suffered no serious reverses. But rivalry between the cantons, and their system of command by a council, always prevented the Swiss from following up their victories strategically, and they never established themselves as a first-class political power. Instead they became the leading mercenary soldiers of Europe. In 1476 they won the two most famous of all their victories, over Charles the Rash of Burgundy, at Granson and Morat.

It was in England, however, that the infantry revolution had first manifested itself. The man responsible was Edward I (1272–1307), conqueror of Wales, victor at Falkirk in 1298, a great military organizer and a fine commander. In his Evesham campaign in 1265 Edward evinced remarkable strategical imagination, timing a series of rapid manoeuvres to prevent two enemy armies joining, and all the while maintaining a river front of fifty miles – until he could dispose of one enemy and then turn swiftly to trap Simon de Montfort in a loop of the Avon. In his Welsh wars (1277–95) Edward again showed his strategic vision, in building a systematic network of roads and castles. He also saw that the Welsh mountaineers could not be conquered by the conventional army of the time, a cavalry host limited to a short period of service in the summer. So he made two innovations of major and enduring importance: he relied on a hired, professional army contracted to serve all the year round, and he exploited the potentialities of the longbow.

The professionalization of armies had started with the increasing dependence on mercenaries. The unsuitability of normal feudal forces in the Welsh situation forced Edward I to abandon that method of recruitment, but in any case the feudal system was breaking down for various economic and constitutional reasons. Specialization and professional armies would be further necessitated by economic factors in the next century, when new types of armour became very expensive, and plague carried off much of the population of Europe.

Edward I's solution to the problem of recruitment was to encourage many of his feudal tenants to commute their service for 'scutage'. He asked his other tenants to bring fewer but better troops, and contracted to pay them after the expiry of their feudal period of service. The contracts or 'indentures' were precise written agreements between a professional officer and the king. They laid down the exact size and composition of the force provided, the place, duration and type of service, the rates of pay, bonuses and so on. Most commonly the force provided was of all arms,

English longbowmen *above* and Swiss pikemen *below* outfought the medieval cavalry

and included such personnel as artificers, surgeons, miners, chaplains and inter-
preters, as well as archers and men-at-arms. The term of service ranged from the old
forty days to 'the king's pleasure'. From 1340 onwards Edward III's armies had no
feudal element. The population of France during the Hundred Years' War was
roughly five times that of England, but because the French stuck to the feudal
system of recruitment they had no proper infantry, and their men-at-arms, although
more numerous, were less highly trained and disciplined than the English.

Edward I's other revolutionary innovation was to make the longbow the chief
English weapon. The English longbow was 6 feet 4 inches in height, and could be
used only by a very tall and strong man; it was made of yew or elm; the arrow was
about 37 inches long. The accurate range was 250 yards, and the extreme range
350 yards. Longbowmen usually wore no more armour than a metal cap and a
quilted tunic. They carried, besides the bow, a sword and sometimes an iron-headed
cudgel. From 1252 onwards all forty-shilling freeholders were required to possess
a bow, and the yeomen thus became a standing archery militia. Archery practice
was at various times compulsory; one form of it was the game of 'rovers' – medieval
golf – in which archers progressed from field to field shooting at one target after
another.

The tactical potentialities of missile fire received their first full recognition in
Edward I's Welsh wars. A rain of arrows might, as a preliminary, unnerve the enemy
and destroy their cohesion, and it could cover the advance of one's own men-at-
arms. In 1282, or Orewin Bridge, the English, led by Edward Mortimer and John
Giffard, defeated the Welsh. The Welsh spearmen were in a strong position,
massed on a slope. But the English surprised them, their longbowmen bombarding
them with arrows from the flank; then, and only when this attack had taken effect,
they launched the charge of their men-at-arms. In 1298 Edward I himself tried out
the new tactics against the Scots at Falkirk. William Wallace was determined to
face the English only from the strongest possible defensive position, and the Scots
were drawn up in four great masses of spearmen, on a steep slope backed by a
forest and fronted by a morass. Edward was short of supplies, was far from his base,
and he himself had two broken ribs. Nonetheless, he decided to attack. The battle
opened when the English men-at-arms on the left and right rode round the morass
and charged the Scots in each flank. The spearmen checked them easily. Instead
of ordering a second charge Edward now brought up his longbowmen, and from
very close range a concentrated archery fire was loosed against particular points
in the enemy masses. Many of the Scots soon fell, and the rest became unsteady. A
second charge of men-at-arms at the weakened parts of the enemy front decided
the battle.

The English defeat by the Scots under Bruce at Bannockburn in 1314 happened
because Edward II reverted to outdated methods, failing to co-ordinate his archers
with his men-at-arms. But this was a temporary lapse. At Dupplin Moor in 1332
Edward Baliol developed the new English system further, by combining archers
with dismounted men-at-arms in a defensive formation. The men-at-arms waited
in the centre for the advance of the enemy. The archers on either wing were thrown

out in a half-moon, scattered thinly in the heather so that they presented no solid body for the enemy to attack. When the struggle became locked in the centre, the archers poured simultaneous volleys into the flanks of the Scots columns. The Scots became unnerved and jammed together, and the second drive of the English men-at-arms was again decisive. The following year Edward III repeated this tactical plan with equal success at Halidon Hill.

In 1337 the Hundred Years' War between England and France began. The issues included the feudal status of the English Duchy of Guienne, Edward III's alleged claim to the throne of France, the recent French support of the Scots, rivalry over the Flemish wool trade, and a long-standing border warfare between English and French sailors in the Channel. From a few disjointed invasions by the English, it developed into a war of attrition, really amounting to the repeated devastation of Artois, Normandy, Brittany and Aquitaine by ruffianly bands of professional soldiers.

The first considerable battle of the war was at sea, off Sluys in 1340. For a hundred and fifty years after Hastings ships had not altered from the Viking pattern, and there had been no large naval operations in northern waters. Then in the thirteenth century there had been a continuous and more or less ferocious war in the Channel. The style of ships had developed, and the flagship of Edward III, the *Thomas*, was about 275 tons, with a crew of 137. Ships now had high sides and raised poops and forecastles. They were generally driven by one large square sail. Tactics at sea corresponded to those on land, as did differences in armament. The French at Sluys fought with swords and pikes and a few crossbows, while the English relied on men-at-arms and above all on longbowmen (firing special arrows tipped with broad heads to slash through rigging and sails). Edward III himself was in command, and he had 147 ships to the 190 of the French. Both sides drew up their ships in three divisions. While the French chained their ships together to make three massive floating platforms for their men-at-arms, the English adopted a more flexible formation – alternate ships containing archers and men-at-arms. The English tactics were to launch a preliminary missile bombardment from long range to weaken the enemy, and then to close – so that the men-at-arms with swords and lances could board the enemy ships. After eight hours of fighting the French broke, and finally they lost seven-eighths of their ships and three-quarters of their men.

Although no great land battle was fought until the war had been going for almost ten years, there were several campaigns during which each side had time to get the feel of the other. The weapons and equipment of the men-at-arms on both sides were very similar. Armour was in the process of transition from mail to plate. The main weapons were the sword, a 14-foot long lance, and the dagger or 'misericord'. The units of organization were the retinues of the knights, which were broken down into 'lances' of three to four fighting men. Both sides had some firearms, but these were as yet tactically insignificant. Where they differed, and where the English held the advantage, was in training, recruitment and quality of infantry. The English professionals were fresh from their successes in Scotland; on the other hand the French feudal levies had experienced virtually no battle fighting during the past twenty-five years. And whereas the few infantry units the French possessed consisted of crossbowmen, the English had a large force of archers, using a weapon which gave twice the range and six times the firing rate of the crossbow.

In 1345–6 Edward III conceived the ambitious strategy of attacking Philip VI of France on exterior lines. The Earl of Northampton and Sir Thomas Dagworth conducted successful campaigns in Brittany, and the Earl of Derby in the south-west. In 1346 Philip bestirred himself to march against Derby, only to be forced to return north by the news, in July, that Edward had landed in north-west France.

On the morning of 26th August 1346 Edward III prepared to meet Philip in battle at Crécy. He had the choice of position, and plenty of time to array his forces. Knowing that he would be heavily outnumbered, and since it suited his tactics, he chose a strong defensive position – a ridge with three terraces in the centre, sloping down steeply for 100 feet to a stream at one end where the French must approach. Edward had no more than 12,000 or 13,000 men to fill a line almost 2,000 yards long. But, if it was safe to leave the terraces thinly manned, this was enough. The main force of the unmounted men-at-arms was placed on the right, well down the slope. The archers were drawn up in three wedge formations on the flanks of the divisions of men-at-arms, the outer two each linking one of the front divisions with a village, and the central wedge connecting the two divisions. The overall proportion of archers to men-at-arms was about two to one. Pitfalls, or *trous de loup*, were dug in front of the Black Prince's division on the right. Edward's command post was a windmill, on the highest point of the ridge. From here he could command the whole English line, as well as the presumed approach route of the French along the road from Abbeville.

Philip's feudal army of 40,000 men, led by a motley galaxy of princes and nobles, appeared at about five o'clock in the evening. Even at a distance the French were seen to be already in some disorder. This became worse when Philip, seeing the English array, decided that he would rather postpone the battle until the next day and gave the order to halt. The order was obeyed by the van of the army, but not by the rear. The men in front were forced on from behind, with no clear orders. Furthermore, the French were approaching the English front from the road at an oblique angle, and had to wheel half left at the last moment to face it directly. Inevitably over the last mile disorder increased to chaos. Descriptions of the French formation as they met the English are most obscure, but it is likely that, at any rate in theory, the French men-at-arms were in three divisions. The Genoese mercenary crossbowmen were in front. The French had the low evening sun in their eyes.

As the French advanced with loud battle cries, confident at least in their numbers, the English waited silently. When the Genoese came within range of the longbow, which was before they could touch their enemy, the first English volley was loosed. In a few minutes the Genoese were in confusion. Terror reigned when the English let off their cannon – the first ever to be used in an important battle. It is recorded that the guns 'made a sound like thunder', and if that was the only impact they made it was nonetheless momentous. The French cavalry, however, was surging forward and many of the mercenaries were ridden down by their own employers,

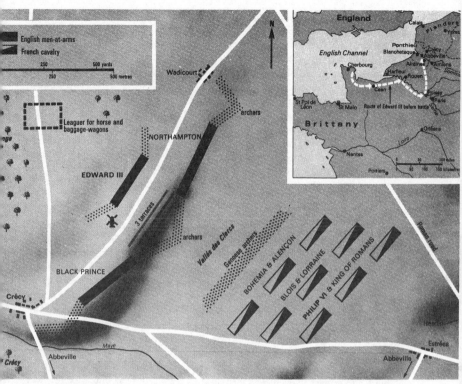

The battle of Crécy

but the longbow continued to work execution among the French men-at-arms.

The continuation of the battle was no more than a succession of suicidal charges by masses of French men-at-arms, and the English reckoned afterwards that from first to last they had fought off fifteen successive attacks. With desperate *élan* the French hurled themselves up the slope, each time heading for the English men-at-arms, partly through outmoded tradition, but actually because neither they nor their horses could face the arrows. The English archers held their position and formation throughout. As each charge began they first loosed volleys to break the enemy into disorder and slow their impetus, and then raked their flanks. Handfuls of the bravest knights in the French army reached the line of the English men-at-arms, only to be cut down by more numerous and fresher men. Each successive wave was muddled and hampered by the retreating remnants of its predecessors. The attacks went on until long after dark, but they grew ever more haphazard and ineffectual, and the English shield-wall, this time, did not waver. Edward never even needed to use his central reserve.

At Crécy a trained, well-armed, confident English army, under a commander who was a tried expert in the most efficient new tactics of the age, defeated a larger army which was hastily raised, diverse, untrained, out of date, and indecisively led. Edward followed up his victory by the capture of Calais, which as a military and commercial bridgehead abroad was to be as valued by England for two hundred years as Gibraltar in a later age. But the strategic result of Crécy in the Hundred Years' War was, above all, moral. The English emerged as the leading military people of Europe. Edward III remained the English commander-in-chief until 1360; another great victory was won, by the Black Prince at Poitiers in 1356, and the morale of the army remained as good as ever. For twenty-two years altogether – a period as long as the Napoleonic Wars – Edward III consistently pursued one strategy, and his soldiers were always confident in his leadership. Furthermore, the continuity and loyalty within the ranks of his high command – Derby, Warwick, Northampton, Hawkwood, Chandos – were outstanding.

War was resumed in 1369. Desultory and unprofitable fighting went on, much of it mere brigandage, until Henry V's invasion in 1415 altered its character. The dominant figure was the Constable of France, Bertrand du Guesclin. His Fabian strategy, of avoiding large pitched battles and pouncing on isolated English columns, worked well, but the English, unbeaten in actual battle, refused to give up. The armour and tactics of the French men-at-arms were somewhat developed after Crécy in an attempt to deal with the problem of the arrow. The transition from mail to plate armour was completed by 1400, by which time a man-at-arms was encased from head to foot in metal. But the quest for security meant a loss of mobility, which more than countered any benefit in the change. At Poitiers in 1356 John II of France dismounted his men-at-arms; trying to beat infantry at its own game without understanding how it had been won, he merely sacrificed his assets of superior mobility and impact. Nonetheless men-at-arms remained dismounted for the next hundred years, and the lance was abandoned. At Agincourt in 1415 the English archers, although handicapped by diarrhoea, had no difficulty in mowing down the French men-at-arms herded together, exhausted and stumbling in the mud.

From 1415, artillery began to affect the character of the warfare. Cannon by now were of cylindrical shape, and guns were able to hurl projectiles of 200 pounds weight. In 1415 Henry V laid siege to Harfleur. When mining failed he resorted to artillery. He had ten cannon, and the chief engineer, Master Giles, organized a steady bombardment, night and day, particularly concentrated against the walls flanking one gate. After twenty-seven days the gate and barbican were in ruins. Master Giles then set alight the woodwork with an incendiary shell, and as the breach was stormed the town surrendered. As Henry V's artillery battered down the walls of Harfleur in 1415 the era of impregnable fortifications passed. There was no reaction in military architecture till the end of the fifteenth century.

After Henry V's death in 1422 the French gradually drove the English off their soil. One of the leading spirits in the French recovery was Joan of Arc, a peasant girl. The Duke of Alençon reported that Joan was an expert at 'the preparation of the artillery'. Maybe Joan did have some God-given military ability; certainly she

By the middle of the fifteenth century artillery was being used for siege warfare

restored the morale of the French soldiery. But the superiority of the French in artillery was perhaps as great a cause of their success. The first great artilleryman was Jean Bureau; in 1449–50, Bureau and his brother conducted, it is said, sixty successful siege operations in the reconquest of Normandy. At the battle of Castillon in 1453 the French army under Bureau's command had 250 cannon, and the cross-fire and enfilade by the French field artillery caused the English heavy casualties.

Already, some years earlier, field artillery had been used in eastern Europe as a third formula for the defeat of heavy cavalry by infantry. John Zizka was the military leader of the Hussite movement in Bohemia, a religious, nationalistic and popular uprising which began in 1419. At the village of Sudomer, with 400 followers and 12 wagons carrying guns, Zizka met 200 royalist cavalry. He deployed his men where the ground gave the maximum flank protection, and arranged his gun-wagons in a leaguer. Victory went to the Hussites. By 1420 the Hussite stronghold of Tabor was organized as a theocratic community on a war footing.

In the following wars Zizka developed his highly original military system. He used ordinary peasant wagons of a suitable size, mounted guns on them, and arranged them in a circle – just as the American pioneers were to do four hundred years later. For defence, the system of wagon leaguers defended by firearms gave him the advantages of a fortress combined with mobility. The wagons were usually sited on a small hilltop. Each wagon carried two or three small guns, and heavier guns were mounted on special carriages. Zizka was the first commander to use field artillery systematically since the experiment of Alexander at the Hydaspes. The rest of the Hussite army consisted of a few cavalry for scouting, and infantry crossbow-men. When Zizka was satisfied with the training of his army he set out for Prague and by the end of the campaign of 1421 the Hussites were in control of most of Bohemia. Zizka himself was blinded by an arrow, but he continued to command, planning his battles on the basis of exact information about the enemy's forces and dispositions given to him in answer to his questions. Zizka himself died of plague in 1424, aged only forty-eight. 'The whole army was overcome by immense sad-ness', and his soldiers were thereafter called 'orphans'. Undoubtedly they had lost a great leader. Zizka was a man of enormous personal courage and force of char-acter. Unfettered by tradition, he ingeniously exploited limited assets to produce an original and successful tactical formula. He was to exercise a powerful influence on tactics and strategy in eastern Europe.

As the fifteenth century wore on gunpowder began to turn all other existing tactical traditions and methods upside down. Of the three weapons which had ruined the heavy cavalryman, the longbow, the pike and field artillery, the last named was to survive longest in its original form. The longbow was to be dropped as the authorised weapon of England in 1595. The Swiss pikeman survived to the beginning of the seventeenth century. But the bowman and the pikeman are equally the ancestors of the post-medieval European infantryman: the marriage of the missile principle with the pike produced the rifle with bayonet; and the alliance of gun-powder with the other resources of the national state produced the beginnings of modern warfare.

9   Asian Warfare

So far our study has not taken us beyond the Near East, but in this chapter on Asian warfare we must range further afield and more widely through time. The Mongols were once a totally warrior society – perhaps the most successful the world has seen. They came from the steppe-lands of Central Asia. They were necessarily tough horsemen, and they were bound to be fighters, since the land was poor and there was continual competition for new territory. From the eternal welter of nomadic movement and conflict a leader occasionally emerged, so strong that he overshadowed the other chieftains and unified the Turkish and Mongol tribes. In the fourth century Attila was such a leader. The most complete and sinister unification in the history of these nomads was the achievement of Jenghiz Khan (1162–1227).

The Mongol peoples were primitive and barbarian. In the past the victory of one tribe over another had normally been followed by destruction and slaughter. Jenghiz Khan quickly showed the superiority of his conceptions by using his victories constructively: to unify the peoples. He elevated his victims to be his subjects, and such was his leadership that they were proud of their new status. He unified the nomads by his willpower and the fear of his strength, but also by offering the prospect of greater rewards. He organized the whole nomad fraternity for war.

Vassalage of a tribe to Jenghiz Khan was not a formality. The great men of the tribe came to serve on his staff or in his guard, tribute was paid to his treasury, and the tribe prepared itself to be a unit in the great fighting force. Princes, chieftains and headmen of tribes were, for purposes of war, commanders of 'toumans' (a unit of 10,000 and the strongest in the army), of thousands and of hundreds. The head of the tribe was responsible for keeping his men permanently trained and equipped according to the regulations laid down, and he had to answer the khan's summons to war instantly. The most senior officers of all, the commanders of armies, were the eleven 'orloks'. When the nomads were unified in 1206 Jenghiz Khan ruled an empire which stretched 1,000 miles from east to west, from the east of the Gobi Desert to the north-east of Lake Balkash, incorporating thirty-one tribes. To this people, peace was nothing but a time in which to prepare for war.

Every man in the Mongol army was a cavalryman. Some were more heavily armed than others, and the equipment of all improved as they became more experienced and richer. There was little protective equipment. The men wore sheepskins, loose leather jackets, and armour of lacquered leather plate. Some wore a shirt of raw silk – which was not penetrated by an arrowhead but was driven by it

into the flesh, so that the wound was less serious. A round shield was used by all
on sentry duty, but in battle only by the shock-troops of the front line and the khan's
guard. The main weapons of the Mongols were a hooked lance, a curved scimitar
suitable for both thrusting and cutting, and two bows – one for use on horseback and
the other for more precise firing on foot. There were varieties of arrow, suitable for
different ranges and against different armour. Besides these, each man had an axe
hanging from his belt; a length of rope which he might use for tethering his horse,
lassoing his enemy, or hauling heavy equipment; a kit which included spare bow-
strings, files for sharpening the arrows, and needle and thread; and a water-tight
skin to carry spare clothes, which could be inflated for crossing rivers. Finally he
had equipment for food – a nose-bag for his pony, his own cooking-pot, and basic
rations of smoke-cured meat and dried milk-curds. Jenghiz Khan ordained that it
was the responsibility of the wife in peace time to see that her husband's provisions
and uniform were in readiness.

The distinctive qualities of Mongol fighting were mobility and co-ordination.
When describing the campaigns of these horsemen who swept through unmapped
lands from China to the Mediterranean it is difficult to measure distances in miles.
Part of the secret of their co-ordination was the nomad's instinct for landmarks and
direction; there was also a well organized system of intelligence and communication.
General information was continually sent to Jenghiz Khan from his subject rulers,
and special messages and intelligence were relayed by the khan's own messengers,
the 'Arrow Riders'. The messengers could cover distances in days which normally
took weeks; their bodies were bandaged for support in their long rides, and they
slept in the saddle. As the Mongol conquests extended it was an important part of
the khan's policy to maintain and protect roads – the old caravan routes which he
knitted into an Asiatic network with regular posts. An army on the march was
preceded by scouts moving several days in advance. Jenghiz Khan also made full
use of spies, and here itinerant merchants were useful.

The urge of Jenghiz Khan to dominate, and the need to provide his peoples with
war, led him to pit the Mongols against the Chinese. He was a careful strategist;
he had no sure intelligence of the strength of China, but he discovered that her
armies were composed of vast numbers of foot-soldiers and that she depended
very much for defence on powerful fortifications. In 1207 the khan led a strong
army into the state of Hsi-Hsia. In the field the Mongol horsemen carried all
before them, but they were checked by the fortified cities. In the next few years
Jenghiz Khan trained some Mongol officers in siege-warfare: in the use of catapults, naphtha, ladders, sandbags and so on; later armies carried missile-throwing
machines, mangonels and catapults, in pieces on pack-animals. By 1211 the Hsia
were conquered; his army had learned a good deal, and Jenghiz Khan launched his
great enterprise against China proper.

A preparatory council was called at the headquarters of the khan. All higher
officers attended and the situation was discussed, the objective made clear, the
grouping of divisions settled, and the plan of campaign outlined. The first troops
to set out were scouts, some 200 riders in pairs, dispersed over the countryside.

The Mongols fought on horseback with a hooked lance or bow, and made effective use of the Parthian tactics of shooting while in simulated flight

Then came the advance-guard – three toumans or 30,000 picked warriors well mounted and each with a spare horse. The touman commanders were Muhuli, Sabutai and Chepé Noyon – the two latter receiving high command before they were twenty-five years old. Behind came the main body in three divisions, totalling about 160,000. Jenghiz Khan commanded the central division of 100,000. His personal standard was nine white yak's tails. Throughout the campaign the commander-in-chief was constantly in touch with all his divisional commanders by 'Arrow' couriers.

The country of the doomed enemy was normally entered simultaneously at several points. In 1211 the Great Wall was penetrated in this way and the divisions advanced along separate lines through Shan-si and Chih-li – on the Peking axis. There was no provision for supplies except what could be found on the way, but that was enough. Each divisional commander had authority to manoeuvre and engage the enemy at his discretion, but the main objective was clear and paramount. The separate columns could very rapidly converge and support each other. The

Mongol army perfectly exemplified Moltke's principle of 'march divided, fight united'.

The tactics of the Mongols were simple. They sought surprise, riding rapidly by day and night and converging their toumans with absolute precision; they might encircle the enemy; they sometimes used the old Parthian tactic of simulating flight, retreating maybe for days while they fanned out before turning and outflanking the enemy. The Mongol cavalry charged in formation under cover of their own arrow and javelin fire. The movement of the formations was controlled by signals – flags in the daytime and lamps in the dark. The troops were in five ranks, the men in the leading two being more heavily armoured. After the first shock the *mêlée* itself was loose and disorderly, each man fighting for himself, wielding his sabre, and pulling down his opponent with his lariat or the hook of his lance.

The first rapid advance into China proceeded in this style, all resistance being overcome. But the weakness of the Mongols against fortifications still remained, and as the masses of the Chinese population barricaded themselves into their cities the war slowed to a stalemate. Some cities fell to ruses. But, like Hannibal before Rome, Jenghiz Khan and his converging Horde were stopped at Yen-king, the capital (later called Peking). This was the situation which prevailed for five years, from 1211 to 1216. Every autumn the Mongols withdrew, and in the following spring they returned, sweeping in separate columns through the open country. Each year their devastation was more terrible and each year they captured more towns, but the major cities continued to hold out. But at last in 1216 the Kin emperor humiliated himself to buy off the Mongols. A vast tribute was paid, Jenghiz Khan received a wife of the Chinese imperial blood, and Muhuli, a touman commander, was left as viceroy and military governor of China. Jenghiz Khan returned to his capital of Karakorum, north of the Gobi Desert, taking the rich booty promised to his warriors and also Chinese craftsmen, technologists and scholars – and slaughtering his useless prisoners.

Having humbled the East and made sure of good order in the heart of his domains, Jenghiz Khan then turned his attention to the West: to the great Islamic power, the Khwarizmian empire which lay beyond the Himalayas. The shah, Ala-eddin Mohammed, was himself a conqueror who ruled from the Persian Gulf and Baghdad to the Himalayas. This was the highest moment of Islamic power: in the far west the crusaders were everywhere retreating. Jenghiz Khan knew little of the Islamic world; Mohammed knew even less of the Mongols – but he did not fear them for he had an army said to be 400,000 strong.

In the spring of 1219 Jenghiz Khan, now aged fifty-six, ordered the Horde to assemble. A quarter of a million men are supposed to have come, better equipped than ever before, each man with three horses; and there was an artillery train carried on yaks. To divert attention from his main concentration the khan sent a force under Juji towards the lower reaches of the Syr Daria river (the Jaxartes of Alexander), which laid waste the trough of country between the Akkum desert and the Alatau range. The shah supposed this to be the main invasion, and sent his son Jelaladdin to deal with it. The Mongols skirmished and then disappeared behind the burning grass of the plain. Mystified, the shah posted troops along the whole line of the Syr Daria. The Khwarizmian defences were thus strong nowhere, and this gave Jenghiz Khan the advantage when his real operations began. The Mongol troops began to move in the autumn. A direct advance was blocked by the mountains which are the highest in the world. The main army set out westwards on the long and arduous ride to the Zungarian Gates, the pass into northern Turkestan. The men were wrapped in sheepskins and kept their insides warm with *koumiss* or fermented mare's milk. To mislead the enemy and as the first part of his pincer strategy, Jenghiz Khan detached a column of 20,000 men under Chepé Noyon to march round the mountains the opposite way and approach the Khwarizmian domains at a south-easterly point – from Kashgar on to Khojent. So perfect was the timing and co-ordination of the Mongol operations that both forces reached their different frontier points in January and February 1220.

Chepé Noyon's column posed an immediate threat to two major Khwarizmian cities, Tashkent and Samarkand, and the shah reacted by moving additional forces into the south. But this was the very moment when Jenghiz Khan with the main body was advancing across his northern frontier in three columns. In February two of the columns of 30,000 each, under Juji and Jagatai, appeared on the shah's left flank, and began to work down the Syr Daria river, destroying the scattered Khwarizmian forces in detail, and moving to join Chepé Noyon's force. At the same time the remaining column of 40,000 under Jenghiz Khan moved due south on Bokhara. Masked by Juji's and Jagatai's columns, Jenghiz Khan's force can hardly have been noticed as it passed into the desert of Kizylkum. The first the shah knew of it was when at the beginning of April Jenghiz Khan emerged from the desert in the south, took Nuruta, and approached Bokhara. On 11th April Bokhara was taken.

The shah had been surprised. His line was turned, his available troops were trapped by columns converging from three directions, and communication with his westerly domains was severed. He himself fled westwards, while the Mongols reunited at Samarkand. Complete success had crowned this campaign of Jenghiz Khan. Extraordinary mobility and endurance, and the brilliant co-ordination of the movements of four columns, each covering and complementing the movements of the others, were the essence of the strategy. At every successive point the enemy had been surprised by superior forces.

It took longer to finish the conquest of the shah's empire. The conquering Mongols advanced more slowly westwards, capturing the cities one by one. Terror was the policy. Jenghiz Khan proclaimed himself in the mosques to be the scourge of God, and the faithful had good reason to believe him. In the Khwarizmian empire only those individuals, technical experts and the like, who might be useful to the Mongols were spared. Otherwise the whole population and its civilization was annihilated. When there were no people to kill, the animals were hunted down and slaughtered. Yet resistance was desperate, and it continued until December 1221, when Mohammed's braver son Jelaladdin lost the last of his troops in a battle by the Indus. Sabutai and Chepé Noyon meanwhile rode on round the Caspian, through the Caucasus towards the Dnieper and Europe before they were recalled by Jenghiz

Khan. They completed the greatest cavalry campaign in history by fighting their way home, passing eastwards and south through the lands of the Russian nomads.

Jenghiz Khan was ready to return to his homelands. He died in 1227. He had made himself by personal force the ruler of a martial race, and then at their head he had conquered the greatest empire of the world, stretching from the Persian Gulf to the Pacific, from the Siberian Taiga to the Himalayas. He was as great as any commander and leader in history. But he was a ruthless barbarian.

After Jenghiz Khan's death, Sabutai returned to Europe and in campaigns of a brilliance which almost match those of Jenghiz Khan he overran Europe to the Adriatic and Poland. After 1241 the Mongols withdrew from Europe, except for Russia. Two more great Mongol conquerors were to arise, Kubla Khan and Timur, who in the second half of the fourteenth century recovered the domination of southern Asia west of the Himalayas. But thereafter the Mongol horsemen never produced another leader, and they returned, little less suddenly than they had appeared, to their original obscurity.

The political history of China is a long story of internal dissension and rebellion, which weakened the state in its continuous struggle to protect the frontiers against nomadic tribes from the north and west. Centuries of such fighting produced a certain military skill. But the Chinese are a peace-loving people and they have not been creative in the art of war. Their great religions are fundamentally pacific. Indeed they have cared to remember very little of the history of their warfare.

Ancient Chinese society was feudal, and the warfare which is heard of before about 500 B.C. was 'heroic' in character; a class of nobles known as *shih* were closely comparable to Homeric heroes, or Red Indian braves. The existence of a code of military etiquette known as *li* indicates that much so-called war was not serious, but fought for amusement, honour and prestige. Mean tactics such as attacking the enemy while crossing a river, or picking an opponent much older then oneself, were condemned! A Chou general challenged the Chin ruler in 632 with the words: 'Will your Excellency permit our knights and yours to play a game?' The champion went into battle driven in a four-horsed chariot; his weapon was a powerful bow; a company of foot-soldiers, lightly armed, followed each chariot. But the period from 403 to 221 B.C. is known as the 'period of the warring states', and warfare was then in deadly earnest. Infantry, composed of tough peasants, became numerous and of far more tactical significance. Foot-soldiers fought with javelins, short swords and bows and arrows. The appearance of iron at about this time brought an improvement in weapons and armour.

About 200 cavalry, on the nomadic model, appeared in Chinese warfare and then chariots gradually disappeared. In the same period there was development in fortification and siegecraft. The instruments of siegecraft were catapults, scaling ladders, and so on – the same as in early European warfare. Fortifications of outstanding strength were developed, the most famous example being the Great Wall, which runs, in parts over mountains and gorges, for 1,600 miles along the nomad frontier south of the Gobi Desert. It is generally some 25 feet wide at the base and

The Chinese, although not naturally a martial race, developed ingenious weapons, such as extendable scaling ladders *left* and fire rockets *right*

17 feet at the top, and 25 to 30 feet high; crenellated parapets stand 5 feet above the walk, and there are regular towers. It was built by policy of the soldier-statesman Shih Huang Ti (246–10 B.C.). The city walls built in the period of the Ming dynasty (A.D. 1368–1644) dwarf contemporary European fortifications. The walls, for example, of Nanking, Sian and Tsinan are 50 to 70 feet thick, and in places 70 feet high.

As early as about 500 B.C. the military experience of the Chinese was distilled in a collection of maxims, *The Art of War* by Sun Tzu. *The Art of War* is regarded as one of the great works of Chinese literature. It is full of mature military wisdom – much of which Europeans were not to learn for themselves until the Napoleonic era. It teaches that the proper object of strategy is the speedy attainment of the political object of the war and a secure peace, not lengthy and destructive warfare. Victory must be gained at the minimum cost in lives and destruction. Though integrity is valued in a commander, ultimately 'all warfare is based on deception'. Characteristic of Sun Tzu's style and wisdom is this advice that he gives to a commander: 'The quality of decision is like the well-timed swoop of a falcon which enables it to strike and destroy its victim'.

Famous commanders in Chinese history include Po Chi, Chang Chien and Tsao Kung, but little is known about them. There is no evidence that Chinese warfare developed significantly, and expansion is likely to have been as much a matter of alliances and cultural conversion as of force of arms. Once the Mongols were established in China, even their military character seems to have been subdued by the deep-rooted aversion to things military which was inherent in Chinese civilization. Although in the time of Kubla Khan (1259–94) the combined Mongol and Chinese arms touched Japan, Burma and Java, these expeditions were not finally successful.

As early as the tenth century the Chinese used gunpowder, and they are known to have used guns in 1356. But in the fifteenth century the great European technological breakthrough in guns and sails set Europeans far ahead of Asiatics in the conduct of war. The Chinese desperately sought to discover the military secrets of the Europeans; they would pay almost any price for guns. It was eventually the Jesuits who instructed them in the manufacture and use of firearms. In the 1640's a German Jesuit, Schall, operated a cannon foundry near the Imperial Palace – on condition that he was allowed to pursue his missionary work. Yet the Chinese were slow to understand and adopt western techniques of warfare. This peace-loving and conservative society of scholars and peasants would not industrialize itself merely for the sake of military strength. The pacific reaction to contact with the Europeans intensified; in the seventeenth century Father Ricci wrote that 'the military is one of the four conditions which are considered mean among them'. The same applied at sea as on land; the Chinese junk was a highly seaworthy and navigable vessel, but it was not a ship of war and never became one. At the end of the sixteenth century the Chinese were persuaded to put cannon on to their junks, but they did not make the necessary mental adjustment. An observer commented: 'Their arquebuses are so badly made that the ball would not pierce an ordinary cuirass, especially as they do not know how to aim.'

This situation lasted until the mid-nineteenth century. It required the humiliation suffered by the Chinese at the hands of the British in the Opium War of 1839–42 to bring realism and to awaken China to the West.

The history of Japan contrasts with that of China in that warfare has always been a prominent element. A great part of Japan is mountainous and infertile, and the high incidence of war among its inhabitants can largely be attributed to competition for the sparse areas of good rice land. A second basic physical factor is that the islands abound with good natural harbours. The Japanese people have thus become tough mountaineers and seamen. Invasions were launched against Korea in the fourth century A.D. However, the prevailing winds and currents in the China Sea generally made it difficult for them to keep contact with the Asiatic mainland, and thereafter, on the whole, Japanese society developed in seclusion and distinctively, with a strong militaristic orientation.

The early Japanese warrior was an aristocratic knight, elaborately armoured and mounted on horseback. Although attended by a retinue he fought as an individual. His chief weapon was the bow, but he used a sword for close fighting. In the eighth century A.D., under Buddhist influence there was a pacifist movement among the upper classes, and an attempt was made to organize the peasants as a huge reserve for national defence. But this did not work because the conscript peasants resented it and lacked equipment. Instead, each province was required to maintain a force of trained regular soldiers. Then, as previously, the fighting men were drawn from the upper classes. The separation of the peasant and the warrior classes in Japan was to become increasingly marked.

In the ninth century Japanese society entered a long phase of feudal development. A weak central government meant independence among the aristocracy and insecurity among the peasantry. At the same time land reclamation was going on, and the strongest men carved out for themselves personal territories. Dependence and loyalty focused on the great estates and on the clans, and private armies were formed. Two clans emerged as the leading rivals, the Taira and the Minamoto, and for 250 years of incessant private wars and rebellions the struggle between these two continued. The Minamoto became supreme on land, and eventually in 1185 they succeeded in defeating the Taira at sea, at the battle of Dan-no-ura in the Shimono-seki Straits.

In two and a half centuries of endless fighting over wild country the Japanese had learned much about war, and the warriors had emerged as a privileged class – known as *samurai*. The chief weapon of the *samurai* was a bow up to $7\frac{1}{2}$ feet long, made of boxwood or bamboo and bound round with cord. The *samurai* also devoted much time to acquiring skill in swordsmanship. They had two types of sword, a single-edged and slightly convex 3-foot sword for fighting, and a shorter one used for decapitating a victim or committing suicide. The sword was regarded as the soul of the warrior. The art of sword-making was perfected in the thirteenth century by two famous swordsmiths, Masamune and Hoshimitsu, who produced perfectly balanced blades of finely tempered steel. The *samurai* also developed *jujutsu*, the art of injuring or killing an enemy by using one's bare hands with the most economical application of muscular force, turning the opponent's weight and strength to his own undoing. The protective armour of the *samurai* was a garment of iron and leather held together with silk or leather cords, and a horned metal helmet. The Japanese never had a proper war-horse; they rode to battle on small, sturdy ponies, which were sometimes also armoured.

Tactical conceptions might involve surprises and ambushes, but for the most part the opposing armies simply sought open battle. Every campaign was initiated by a human sacrifice to the God of War. *Samurai* battles had a strong ceremonial character. Notice of intention to attack the enemy was given by firing a single arrow and raising a special chant. Signals were given by means of flags emblazoned with figures such as dragons, and by the beating of drums and gongs. Before the fifteenth century a battle resembled a gigantic multiple fencing match. Each *samurai*, selecting an individual opponent, would proclaim his name, titles and achievement, and would probably insult his enemy. The duellists would then fight to the death without interference.

A code of individual etiquette, and of solidarity and feudal obligation, developed in the *samurai* class. This was called *Bushido*, or 'the Way of the Warrior'. The *samurai* had to die for his lord. He was bound also to fight to the death rather than surrender, and if he did surrender he was an object of utter contempt, unworthy of

The *samurai* acquired great skill in fighting with their single-edged slightly convex swords

treatment as a human being – hence, perhaps, the Japanese treatment of their prisoners in the 1939–45 war. If a *samurai* was dishonoured he must commit suicide by the form of *hara-kiri*, disembowelling himself with his own sword. Instances are recorded of hundreds of *samurai* committing mass suicide rather than allowing themselves to be taken prisoner.

Yorimoto, the Minamoto victor in 1185, proved himself to be a considerable soldier-statesman, for he succeeded in establishing a strong central government while maintaining Japanese feudalism in its military character. In the next century Japan was strong enough to face the Mongols. But a new line of shoguns took power in 1338, and they had no claim to the loyalty of the feudal and military lords. Turmoil was thus the condition of Japan when she first made contact with the western world in the sixteenth century. The Japanese quickly appreciated the superiority of European firearms over their own bows and arrows, and before 1600 the Japanese themselves were manufacturing arms.

At this same time the country was at last again brought under one strong political authority. The progress from anarchy to unity was the work of three men who worked together. Nobunaga was a statesman and military administrator who began to westernize Japanese armaments. Hideyoshi was an outstanding general, a man of patience, powers of organization and leadership; his achievement in his own country was great, but he then attempted to conquer Korea and in this he was eventually thwarted by the naval superiority of the Koreans, with their fleet of 'tortoise-shell' ironclad ships commanded by a remarkable admiral, Yi-sun. Finally in 1600 Iyeyasu, also an able general, established the Tokugawa shogunate.

The strange policy of the Tokugawa was to freeze Japan's social and political institutions and to isolate her from the rest of the world. This gave her 250 years of peace. But during that time her technology fell further and further behind that of the rest of the world, and her army of *samurai* became an outdated and ineffective fighting force. In 1853, however, a squadron of American ships appeared, and the Japanese also were compelled to make a positive response to the modern world of the West.

The course of warfare in India has been dictated to an exceptional degree by the natural factors of geography, population movement and climate. Between the Himalayas and the Vindhya range in central India lies Hindustan, a vast fertile plain with no natural defences. Before the British assumed control no power took responsibility for guarding the north-west frontier, and from earliest times immigrant peoples crossed the passes. In due course Greeks and then Turks, Huns, Mongols and Persians came the same way. Between 2400 B.C. and A.D. 1500 the actual inhabitants of India were everywhere defeated by the foreign invaders and pushed southwards, the invading movements being generally halted by the Vindhya mountains. In southern India large areas are hilly and dry – unsuitable for the movement of considerable bodies of people. This country lends itself to resistance against both invasion and internal government by loose-fighting warriors such as the Marathas.

War was most prominent in the politics and literature of the ancient Hindus. Yet the documentation available allows us to gain only a very imprecise understanding of this military history. Kautilya, author of a manual of statecraft called the *Artha-sastra* (c. 100 B.C.), is a useful authority for, significantly, he includes a military treatise of some merit within his political theory. But in the Sanskrit epics, such as the *Mahabharata*, it is difficult to distinguish between what is historically authentic and what is literary fantasy. The *Mahabharata* is comparable to the *Iliad* and the *Nibelungenlied*, a great epic poem on war.

From the dimmest period of the past to the nineteenth century A.D. the bow was the chief weapon in India. Arrian describes the Indian bow in 326 B.C.: 'The Indian infantry have a bow equal in length to the man who carries it. Nothing can withstand [an arrow] shot by an Indian archer, neither shield nor breastplate.' Later on the sword rose in esteem, and club and spear, discus and sling were among other weapons also used. Chariots, with crews of from two to 12 men, were in use for many hundreds of years. Indian horses, however, were of an inferior breed, and the disasters at the hands of the Greeks and Turks were defeats of armies having a poor cavalry element by armies consisting essentially of good cavalry – this despite the fact that Indian armies in the first century B.C. are the first cavalry to have been equipped with the stirrup. Shields were carried by all except archers and the very poor. They were made of the skins of oxen or tigers and of bamboo or matted creeper, and were decorated with emblems. Only a minority had body armour; a type of chain armour existed, but padded coats of quilted cotton were more often used.

King Paurav, who was defeated by Alexander at the Hydaspes in 326 B.C., came to battle mounted on an elephant. From then until the seventeenth century A.D. elephants were to be regarded as the chief striking power in Indian armies. Chandragupta Maurya (322–298) had an elephant corps 9,000 strong. Each elephant carried a driver and generally three warriors armed with bows and arrows – though javelins, knives, pots of oil and stones might also be used. The animals themselves were elaborately equipped with mail armour and carried bags for ammunition, as well as necklaces, rugs and heraldic devices.

Elephant drill included *samyana* (moving forward and sideways, or making serpentine movements), *vadhavadha* (trampling down and killing), *hastiyuddha* (fighting in formation) and other training. Elephants had strength and a terrifying appearance. They could trample men under foot, batter down obstacles, and strike terror into the hearts of inexperienced soldiers and untrained horses. But they had too many defects to be trustworthy as the chief offensive force in battle. They were always difficult to control, and there were numerous instances of panic-stricken elephants turning and causing chaos in their own forces.

The most common time for beginning a campaign was October, after the monsoon, though political conditions might alter the timing. Espionage, both diplomatic and military, was highly organized. It is extremely difficult to determine from the various authorities the deployments and tactics used in battle. The poet of the *Mahabharata* gives free rein to fantasy in describing formations called 'heron', 'hawk' and 'crocodile', and in remaining consistent in his metaphors to the most minute detail. Kautilya talks a little more realistically of four basic formations, the 'staff', 'snake', 'circle' and 'detached order', each with its own variations. Clearly there were numerous theoretical battle deployments.

It will be understood that the warfare of the ancient Hindus is not a very fruitful area of study. The main weaknesses in the composition and organization of their armies were excessive reliance on elephants, poor cavalry, and a feudal method of recruitment which militated against unity of command and standardisation in equipment and organization. Even the more successful commanders, such as Chandragupta Maurya who drove out the Greeks, and Skandagupta and Yasodharman who repelled the Huns, seem to have lacked vision and had little strategical or tactical sense. The passes of the north-west frontier were not held, and armies

The Indians relied largely upon elephants in battle. A suit of eighteenth-century elephant armour, worn in the battle of Plassey

moved sluggishly. Hindu wars were petty affairs, fought with reserve – affairs of politicians, which were ignored by the peasants cultivating the fields. Hindu civilization by A.D. 1000 was complacent and conservative. These weaknesses were exposed by the Islamic invaders.

The Turko-Islamic conquest of India developed in a pattern. It was a gradual process which began in the tenth century and was completed only in the seventeenth – the wild Turkish tribesmen being continually lured to invade a rich and disunited country. The Turks would begin by making raids across the frontier; these developed into invasions, in which the nearest Hindu king was defeated in pitched battle. The first conquest was the springboard for the next advance, and the Hindu territories were gobbled up successively as the forces of Islam progressed south and eastwards. Only in the seventeenth century did the tribesmen of the Assam jungles halt the then

A Hindu army on the march moved to the music of a band

decadent Moghul forces. As the invaders of the earlier waves settled and became Indians, they themselves were swamped by succeeding waves from the north-west. Each separate advance was usually short, but occasionally an outstanding Moslem conqueror swept all before him in a devastating tide. Four names stand out: Mahmud of Ghazni (997–1030), who is said to have led seventeen campaigns in India; Shihabuddin Ghori, victor at Tarain in 1192; Timur, the Mongol, who swept through Hidustan in five months during 1398, sacking Delhi but then returning to his capital at Samarkand; finally Timur's descendant, Babur the Tiger, who invaded India in 1525, defeating his enemies at Panipat and Sikri.

The Turks possessed in outstanding measure the essential martial qualities which the Hindus lacked. They found complacency and tolerance, and opposed these with the vigour of a barbaric people fired by fanatical devotion to the faith of Islam. The Turks had energy, social solidarity, a fatalistic contempt of death, and sobriety. With these they also had mobility, being mounted on fast, tough Turkoman and Arabian horses. Their armies were in fact hordes of mounted archers, in the old and effective tradition of the Parthians, the Huns and the Mongols. Their composite bow was as good as any weapon of the Hindus, and they used it to better effect. They were able to produce senior officers of high military intelligence, and occasionally

The Turko-Islamic invaders pursued the Hindus across the Ganges with guns in 1565 commanders of genius. The essence of Turkish strategy was controlled mobility over large areas. Their tactics, as in the West, were normally to harass and exhaust the enemy by means of clouds of encircling, elusive mounted archers, and then to clinch victory by a charge of heavier cavalry.

But as the Turkish peoples settled in India so they lost the original *élan* of the steppes, and to some extent became absorbed in the ancient, rigid ways of their new land. The use of elephants was adopted, and although cavalry remained well regarded mobility declined. Furthermore, the advent of firearms affected their warfare. Already Babur's army was different from those of his predecessors. He had fewer Turkish horsemen, although these remained the *élite* troops; he had contingents of native Indians, fighting with their traditional bows, swords and spears; and he had infantry armed with match-locks and falconets mounted on carts. Babur used guns skilfully – particularly at Sikri where (like Gonzalo de Córdoba) he drew the Rajputs to dash their forces against a strongly entrenched position defended by infantry and guns. But the Turks in India shared the liking of their westerly cousins for excessively large guns; some cannon later manufactured in India weighed 40 and even 50 metric tons. Yet as late as the Mutiny of 1857 some Indian troops were using the bow and arrow as effectively as the handgun.

The battle of Talikota in 1565, which established the power of the Moslems over the Hindus in the Deccan, shows a later Moslem Indian army at its best. Husain Nizam Shah was undismayed by the fourfold numerical superiority of his enemy. His artillery was greatly superior and he positioned it forward, screening it with Turkish horse-archers who lured the enemy towards them. His cavalry was well equipped and trained, being formed into divisions with a powerful reserve to deliver a final decisive charge.

By the eighteenth century the Turko-Islamic forces had absorbed too many traditional Hindu characteristics; this was shown when the forces of Nizam-ul-Mulk were defeated by the Marathas, who fought much in the style of the original Turkish invaders of India. They were Hindus from south-western India, hardy frugal people, unlike the dwellers of the rich north – and they had been forged into a new military force by Sivaji in the mid-seventeenth century. They were at their best in the eighteenth century, and the Palkhed campaign of 1727–8, in which Baji Rao I outgeneralled Nizam-ul-Mulk, is a masterpiece of strategic mobility. Baji Rao's army was a purely mounted force, armed only with sabre, lance, a bow in some units, and a round shield. There was a spare horse for every two men. The Marathas moved unencumbered by artillery, baggage, or even handguns and defensive armour. They supplied themselves by looting.

Baji Rao resented the Nizam's rule over the Deccan and it was he who struck the first blow. In October 1727, as soon as the rainy season ended, Baji Rao burst into the territory of the Nizam's supporter, Asaf Jah. The lightly equipped Marathas moved with great rapidity, avoiding the main towns and fortresses, living off the country, burning and plundering. They met one reverse at the hands of the Nizam's able lieutenant, Iwaz Khan, at the beginning of November, but within a month they had fully recovered and were off again, dashing east, north, west, with sudden

The last stand of the Kusunoki. A print by Kuniyoshi depicting the battle of
Shijo Nawate, 1348

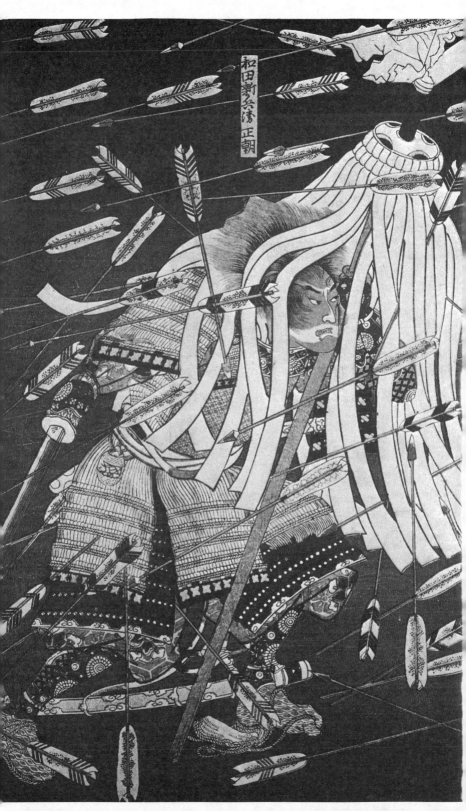

changes of direction. The Nizam had mobilized his forces, and for a time pursued them, but he was bewildered by the swift unpredictable movements of the enemy, and his men became exhausted. At the end of January the Nizam changed his strategy; he gave up the pursuit of the elusive Maratha forces and instead made direct for their heartland around Poona, which he captured and ravaged. But Baji Rao resisted urgent calls to come back, and instead countered the Nizam's move by in turn threatening his capital, Aurangabad. The Nizam predictably evacuated the Poona district and returned to rescue Aurangabad. As the Nizam once again endeavoured to catch Baji Rao, the Marathas harried and circled round his forces. The Nizam preserved his army intact, but in March 1728 he gave up. The Marathas returned home laden with plunder, and by the peace terms some of their territorial claims were conceded.

Mention should be made of fortification in India, for some Indian forts such as Agra, Daulatabad and Mandu were as powerful as the best in medieval Europe. The hill on which Mandu stands rises 1,000 feet above the plain. The fortifications were built by Shah Hoshang Ghori (1406–35). The basic strength of Mandu was a powerful crenellated wall of grey basalt built round on the edge of a cliff above an escarpment, strengthened at points by bastions and with a number of strongly defended gateways. A wide and deep gorge runs up from the east side into the centre of the city; this was defended by a causeway, called the Seven Hundred Steps, built across its mouth. The main entrance was on the north side, where a path, barred by three successive gates, wound up the moderately steep slope. The topmost, the Delhi gate, is a magnificent vaulted structure; the gates on the south-east and south-west are also particularly strong; the passage of Tarapur gate is narrow and steep, with the defence assisted by right-angled turns within the gateway. The doors were plated with iron and protected against the assault of elephants by iron spikes. An assailant who forced the passage would come under attack from the rear by the defenders of the west wall. Indian siegecraft was a matter of catapults and later of heavy artillery, but the most successful strategists generally skirted round the great strongholds.

In the mid-eighteenth century the stage in India became clear for the imperial struggle between Britain and France. A Frenchman, Joseph Dupleix, was the first European to train Indian troops in the European method of war in any numbers and with any success. However, the British East India Company very quickly learned to play the same game. Stringer Lawrence began to raise 'sepoys' – the name given to Indian troops trained by Europeans and retained in their service – and Robert Clive emerged as a diplomat and soldier even abler than Dupleix. Clive's most famous victory was against Suraj-ud-Dowlah's army at Plassey. Clive had about 800 Europeans, some 2,000 sepoys, and 8 pieces of artillery to set against 34,000 foot, 15,000 horse and 53 cannon. The odds seemed hopeless. But the British were well positioned in the shelter of a mango grove, and a heavy fall of rain put the Indian artillery out of action; the generalship on the Indian side was so bad that the battle was little more than a skirmish and a rout. The way was thereby opened for the expansion of British dominion over the native peoples of India.

Akbar's forces besiege Rauthaubhor Fort, 1568. A Moghul painting for the Akbarnama

10   The Ottoman Turks

The beleaguerment of medieval Europe by barbarians was hardest to raise in the south-east. By A.D. 1000 the aggressors from the north had been assimilated, and by 1500 technological progress had enabled western Europe to adopt an offensive world strategy. But the Turkish assault on the south-east was more formidable and prolonged. The crusades may be regarded as a series of defensive sorties; the first of them took the enemy by surprise and was a success, but subsequently each one was increasingly hesitant. The failure of medieval Europe's most vigorous counter-attack indicates the strength of this particular enemy.

The Turks were a group of semi-nomadic peoples, who had advanced towards the eastern Mediterranean from central Asia, driven by Mongol expansion and lured by the failure of Arab power. Their western spearhead had infinite resources of manpower. By contrast Europe's population, previously stagnant, was greatly reduced between 1347 and 1351 by the Black Death. Moreover Turkish morale was good; there could be no hope that the Turkish warrior, a fiercely dynamic Moslem, would be disarmed and converted by the insipid *élan* of chivalry, or by the passivity of Orthodoxy and the dying civilization of Byzantium.

The native Asiatic technology of war had throughout history been superior to that of Europeans – except in one phase, when Alexander produced a cavalry with mobility as well as stamina and tactical purpose. Otherwise, at every great clash in the Levant, Asiatic mobility had triumphed. Carrhae and Hattin tell the same story, and in the High Middle Ages as the European men-at-arms became heavier and heavier the perennial nomad light horse found it still easier to run circles round them. The continuing success of the Turks in the age when Europe was expanding on other fronts is similarly to be explained by a technological factor: that the Turks grasped as quickly as any Europeans the revolutionary implications of firearms.

The victory of the Seljuk Turks over the Byzantines at Manzikert in 1071 opened the way for the Turkish advance into Asia Minor. Turkish chieftains and their followers were looking for homes, but they were also inspired by their faith as *ghazis*: warriors for the Moslem faith. They obeyed the *futuwwa*, a military and moral code as formal as chivalry, and more dynamic. The Ottoman state originated as one among many small *ghazi* powers. Soon after the fall of the Seljuks in 1243, the Ottomans emerged as leaders of the Turks. This was due to their westerly position, but also to the genius of their early leaders, who knew how to organize and where to lead the energy of the westward-flooding Turks.

Europe was in no condition, then or later, to repel the Turkish threat. The end of the political and military power of Byzantium had been signalled by the crusaders' sack of Constantinople in 1204. The former subject peoples of Byzantium, the Bulgars and the Serbs, had no love for her. The peoples of western Europe at first failed to understand that Byzantium was doomed without their help, and when they did realize it they hardened their hearts. The Europeans knew in any case that they were faced by a superior military power. When they did oppose the Ottoman advance, the depressing experience of the crusades was confirmed by a succession of resounding defeats.

In 1301 Osman started to clear the Byzantines out of Asia Minor, his cavalry meeting no effective opposition as they swept over the countryside. By 1356 the Turks were ready to cross into Europe. For the time being they were content to skirt round the great city of Constantinople. The advance towards the Danube was then pressed forward, the stages being marked by the victories over the Serbs at the River Maritza (1371) and Kossovo (1389), and by the destruction by Bayezit I of a crusader army composed mostly of Hungarians at Nicopolis (1396). Constantinople was surrounded and doomed – though three times the Turks prepared the final siege and were distracted.

There was no distinction in the Ottoman state between civil and military functions – it owed its origin to a conquering drive, and developed as an organization for further conquest. The sultan was commander-in-chief as much as emperor, and the heads of governmental departments constituted his military staff. The soldiers in the Turkish army owed their duty to the sultan as an individual rather than to the state. The system was comparable to the European feudal system, but it worked a great deal better. The bulk of the army was a regular militia, settled on land in return for military service as required. Feudal troops, which were cavalry, constituted the main reliable mass of the army. There were also hordes of irregular troops, infantry called *bashi-bazouks* and cavalry called *akibi*, who were unpaid and fought for plunder. The *élite* troops of the Turkish army were the sultan's own corps of guards, the 'Janissary' infantry and the 'Spahi' cavalry.

The Janissaries were professional infantry, a remarkable fact considering the circumstances of their institution – organized by a people whose only tradition was of cavalry and at a time when infantry was despised in most of the West. Maybe the last-ditch stand of the Byzantine legions had taught Orkhan to appreciate the potentiality of a good infantry force. The method of recruitment to the Janissaries was extraordinary, but, as it turned out, sound. They were taken as children from Christian families and trained in special communities. They received in their monastery-barracks an education which made them fanatical Moslems. They were also given the best physical education possible, and were highly trained in the handling of their weapons. As the sultan's own guard, they occupied a privileged position in the state, but otherwise they were not pampered – receiving little pay, being strictly subject to the Moslem rules of temperance, and being expected to maintain absolute devotion to their profession of arms and their allegiance to the sultan.

At the height of their greatness, in the first half of the sixteenth century, the Janissaries numbered between 12,000 and 15,000. The titles of the officers were

The Spahis were the *élite* Turkish cavalry

taken from the titles of household departments – for example, 'chief soup-maker' and 'chief of the bloodhound keepers'. The original weapon of the Janissaries was the bow, a short composite weapon which far outranged any other type. But as soon as the arquebus appeared as a practicable weapon it was adopted. Sabres and daggers were also standard equipment. Other weapons at various times used by them as well as by the *bashi-bazouks* included slings, crossbows, javelins, lances, straight swords, pikes, axes, maces, scythes, flails and whips. The men were not heavily laden with protective armour. In the fifteenth and sixteenth centuries they had a small round shield, a metal helmet shaped like a *fez* with a sharp point on top, and possibly some light mail. There was a colourful uniform for each section; they also went in a great deal for tattooing.

The mass of Turkish forces were horsemen, and of these the Spahis were the *élite* cavalry, a nucleus for the rest. In the 1520's the Spahis numbered between 10,000 and 12,000. Each man was responsible for recruiting and training between two and six additional horsemen; these he brought to battle rather as a western knight was accompanied by his 'lance'. The chief weapons of the Turkish cavalry were bow, lance and short sword. They had no defensive armour. Besides the cavalry there were also specialist corps of marines, gunners, armourers, smiths, commissariat officials, and bandsmen.

The theoretical total of men of all arms and functions in the Turkish army in its heyday, under Mehmed II (1451–81), Selim I (1512–20) and Suleiman the Magnificent (1520–66), was in the region of 300,000 men, and such was the organization of the Ottoman state that mobilization was remarkably rapid and complete. The professional nucleus of infantry and cavalry numbered at least 25,000. European observers were profoundly impressed; Giovio wrote: 'The Turks surpass our soldiers for three reasons: they obey their commanders promptly; they never show the least concern for their lives in battle; they can live a long time without bread and wine, content with barley and water.'

In 1451 Mehmed II became sultan. He was nineteen years of age, taciturn and cruel, inclined to drink, but resolutely ambitious and a capable soldier. His chief aim at his succession was to complete the conquest of the Byzantine empire by capturing Constantinople. That he suceeded in doing this in 1453 is not remarkable; the city had long been encircled, and the Turks brought an army of 100,000 to besiege its fourteen miles of walls garrisoned by 7,000 men. The fall of Constantinople to the Turks is principally significant in that it meant the final extinction of the civilization of Greece. It is also interesting in that it showed very clearly that the age of chivalry had passed; no Christian force attempted to raise the siege. From the military point of view the chief point to note in the siege is that it was a landmark in the history of artillery.

The main reason for Europe's inability to repel the Turks was that the Ottoman invaders were just as advanced as any other people in the use of firearms. In 1452 a Hungarian engineer called Urban came to the emperor Constantine, offering his services as the best maker of cannon in the world. But Constantine could not pay him what he asked nor provide the necessary raw materials. Urban therefore, the first of many renegade westerners who were to sell their services as technical advisers to the Turks, approached the sultan. Mehmed offered him four times the salary he had asked and gave him all the technical assistance he needed. By the beginning of 1453 Urban had produced at Adrianople the largest cannon ever seen, with a barrel nearly 27 feet long, and capable of throwing stone balls of over 1,000 pounds weight. When it was tested the projectile travelled a mile, and the bang caused pregnant women twelve miles away to have miscarriages. Mehmed was delighted, and Urban's monster-cannon set out for Constantinople drawn by sixty oxen. At the siege it broke down, but that did not matter because of the efficiency of the other Turkish artillery.

The Turks kept up a ceaseless bombardment of Constantinople for six weeks, concentrating fire on the most vulnerable points in the walls. Some of their cannon were exceptionally large, and these were difficult to get into position as well as to maintain on their platforms – particularly when rain made the ground soft. Since the barrels cracked if they were not left to cool between shots, the larger cannon could not be fired more than seven times a day. But every shot did tremendous damage.

Within a week the outer wall of Constantinople was completely destroyed at several points. Thereafter the gallant defence worked night and day to repair a stockade and earthwork behind the outer wall. But the bombardment, unhurried and relentless, gradually destroyed the fortifications. The Turks demonstrated their technical ingenuity by floating cannon on platforms attached to a pontoon bridge across the Golden Horn, thus reinforcing their bombardment from a new angle. Twice when Mehmed thought that his bombardment had already done enough he was mistaken, for the first two Turkish assaults were beaten off. But the third time he succeeded.

The capture of Constantinople was the prelude to a period of dramatic advance by the Turks and the height of their military greatness. Greece and Serbia were for the first time effectively conquered during the next fifteen years. The resistance of the Albanians, led by George Scanderbeg, at last collapsed in 1468. The limit of Turkish expansion in the west was set for the time being by Mehmed's failure to capture Belgrade. Mehmed, though cruel to individuals and rigorous in the exaction of tribute, was however in many ways a liberal conqueror. The Orthodox religion was tolerated, and the major monuments of Greek and Byzantine architecture were not molested structurally. (It was not until the Venetian siege of the Acropolis in 1687 that the Parthenon, used by the Turks as a powder magazine, was ruined by an explosion.)

During this time the advance of Turkish power on land had been balanced by the development of naval strength in the eastern Mediterranean. From the first, as a natural extension of the original *ghazi* drive, some Turks had taken to the sea as corsairs. When the expansion into Europe began it became necessary for the Ottomans to have a navy, if only to protect the crossing of the Bosphorus; thereafter Turkish seapower grew, and a definite policy was formulated for controlling the trade of the Levant. The chief European naval power in the Mediterranean at this time was Venice. Pietro Loredano destroyed a large part of the Turkish fleet off Gallipoli in 1416, but trade was the great concern of Venice; from 1430 in any case Venice was preoccupied with struggles with rival Italian states, and again owing to the disunity of their enemies the Turks were able to make progress westwards. One of Mehmed II's soundest reasons for confidence in besieging Constantinople was that he had a strong fleet to cut the sea communications of the city.

The Turks of course had no native seagoing tradition of their own, and when they reached the Mediterranean they adopted without criticism or modification the ancient Mediterranean naval tradition of the galley – not only in ship design but also in tactics. Fundamentally, little ever changed in galley warfare between the battles of Lade in 494 B.C. and Lepanto in A.D. 1571.

The Greek and Roman trireme had been taken over as the basic ship of war by the Byzantines, who called it the dromon, and increased it in size till it ranged in displacement from 78 to 175 tons, with from 100 to 200 rowers. Venice and Genoa had latterly become the leading Mediterranean sea powers; they called their ships 'galleys' and used only a single tier of oars. Galley tactics were simple and had been stereotyped by their most efficient practitioner, Ruggiero de Lauria, in the Sicilian wars of the end of the thirteenth century. The principle was to advance in line or crescent formation, to ram the enemy in the hope of damaging his oars, and then after a bombardment to board and capture the ship. The majority of the fighting men were slingers and crossbowmen. Refinements in assault included the use of liquid soap to make the enemy's decks slippery, and of broad-tipped and incendiary arrows to damage his rigging. The only subsequent changes were that the size of galleys increased slightly and *ballistae* were replaced by small cannon as bow artillery. Tactics did not change, and the outcome of fighting continued to depend on the 'grapple and board' method. When the Turks at last captured Constantinople they gained a great ship-building centre.

The victorious campaigns of Selim I (1512–20) against Persia and Egypt were part of an overall strategy to gain control of the eastern Mediterranean and the Near East. He decided it was essential to meet the challenge of Spanish power along the north coast of Africa; the occupation of Egypt was the first stage in this strategy. It was followed up in 1519 when Khairredin Barbarossa, the foremost pirate of the Barbary coast, was induced to give his allegiance to the sultan, and was appointed *beylerbey* of Algiers. There then remained in the Mediterranean one glaring weakness in the Turkish lines of communication: the continued possession by the Knights of St John of the island of Rhodes. But Rhodes fell to Suleiman the Magnificent, after a heroic defence against massive siege operations, in 1522.

In 1525–6 Suleiman led a major Turkish campaign on the Danube front. There was no united opposition from the barons of the frontier nor from the states of eastern Europe. The armies of Suleiman and King Louis of Hungary met on the plain of Mohacs. Suleiman's army of 70,000 was drawn up in a deep formation; two lines of cavalry were backed by the Janissaries and Spahis. The Christian army of only 35,000 was in two long lines of mixed horse and foot. The first cavalry attack of the Hungarians appeared to throw the Turks into disarray, and Louis ordered a general advance. But he had misjudged the depth of the Turkish army, and the Hungarians who penetrated to the rear of their enemy were destroyed without difficulty by the Janissaries. The victory was complete.

In 1529 the Turks advanced with fire and sword and laid siege to Vienna. But a desperate defence and the onset of winter determined Suleiman to abandon the siege, since he was now so far from home, and he had more fighting to do on his eastern frontier. The furthermost boundaries of the Ottoman empire established by Suleiman extended almost to the gates of Vienna in Europe, almost to the straits of Gibraltar in north Africa, down both sides of the Red Sea, and to the shores of the Persian Gulf and the Caspian Sea.

In the last third of the sixteenth century the tide began to turn against the Turks. Venice appealed for help to Rome and Spain, and in 1571 the three powers prepared a united fleet under the command of Don John of Austria, aged twenty-six. At Lepanto in that year the Christian fleet of 200 galleys and 30,000 fighting men inflicted an overwhelming defeat on a comparable Turkish fleet. In Oliver Warner's words: 'At Lepanto, as in most earlier naval battles, the fleets were like armies. Their formation was rigid; the commanders were military; and tactics were based on experience by land. The sailors got the ships where they were wanted: the generals and their soldiers fought it out.'

Lepanto was a negative victory; it preserved the western Mediterranean from complete Turkish dominance, but it was followed up by no strategic offensive by the Christian powers. A new Turkish fleet was rapidly built, and until the English and Dutch fleets began to operate in the Mediterranean in the 1650's the Turks continued to terrorize those waters. Turkish seapower was, however, in decline, the principal reason being a failure to keep abreast with technological development in Europe. The Turks and the Italians continued to use galleys right up to the early nineteenth century.

The Turkish army too entered a decline marked by technological backwardness. As firearms developed in western Europe with the introduction of good field artillery and the bayonet the Turks failed to follow suit. They retained their old weakness for enormous and unmanageable cannon. There was also a failure of leadership, as too many sultans abandoned their responsibilities as rulers and commanders-in-chief, and gave themselves over to pleasure. In 1582 Murad III forced the Janissaries to admit to their ranks the acrobats and wrestlers who had delighted the people at the festivities occasioned by the circumcision of his son. Discipline, morale and efficiency declined. At St Gotthard in 1664 the Germans under Montecucculi, a commander who had learned all the lessons of the Thirty Years' War, inflicted a defeat on the Turks which was the decisive turning-point in their military history. Their last serious aggressive demonstration in Europe was the unsuccessful siege of Vienna in 1683. By the eighteenth century the Ottoman empire was hard put to defend its frontiers.

In the east the Turks extended their conquests into Persia

11 The Greatness of Spain

In the history of European warfare in the sixteenth century the leading nation was Spain. She took a major part in all the important nationalistic-dynastic wars of the century; furthermore, in the new commercial offensive of European imperialism the ships of Spain, with those of England snapping at their heels, were responsible for the tremendous development and expansion of the strategic and diplomatic horizon of Europe to include the Atlantic and the newly colonized continent of America.

In the development of military and naval technology and tactics Spain was again a leader. The overriding question at the beginning of the sixteenth century was what was to be the future of guns. At the battle of Cerignola in 1503 Gonzalo de Córdoba, the *gran capitán*, demonstrated that the handgun or arquebus would for the foreseeable future be the dominant weapon in battle. Land warfare after about 1525 became almost entirely a matter of manoeuvre and siegecraft, open battles on any large scale being avoided. But of the three outstanding military commanders in the European wars of the later part of the sixteenth century – Alexander of Parma, Ambrogio Spinola, and Maurice of Nassau – the first two were in the service of Spain. The forays of Europeans over the seas of the world in this period were made irresistible by the development of the sailing ship armed with cannon – described by Cipolla as 'essentially a compact device which allowed a relatively small crew to master unparalleled masses of inanimate energy for movement and destruction'. Here the most creative individual, in the navigation and tactics of these revolutionary ships, was an Englishman – Francis Drake. But Spanish seamen, though outclassed at the defeat of the Armada in 1588, had been as ready to experiment as any.

The explanation of the rise of any people to military greatness must ultimately be obscure, but one or two preconditions to the greatness of Spain stand out. Castile was a barren country and bred a tough people. The Spaniards had just completed the work of three centuries in reconquering their country from the heathen Arabs. They were thus left with an impetus of military success. Economic demands were not likely to distract their energies from war, since the pastoral economy of the countryside needed little labour. Besides, war was expected to be profitable.

During the Italian wars, which we are about to consider, for the first time a distinctly modern attitude to war can be discerned. It was an age of political realism, the age of Machiavelli and *raison d'état*. New systems of international law, diplomacy and secret service developed. Old clichés died hard, and for a long time firearms were denounced as a cowardly and unchivalrous threat to Christian morality and the social order. The point was, however, that they worked, and they were used. In the military theory of the *Nef des Princes et des Batailles* (1502) Robert de Balzac

The Spanish became the dominant military power in Europe and founded a great empire overseas. A detail from a mural depicting the capture of Oran from the Moors epitomized the new attitude. Behind a smoke-screen of conventional moralizing he stresses the efficient use of firearms and modern formations, and the necessity of ruthlessness in such matters as the maintenance of discipline and scorched earth policies. He encourages the keeping of treaties, but warns his readers never to rely on the honour of other powers. With the same freedom from sentimentality he observes that 'success in war depends on having enough money'.

In 1494 Charles VIII of France invaded Italy. In 1495 Gonzalo de Córdoba was sent to defend Spanish interests in southern Italy. The details of the wars of the next sixty years make a tedious story of hit-and-run invasions and a kaleidoscopic complex of alliances and fratricidal counter-alliances. The Italian wars developed into a wider conflict between the Valois and Habsburgs, but from the military point of view the interest is concentrated in certain campaigns and battles of the earlier phase.

In 1495 the victory of Charles VIII at Fornovo against the combined armies of Venice and Milan ended the somewhat absurd era of *condottiere* warfare. For the past two hundred years the wars of the Italian cities had been conducted by bands of cavalry under professional soldiers known as *condottieri*. Many campaigns had by this time become so 'scientific' that battles were no more than manoeuvres, in which armies would surrender as soon as they were technically outflanked or cut off from their base. The Italians therefore got a rude shock when the French with their Swiss mercenaries crossed the Alps, with the intention of taking towns by storm and slaughtering prisoners. Charles VIII's irresistible progress up and down the length of Italy in 1494–5 showed what artillery could do. In recent years Jacques de Genouillac had made certain technical improvements to artillery weapons, including the introduction of gun carriages, of trunnions to elevate guns, and the use of metal instead of stone cannon balls. City walls were still of the medieval type, high and defended primarily by crossbowmen, and the Italian cities could make no effective defence against Charles's siegecraft. In 1515 also, at Marignano, the first great defeat of the Swiss by the French under Francis I, field artillery played a crucial part.

High hopes were now raised for field artillery, but they were not fulfilled. Machiavelli was right in arguing that the immobility of field artillery was such that an intelligent tactician should be able to deal with it. To make them more formidable, guns were being made ever larger. For the purpose of battering down walls this was sound, but there was as yet no differentiation between cannon for use on the field and cannon for siegecraft. Mobile and rapid-firing field artillery was not developed until the seventeenth century.

By the beginning of the Italian wars the handgun had at last been developed into a weapon of very great potentiality. In the Hundred Years' War it had been so unwieldy and inefficient as to be virtually unserviceable, two men being required to operate it; but recently there had been improvements. The weight was reduced to 30 pounds, and its butt so shortened that one man could support the gun against his shoulder. The barrel was lengthened to over 3 feet and the calibre reduced, thus giving range and accuracy. But the most important development was the invention of the match-lock. Previously the method of firing the gun had been to apply a smouldering piece of impregnated fibre called 'match' to the touch-powder. To do that, while at the same time holding the gun in the position of correct aim, required a virtuoso juggling performance. The match-lock now gave the gunner the chance to be efficient, by making the firing automatic. The match was clipped to a cock, which swung over to ignite the touch-powder when the trigger was pulled. The handgun fitted with the match-lock was known as an 'arquebus'.

The man who first recognized the tactical potentialities of the arquebusier, the infantryman armed with a handgun, was Gonzalo de Córdoba. He greatly increased his force of arquebusiers and equipped them with the latest guns, each man also having a bullet pouch, a match, cleaning materials, a ramrod, and powder in small tubes hung on a bandolier. In addition they were armed with a sword and protected by a helmet and cuirass. Gonzalo considered that sufficient arquebusiers strongly entrenched would be able to check the assault of any number of crossbowmen, pikemen or cavalry – just as the English longbowmen had done. The arquebusiers would need to be backed by pikemen, who were the best hand-to-hand fighters of the time; these would reinforce them should the enemy succeed in closing, and would

Field guns played a decisive part in the battle of Marignano

148 A CONCISE HISTORY OF WARFARE

be necessary in counter-attacks. The most important cavalry were light javelinmen known as 'genitors', useful for scouting, skirmishing and harassing the enemy.

Gonzalo's system was tested against the French at Cerignola in April 1503. The Spanish infantry units – a few ranks of arquebusiers in front and the pikemen behind them – were entrenched on the lower slopes of a hill. Just below ran a ditch, the bank of which was raised into a sort of rampart with earth and vine-props. Gonzalo induced the enemy to attack him by sending out clouds of genitors who harassed the French and drew them forward. The French men-at-arms and pikemen made a headlong attack, thinking that the force of their rush would break the meagre-looking stationary Spanish line. As they came within range the Spanish arquebusiers opened heavy fire. The leaders of the advancing columns were shot down or fell into the ditch. The French assaults were repeated but with the same result. Only when it was clear that victory was in sight did Gonzalo order his men forward from the line of their entrenchment – to complete the destruction of the enemy. Gonzalo de Córdoba raised the infantry soldier armed with handgun to the status of the most important fighting man on the battlefield – a status which he was to retain for over four hundred years.

Gonzalo's outstandi 1g military ability and leadership were again evinced at the end of 1503 in the campaign and battle of the Garigliano. The French remnants of Cerignola had been heavily reinforced, and in October Gonzalo tailed a French army twice the size of his own down the valley of the Garigliano. The enemy were heading for Naples, but because of torrential autumn rains they decided, rather than attempt the mountain route, to make for the coast and then proceed along it. When Gonzalo realised this, he moved his army through the mountains at top speed to get across the river before the enemy, and early in November he confronted them across the swollen lower reaches of the Garigliano. The French threw a pontoon bridge across, but were driven back by the artillery and arquebus fire of the Spaniards. The weather was worsening, and after one more attempt to cross the river the French gave up trying.

A deadlock of six weeks followed, during which both sides sat fast, guarding the muddy banks of the Garigliano – the weather continuing exceptionally wet and cold. Gonzalo knew that it would be fatal to retreat even as far as the drier foot-hills, since once the superior forces of the French crossed the river Naples was doomed. Morale now played a decisive part. Gonzalo himself lived in a hut about a mile back, and visited the forward positions daily – exhorting and keeping his drenched and inactive army in good heart. On the other hand, the French officers rapidly lost interest, many of them retiring to live in comfortable quarters in the nearest towns, while the commander-in-chief, the Marquis of Mantua, developed a diplomatic 'fever' and handed over his command to the Marquis of Saluzzo. The soldiers soon became thoroughly demoralized; many deserted, and their lines straggled farther and farther back from the mud of the river bank. In such weather it seemed highly improbable that the Spaniards, who were outnumbered and had hitherto adopted the defensive, would attack; consequently French vigilance was neglected.

The deterioration of the French was perceived by Gonzalo, and he planned a surprise attack. Well behind the lines the parts of a pontoon bridge had been prepared, under the supervision of the remarkable specialist in gunnery and engineering, Pedro Navarro. The parts of the bridge were made small and light enough to be carried on mules, and they could be fitted together quickly. At Christmas there was a two-day truce, and some fraternization took place between the armies – the French soldiery continuing their celebrations for several days. On 27th December the mass of the Spanish army and the components of the bridge were moved up to the north end of the Spanish position, opposite the extreme left of the French at the village of Sujo, where the river was a little narrower, the ground less wet, and preparations could be concealed. The assault was planned for dawn on the 29th. In command of the bridge-builders and the van was Alviano; Gonzalo commanded the 'main battle'; the rear units occupied the trenches along the river opposite the main force of the French, with orders to cross at that point if the battle went well.

The scheme worked as planned. The bridge was laid by dawn, and the few French infantry at Sujo were not even under arms to resist the light horse of the Spanish van when they fell upon them. Alviano dashed on downstream through several villages occupied by Swiss infantry, who were not given time to form up for battle. The French men-at-arms were mostly well back from the river, and Saluzzo was able to collect only a small party, which made one charge – but in vain. The genitors pursued the enemy for ten miles before a considerable body of French succeeded in holding them in the defile of Formia. Gonzalo's infantry of the 'main battle' were already at hand, and behind them the rearguard had crossed the river. The only real battle of the Garigliano took place in the defile. After an hour's hard fighting the French broke, and the chase and captures of men and guns continued as far as Gaeta.

The Garigliano was a victory of great diplomatic significance and a fitting crown to the military career of the 'Great Captain'. Gonzalo de Córdoba died in 1515. Spain continued to increase the proportion of arquebusiers in her forces, and their effectiveness was repeatedly demonstrated.

The victory of the Spaniards under Prosper Colonna over the Swiss at Bicocca, for example, in 1522 was won by following Gonzalo's pattern of Cerignola. Colonna prepared a very strong defensive position, where a sunken lane ran between the edge of a garden and some fields. He built up the bank of the garden side into a rampart, mounted some artillery on it, disposed his arquebusiers four deep to man the rampart, and in rear of them placed continuous units of pikemen. As the Swiss pikemen advanced across the fields they were mown down first by artillery and then by arquebus fire. Those who succeeded in pressing forward to jump down into the lane found themselves trapped in an abattoir, and were slaughtered by the arquebusiers who were so high above them that the Swiss pikes could not even touch them. Eventually the Spanish pikemen descended to finish them off. Bicocca was a day of total disaster for the Swiss; thereafter they never recovered their former confidence and pugnacity. At Zürich the reformer Zwingli, who had been an army chaplain at the first defeat of Marignano, found sympathetic audiences in his denunciation of the demoralizing mercenary trade. Lack of alternative employment in their own country, however, compelled the Swiss to continue providing recruits for all the armies of Europe in the sixteenth century.

For the Spaniards, by contrast, Bicocca was a total vindication of their new system. Having defeated the most renowned infantry in Europe, the Spanish arquebusiers gave further notable evidence of their prowess by the victory under the Marquis of Pescara over the French cavalry outside Pavia in 1525. Here they did not win by waiting behind good cover for an attack; they defeated the French by surprising them on open ground, turning their flank, and then pouring unremitting volleys into the massed ranks of cavalry. The enemy infantry was also all but destroyed.

Gonzalo de Córdoba's system had now been proved repeatedly against cavalry and all types of infantry. Crossbowmen and mounted men-at-arms began to disappear rapidly from almost all European armies, to be replaced by arquebusiers and pikemen. Pikemen everywhere adapted themselves perforce to a new tactical

The battle of the Garigliano

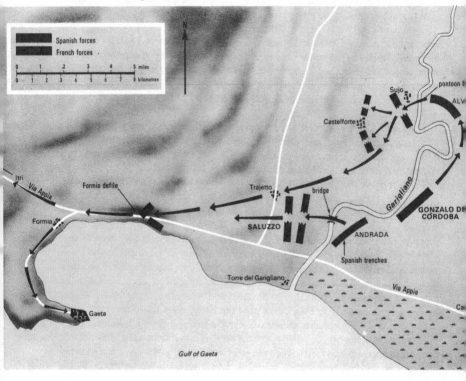

function: of backing arquebusiers rather than themselves leading the attack in *échelon*. Body armour offered no effective protection against the new bullets, and, since it conduced to immobility, after passing through an ornamental phase it was largely abandoned. The defensive power of arquebusiers, above all, was now the most prominent tactical consideration in the minds of commanders, and once again the defensive in warfare became dominant, with the result that after Pavia large-scale open battles on land became extremely rare.

The Habsburg-Valois wars ended in 1559, but in 1562 the French wars of religion began. They were fought ostensibly over the right to worship according to the dictates of conscience, but their most important outcome was the success of Henry of Navarre in maintaining the absolute authority of the crown. They have been described by V. H. H. Green as 'inextricably confused, tedious if considered in detail, occasionally revealing intense devotion to principle but more often complete lack of it'. At the same time, after 1568, the Dutch were fighting to gain independence from Spain. Had Spain's other problems not prevented her from concentrating her force to crush the revolt, the Dutch would certainly have lost; but, as it was, they threw off their yoke in a struggle of epic endurance.

These wars saw the definition of the innovations which had appeared in the Italian wars. They were fought very largely by mercenary troops, and all armies were of mixed nationality. The legacy of Gonzalo de Córdoba made defensive tactics normal; commanders preferred manoeuvre, feinting and seeking to attack the enemy on the march, to cut his communications or starve him out – rather than frontal attacks. The Dutch war was fought, in any case, over a terrain of bogs, dykes and canals, appropriate mainly for defensive campaigning. Much poor leadership and unsound military theory was a reason for the poor conduct of the fighting in France. The French soldier, La Noue, complained about his countrymen, 'The young have been reading too many romances of reckless adventure, full of *amours déshonnêtes* and objectless fighting. The old have been reading and rereading Machiavelli.'

The generalship in the early years of the French wars was indeed remarkable for sustained incapacity: at the battle of Dreux (1562) each side captured the other's commander. No state, except Spain, could recruit or afford to pay more than a very small regular national army, and the high proportion of mercenary troops in all armies largely accounts for the general lack of initiative, offensive spirit, and strategic unity of purpose. Even the national troops of Spain were inclined to go on strike when their pay was not forthcoming; the mutiny of 1576 caused terrible damage to Antwerp. Lack of funds was a cause of numerous campaigns petering out. The ablest soldier of the time was Parma. But he seldom had enough funds, and at times orders from the king of Spain, with typical disregard of strategic continuity, prevented him from carrying out his main task of defeating the Dutch rebels: in 1588 he was told to stand by for an invasion of England, and between 1590 and 1592 he was sent to France.

During the fifteenth century siegecraft had got the better of fortification. The situation changed in the sixteenth century, as military architects at last reacted constructively to the existence of artillery, and scientific fortification developed rapidly along new lines. Once again fortifications became well-nigh impregnable. Together with the defensive pattern in tactics and the shortage of funds common to all the governments of Europe, this factor led to the prevalence, after the Italian wars, of defensive strategy – or at any rate of long-term strategy and political manoeuvre in preference to quick results by force of arms. People naturally retired into their safe fortresses, and opposing commanders did not dare leave them unreduced. After Pavia (1525) the annals of warfare are increasingly a record of sieges, culminating in the three years' beleaguerment of Ostend (1601–4) by Spinola.

The chief principle in the new fortifications from the 1520's was to build them compact and low, indeed partly below ground level, so as to be a difficult mark for artillery, and thick enough to withstand bombardment and also the recoil of their own guns. The outworks were strengthened with covered ways and glacis, and by making larger ditches. Cannon were to be used for defence, and walls were built with bastions, redans and hornworks in order to command as wide a range as possible.

There was no development in artillery to compete with the increased strength of fortifications, and the design of muzzle-loading cannon remained basically unchanged for three hundred years. English artillery ranged through sixteen sizes, from the 'cannon-royal' weighing 4 tons and firing a 75-lb shot, to the 'rabinet' which weighed 300 lbs and fired a 5-oz shot. The cannon used in ships were from the smaller range, such as 'culverins' and 'sakers'. In the early sixteenth century, when Henry VIII decided that he wanted to acquire 'cannon enough to conquer hell', he had to order them from the Flemish manufacturer, Hans Poppenruyter – an indication of English military backwardness at that time. But in 1541 the Rev. William Levett began to make iron cannon in Ashdown Forest. Though iron guns were brittle, very heavy, and generally less efficient than bronze, they were much cheaper. The best cannon at this time were German; the Germans also invented the mortar, a short gun designed to lob a shot on to the enemy. Spain had no efficient manufacture of artillery, and thereby suffered a significant disadvantage.

In siegecraft, treachery or guile or starvation were generally more successful after the Italian wars than bombardment. The firing rate of artillery had not yet surpassed that of the *ballista*. In 1546 Niccolo Tartaglia, a Venetian, published an important treatise on ballistics, teaching the artilleryman to estimate range and elevation with the use of a quadrant. Although siegecraft was such a laborious business, with the odds piled against the besieger, the wars of this period did produce two masters – Alexander of Parma and Maurice of Nassau.

Maurice's method was to achieve surprise if possible and concentrate an intense artillery fire on a small section of the *enceinte* to create a breach. He would persuade his victims to surrender by allowing them the full honours of war and by forbidding pillage.

In such open fighting as took place, until at least 1600, the Spanish infantry – arquebusiers, musketeers and pikemen – were the best in Europe. One notable feat – more remarkable than Wellington's crossing of the Bidassoa in 1813 – was the march of 3,000 men under Mondragon to relieve Tergoes in 1572. They waded for six miles through water up to the waist and over, knowing that if the tide came in before they were across they would all be drowned. The introduction of the musket towards the end of the century made no difference to tactics. It was a handgun of greater range and accuracy than the arquebus, but it had the disadvantages of being so heavy that it had to be rested on a fork, and of having a firing rate appreciably slower even than the forty rounds an hour of the arquebus. It is an interesting reflection on the age that in 1534 the number of chaplains in a brigade (3,096 men) of the Spanish army was 13, while the number of medical staff was 3. There was a tendency during these years to reduce the size of units, in both infantry and cavalry. In place of the enormous units of Gonzalo's day, smaller 'regiments' commanded by 'colonels' appeared in the Spanish army.

The publication of *Don Quixote* in 1605 finally ridiculed into extinction the armoured knight of the age of chivalry. The javelin was replaced as the weapon of light cavalry by the pistol, first conspicuous in the campaign of Mühlberg in 1547. The pistol was detonated by a 'wheel-lock', which worked like a cigarette lighter. The best pistoleers were the Germans, known as *reiter* – each of whom carried three pistols, in holsters, and wore black armour. Their characteristic tactical manoeuvre was the 'caracole'. Each line in succession rode up to the enemy, fired, and then swerved off – to reload and form up again in the rear. It was a hazardous system, since the complicated manoeuvre could lead to confusion, and it took a brave man to ride up close enough to the enemy to be within effective pistol range. This deep formation contradicted the principle of shock tactics, since the impetus of the back ranks was wasted, and if the enemy had cannon or even arquebuses the casualties among the *reiter* were bound to be heavy.

Maurice of Nassau did not neglect cavalry in his general improvement of the Dutch forces. At the battle of Turnhout (1597) the Dutch cavalry drove the Spanish cavalry off the field, and then turned in conjunction with their infantry to break the enemy's foot. At Nieuport in 1600 it was the clear superiority of the Dutch horseman which decided the greatest battle since Pavia. Henry of Navarre was a daring, rash, but on the whole successful cavalry leader, who believed in winning victories by dashing charges in the style of Pappenheim and Murat. His defence of the defile of Arques in 1589 is also a classic of its type. But whenever they clashed Henry was outclassed by Parma, a master of economic strategical manoeuvre.

The history of naval warfare in this period is more rewarding. In the fifteenth and sixteenth centuries Europe at last broke out of its beleaguerment by alien peoples – Goths, Arabs, Vikings, Mongols, Turks – which had gone on throughout the Middle Ages. There is no simple explanation for the new advance of Europeans across the seas of the world. The navigators and *conquistadores* were generally conscious of wanting to bring Christianity to the heathen world and to perform great deeds for themselves and their countries. Curiosity drew them further, but the strongest urge of all was the desire to become rich. European imperialism was a commercial affair, backed by speculators and carried forward by adventurers.

Francis I of France only meant to be rude when he called Manoel of Portugal *le roi épicier*, but in fact his analysis was correct. If commerce supplied the energy, and religion the pretext, the means lay in the new developments in technology, in sailing ships and guns.

The first offensive drive came from Spain and Portugal. In 1493, the year after the final defeat of the Moors, Columbus' voyage suggested an outlet for Castilian energy in a new world. The European empires founded in the sixteenth century – Spanish, Portuguese, English and Dutch – remained essentially maritime trading empires. The Europeans were not numerous enough to occupy in a real sense the vast interiors of the new continents, nor did they have the same overwhelming technical superiority in land warfare over the non-European peoples as they had at sea.

The square-rigged sailing ship, armed with cannon and manned by sailors with advanced navigational knowledge and skill, was the key to these adventures. The Portuguese made the first crucial navigational discoveries. Prince Henry the Navigator patronised seamen and collated knowledge in the 1430's and 1440's. Improvements in the cut of sails made it possible to tack against the wind, and by 1456 the Portuguese were using astrolabe, quadrant and cross-staff. Schools of navigation were set up at Lisbon and Seville. However, there was still no way to measure longitude, and charts remained rudimentary. The caravels of the fifteenth century had far to evolve, but already no other ships in the world could rival their combination of mobility and destructive power. In 1509 the Portuguese under Francisco de Almeida shattered the combined Egyptian and Gujerati fleets off Diu, and thus replaced the Arabs as the dominant seafaring people in the Indian Ocean.

The Spanish conquests of Mexico and Peru (1519–33) were not strictly military episodes, for both were gigantic bluffs. Cortés and Pizarro, each with bands of adventurers under 1,000 strong, only a few horses, and firearms which were not particularly up-to-date, took over the empires they coveted by playing on the superstitious fears of their enemies. It was fear of strange white gods mounted on horses and wielding instruments of thunder and lightning which really caused the Indian rulers to capitulate with hardly a blow, while their terrorised subject peoples welcomed the release. The introduction of smallpox by the Europeans to the American continent also played some part in destroying their enemies' resistance. But the story at any rate merits a prominent place in the annals of courage, leadership and psychological warfare.

On the occasions when Spanish arms did clash with Indian in South America, their technical superiority was demonstrated. The Indians had only slings, bows, obsidian-headed spears, and axes, whereas the Europeans had guns, steel swords, and horses. The Aztec capital of Tenochtitlan (site of Mexico City) was built on an island in the lake of Texcoco. For the final siege in 1521 Cortés had thirteen 42-foot brigantines constructed to support the assault of his men along three causeways. Each had a crew of twenty-five men, armed with arquebuses and cross-bows, and a small cannon mounted in the bows. Cortés regarded his brigantines as 'the key to the whole war', and committed to them a third of his total force and almost 80 per cent of his artillery. They did indeed play a vital part in the combination of blockade, bombardment and assault by which Tenochtitlan was reduced. The brigantines annihilated a vast Indian fleet of canoes by ramming and gunfire. They performed the tactical function of cavalry in supporting the flank and rear of assault forces on the causeways, and at night they guarded the men at rest. They carried out supply and liaison duties, severed the enemy's communications, and formed pontoon bridges. Eventually their bombardment destroyed the native fortifications, and they penetrated along the canals which led into the heart of the city. Cortés' siege of Tenochtitlan was a sustained amphibious operation, original in conception and brilliantly executed. Even such an improvisation demonstrated the overwhelming power of guns and sail combined.

Warlike competition between the European imperial powers themselves was bound to arise sooner or later, and certain rich areas, notably the Caribbean, became areas of rivalry between aggressively monopolistic powers. In 1580 the thrones of Portugal and Spain were united, thus producing a single very powerful navy. Spain's chief rival in this period was England. Sir Walter Raleigh summed up the strategical attitude of all concerned in the maritime competition: 'Whosoever commands the sea commands the trade; whosoever commands the trade of the world commands the riches of the world, and consequently the world itself.' In the 1540's and 1550's the Spaniards developed the silver mines of South America. The whole lucrative Spanish trade was tempting, particularly to adventuresome piratical 'privateers', and a slump in the north European market in the late 1540's gave a particular stimulus to the English to investigate the New World.

The development of British seapower in the sixteenth century was a haphazard process. The most important factor at the outset was that, being on the edge of the Atlantic, the English nautical tradition was of sail rather than oars. Henry VII (1485–1509) increased the size of sailing vessels to about 100 tons; it was he who made Portsmouth the home of the British navy and built there the first dry dock; he also encouraged navigators, and as a matter of policy supported a new class of rich man – whose enterprise was to build British maritime power in the years to come. Henry VIII (1509–47) took the most important technical steps forward. Having acquired some new cannon he found that they were too heavy to go in the flimsy gun castles of his carracks; he therefore installed them along the cargo deck, cutting holes in the freeboard. Henry's ships were thus the first to be armed with a broadside. Henry VIII also made his ships more manoeuvrable by removing the gun castles altogether and streamlining the hulls so that they could sail closer to the wind. The new type of sailing ship, with vastly developed offensive power and manoeuvrability, was called the 'galleon'. By 1550 there were galleons of 600 tons, and by the 1580's there were some, such as the *Triumph*, of over 1,000 tons. These were the ships of Hawkins and Drake. Smaller armed sailing vessels, called 'pinnaces', were also used. To supplement the Lord Admiral, Henry VIII also set up a bureaucratic system: the Navy Board and Comptroller. In the 1550's the Spanish adopted the galleon to protect their Atlantic shipping.

The chief figure of the period before 1569 was Sir John Hawkins. He improved the design of the galleon, and raised fleets by subscription, which for a while poached very successfully in the Caribbean. Then in 1568 came the disaster at San Juan de Ulúa. The English were making repairs to their ships in the harbour when they were set upon by a large Spanish force, and only a very small part of the expedition got back to England. This was a turning-point. Queen Elizabeth made it clear that she supported the activities of privateers. The antagonism of commercial rivalry was sharpened by religious differences and by a mounting record of maltreatment of prisoners by the Spaniards.

Francis Drake now emerged as the leading seaman of the galleon age. In twenty years of successful enterprise his name became a terror to the Spaniards and a byword at home. In 1572-3 he avenged the events of San Juan de Ulúa, when he made a successful raid on Nombre de Dios, a key point in Spain's maritime communications. Several months were then spent in pillaging the Spanish Main and destroying shipping. At one point he took to the land and in alliance with the natives captured a valuable Spanish silver caravan. Between 1577 and 1580 Drake made his famous 'circumnavigation' of the world.

But the end of the easy period had come. English ships and seamen were better than ever before, but the Spaniards had also taken measures to deal with the marauders. Their cargo ships had been made larger and were equipped with guns. They adhered strictly to the convoy system; two great fleets left America for Spain at fixed times of the year, accompanied by a powerful protecting squadron of galleons. For a long time the Spaniards, being a Mediterranean people, had been reluctant to abandon the oared ship for the sailing ship. If endurance was the key to strategy, mobility was essential for tactics. Against the Turks, as at the great Mediterranean sea battle of Lepanto (see Chapter 10), in 1571, the Spanish fleet still consisted wholly of galleys. Gradually, however, the qualities of sailing ships were admitted.

In 1585 war was officially declared. Unlike in previous wars in English history, when fleets had been used merely to transport and assist troops to fight on land, there was now a genuine naval strategy. British ships were used systematically to cut the vital maritime links of the enemy – a strategy of indirect approach comparable to that used by Sparta to defeat Athens in the last ten years of the Peloponnesian War. The communications between the Spanish armies in the Netherlands and their home base were attacked; the military expedition sent to aid the Dutch in 1585 was a complementary part of the strategy. At the same time England continued Drake's policy of cutting off Spain's American resources. In 1585 Drake sailed for the Caribbean with 20 ships and 2,300 men, his object being to capture the Spanish emporium of Havana. He succeeded in causing much damage to Spanish shipping and installations, but he did not have enough men to achieve complete success.

Elizabeth proved to be an inspiring national leader. She was short of money and had hitherto conducted her maritime policy by subscribing to private joint-stock enterprises, such as Drake's expeditions. But now the British fleet was also built up again.

The Spanish strategy in the war was to destroy the saboteurs of the empire in their nest, and strike a blow against heresy, by invading England with a great

Armada in conjunction with Parma's army from the Netherlands. Rumours of these preparations spread through Europe, and in 1587 the English made an attempt to nip the invasion in the bud. Leaving a flotilla to watch the Flemish coast, Drake sailed to Spain with 23 ships, on his most brilliant mission of all – 'the singeing of the king of Spain's beard'.

In the harbour of Cadiz he found about 80 ships of various kinds being fitted out. Seizing the advantage of surprise, he sailed his ships into the harbour, and destroyed all that he could find; altogether the Spaniards lost 30 ships. Drake's Cadiz expedition is the first example of a future essential of British naval strategy: the interception of the enemy on his own coast. A direct consequence of this episode was the Spanish decision finally to abandon galleys for galleons; all preparations for the Armada had to begin again. In 1588 Drake urged that his offensive-defensive strategy should be repeated. But the queen's hesitation, followed by unfavourable winds, confined the English fleet to home waters.

The Armada which finally set out for the English Channel in May 1588 was a seemingly imposing force. The main fighting strength of each side was equally strong: 60 to 70 galleons, with a core of about 20 very powerful ships. The largest

The oar-propelled galley remained the principal vessel in the Mediterranean, but it was gradually being replaced by the galleon, fitted with sails

ships on either side were of about 1,000 tons. The Spanish vessels, however, were higher out of the water, with large forecastles, which rendered them considerably less manoeuvrable than the lower English galleons. And, very important, the English had more seamen experienced in sail.

The quality of command on the English side was also superior. The Duke of Medina Sidonia and Lord Howard of Effingham were titular commanders. The real Spanish commander was Diego de Valdez, a sailor of great experience, but unable to control his subordinates. The English had Drake, then in his prime.

There were considerable differences between the armament of the fleets, which coresponded to differences in tactical approach. The tactical intent of the Spaniards was to bombard the enemy from short range so as to damage his rigging and the fighting capacity of his men, and then to close, grapple and board. They therefore armed each galleon with about 40 heavy, short-range guns. The purpose of the English was to bombard the hulls of the enemy ships when on the 'downward roll' and from as long a range as possible, in order to sink them. They therefore armed their ships principally with lighter-shotted, long-range 'culverins'.

On 19th July 1588 the Armada appeared off the Lizard. For some time a south-westerly wind had confined the English fleet to Plymouth Harbour, and its officers to playing bowls. But on the 20th the English ships beat out of harbour towards the Armada. Drake was determined to steal the initiative by getting to windward of the Spaniards. The first instance of the superiority of the English as seamen came when their fleet beat across the enemy's front on short tacks to put themselves to windward. The Armada, in its westward-trailing crescent, could now be compelled to fight a rearguard action at the English convenience all the way up the Channel.

This was, in fact, what happened during the next five days. The English decided to exploit their superior mobility and firing range, tailing the enemy, and day after day picking on the weathermost ships in their rear. At first they pounced in small groups; later the fleet was organised in four squadrons – the beginning of coherent fleet tactics. Time and again the English ships outsailed the enemy. But their chosen tactics worked no more than did those of their enemy. The English guns proved to be too light to inflict any serious damage from the distance which was regarded as safe. The Spanish tactics, which were hardly adapted from the medieval galley system, were a failure; not one of their ships ever closed with the English on its own terms.

The English got the better of the struggle by virtue of superior seamanship, aided by the distinct incompetence of the enemy. Having gained the first initiative, Drake kept the windward position, thanks to the consistent blowing of a 'Protestant' wind. By anticipating minor variations in wind and water, on the 25th he forced the Spaniards to go past the Solent and head on up the Channel, with no further possibility of finding the safe anchorage which they needed – since Parma had not synchronised the assembly of his troops on the Flemish coast. The decisive moment came when the English dispersed the Armada with fireships off Gravelines before dawn on 29th July. The Spaniards panicked, and at last the English were able to get in among them – thanks to the Spanish inefficiency in running out of ammunition.

The greatest losses that the Armada finally suffered were from storms as the broken fleet fled round the north of Scotland.

During the fifteen years of the war which remained, the full results of the English victory were thrown away through failure to follow a resolute strategy. In an amazingly short time the wealth of Spain raised up a great new fleet of galleons. At the very same time, as so often happens after a major victory, English naval expenditure was cut down, and disgracefully inadequate expeditions were sent out. Grenville's celebrated action off Flores in the Azores in 1591 should never have happened. When peace came in 1603 England had lost the dominance of the seas gained for her by Drake. Never once did the privateers achieve their dream of capturing a great Spanish treasure fleet.

It did not matter over much, for by this time other factors, particularly inflation, were causing Spain to decline. The task of ruling such an immense empire, and defending it against predators of all nations, was exhausting. The defeat of the Armada followed by defeat by the Dutch sapped morale. Nonetheless, for some considerable time to come the efficiency of Spanish arms, both on land and sea, continued to command general respect.

Handguns consisted of the arquebus and musket and the lighter pistol. The charge in an arquebus or musket was detonated by a smouldering match; that in a pistol, however, was fired by a milled wheel striking a piece of pyrites—known as a wheel-lock

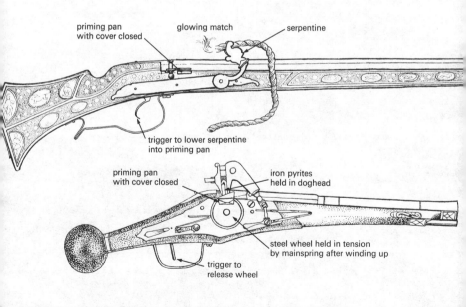

priming pan with cover closed

glowing match

serpentine

trigger to lower serpentine into priming pan

priming pan with cover closed

iron pyrites held in doghead

steel wheel held in tension by mainspring after winding up

trigger to release wheel

12 European War in the Seventeenth Century

The subject of this chapter is warfare in the period of the Thirty Years' War, the English civil war, and the Anglo-Dutch wars at sea. The period produced one of the great captains, Gustavus Adolphus, king of Sweden. It also produced Wallenstein, Pappenheim and Rupert, Condé and Turenne, Cromwell, Tromp and Blake. It was the age in which offensive tactical systems involving the use of firearms were first successfully developed. Furthermore, a great widening of the scale and scope of warfare took place – in strategy, organization, and its impact on national life.

Philip II had dominated western Europe with 40,000 men, whereas Louis XIV needed 400,000 for the same purpose. The increase in the size of armies was originally a result of the enlarged range of strategy and the growing wealth of states. An arms race ensued, so that even Brandenburg increased its number of men under arms from 900 to 80,000 within a hundred years. Armies were also beginning to be permanent. In order to garrison frontiers and to be ready for winter campaigning, it became the practice of most states to keep their best troops on a regular basis all the year round; new tactics in any case required longer training.

As the scale of war increased, its economic implications became greater. It was now much more expensive to be an effective military state: Gustavus Adolphus allocated over half of his budget to military expenses. The area in which an army was quartered, whether or not it was hostile, was likely to be bled of its resources of food, fuel and other needs. But there were benefits. The necessity of feeding great armies was a stimulus to agriculture, and the demand for armaments provided a field for industrial expansion. Sweden, for example, in the second quarter of the century found a profitable use for her natural endowments of metal ore, her charcoal-producing forests, and her rivers which could provide power and transport, and exports of Swedish cast-iron guns rose enormously. This trade assisted Swedish shipping to develop. War provided a major source of employment, in associated industries, in the fighting forces and in the attendant bureaucracy; and smaller and poorer countries, such as Switzerland and Scotland, could sell manpower to the great states.

There were interesting social implications. War now became one of the chief occupations of the masses, with cavalry regiments open to all who could sit a horse and operate a gun. Nevertheless the structure of armies hardly allowed any social mobility. Everywhere the poorer nobility and gentry of Europe saw an opportunity for self-preservation; they annexed the officer corps as the exclusive preserve of their caste, developing their code of honour and the duel, privileges and duties. Militarism was born.

Armies now increased greatly in size. An imperialist army on the march during the Thirty Years' War

The administrative and political implications of the growth of armies and navies were also significant. G. N. Clark writes, 'Just as the modern state was needed to create the standing army, so the army created the modern state.' The demands of finance, recruitment and equipment forced governments to develop their bureaucracies and interfere increasingly in the lives of their subjects; for example, the need for standardization in gunpowder and calibres made it necessary to institute arms' monopolies and state supervision. The strengthening of governments led, in most countries, to the suppression of democracy – in France and, most strikingly, in Prussia, where the *Intendantur der Armee* became the nucleus of the whole government. Most of the armies of the seventeenth century were state armies, not national armies; and in no country except England was the commander-in-chief of the army, the king, made responsible to the people.

In an age of developing absolutism the range of strategy, despite bad communications, increased. A greater mobility and range were in any case called for when the development of offensive tactics encouraged commanders to seek out the enemy and destroy him in battle. The new massive armies could only with difficulty live off the country over which they were operating, and it became essential to guard one's own supply and trade lines. Conversely it was desirable to deprive the enemy of his. More positively, war was seen as a means to wealth. It was believed that the richest nation would be the one which, by fair means or foul, annexed for itself the largest share of the world's resources of materials and manpower. Logistical capacity now began to catch up with political imagination. The operations in the Thirty Years' War ranged all over central Europe: the Spaniards schemed to seize Göteborg, and Prince Piccolomini marched from Flanders to Bohemia. Gustavus Adolphus was a master at combining short-term strategy seeking a decisive battle with the longer-term strategy which sought to drive the enemy back on all fronts.

In the Thirty Years' War, which began in 1618 in Germany, politics was interwoven with religion. The war developed into a struggle to dominate Europe, between the Holy Roman Emperor Ferdinand II, supported by Spain and Bavaria, and France supported by various Protestant states as well as by the Pope. Richelieu, chief minister of France, produced a master-stroke when in 1630 he won Gustavus Adolphus of Sweden as an ally.

In 1630 Gustavus Adolphus was thirty-six years old. He had become king at the age of seventeen, and since then had been frequently at war with Denmark, Poland and Russia to prevent any of them dominating the Baltic. Study of the science of war had balanced his practical experience. His studies had included Xenophon's *Cyropaedia*, which Liddell Hart considers to be 'perhaps the greatest of all military text-books'. He also kept in touch with scientific and technological developments. His ideas on organization, training and tactics were original and brilliant; furthermore he was energetic and efficient in applying them. As a man he was passionate and brave, much liked and respected by his people, outstandingly humane, and motivated by high convictions without being bigoted. As was said, his great military achievements 'were ever attended by devotion within and circumspection without. He first praised God, and then provided for man, at once having an eye on his enemies' next designs, and his soldiers' present necessities.'

The basis of Gustavus' success was his understanding of administration and organization. Sweden could not afford a mercenary army large enough to face the combined armies of her enemies, and Gustavus therefore introduced a system of conscription – eventually creating the first national army to be raised, paid, fed and equipped by the state. Using clergy and local juries as recruiting sergeants, he raised over 40,000 Swedes who were 'strong of limb, and, so far as can be ascertained,

Germany at the time of the Thirty Years' War

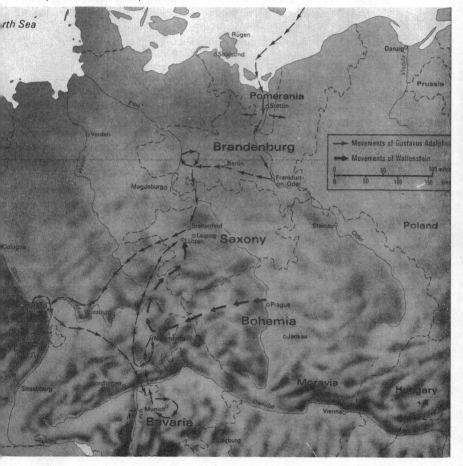

courageous – in years from eighteen to thirty'. Workers in 'reserved occupations' such as transport and munitions were exempted. Some men were paid in grants of land or tax remissions. Apart from being economical, it remained essentially a national army, and so its morale was higher than that of its predominantly mercenary opponents.

In composition and equipment the Swedish army differed from the others of Europe in that it corresponded with the king's tactical conceptions – the chief of which was the supreme importance of firepower and mobility. He made the musket the chief weapon and greatly increased the proportion of musketeers to pikemen. At the same time, following the example of Maurice of Nassau, he created smaller units and sub-units. Thus a company consisted of 72 musketeers and 54 pikemen; there were four companies in a battalion, eight battalions in a regiment, and two to four regiments in a brigade. The musket was shortened and lightened so that the rest was unnecessary; the loading drill was simplified; and the wheel-lock and the paper cartridge were made standard equipment. The pike was shortened from 16 to 11 feet, and armour reduced. Cavalry consisted of cuirassiers armed with sword and pistol, and dragoons who were mounted musketeers.

Gustavus was the first great commander to recognize the importance of field artillery, and he made it a third essential arm. He was assisted by a brilliant general of artillery, Torstensson. Field guns were made shorter with lighter carriages to assist mobility, becoming distinct from siege guns. Calibres were reduced in number and standardized. Field guns weighed 12, 18 or 27 cwt; there were also 4-pounders, called 'regimental' guns, which could be moved by one horse or three men, and fired eight rounds of grape or canister to every six shots of a musketeer. There was a corps of engineers, and civilian experts were called in when necessary. Standard equipment included new aids such as field-glasses and maps.

Drill was practised as an aid to discipline and efficiency in the junior ranks and for the soldiery. In a large army consisting of small units officers were naturally more numerous and important than in the past, and the concept of rank and hierarchy emerged. As Michael Roberts observes, the army was seen not as a brute mass nor as a collection of aggressive individuals, but as a complex organism each part of which had to respond intelligently to impulses from above. Senior officers had to have a working knowledge of science, geography, and even diplomacy; for these reasons several military academies were founded in Europe during the seventeenth century. Gustavus was intolerant of inefficiency, and ready to promote officers for their merit; N.C.O.'s had never been given so much responsibility and initiative since Roman times. Tactics now demanded flexible manoeuvre and good fire-discipline, for both of which training was necessary. A step to achieving uniformity, as well as *esprit*, was the introduction of uniforms and badges.

Warm uniform, introduced by Gustavus, did much to ensure a good state of discipline and morale. This was likely to exist anyway in the Swedish army, in which the men were selected from the best of the national youth, led by bright young officers under an inspired commander. But such a vital matter was not left to chance, and in his *Articles of War* Gustavus forbade drunkenness, whoring and profanity. Punishments for small offences were humane, flogging being forbidden; but pillage, rape and 'despising divine service' were punishable by death.

The commissariat was organized on new and business-like lines. Standardization of weapons meant that they had to be provided by the state rather than, as in the past, by individual soldiers. It was practically impossible for a seventeenth-century army to live off the country, and for reasons of humanity it was undesirable. Gustavus' reforms included an intelligent system of requisitioning, with supply depots at appropriate centres. In principle, too, he quartered his army in fortified camps, like the Romans. These reforms were to cut down wastage and atrocity; they would do away with the need for the army to disperse over the countryside in search of forage and quarters; and mobility would be gained by reducing the huge numbers of camp followers. In practice the system did not always work, and the Swedes were often reduced to pillage and forced billeting. But the system was a great step forward in principle. Gustavus also made valuable innovations in the medical services; he provided a surgeon for each regiment, and allocated a tithe of all captured material for the maintenance of military hospitals.

The twin objects in the foreign policy of Gustavus were the strengthening of Swedish power and the defence of Protestantism. By 1630 the two 'Catholic' Imperialist armies of Wallenstein and Tilly occupied all Germany up to the Baltic. Gustavus decided to take the offensive; the long coasts of Sweden would be difficult to defend, and the king did not wish his people to suffer. In the wide expanses of Germany the numerical superiority of the enemy would count for less. As Gustavus reckoned: 'He has an extensive country to occupy, and many cities to guard, which requires a large number of troops, It is not well to lose sight that the power of the enemy is more in fame than in the reality, and that the loss of a single pitched battle would render his position very critical.' He was to be proved right; but it was a bold calculation. Gustavus landed at the mouth of the Oder in the summer of 1630 with only 13,000 men to oppose combined enemy forces totalling 100,000.

Infantry formation used by the army of Gustavus Adolphus

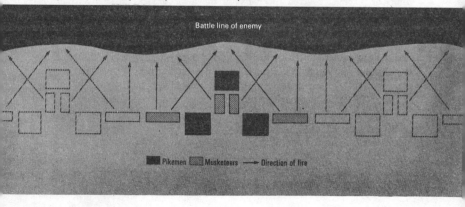

Battle line of enemy

Pikemen   Musketeers   ⟶ Direction of fire

But at that moment the emperor dismissed Wallenstein – whose power he feared. Half of Gustavus' enemies were thus removed from the scene without a blow, and the Swedish army was actually able to recruit numbers of Wallenstein's out-of-work soldiers.

The Protestant princes in Germany remained too cowed to help him, and Gustavus' strategy was to progress cautiously and methodically – adjusting his strategy to his resources. He spent the first year in operations on the southern Baltic coast, securing his base and communications and gradually bringing more men over into Germany. In May 1631 he was ready for battle, and moved south. Gustavus gained the support of the Saxons, and in September his allied forces met Tilly's army at Breitenfeld, five miles north of Leipzig.

Tilly had hoped to defer battle, but he had been more or less forced into it by his impetuous second-in-command, Pappenheim, who had gone forward to reconnoitre, and reported, untruly, that the enemy were approaching so fast that battle was inevitable. This contrasted with the Swedish king's careful reconnaissance and preparation. The system by which orders and information were communicated in the Swedish army was a model in form, each numbered paragraph covering one point concisely, clearly, and in a logical sequence. This system helped to secure mutual protection, and economy and concentration of force in attack. At Breitenfeld Gustavus joined battle at his own time and when the enemy was ill prepared.

He had 47,000 men, of whom 37,000 were his own Swedes; during their long service together he had instilled in them his own tactical conceptions, at training and in battle. It was Gustavus who first developed a tactical system for the age of firearms which combined security with a successful offensive formula. Firearms were to provide the chief striking power of infantry, and the number of musketeers had been accordingly increased. The pike again became an offensive weapon, but the chief function of pikemen remained to cover the musketeers from attacks while loading. An efficient and flexible T-shaped formation was devised for the infantry, combining musketeers and pikemen. The advanced central block of pikemen formed a breakwater in defence and a spearhead in attack, while the other units of pikemen covered the flanks of the musketeers. The latter, while fully protected, could assail the enemy front with volleys at any point, and bring converging fire to bear from different angles. Mobile field artillery with its rapid rate of fire supplemented the missile shock of musket fire, and was highly effective against massed formations. Furthermore, the smoke from the guns could to some extent obscure the movements of the troops behind. A third element of shock was provided by the cavalry – the caracole of pistoleers was abandoned and replaced by a charge at the gallop, with the sword as the cavalryman's chief weapon and the pistol used as a supplementary weapon in the *mêlée*. This was a return to the proper use of the speed and weight of cavalry. Cavalry fulfilled a twofold tactical function: the preliminary clearing work in front to make way for the infantry assault, and delivering the decisive shock attack. Realizing that a mass formation is a waste of manpower, being unmanoeuvrable and vulnerable to gunfire, Gustavus used a linear disposition – repeating T-shaped infantry formations and small cavalry

The Spanish Armada. A detail from a sixteenth-century oil painting design
for a tapestry

die Belägerüng Wien Von Türggn
16 83

squads, and backing them with reserves. The pikemen were arranged six deep, the cavalry four deep with intervals between the files, and the musketeers three deep. Firepower, movement and shock could be directed economically and freely.

The battleground at Breitenfeld was a slightly undulating plain, bare of trees. To face the 47,000 strong allied army, the Imperialist army of Tilly consisted of 40,000 men: 30,000 foot and 10,000 horse. Tilly was a good commander in the conventional Spanish tradition, a man of over seventy. He drew up his army in one or two lines of 'tercios', seventeen solid squares fifty men deep, with the infantry in the centre and the cavalry on the wings. The armies faced each other on a front of over two miles. Although there was little difference between the two armies in numbers, the Imperialists were at a clear disadvantage in artillery – having about 26 guns to their enemy's 54 or so. Both commanders were experienced and confident. The outcome of the battle would depend upon which of two different tactical systems proved to be superior. One relied on mass and the other on mobility; once again, the phalanx was challenged by the legion. Early on 17th September 1631, after prayers had been said and Gustavus had addressed his officers, the Swedish army advanced. A marshy stream had first to be crossed, but Tilly failed to take advantage of this moment to fall on the Swedes and the crossing was made virtually without incident. The first main phase of the battle was a cannonade, which began at noon and lasted for over two hours. The Swedes gained an advantage here as their artillery fired about three rounds to every one of their enemy. Eventually the Imperialist cavalry on the left became so galled by this fire that Pappenheim, in command on that flank, could restrain himself no longer; without any orders from Tilly, he moved with 5,000 men a little farther to his left, and then launched a charge against the Swedish right flank. Their training for manoeuvre and their flexible formation now paid off for the Swedes. Gustavus quickly wheeled up his reserve line of cavalry to form a right angle with the front line. In seven vain charges against this bastion of mingled horsemen and musketeers Pappenheim's cuirassiers disintegrated. Then Baner counter-attacked, and drove the Imperialist left wing of cavalry from the field.

Meanwhile, fortunes at the other end of the battle were swaying in the opposite direction. Fürstenberg's cavalry on the Imperialist right wing attacked and within half an hour had put the Saxons to flight; this left the remaining Swedes outnumbered and with their left exposed. So far Tilly can hardly be said to have been in control of his army, but now he realized his advantage. Observing that his right overlapped the enemy whose left was weakly formed, he ordered it to move round and attack the Swedish rear, while his centre of heavy infantry moved to their right to attack the Swedish left in flank. But as this massive Imperialist manoeuvre began, Gustavus demonstrated both his own quickness in tactical reaction and that his articulated formation was superior to his enemy's masses. He immediately ordered Horn to wheel his men left to face Tilly's new front; at the same time he brought across two brigades of infantry from the second line in the centre to reinforce the left. Since Gustavus' small units manoeuvred a great deal faster than the Imperialist squares, Tilly lost what had momentarily seemed to be a definite advantage.

The relief of the last Turkish siege of Vienna. A detail from a seventeenth-century painting

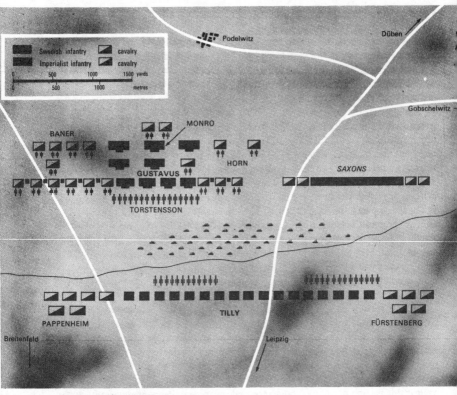

The battle of Breitenfeld

Monro, the Scots commander of one of the Swedish central brigades brought over to the left, describes how the fighting now took place:

> The enemies Battaile standing firm, looking on us at a neere distance, and seeing the other Briggads and ours wheeling about, making front unto them, they were prepared to receive us with a salvo of Cannon and Muskets; but our small Ordinance being twice discharged amongst them, and before we stirred, we charged them with a salvo of muskets, which was repaied, and incontinent our Briggad advancing unto them with push of pike fell on the execution.

This was the hardest phase of the fighting, and the outcome of the battle hung on its progress. Gustavus decided to risk all in a decisive blow. His right wing had been secure since the defeat of Pappenheim; he now brought across four cavalry regiments and himself led them in a great charge up the slope towards the enemy's artillery, sweeping through the guns and round into the Imperialist left. The enemy's artillery being captured, Torstensson turned it against them, thus bringing converging fire to bear from the right and from the Swedish guns in the centre. While this was going on, the attack by the Swedish left against Tilly's centre continued. Assailed on their front and on their left simultaneously by infantry, artillery and cavalry, the close-packed mass of the Imperialist infantry fought on bravely – but in the end were defeated, and broke. The pursuit by the Swedish cavalry did not last long. The final losses of Tilly's army were 13,000, and the whole of its artillery and baggage train.

Gustavus consolidated his victory by occupying the Rhineland, thus breaking the Spanish link with the Netherlands and checking the schemes of Richelieu. His second great victory was against Wallenstein's army at Lützen in 1632. But in this battle Gustavus himself was killed. The career of Gustavus parallels that of Alexander the Great. His historical significance is above all as the founder of modern military organization.

Wallenstein, although defeated in battle, was now left as the most powerful man in northern Europe. A self-made man, early in the war he had offered to raise and equip, at no charge, an army of 50,000 men for the Imperial service. By 1627 Wallenstein had overrun Germany up to the Baltic. Ferdinand then dismissed Wallenstein. He sent Ferdinand his plan of an alliance with Denmark in order to strike by sea at Gustavus' base, but it was rejected. By 1632 all that he had gained for the Imperialist cause had been lost, and he was recalled.

Wallenstein's campaign before Lützen was a brilliant strategical operation. He did not strike directly at his main enemy, but concentrated first on dealing with the Saxons. Having deprived Gustavus of his chief ally, Wallenstein still did not attack him, but moved north against his communications. Gustavus was forced to leave Bavaria and follow, with Maximilian of Bavaria tailing him. At Nuremberg the two armies entrenched opposite each other, each seeking to starve out the other. Gustavus wanted a battle, but Wallenstein refused. Finally Gustavus, desperately short of supplies, launched a heavy attack on the enemy's entrenchments. The Swedes were repulsed, and yielding to hunger and superior willpower Gustavus retired and moved south to the Danube. But the battle of wills was renewed. Wallenstein turned north and headed for Saxony, seeming to threaten the source of Gustavus' communications on the Baltic coast. The plan worked: Gustavus was again drawn right away from the Imperialist territories in the south, and doubled back. Then he made up for his failure; he brought Wallenstein, when he did not expect it, to battle at Lützen.

By 1633 Wallenstein had reconstructed his army, making good the losses of Lützen and a complete Imperialist victory seemed certain. He defeated the Swedes at Steinau, and would have cut them off from the Baltic; but Ferdinand nervously recalled him to protect the south. In 1634 Wallenstein was assassinated. Wallenstein is not easy to evaluate. He was a poor tactician, and as an organizer he was not in the class of Gustavus. But he was a very able strategist; and he had a clear political object: to bring about a peace which could last. He was an outstanding military and political adventurer. He went into the war to make money, and succeeded; he was also something of an idealist, practising religious tolerance and urging the unification of Germany. It required a powerful personality to outwill Gustavus Adolphus, to attract thousands of followers with ease, to make the Holy Roman Emperor accept a humiliating contract, and in Richelieu's words 'by his sole presence and the severity of his silence' to make men obey him.

The war did not end till 1648. From 1643 the modernization of the French army was undertaken by Le Tellier, minister for war, along the lines of efficient state control, and in that year the 21-year-old Duc d'Enghien, later Prince of Condé, dispelled what remained of Spanish military prestige by his victory at Rocroi. Under Condé's command French soldiers continued to learn the new tactics of fire and movement. France had another fine commander in Turenne. When peace was established France had probably gained most, with her frontiers fixed along the Pyrenees and part of the Rhine, and her army the most powerful in Europe. Sweden and Brandenburg also emerged as major powers.

The fate of the people of Germany was perhaps the gravest consequence of the Thirty Years' War, because it had been fought over their country by great armies and in spite of the efforts of Gustavus and Wallenstein devastation had for thirty years been a logistical necessity. Before ever the war had begun Hugo Grotius had foreseen this situation and had written his *De Jure Belli ac Pacis*, putting forward a code of international conventions which might to some extent mitigate the horrors of war. But even the limits of conduct that he suggested were appallingly wide; for example, he accepted the necessity of killing prisoners of war and even civilians. Religious passion was not necessarily a civilizing influence as Gustavus had hoped, and no moral sanctions prevailed against political and logistical necessity. The sack of Magdeburg, during which 30,000 people were burned to death, was the single most horrifying episode of the war. But the cumulative horror was even worse. Eight million people in Germany perished. German Protestantism was preserved, but in other respects German civilization suffered deeply.

In 1642 civil war began in England. An antagonism had long been developing between King Charles I and certain prosperous and articulate sections of his subjects – Puritans who demanded liberty for their own conscience and a state Church which was less Catholic in tendency, and Parliamentarians who demanded a more liberal and competent regime than the inefficient absolutism which Charles was setting up. Charles found most of his support in those areas of England farthest from the capital; the supporters of the Great Rebellion were mostly in the manufacturing centres and seaports, particularly London. The majority of the English people committed themselves in advance to neither side.

Both sides regarded control of London as the key to victory. At the outset of war neither side could raise more than a handful of good quality troops. The Parliamentarians had an advantage in material resources and seapower, which lasted; the Royalists had an initial advantage in their cavalry, commanded by Prince Rupert of the Rhine – but this advantage was soon to be offset by the rise of Oliver Cromwell.

Cromwell was a country squire from East Anglia. In 1642 he was forty-three years old and had no previous military experience. He was a Puritan, energetic, hot tempered and forthright. He was present as a cavalry captain at Edgehill in October 1642, and his experience in that clumsy and bloody battle gave him furiously to think.

Cromwell saw that Parliament must raise a cavalry force capable of beating that of the king. Rupert had followed Gustavus in substituting the charge of cavalry, sword in hand, for the caracole of pistoleers, and he himself was a fine leader – courageous, headstrong, and flamboyant with his scarlet coat, his black horse, and the pet monkey which the Puritans called 'the little whore of Babylon'. In the winter of 1642–3 Cromwell raised a regiment of cavalry in East Anglia, being highly selective in his recruitment. No 'decayed servingmen and tapsters and such kind of fellows' would do, nor 'that which you call a gentleman and is nothing else'. His principle was that 'A few honest men are better than numbers. I had rather have a plain russet-coated captain that knows what he fights for, and loves what he knows.' Religion was the foundation of his discipline, and training was rigorous. The men were armed with a sword, a carbine, and a pair of pistols – being trained to use them all with the utmost proficiency. Their defensive armour consisted of back and breastplates, a helmet and a buff coat. They were regularly paid, and strictly disciplined – swearing and all marauding (except damaging churches) being severely

The Thirty Years' War brought terrible devastation to Germany. A view of the battle of Lützen

punished. The regiment had its first blooding in a clash at Grantham in May 1643, when, in Cromwell's words, 'We came on a pretty round trot, they standing firm to receive us; and our men charging fiercely upon them, by God's providence they were immediately routed.'

Sir Winston Churchill once referred to me as a Cromwellian figure, because, as he said, I always tried both to praise the Lord and to pass the ammunition.

The real test of Cromwell's 'Ironsides', as they came to be known, did not come until July 1644 at Marston Moor. The battle had hardly opened before Rupert's charge swept three-quarters of his enemy off the field. But Rupert led the pursuit too far, and that quarter of the Parliamentary army which had stood firm included Cromwell's regiment. Charging knee to knee at a fast trot rather than a wild gallop, the front rank holding their fire till the last moment, they fell on the flank of the king's infantry, and after a long, hard fight destroyed them.

Cromwell's reputation, as a trainer and as a leader of cavalry, was now made. In the following winter he persuaded Parliament to overhaul its forces and create a New Model Army. The cavalry consisted of eleven regiments, each 600 strong, armed, equipped and trained in the same manner as the Ironsides, except that the carbine was generally discarded. There was also one regiment, 1,000 strong, of dragoons; these were equipped with musket and sword, mounted for transport and skirmishing but generally fighting on foot. The infantry force was twelve regiments, each over 1,000 strong, the proportion of musketeers to pikemen being two to one. The musket used was the new shorter and lighter weapon, and the match-lock was replaced by the wheel-lock and flint-lock. The latter, the detonation of which was caused by the spark from a piece of flint striking a metal plate, became the more common, being cheaper and more reliable. The range of the musket was at least 400 yards, but in battle it was used at closer quarters. The musketeers of the New Model Army wore no defensive armour; they had red tunics, which were to remain the uniform of the British army until the end of the nineteenth century. The defence of the musketeers was afforded by the pikemen, who used a 16-foot long weapon; they also had swords and heavy defensive armour. The infantry of the New Model fought in linear formation usually six deep.

Regarding artillery reorganization, there were four grades of field guns, ranging from the 'culverin' which discharged an 18-pound ball to an extreme range of 2,100 paces once every six minutes, to the 'drake', a 3-pounder which could be fired every four minutes. The English field-artillery was probably less mobile but more accurate than the Swedish. A powerful siege-train was also built up. Each gun crew consisted of the gunner and two assistants who attended to the powder and shot.

The authority of the commander-in-chief of the Parliamentary army was absolute. Officers were considered for promotion by seniority but the unfit were ruthlessly rejected, and for the only period in the history of the British army before the late nineteenth century it was possible for a good man of humble birth to rise to officer rank. Recruitment was almost entirely voluntary; discipline retained its religious character. The post of 'Scout-Master-General' (head of intelligence) was upgraded, and sound administration was considered of first importance. William Clarke, who began as secretary to General Monck, became so indispensable in the running of the administration of the army that after the Restoration he was kept on as 'Secretary at War' – the office from which the later ministry developed.

In June 1645 the New Model Army defeated the Royalists decisively at Naseby. The course of the battle was a repeat of Marston Moor, Rupert sweeping the field initially, but Cromwell in a mood of religious excitement standing his ground – then charging at the right moment and retaining control of his troops to the end. From the evidence of Marston Moor and Naseby Cromwell emerges as a fine cavalry commander. His development into a great general belongs to the period after the defeat of Charles I, when fighting continued against Scots and Royalists.

To achieve his victory at Preston in 1648 Cromwell marched 250 miles in twenty-six days through rough country in filthy weather in order to catch the enemy off balance. Having beaten them, he then pursued them relentlessly to ensure that they would never reform as an army. At Dunbar in 1650 Cromwell was caught at a disadvantage, hemmed into a valley by the sea, and opposed by an able commander, Leslie, whose forces outnumbered his own by two to one. His men were becoming demoralized by foul weather and the Fabian tactics of the Scots. But Leslie also had his problems – in the weather and the Scots churchmen who kept urging him to 'fall on'. Allowing himself to be bullied into it, Leslie abandoned his position on the brow of a hill, and moved his army down to stretch in a three-mile arc from the foot of the hill to the sea. Cromwell reckoned that this development gave him a chance to attack and fight his way out. The Scottish army presented a straggled target; the compact and disciplined English army might be able to catch by surprise the enemy right wing nearest to the sea, and then turn inwards and roll up the centre. Unsuspicious, the Scots passed a stormy night in no state of preparation for battle. At dawn the English van fell on them. For a minute or two the Scots could not even reply to the English fire because their matches were not alight. Hard fighting followed and the first two waves of English foot were repulsed; then Cromwell threw in his reserves. They came 'seasonably in', and a witness commented, 'I never beheld a more terrible charge of foot.' It proved decisive. The cavalry rallied, and the Scots were, as Cromwell said, 'made by the Lord of Hosts as stubble to our swords'. The whole battle was over in an hour; 3,000 Scots were killed, 10,000 taken prisoner, and 15,000 arms captured on the field. The victory was a brilliantly calculated surprise operation – a triumph of nerve and of discipline.

Probably the most remarkable of all Cromwell's military feats was the strategy which led to the battle of Worcester in 1651. In June that year he found Leslie with his Scots very strongly positioned in the hills south of Stirling. He was anxious to move him, and this he did by abandoning his own base, and crossing the Firth of Forth to cut Leslie's communications with the north. Leslie was thus faced with the alternative of fighting in his now weak position at Stirling, or of moving south. He fell into the trap designed for him, and invaded England. Cromwell had calculated that the Scots-Royalist army would gather little if any popular support as it marched south, while he himself could call on large reserves of troops in England. The Royalists advanced as far as Worcester, their forces gradually dwindling until they totalled only about 12,000. Cromwell, moving southwards, took a more easterly route, concentrating other forces on the Worcester area from various directions. The Royalists were harried from behind, blocked in front on the London road, and finally trapped when Cromwell reached Evesham, a few miles east of Worcester. There by the end of August he had assembled 28,000 men. The battle which took place a few days later was stiff, but its result was a foregone conclusion.

Worcester ended Royalist armed resistance, and from then until his death in 1658 Cromwell was ruler of England. His political career turned out to be self-defeating, for, while he desired to give his country acceptable constitutional government, the only basis of his power remained the army. Strained by this dilemma he dissatisfied both soldiers and civilians. His military courage and caution turned to political blustering and hesitancy. Absolute conviction of his own rightness and a passionate desire for righteousness had served him as a soldier, but betrayed him now. It is sad that Cromwell should be remembered more for his unfortunate dictatorship than for his idealism, his courage, and his genius as a trainer and commander of cavalry and as a strategist. But one feature, at any rate, of his rule was to prove enduring and beneficial. This was the development of English seapower and imperialism.

The leading maritime people of the first half of the seventeenth century were the Dutch, who had exploited an advantageous geographical situation and a native flair for commerce and seamanship. By 1650 they were at the height of their prosperity. The success of the Dutch, however, had been built during the time when England and France were concerned with checking the power of Spain. When Spain ceased to be a menace the Dutch found themselves facing competition, above all from England. Strategically England had an unrivalled position for the pursuit of an ambitious maritime policy. France had to concentrate primarily on problems inside Europe. The Italians still went to sea in galleys. The Dutch were a small, rather disunited people, and they also had to protect their land frontiers. But England was an island, well placed off the coast of Europe to keep an eye on her northern rivals, and from an interior position able to intercept their fleets. She also happened to have exceptionally good harbours and safe coasts.

After the civil war an aggressive naval policy was undertaken by Cromwell, supported by commercial opinion. The English passed three Navigation Acts, excluding the Dutch from their trade, in the hope of making inroads on their rival's monopolies. Fearing a retaliatory threat to English ship-building supplies from the Baltic, Cromwell opened up the timber trade with North America and sent an expedition to seize Jamaica. At the same time a big ship-building programme was launched. By 1652 thirty new ships had been added to the fleet of thirty-six inherited from Charles I.

The design of warships in this period was a development of the Armada galleon. In the 1650's ships carried between 30 and 60 guns; then the three-decker came to stay, and between 1660 and 1670 nine ships of over 1,000 tons were built in England. Because of the shallowness of their coastal waters the Dutch had to build ships

A naval engagement in the Anglo-Dutch wars at the battle of the Gabbard

with less draught. Their ships could thus not support more than 80 or 90 guns at the most, and they sailed less well to windward. The Dutch had developed rigging considerably since the sixteenth century, increasing sail area by adding mizzen topsails and fore and aft staysails. Rig was to alter very little thereafter before Trafalgar.

Guns, too, reached by 1670 the form which they were to keep for nearly two hundred years. They were now cast in one piece, with a smooth bore and the outside of the barrel tapering from breech to muzzle. The gun was elevated or depressed by levering the breech of the barrel, and then inserting underneath it a wooden wedge marked in degrees. The gun was trained right or left by levering the whole carriage round.

In 1652 war broke out. The English fleet had better ships and better weapons; the Dutch ships with their shallow draught could use the lines of sandbanks in the Channel for refuge. Each side mobilized about eighty sail. The Dutch admirals were probably the two best seamen in the world – Marten Tromp, a fine leader and a quick, cool thinker, and Michael de Ruyter, a resourceful seaman, and a carto-grapher and mathematician. While most of the Dutch officers were merchant captains of great experience, in the English fleet the senior officers were soldiers by training, good fighters but inexperienced at sea. The English commander was Robert Blake, a colonel of artillery, who took to naval warfare at the age of fifty. The strategy of the English was to gain naval control in the English Channel, and at the same time to protect their own merchant convoys. Both sides sought to destroy the enemy's fleet in battle.

The English fleet in theory used the line-ahead formation for tactics, but seamanship and discipline were not yet good enough for this to work; in practice their ships fought like the Dutch, in squadron clumps, relying on each other for mutual support and seeking to isolate one of the enemy, then to bombard and board. Both sides recognized the advantage of the leeward position in battle but the Dutch, being better seamen, usually managed to get it. They exploited their advantage by firing on the upward roll to damage the enemy's rigging, making it impossible for him to escape to windward. These Dutch tactics paid off in the early battles of the war, for example in November 1652 when Tromp defeated Blake off Dungeness. After the battle he hoisted a broom to his masthead to indicate that he had swept the seas clean of the enemy. But in February 1653 Blake reversed the situation with his victory off Portland. The English were outnumbered, but their warships were better and they were not hampered by a merchant convoy. A running fight took place between Portland and Gris Nez. The first day was indecisive as the English fleet was still scattered, but by the next morning the English had assembled and the Dutch began to run short of powder. Tromp fought a masterly retreat, his warships putting up a stubborn rearguard action, until eventually ammunition ran out and the retreat became a rout; he avoided total disaster only by brilliant seamanship, extricating himself with the loss of only 11 warships and 30 merchantmen. From now on the English became better trained in their line-ahead tactics and after the death of Tromp the Dutch were forced to sue for peace early in 1654.

The English now realized that naval warfare required a modernized administration, the right ships and professional seamen. This meant state control. The shipbuilding programme was pressed forward and by 1660 the fleet consisted of 230 ships. The state appointed commanders, provided dockyards, and became responsible for maintenance and recruitment – chiefly by the press-gang method. Conditions for seamen were improved, their pay was put on a monthly basis, and official care introduced for the sick, wounded and disabled. Meanwhile the Dutch navy remained comparatively decentralized for two main reasons – the confederate political structure of the United Provinces, and commercial preoccupation which was not compatible with specialization for war. Charles II carried on Cromwell's maritime policy after 1660, giving his fleet the title of 'Royal Navy'. In 1673 Samuel Pepys assumed control of administration as Secretary of the Admiralty Office. He introduced important reforms, including examinations and a minimum period of service for officers – thus laying the basis for a full-time professional corps of naval officers.

England was again at war with the Dutch in 1665, and in 1667 de Ruyter in a brilliant operation sailed up the Thames and captured or destroyed the best part of the English fleet which was laid up. A third Anglo-Dutch war took place between 1672 and 1674, in which France was allied with England. The Dutch and French fought on from 1674 to 1678, and during these years of neutrality England overtook the Dutch as a maritime and commercial power. But now she had to face France.

13   Marlborough and his Times

John Churchill, Duke of Marlborough, lived from 1650 to 1722. He was a military genius with great diplomatic skill, and it was he who was responsible for the rise of the British army to become one of the foremost armies in Europe. In this chapter we shall see the eclipse of Sweden and the temporary decline of France. We shall also see the effect on warfare of fortification, as developed by Vauban; it was Marlborough who prevented this factor from paralysing generalship. It was an age of cavalry; but the introduction of the bayonet raised the status of the infantry soldier and caused the end of pikemen.

The central factor in the politics of Europe after the Thirty Years' War was the aggressiveness of France under Louis XIV. Of the various individuals who have set out to dominate Europe, none ever made a more long-standing nuisance of himself. He unleashed four major wars: the War of Devolution (1667–8), the Dutch War (1672–8), the War of the Grand Alliance (1688–97), and the War of the Spanish Succession (1701–13). His aims were *la gloire*, wealth, the expansion of France to her 'natural frontiers' on the Rhine, the Alps and the Pyrenees, and the breaking of the Habsburg ring. All the other states of western Europe united to resist the French, but in the first three of these wars they were unable to succeed. France had a larger population and more natural resources than any other country; she also had interior strategic lines, and centralized absolute government. Furthermore, some of Louis' servants were exceptionally able.

Colbert was the minister chiefly responsible for France's finance and her navy. After the Dutch wars, warships did not change in basic design. A nation could gain naval superiority only by increasing its numbers of ships and bases, and by improving its organization. Colbert enlarged the French navy from 20 warships in 1661 to over 270 by 1690, and these defeated the combined Anglo-Dutch fleet in 1690 off Beachy Head. In 1692, however, the allies got their revenge at the battle of La Hogue; from then on England was the leading naval power, and in the War of the Spanish Succession she had absolute command of the seas.

In the administration of the army Louvois followed the tendencies, begun in the time of Gustavus, towards increased size, centralization, uniformity and professionalization. Condé had won the battle of Rocroi in 1643 with an army of 23,000 men; in 1672 Louis XIV invaded the Netherlands with 120,000. Of these, 75 per cent were now infantry, with their own field artillery. In recruitment and organization, corruption and feudal traditions were as far as possible eliminated. Inspectors, such as the famous Martinet, saw to this, as well as supervising training and enforcing strict discipline. A system of magazines was set up for supply. The army was intensively drilled. The match-lock was replaced by the flint-lock as the standard infantry weapon. Corps of grenadiers were organized, the status of engineers was upgraded, and artillery was integrated more closely with the rest of the army. The real basis of power at this period was military, the security of a dynasty being closely related to the size and strength of its standing army. It was the efficiency of the French War Office which made possible the successes of French armies in the field before the 1690's.

Finally, the generalship of Condé and Turenne achieved these successes. The talents of these two commanders balanced each other well, for Condé was a battle commander whereas Turenne was exceptional as a strategist and organizer. Enterprising, yet cool and comprehensive in his judgement, Condé inspired his men on many battlefields for thirty years after Rocroi. However, in the warfare of this age, when communications were poor and strong fortifications favoured the success of another type of general, it was the man of more patience and forethought, Turenne, who rose to greater distinction. In the civil wars of the 1650's, when he fought against Condé, he emerged as the better soldier.

The supreme ability of Turenne lay in manoeuvre. His object always was to produce a battle situation on the most favourable terms, and at the time and place of his choosing; with this end in view he trained his men to march long distances. His plans were always made with care and imagination; his soldiers knew this and trusted him, because his victories were won with a minimum expenditure of human lives. Between 1653 and 1658 in the civil wars, opposing an army commanded by Condé and superior in numbers and equipment, he succeeded in keeping his army together and made up for weakness in numbers by mobility, keeping touch with the enemy and hampering his activities until he should be strong enough to beat him in battle.

Later Turenne increased his range, making fuller use of time and space; his 'audacity', as Napoleon observed, 'grew with years and experience'. His greatest achievement was the Turkheim campaign of 1674–5. Turenne's role was to hold the enemy allied forces on the German Rhine front while the French offensives were launched elsewhere. He was forced to withdraw in November, because the enemy had received heavy reinforcements. While he moved back into Lorraine, the enemy forces went into winter quarters, scattered through Alsace. The weather was bad, supplies were short, and nobody expected any further fighting. But Turenne saw an opportunity for a surprise victory. Scraping together additional forces he brought his own numbers up to 33,000 to face the enemy's 57,000. Then at the end of December he moved through the mountains to outflank the enemy, and debouched from the Belfort Gap into Alsace. The allies could concentrate only a small part of their forces in haste, and Turenne fell on them at Turkheim. Within ten days not a single German remained on the left bank of the Rhine.

This was a time, however, when limitations were imposed on positive generalship by the power of fortification. After the disappearance from the scene of Condé and Turenne by 1675, the leading military figure was an engineer, Sebastien de Vauban.

In an active career of over forty years Vauban was responsible for the systematic fortification of the vulnerable parts of the frontiers of France. I have carried out many reconnaissances of the gap between the Jura and Vosges mountains where Vauban fortified Belfort and Neuf Brisach. In the past the Belfort Gap has been an avenue of approach from the east and had to be well defended. Today it has no strategical value, because of air power and the range of modern weapons. The area which it was most important for the French to bar was Flanders, a plain where the maritime enemies of France could converge their forces and operate unimpeded by natural obstacles. Here by 1702 more than thirty large fortresses of the first class and some fifty lesser fortified towns and citadels in the hands of France made a formidable barrier.

Vauban developed the art of fortification into a geometric exercise, and succeeded in making the defence too formidable to allow frontal assaults by irreplaceable soldiers. He retained the traditional groundplan for a fortress: inner enclosure, rampart, moat and outer rampart, but varied and elaborated the details. A fortress could last intact only until the main body of its fortifications had been breached, and the result of a siege was thus in large part a question of which side could best hold out. He built ramparts of earth since large ones could be built more cheaply and easily and stone shattered dangerously. He extended the outworks as far as possible. He thus compelled the enemy to begin his siege operations at a distance,

Vauban brought fortification and siege warfare to a fine art. A model of Neuf Brisach

and multiplied the obstacles in his way so that the difficulties in gaining ground never ceased.

Vauban's geometrical skill and practical eye for ground enabled him to design fortifications in such a way that every face was flanked and supported by the works behind and beside it. The basic element in the design, multiplied and varied in scale, was an outward-pointing triangle with its inner side missing. The outward point made a difficult target for the enemy and forced him to concentrate his forces vulnerably, while each face was so angled that the area of wall between it and the face of the next salient could be covered by enfilade fire. This was the principle of the great bastions on every angle of the main polygon. The large bastions were interspersed with smaller ones along the curtain, close enough together for each to be able to cover the next with small-arms fire. Other triangles, widely varying in size, stood in a dry moat, projected farther forward, covering each other, and covered from behind. Repeated complexes of fortification of this type often extended 300 yards from the central rampart and made powerful obstacles to a siege.

Vauban was also a master of offensive siegecraft. Before his time the usual method of investment had been to approach the walls with zig-zag trenches until the guns were in range. Since the enemy could concentrate their fire on the sap-head, this was costly of life and ineffective. Vauban's innovation was the use of parallel trenches connected by zig-zags. The besiegers could now converge their fire against points in the defence, and more simultaneous separate assaults could be launched. He also introduced the use of ricochet fire, plunging shot over the first parapet to drop on to the defenders behind it. It was still the custom, once a breach had been made, to invite the defenders to surrender with the honours of war. If they did not, the place was stormed, and generally no quarter was given.

Vauban's methods of fortification and siege remained standard until the later nineteenth century, when the increasing range of artillery changed the problems of defence and attack. Fortifications of this type were not impossible to overcome, but a successful siege would always require time, intelligence and determination. By the end of the seventeenth century the intensive fortification of the French frontiers was slowing the pace of warfare, and the French strategy seemed to be successful. But in the War of the Spanish Succession the armies of the allied enemies of France were commanded by a man capable, when he was given the chance, of transcending the contemporary limitations of warfare. This man was Marlborough.

Marlborough had seen a wide range of professional service, including service as a colonel of infantry under Turenne in 1674–5. As a man he was difficult to get to know, and his private moral record has certain blemishes; but against this can be set his devoted care at all times for the men under his command, and the tireless service of his country. He was an equable man and unfailingly courteous and charming. He had a complete mastery of his profession, and while he saw the problems of the war in perspective as a whole, he also overlooked no essential detail, tactical or administrative.

This was a time when the art of command was meeting increased complications.

While the size of armies and the range of strategy continued to increase rapidly, the organization of the administrative machine did not keep pace. Furthermore, communications in Europe were slow and politics complex, so that a commander, particularly of an allied army, had many responsibilities as a diplomat. At the same time he had to deal with politicians in the home country. In the exercise of command, Winston Churchill, Marlborough's own descendant, has written of the dynamic sum of numerous constantly shifting forces which had continually to be comprehended: 'All the factors which are at work at the time; the numbers and quality of the troops and their morale, their weapons, their confidence in their leaders, the character of the country, the condition of the roads, time, and the weather: and behind these the politics of their states, the special interests which each army has to guard.'

Command was personal and direct; a commander-in-chief could survey his whole battle area, and transmitted his orders by a system of gallopers and orderlies. In battle, he sat his horse in the thick of the activity and often under fire, keeping in mind the position and fortunes of every unit on a four or five-mile front, studying the enemy, and adjusting his dispositions to the developing tactical situation.

Armies were cosmopolitan. Of the 40,000 men voted by Parliament as England's contribution to the allied force at the beginning of the war only 18,000 were British. In contrast to France, anti-military feeling was strong in England where, after the experience of the seventeenth century, a standing army was regarded as a threat to liberty. The English Parliament jealously scrutinized the ordering of the armies which it authorized, and recruitment was difficult. Even the glorious successes which her armies were to gain did not alter England's attitude. There was only very limited conscription, and its object was largely regarded as the provision of suitable employment for criminals and ne'er-do-wells. Regiments were raised and equipped by proprietary colonels after whom they were named, and normally consisted of a single battalion of 700 to 900 men. There was frequently a good deal of fraud in administration – as officers drew pay, provisions and equipment for non-existent troops while those which did exist were often cheated of their due. Indeed, in 1712 Marlborough's enemies in Parliament brought charges of peculation against him; but the charges were disproved.

The Bank of England had been founded in 1694, and in this respect the English and the Dutch were at an advantage over France in the war. The war provided a stimulus to financial development, as well as to diversification of trade and industry. It was not unduly destructive either, for the memories of the Thirty Years' War caused men to mitigate horror as much as possible. Some plundering took place, but there was very little systematic destruction. Discipline was strict; supply magazines were organized and careful attention was given to the provision of good quality equipment such as boots and warm uniforms. The army formed a very small proportion of the total population of a nation, and was divorced from it. G. M. Trevelyan wrote: 'Europe was too ill-organized and too poor to pay a heavy blood-tax, and her credit system was too primitive to draw large drafts on the wealth and happiness of future generations.'

This was a great period of cavalry, even although open battles were comparatively rare and commanders put their main trust in infantry. The French cavalry still clung to the remnant of the sixteenth century tradition of the caracole, relying on firearms as much as on the sword. But the English cavalry as trained by Marlborough perfected the tactics of Gustavus and Cromwell, being trained to charge in a line three deep, advancing at a 'full trot' rather than at a gallop, and using only the sword. At first the cavalrymen wore no body armour at all, but in 1707 Marlborough introduced a cuirass in front. Dragoons might charge as cavalry, or ride only to the scene of action and fight on foot as musketeers.

Two important changes had recently taken place in the equipment of infantry. Since 1650 the flint-lock musket had replaced the match-lock as the standard infantry weapon; it functioned better in wet weather and gave a higher rate of fire. Secondly, the bayonet had been developed. At first the knife was plugged in to the muzzle of the musket. The vital change came with the invention of the ring bayonet in 1678; this clipped on to the outside of the barrel, allowing the soldier still to fire his weapon. It was not long then before pikemen became redundant because the musketeer could now perform their function for himself. For the next hundred and fifty years infantry soldiers were to fight armed only with flint-lock muskets and bayonets, carrying leather pouches holding between 40 and 60 paper cartridges, and wearing no defensive body armour.

The new battalions, unencumbered with match and clumsy pikes, had a greater mobility than before. Mobility, and the reliance on firepower rather than shock, increased the possibility of good troops winning against numerical odds. Marlborough fully appreciated this, and he paid great attention in the six winter months outside the campaigning season to training his infantry in efficient marksmanship and volley firing by platoons. Regiments were drilled to form hollow squares when attacked by cavalry. Besides musketeers every regiment contained a company of grenadiers, who were selected for their physical qualities, and were to some extent storm troops. Linear formations were now normal, being designed to exploit the new firepower to its fullest extent. Linear tactics demanded courage, experience and practice: as extensions became wider in the face of the increased power of small-arms fire, so the soldier might be separated from his comrades; when this happens fear appears; hence the importance of discipline.

Marlborough furthered the integration of artillery with other arms begun by Gustavus. Colonel Blood's artillerymen performed outstanding services for him. The problems of ground which they surmounted in 1704 when marching through the Black Forest to the Danube and fighting among the marshes of Blenheim were formidable. At long range field artillery fired cannon balls, and at closer quarters grape shot. The heavy siege trains were distinct from the field artillery. Marlborough placed great value on the tactical use of field artillery.

In the War of the Spanish Succession Marlborough was Captain-General of the Confederate Armies of Britain, the Dutch United Provinces, Austria, Baden and other minor German powers. He faced a difficult strategic situation. France and Spain were united, able to operate on interior strategic lines, and in 1703 were

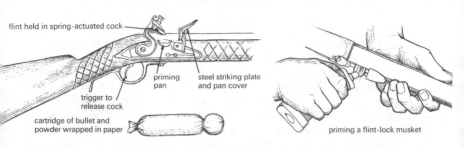

flint held in spring-actuated cock

priming pan

steel striking plate and pan cover

trigger to release cock

cartridge of bullet and powder wrapped in paper

priming a flint-lock musket

The area of Marlborough's campaigns *below*. During this period the flint-lock replaced the match-lock as a means of firing the musket *above*

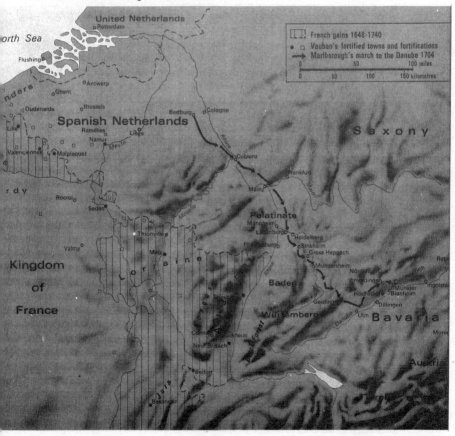

French gains 1648-1740
Vauban's fortified towns and fortifications
Marlborough's march to the Danube 1704

0   50   100 miles
0   50   100   150 kilometres

United Netherlands
Rotterdam
orth Sea
Flushing
nders
Ghent
Antwerp
Oudenarde
Brussels
Bedburg
Cologne
Spanish Netherlands
Lille
Ramillies
Liège
Rhine
Valenciennes
Namur
Meuse
Malplaquet
Saxony
Coblenz
rdy
Frankfurt
Rocroi
Main
Sedan
Mainz
Moselle
Palatinate
Mannheim
Ladenburg
Thionville
Heidelberg
Valmy
Metz
Philipsburg
Sinsheim
Gross Heppach
Mundelsheim
Kingdom
Nördlingen
Retr
of
smedingen
Münster
Ingolstadt
France
Baden
Höchstädt
Blenheim
Geislingen
Dillingen
Württemberg
Danube
Ulm
Bavaria
Strasbourg
Munich
Colmar
Gunzkheim
Neuf Brisach
Austria
Belfort
Jura
Besançon

Lorraine
Black Forest

joined by Bavaria. On the northern front France had possession of the great barrier of fortresses in the Spanish Netherlands, guarded by an army of 90,000 men. In the south the Spaniards were in Italy. In the east by 1703 there was nothing except their own disagreements to prevent the Bavarians and the French, under Villars, from marching on Vienna with overwhelming force.

The allies were split into two widely separated blocs, and disagreed over policy. Marlborough's first difficulty was with the Dutch who wanted to keep their army close to their own home country. Time and again his projects were vetoed. This handicap, combined with occasional lack of support from the British politicians, placed Marlborough at a disadvantage compared to the enemy commander-in-chief, Louis XIV, who had absolute authority and a centralized war-machine. The strategy adopted in the south was to send a military expedition to Spain, and a British fleet into the Mediterranean in order to command the seas around the theatre of war and confine the enemy to a land strategy. Gibraltar was captured in 1704. Marlborough himself in the Low Countries planned to draw the war farther east, in order to remove the immediate threat to the Dutch, to co-ordinate operations with the Austrians, and to attack France on her more vulnerable north-east corner. By 1703 Austria was in extreme danger. Marlborough decided to seek a decision with the French on the Danube, and thus defeat their threat against Austria.

The idea had everything to recommend it. Vienna was threatened from Ulm (on the Danube) by a combined Franco-Bavarian army of 45,000 men (soon to be brought up by reinforcements to 57,000) under the elector Max Emanuel and Marshal Marsin. It was vital to save Vienna, for if Austria were to be knocked out of the war the French would be able to concentrate their whole effort on the northern front. Since a defensive or slow moving war suited Louis XIV, in his powerfully entrenched central position, the allies must clearly take the offensive. But there were two practical difficulties. The Dutch politicians were immensely timid; and, secondly, if the allied armies were to reach the Danube they had to march across the French centre with their flank exposed. Marlborough's method of achieving his object was to act fast, and to deceive both friend and foe. He told the Dutch that his campaign was going to be on the Moselle and with the greatest reluctance they gave him a contingent. His true destination was a secret known only to a few top political figures. The Margrave Lewis of Baden promised his support, and from Vienna Prince Eugene set out to meet Marlborough.

The march of Marlborough's 40,000 men began in May 1704. Speed was the secret of success, and it was much aided by sending the heavy artillery and supplies by water. 'There were', as Trevelyan writes, 'two stages in the deception of Europe.' The first was as far as Coblenz, where the army was expected to turn up the Moselle, and enormous stores had been collected to give this impression. But when Coblenz was reached the army marched on south and the stores were sent after it up the Rhine. Even now its apparent destination was not the Danube, but Alsace. The reactions were immediate. Villeroi removed his army from the Netherlands, first to cover the Moselle, and then to join Marshal Tallard in the defence of Alsace.

Only on 3rd June did the secret come out; on that date the cavalry continued south-east towards the Danube.

This great march, of large numbers of men over long distances, was a fine example of administrative ability. Marlborough had worked at top speed since the early spring to make the diplomatic and administrative arrangements for his campaign. The permission and assistance of all the German rulers concerned had been assured. Bridges were all in good condition at the right points, and provisions were ready where they were needed. Credits had been arranged with German bankers, everything being paid for on the nail – with the result that the army was well received by the people of the country. New boots awaited the army on the threshold of Bavaria.

Mid-way between the Rhine and the Danube Marlborough was joined by Prince Eugene. A skilled tactician and a gallant leader, Eugene was probably at this time better known than Marlborough, since by his victory of Zenta in 1697 he had driven the Turks out of Hungary. He was to prove an ideal second string to Marlborough, for while he had great military skill and experience, and a welcome spirit of enterprise, he was ready to defer to the superiority of genius. A day or two later Marlborough was joined by a third commander, the Margrave Lewis of Baden – also an experienced soldier, but unenterprising and obstinate.

The strategy agreed was that Eugene should move to the Rhine to hold the armies of Villeroi and Tallard in play, while Marlborough and the Margrave advanced eastwards to make Bavaria change sides. Marlborough and Lewis were to exercise command over their combined army on alternate days – a curious plan; however there was a definite understanding that the prevailing direction of the campaign lay with Marlborough.

Eugene departed towards the Rhine and the main army went on its way. On 1st July, Marlborough with 70,000 men arrived at Amerdingen on the Danube, while Marsin and the elector were on the south bank ten miles farther upstream. Marlborough was now between his enemy and Vienna.

Marlborough had already made up his mind that his first move must be to capture Donauwörth, fifteen miles downstream to his east, because the possession of it would secure for him a new line of communications northwards into the friendly area of central Germany, as well as placing him astride the Danube, with a bridge into Bavaria. He had no time to lose. Tallard with his 60,000 men was on the point of advancing eastwards across the Rhine from Strasbourg, and Eugene with only 30,000 could not hold him. Even more urgently, Marsin had seen the crucial importance of Donauwörth; already on 30th June some 14,000 men had been sent ahead to hold the place, and the main army was ready to move. Marlborough had a ten-mile start over Marsin, and on 2nd July at dawn he set out eastwards to capture Donauwörth.

The troops had fifteen miles of appalling road to cover, and at the end of it formidable fortifications to storm. The key to Donauwörth was the Schellenberg, a high-domed fortified hill by the wall of the town. It was taken at the end of the day after an hour-and-a-half's very bloody fighting: men were 'slaying or tearing at the muzzles of guns and the bayonets which pierced their entrails'. The advance guard went straight into the assault on a steep and narrow front, forcing the defenders to concentrate at that spot while the remainder of the army moved round to attack from behind. It was a most costly victory, but Marlborough knew when the potential gains were big enough to be worth the casualties; he also knew that soldiers will accept casualties provided they win victories – though there are limits to the sacrifice of men's lives. Roads were now open where Marlborough wanted, behind and in front, and he was firmly placed between the French and Vienna.

The information of Tallard's crossing the Rhine was reported to Marlborough within two days of the event. It was urgently necessary to detach Max Emanuel from his alliance with the French, and to achieve this the allied army systematically devastated Bavaria in July. But the elector was prepared to let his people suffer for a while as he expected relief from Tallard, and this unpleasant war measure served no useful purpose. By early August Tallard had joined forces with Marsin and Max Emanuel, and on the 10th they set out northwards to cross the Danube at Dillingen. Tallard, the commander-in-chief, was intelligent and much respected, but was a diplomat rather than a professional soldier, and he did not have a really firm control over his army. On the 11th, Eugene, who had come east too, wrote to Marlborough from Münster outlining the situation. Marlborough hastened to rejoin Eugene: for three years he had desired the opportunity of meeting the French in full battle.

By 12th August the French and Bavarians were encamped at Blenheim, on the Danube some five miles upstream from Münster. They did not want a battle, nor did they expect the allies to seek one for their position was strong. Furthermore, as they knew, Lewis was away besieging Ingolstadt with 15,000 men. But in fact Marlborough had purposely disembarrassed himself of his slow colleague to give himself the freedom to fight. During that day Marlborough and Eugene surveyed the situation from the church tower of Tapfheim.

The two armies, French and Bavarian, were encamped on an open plain recently harvested, just behind a marshy stream called the Nebel which flowed into the Danube from the north. They were spread across a front of four miles: Tallard's own army was positioned in the two miles between the village of Blenheim on the bank of the Danube and the village of Oberglau, while between Oberglau and Lutzingen lay the army of Marsin and the elector. North of Lutzingen were wooded hills. With both flanks thus protected, the villages forming bastions, and the Nebel marsh in front of them, the armies were in a strong defensive position. They also had a superiority in artillery. Otherwise the opposing forces were more or less equally matched, each being between 50,000 and 60,000 strong.

It seemed to Marlborough and Eugene that the dispositions of the enemy armies were unsound. They were disposed separately, each with its cavalry on the wings, except that Tallard, having no room on his right because of the river, had placed all his cavalry on his left. This meant that the centre of the combined armies around Oberglau was predominantly composed of cavalry. It was admittedly perfect ground for a cavalry battle, but the relative dispositions of the French cavalry and infantry did not make sense. A second weakness in the French layout was that Tallard was about 1,000 yards back from the Nebel. Two basic tactical principles have always

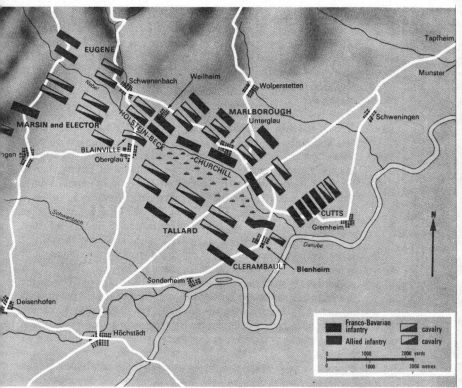

The battle of Blenheim

formed part of my military thinking: a force within striking distance of an enemy must be suitably disposed with regard to its battle positions, being ready *at all times* to fight quickly if surprised; secondly, an obstacle loses 50 per cent of its value if you stand back from it, allowing the enemy to reconnoitre the approaches and subsequently to cross without interference. (The first of these principles stood me in good stead at the Mareth Line in 1943 and on the Rhine in 1944, when rather than attack the British and Canadian armies under my command the Germans attacked the Americans who had left a gap between their forces of 100 miles across the Ardennes. As regards the second, during the withdrawal operation in Belgium back to Dunkirk in 1940. I always took the greatest care to ensure that the Germans were prevented by fire and patrols from reconnoitring closely the various river obstacles held by my division; as a result we had no difficulty in holding our positions until the time came to withdraw farther.)

But let us come back to Blenheim. Tallard's French army was within easy striking distance of the allied armies of two formidable generals, and he took no precautions against surprise. If he had pushed his leading troops forward to the river bank on 12th August, the bridging operations by Marlborough's army and the subsequent crossing would have been rendered very difficult. Marsin and the elector acted far more sensibly on the northern part of the front; they held the firm ground close to their edge of the marshy river, so as to destroy the enemy before they could form up after wading across.

Marlborough and Eugene noted all this and they decided to attack the enemy by surprise the next morning, 13th August. The advance of the allied armies began before dawn, and as the sun rose nine columns of soldiers debouched into the plain, and fanned gradually out into their battle formation. The Danish and Prussian infantry and the Austrian cavalry, all under the command of Eugene, moved northwards towards Lutzingen to form the right wing. The main force of British, Dutch, Hanoverians and Hessians, under Marlborough's command, advanced straight on down to the east bank of the Nebel. If Tallard had not expected an attack, by 7 o'clock he could no longer doubt that it was coming. Hastily the French aroused themselves to activity, their minds confused by the urgency of the crisis.

The surprise had been successful, and the enemy dispositions were found to be dictated, as Marlborough had hoped, by the positions of their tents. Blenheim was strongly defended by 27 battalions of infantry. Between Blenheim and Oberglau the French had 44 squadrons of cavalry in two lines, supported by 9 infantry battalions and 4 squadrons of dismounted dragoons. Oberglau was defended by 32 cavalry squadrons and 14 infantry battalions. On the left there were 32 cavalry squadrons and 17 infantry battalions, and then at Lutzingen 51 cavalry squadrons and 12 infantry battalions.

While Eugene's columns made their way over the wooded and broken ground towards Lutzingen, Marlborough watched the Franco-Bavarian dispositions unfold. The enemy's right was particularly strong, with great strength deployed in the two villages of Oberglau and Blenheim. While Eugene was to engage the enemy vigorously in the north and turn that end of their line if possible, the decisive part of the battle was clearly to be fought out between Marlborough and Tallard farther south. Marlborough expected Tallard to dispute his crossing of the Nebel and he deployed for attack accordingly in an unusual formation of four lines. In front, 17 battalions of infantry were to cross the Nebel and gain the west bank; behind them, two lines of cavalry, the first of 36 squadrons and the second of 35, were to make the main assault; the last line of 11 battalions of infantry were to wait east of the Nebel to cover a possible cavalry withdrawal. At the outset of the battle the chief effort of the attack was to be made against the two villages. This would surprise the enemy, in the same way as the attack against the strongest part of the Schellenberg had done; and if the garrisons of the villages could be contained, they would be unable to counter-attack in flank the advance of the cavalry to break the centre of the Franco-Bavarian line.

The first action, at 10 o'clock, was the advance of Lord Cutts's column of infantry over the Nebel opposite Blenheim, where the banks of the stream were comparatively firm. But the main attack could not begin until the right, under Eugene, was in position. For four hours, until noon, an artillery duel was carried on causing considerable casualties, while the allied sappers worked to produce six passable bridges over the stream, and prayers were held among the men. Marlborough inspected the lines, and at one point was hidden from view by the dust of a cannon ball falling near him. The sun was hot, and all waited tensely. At last, shortly after noon, Eugene was ready, and Marlborough ordered the attack forward.

On the left the first of Cutts's brigades moved forward against Blenheim, with orders not to fire until they reached the French palisades. A third of them were destroyed by a French volley from 30 paces, but two more brigades reinforced the attack. The Marquis de Clérambault, in command of the French in Blenheim, had already called up 7 battalions to support his first 9. The fighting went on, as bloody as it had been at the Schellenberg, and with as good effect. Then Clérambault lost his head, and called in his last reserve of 11 battalions. The allies continued to assault, but could not penetrate into the village. Nonetheless they were carrying out their appointed function – of containing the enemy. With the 12,000 additional soldiers who had joined the original garrison, the French were so congested in the village that freedom of movement was impossible. Marlborough ordered that the enemy forces in Blenheim were to be held there, so that they would be unable to take part in the battle elsewhere.

While this was done on the left with hard fighting all day, Eugene was playing a comparable part on a broader front on the right. The whole day long he fought his fierce containing action between Oberglau and Lutzingen, at the same time watching the primary battle farther south, ready if necessary to feed into that area any troops which Marlborough might need – even though he himself could ill spare them.

The decisive developments were taking place in the centre, at Oberglau and south of that village. Marlborough himself commanded here, keeping an eye on the events at Blenheim but concentrating his attention on the centre. He was excellently served by his subordinate commanders, notably Lord Orkney, and his own brother, Charles Churchill. Tallard, by contrast, moved to and fro to the different parts of the battle front, without being fully in control anywhere, and not really comprehending what was going on.

It was now clear that Tallard had made a serious mistake at the very outset of the battle in allowing his enemy's first lines of infantry and cavalry in the centre to cross the Nebel unmolested except by artillery fire. He did not launch a cavalry charge until the allied troops had formed up on his side of the stream; and though the fighting was hard they were not driven back. Indeed, more troops then crossed and the allies began to gain ground, with their superior numbers and better tactics – infantry and cavalry working in a close combination developed in previous training. The cavalry charged in front; the infantry were in reserve behind them, drawn up with spaces in their lines through which the cavalry might withdraw to re-form for the next charge, while they poured volleys by platoons into the oncoming enemy horsemen. Practised in the use of their bayonets, these infantrymen could also stand up to cavalry at close quarters very successfully. The French infantry in this part of the battle were 9 battalions of young recruits who, as Trevelyan says, 'knew nothing of battles except how to die at their post'.

The high point of the battle came when, in the early afternoon, 10 battalions of allied infantry under the Prince of Holstein-Beck advanced to storm the village of Oberglau. Nine defending French and Irish infantry battalions commanded by the Marquis de Blainville made a desperate counter-attack from the village and drove their assailants back to the Nebel. The right flank of Marlborough's centre was suddenly open to attack, and his army in danger of being split. Marsin, spotting this, immediately gathered a force of cavalry near Oberglau. Marlborough, seeing the danger, sent an urgent call to Eugene for a cavalry reinforcement. As Marsin's men began their charge down towards the Nebel, the cavalry brigade duly sent by Eugene came up in the nick of time to hit them in flank and turn them away. Holstein-Beck's infantry now rallied, and returning to the attack forced their opponents back into Oberglau and penned them there. The allies now had the winning of the battle in their hands. Large numbers of the enemy were bottled up in Blenheim and in Oberglau, the enemy's left was held by Eugene, and it now only remained for the allies to concentrate overwhelming strength in the centre to gain a complete victory.

But Marlborough bided his time, holding the situation in the centre so as to let his men get their breath, reorganizing the tactics of the whole battle front, and drawing up his formation for the decisive blow. Eugene still had a lot of hard work to do on the right, but soon after 4 o'clock his men were working round and beyond Lutzingen. Meanwhile Marlborough had brought the last of his troops across the Nebel, and on the front between Blenheim and Oberglau he drew up first two lines of cavalry totalling 90 squadrons, and then 23 battalions of infantry in another two lines. In front of him Tallard had only 60 squadrons at the most and 9 battalions. When at last he realized Marlborough's tactics he brought up his infantry and sent them forward to the south of Oberglau to block the attack. Marlborough, not yet having completed the deployment of his cavalry, sent 3 battalions and some artillery against them. Momentarily the French infantry had the better of the encounter; but their cavalry did not charge to use the advantage. At 5.30 o'clock Marlborough was ready. Almost the last of the 9 brave French battalions were blasted out of the way by the artillery, and the allied cavalry launched their charge.

From the higher ground at Lutzingen the combatants of both sides could see the scene on the plain. As the allied cavalry moved forward in a great line, thigh to thigh at a medium trot but gathering pace, the French cavalry came forward to meet them. Even had they not been outnumbered they would have been beaten, for their charge was a dash of individual squadrons pausing at the last moment to fire their *fusils*. As the French paused the allied cavalry increased their speed, hitting their opponents with all the shock of speed and combined weight, relying on the sword to kill. Such gaps as appeared in the allied front line were instantly filled from behind. The French were borne back, at a speed which soon rose to the gallop of flight.

The fugitives from the French centre were driven to the Danube, being hurled over precipices and into marshes. Marshal Tallard, dutifully making his way to Blenheim, was captured and brought to the allied commander-in-chief. Marlborough at that moment scribbled a note from the saddle, on the back of 'a bill of tavern expenses', to his wife Sarah: 'I have not time to say more, but to beg you will give my duty to the Queen, and let her know Her Army has had a Glorious Victory. Monsr. Tallard and two other Generals are in my coach and I am following the rest.'

At the moment when the French centre had broken, Lord Orkney had wheeled off his English and Scots, and joined Cutts and Churchill in the investment of Blenheim, sealing the village round to the banks of the Danube. Clérambault panicked and leaped into the river, being drowned, and at 9 o'clock in the evening the French officers in Blenheim capitulated. The 9,000 unwounded troops of the enemy in the village were gathered in. Oberglau had already been deluged in the great advance. Seeing what was passing, Marsin and the elector, themselves far from beaten yet, had by 7 o'clock begun an orderly retreat westwards. They were not pursued; Marlborough had no reserves, it was almost nightfall, and he had to deal with many prisoners. His army itself had lost about 4,500 killed and 7,500 wounded, or 20 per cent of its strength. The French losses were about 40,000, including 14,000 prisoners, and 60 guns.

The campaign to the Danube and the battle of Blenheim were profoundly decisive in their consequences. At the beginning of 1704 Louis XIV had been within an ace of achieving his ambition to dominate Europe; Spain, the Spanish Netherlands and Italy were in his pocket, and Austria seemed doomed. But after 1704

Marlborough's army broke into the French entrenchments at Malplaquet

he stayed on the defensive, knowing that his army was now outclassed and his economy exhausted – and seeking only an honourable peace to preserve his frontiers. Marlborough had dispelled a shadow which had hung over Europe for more than forty years. British soldiers, for the previous two and a half centuries almost unknown on the Continent, had now gained their reputation as the best in the world.

But the war was not yet over. From 1705 to 1711 Marlborough had to fight in the Low Countries. Battles were hard to bring about, although he won three more great victories, at Ramillies (1706), Oudenarde (1708) and Malplaquet (1709). In 1708 he proposed to follow up his victory of Oudenarde with a direct advance on Paris, but the other generals would not have it and insisted on besieging Lille. But even in this uncongenial warfare of sieges and small manoeuvres Marlborough's genius excelled, in the economy of his manoeuvres to anticipate and parry the enemy's next move. In 1711 he was relieved of his command for political reasons.

There are two lesser commanders of the War of the Spanish Succession who are also worth noting. The first is the Earl of Peterborough, commander of the British expedition to Spain in 1705. His dramatic successes, achieved with a handful of troops, were due to boldness and effrontery, fertility in stratagem, and the prodigiously bad generalship of the other side. Peterborough captured Valencia without firing a shot, having induced Las Torres, the Spanish general, with 7,000 men to retreat for a month before a force which never numbered more than 1,300 and at one point was as little as 150 men: Las Torres was allowed to 'capture' certain officers who 'warned' him of the imminence of Peterborough's huge army.

A more important figure is Marshal Villars. It was he who placed Vienna in peril by his victories at Friedlingen in 1702 and Höchstädt in 1703. Villars, however, was a professional soldier rather than a courtier, and his hot temper and bluntness endeared him more to his men than to his political masters. For some time he was forced into obscurity. But from 1709 he held the major command on the northern front. He could not actually get the better of Marlborough, but he put up a very strong defence. He was audacious and willing to fight battles, yet cautious to the right degree. In 1709, when his army was the last French line of defence before Paris and considerably outnumbered, and although he was badly wounded in the battle himself, he managed to make Malplaquet a Pyrrhic victory for Marlborough and the allies. In 1710 and 1711 he continued to hold off the enemy by his *Ne Plus Ultra* line of earthworks across from the coast of Picardy to Namur. When Marlborough had departed from the scene Villars definitely got the better of Eugene in 1712, defeating him at the battle of Denain and pushing the allies back. Having lost every campaign of the war, the French thus won the last. Thanks to the holding power of Vauban's fortifications and to the generalship of Villars, France secured very reasonable terms at the final Treaty of Utrecht in 1713.

Besides the War of the Spanish Succession Europe had to endure the Great Northern War (1700–21) between Sweden and Russia. The Muscovite state was bound to expand, if only to find defensible frontiers, and this was not its first clash with Sweden, the great power of the north.

Charles XII of Sweden was heir to the military tradition of Gustavus Adolphus. He loved war with all its rigours and perils and, having great powers of endurance, was willing to perform himself all the unreasonable feats he demanded of his soldiers. But he was so unwise as to engage in war with Russia. Peter the Great adopted the time-honoured strategy of evading battle and luring his enemy on into the vast open spaces of Russia, bringing him up against the problems of distance, climate, devastation and the harrying of lengthy communications. Charles violated most of the principles of generalship. The winter of 1708–9 was exceptionally severe and the Swedish army suffered terribly. The final disaster came in 1709 when the Swedes were besieging Poltava in the Ukraine; Peter closed in on them with a greatly superior force; Charles himself was wounded and fled south to the protection of the Turks, and his army surrendered. Later he returned to Sweden, and he went on fighting until he was killed in 1718. The Great Northern War ended in 1721 with the Treaty of Nystadt; this marked the eclipse of Sweden, and the emergence of Russia as a new great power in Europe.

So much for Charles XII. Some writers have considered him to be one of the great captains, because of his leadership and victories in the field. I do not agree. The credit for the most spectacular of the Swedish victories in the war, Narva in 1700, belongs more to General Rehnskjöld who designed the attack than to Charles. Charles never had any clearly defined strategy, and he underestimated the Russians – as both Napoleon and Hitler were to do later. His attitude to politics was irresponsible, to say the least; he had little regard for the lives of his soldiers; and he brought Sweden to the brink of ruin.

The Swedish army defeated the Russians at the Dvina in 1701

14 European War in the Eighteenth Century

The competition for empire between Britain and France in the eighteenth century was predominantly a question of naval strategy and economic warfare – for the first time on a world scale. The Treaty of Utrecht in 1713 ended the French attempt to dominate Europe, but left wide open the other great source of friction, the question of trade and colonies. The years between 1713 and 1739 were years of general expansion in ships, trade and bases. Tension steadily arose in certain key areas: the Mediterranean, West Africa, North America and India. A succession of incidents led to the first outbreak of war, the war of Jenkins' Ear (1739–44) in the Caribbean, which merged with the wider War of the Austrian Succession (1740–8). After a pause to gather strength the struggle was reopened in the Seven Years' War (1756–63); and again carried on in the War of American Independence (1775–83). William Pitt recognized the advent of the era of world war, when he spoke of 'winning Canada on the banks of the Elbe' – literally by using his Prussian ally to divert so many French troops that the French were weak in America.

France had a population in the eighteenth century of around 20 million, whereas England's was only five, but the advantage of Britain's geographical position outweighed this numerical disadvantage in the oceanic struggle. France had always to give her primary diplomatic and military attention to Europe. Britain, on the other hand, could be content in that theatre with subsidizing diversionary allies – Austria and then Prussia. Marlborough's army was allowed to decline, only small forces being sent to the Continent – where often they played an undistinguished part. The navy was the chief strength of Britain in the eighteenth century.

As so often happens in years of peace, Britain's navy had been allowed to fall into bad condition before 1739. In that year only 80 fighting ships were fit for service, and of these not more than 35 were actually in commission. The French had 51 warships, which had all been constructed fairly recently; an English expert wrote 'it is pretty apparent our 70-gun ships are little superior to their ships of 52 guns'. There was little progress in ship design in the eighteenth century, except for the introduction in 1761 of copper sheathing for the ship's bottom to increase speed and sea-endurance. The frigate was introduced in this period as a fast cruiser.

The French aimed to avoid battle while protecting their commerce and extending their colonial possessions on land. In contrast, British strategy was offensive, aimed at cutting the enemy's communications and destroying his fleet at sea. Tactically both sides adhered to the line-ahead formation, and the British Admiralty's 'Permanent Fighting Instructions' actually laid down that no ship should in any circumstances break the line to seek a *mêlée* with the enemy. The rigid tactics of the line, however,

Colonial expansion led to an increase in sea warfare between the great powers.
The escort of a Spanish treasure ship intercepted by an English squadron in 1708

precluded the possibility of a decisive victory, and British naval victories between 1692 and 1782 were won by men who dared to ignore the official rule, and broke the line to hunt down and destroy the enemy.

In 1739 the French and British naval personnel seemed about equally bad in quality. The high command in both navies was vitiated by the system of purchasing commissions and by appointments through social influence. The crews were largely recruited by press-gangs; the best men were those stolen from the merchant navy. Dr Johnson considered that a man who would voluntarily go to sea would as voluntarily go to hell. However, when the test of war came British sailors proved to be better than the French or Spaniards. In 1739 Admiral Edward Vernon captured the castle and harbour of Porto Bello on the Panama isthmus in a fine amphibious operation. And between 1740 and 1744 Commodore George Anson made his great voyage. Anson was sent in 1740 with a squadron of six ships to harry the Spaniards in America and the South Seas. By his powers of leadership Anson surmounted the handicaps of poor quality men and equipment, and eventually returned with only one ship, but the richest prize cargo in history. This voyage was the training ground of several sailors of future fame. In 1747 Anson commanded at the first battle off Cape Finisterre, when he gained a victory by breaking his line at the right moment. His strategic conception was to destroy the enemy at sea as well as blockade his main ports.

From 1745 until his death in 1762 Lord Anson was at the Admiralty. He introduced important reforms and under his guidance the British navy emerged from its decayed state. The dockyards were reorganized, and the conditions of the ships improved – their number being raised to 100, almost double that of France and equal to the strength of the combined navies of France and Spain. The recruitment of seamen was assisted by the introduction of bounties, and discipline was tightened. Corruption was to a great extent removed, and numerous able young men were given the chance to rise to the top of the service.

When the Seven Years' War began in 1756 Britain was thus strongly placed against France at sea. Yet because of ministerial bungling the first developments of the war were disastrous for Britain. Minorca was lost by a weak British fleet, and a scapegoat was made in Admiral Byng, who was tried by court-martial and shot – it was suggested by Voltaire 'pour encourager les autres'. The real encouragement to Britain came, however, with the accession to power in 1756 of William Pitt (later Earl of Chatham), a great war leader and statesman. Like Churchill, Pitt came to power at a dark hour in England's history, and like Churchill he rallied and led the British people by his superb oratory. He saw that Britain's true interest in this war lay in commercial empire. The chief importance to England of the war in Europe was that it might divert France's attention and resources from the war in the rest of the world, and to this end Pitt subsidized Prussia with money but gave the minimum of direct military intervention. Thus Britain's strength was saved, and her great effort could then be made in India and North America.

The English colonies in North America were confined to a narrow north-south strip between the Alleghany Mountains and the Atlantic. To the north the French had Canada and to the south Louisiana. It was their aim to occupy the valleys of the Ohio and the Mississippi in order to connect their colonies and prevent English expansion to the west. The British sought to upset this strategy by cutting the Atlantic communications of the French, and by forcing their way westwards. Pitt decided in 1757 to conquer Canada. The French navy was as far as possible put out of the war by the blockades of Brest and Toulon, and by raids all along the French Atlantic coast. Louisburg fell to a first-rate inter-service operation in 1758. In 1759 the whole British effort was concentrated on the advance up the St Lawrence towards Quebec, and the command was entrusted to Major-General James Wolfe, aged thirty-two.

Wolfe had first seen active service at the age of 16 at the battle of Dettingen, and at twenty-three he had commanded the Lancashire Fusiliers. He was a dedicated soldier, though he was also cultivated in other fields. Although loyal to his superiors and deeply patriotic, he was inclined to be outspoken and critical. Fortunately he was generally right, and, equally fortunately, Pitt was sensible enough not to allow his advance to be blocked by resentful senior officers.

The capture of Quebec in 1759 ranks among the most brilliant amphibious operations in history. Not the least brilliant part of it was the first passage of the fleet, commanded by Charles Saunders, through the currents and shoals of the St Lawrence. At the end of June, Wolfe and 9,000 soldiers disembarked on the south side of the river. Quebec was opposite them on the Heights of Abraham, defended above and below by 16,000 men and with powerful artillery support. Wolfe's great assets were command of the river and hence the possibility of surprise. The French sat tight. For weeks Wolfe looked for a way of taking Quebec which should not be obviously suicidal, and by the end of July he began to despair. His personal health was extremely bad. In August he received a reinforcement of 1,200 men, and at the beginning of September he decided to risk an attack by a small, winding path which climbed the cliffs a mile and half up-river from Quebec, and which seemed so inaccessible that the French had defended it only by a small piquet. On the night of 12th–13th September the army was floated across the river and made a surprise landing; at dawn it appeared on top of the Heights. The battle, and the fate of

The musket with socket bayonet replaced the pike to give the infantryman a double-purpose weapon

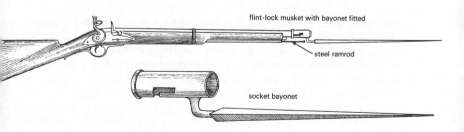

flint-lock musket with bayonet fitted

steel ramrod

socket bayonet

Canada, was decided briefly by one perfectly timed volley. Wolfe himself was killed.

The student of war and of human nature will find much of value in Wolfe's early years of striving and preparation to fit himself for the opportunity whenever it might come. When it did come he was ready. Like Nelson he proved that a great spirit can be found in a frail body.

The capture of Quebec was only one aspect of the success of British arms in 1759. In that year Pitt's strategy bore fruit not only in the conquest of Canada but in a series of victories all over the world. At Minden in Europe the English infantry contributed to an allied victory. Boscawen defeated the French Toulon fleet at Lagos and Hawke shattered the Brest fleet at Quiberon Bay. Guadeloupe in the West Indies and Goree in West Africa were taken. Early in 1760 the battle of Wandewash dealt a heavy blow to the French position in India. The rest of the war until 1763 was, from England's point of view, a mopping up operation, and the exclusion from office of Pitt in 1761 made no difference. By the Peace of Paris in 1763 almost all the English gains of the war were confirmed, and Britain emerged as the leading imperial power of the world.

Britain, as usual after winning a great war, then neglected her military and naval strength. Her conduct of the War of American Independence (1775–83) is in marked contrast to the record of the Seven Years' War. It was above all the complete lack of good military and political leadership which prevented England from quickly crushing what began as a thinly supported revolt. It is a nice point which were the worse equipped and worse led: the American troops or the British. However, George Washington matured as a leader although he was never a remarkable soldier, and the Americans adapted themselves better to fighting in the type of country involved. Whereas the British troops fought in red coats and drill formations, the Americans camouflaged themselves in green and fought largely as irregulars. The decisive factor in the war was the intervention against England in 1778 of France, followed by Spain and the Dutch United Provinces. The reconstructed French navy with its allied fleets could not be contained by the British navy. The war was now another world war, and Britain was desperately pressed to preserve her far flung colonial possessions. With his sea communications cut and Washington's large army behind him, General Cornwallis in command of the main British force in America was compelled to surrender at Yorktown in 1781. England was fortunate that by the Treaty of Versailles she lost little more than her American colonies.

The eighteenth century was the age of reason and complacency which fell between the religious fanaticism of the seventeenth century and the nationalist fanaticism of the nineteenth. Most wars in Europe were fought for dynastic reasons, and their objectives were thus limited. The conduct of war was restricted by convention, and the strategical and tactical emphasis was on manoeuvre and the avoidance of overmuch fighting – not on seeking out the enemy to destroy him. Siege warfare took up a great deal of time. Armies, growing ever larger, were immobile and expensive. As far as possible war was prevented from affecting civil life. Armies were recruited

An Anglo-Dutch naval engagement. A detail from 'The Four Days' Fight, 1666' by Abraham Storck

from nobles and vagabonds, the only willing and available classes, and nationality made little difference to allegiance. Hard training, and discipline and rigid rules, were necessary to instil just a minimum of competence and to prevent desertion. The officer corps was permeated by corruption and indolence, and was separated from the men by the gulf of snobbery and incompetence. With such limitations eighteenth-century war was, on the whole, mediocre. It was not, however, impossible for genius to achieve something in these conditions, as the careers of Maurice de Saxe and Frederick the Great amply demonstrate.

Saxe, having served under Eugene and Peter the Great, made his first reputation by his surprise night attack and capture of Prague, and became the leading French commander in the War of the Austrian Succession (1740–8). In 1745, though so ill that he was unable to mount his horse, he won his most famous victory, over the British at Fontenoy. He should chiefly be remembered for a remarkable work on the the art of war published in 1757 seven years after his death – *Mes Rêveries*.

In *Mes Rêveries* Saxe exposed almost every one of the weaknesses of eighteenth-century war. He condemned slavery to conventions, and above all immobility. He declared that too much time was wasted over the fortifications of cities, and that it was better to defend strong natural sites. He laid down that mobility, that is to say rapidity of movement, ease of manoeuvre and efficiency of supply, was the pre-condition of decisive success. His ideal army in the eighteenth century would consist of 46,000 men, for 'multitudes serve only to perplex and embarrass'. Such an army must be flexibly organized, on a legionary or divisional system, use being made of light-armed troops. The commander must create his opportunities and not wait for them to appear, he must concentrate strength against weakness, and he must pursue the enemy to destruction. Saxe clearly understood the factor of morale, and the delicate balance between the will to go forward and the instinct to go back. He urged that simple things could be great aids to morale: armour, music, badges, regimental tradition, national service, and promotion by merit. The fact that all these things are now commonplace, but were then extraordinary, testifies to the rare quality of Saxe's military mind.

In 1740 Frederick II, 'the Great', became king of Prussia. The background to Frederick's military achievements lies in the work of administrative and social organization carried out by two of his predecessors, the Great Elector Frederick William (1640–88) and King Frederick William I (1713–40). The original scattered lands of Brandenburg and Pomerania were economically poor and had no natural defences, and if the Hohenzollern rulers were to retain the strong political position left to them by the decline of the Habsburgs in the Thirty Years' War they must construct a strong state and an army. This was done. The Great Elector made himself absolute master of a single administrative machine, centred on the army supply organization, the *Kriegskommissariat*. This process was made possible by a bargain struck between the ruler and the nobles or 'junkers'. In 1653 the junkers gave the elector absolute power and the financial means to maintain a standing army, on the conditions that the officer corps should be their exclusive preserve and that the peasants on their estates should be reduced to serfdom. The middle classes east

The Duke of Marlborough gives orders to an aide-de-camp at the battle of Malplaquet. A tapestry at Blenheim Palace of the Elbe were too weak to oppose this. Such was the origin of Prussian absolutism and militarism.

The new Prussian army emerged to European significance with the victory against the Swedes at Fehrbellin in 1675. The Prussian state increased enormously in strength in the reign of Frederick William I, who doubled the budget and increased the size of the army from 38,000 to 80,000 men. Frederick II before his accession in 1740 had been more interested in French literature and flute playing than in battle drill, but as king he quickly became a hard realist.

Prussia's trump cards were her army and her king. Her population was only twelfth among the states of Europe, and although the nuclei of the regiments were conscripted from the provinces of Prussia the majority of the men in the army were raised abroad, if necessary by kidnapping. The first function of the Prussian bourgeoisie and peasantry was economic production. The officers in the army were mostly Prussians of noble birth, and Frederick relied on them more than on his men. Every junker family sent at least one son to the cadet school; the officers were inculcated with *esprit de corps* and patriotism as well as discipline, and were given a practical military education. Frederick considered that the best he could do with the men was to drill them until each man was a highly efficient automaton, 'more afraid of his officers than of the dangers to which he is exposed'. This ruthless military training had two valid objects. First, in an army composed largely of foreigners lacking in goodwill and morale, it was only compulsion which could produce discipline, alertness and cohesion. Secondly, Frederick knew that mobility was the key to victory in the conditions of the time, and that battle drill alone would produce it. The formations and evolutions of the parade ground were those of the battlefield. The chief weapon of the Prussian army was the bayonet-carrying musket of Marlborough's time.

In 1740 Frederick invaded the neighbouring Austrian territory of Silesia. His only excuse was that Silesia would be an invaluable economic and strategic acquisition. This aggression began the War of the Austrian Succession in Europe. The political implications rapidly widened, but Frederick kept his eye on his main objective. By the victories of Mollwitz (1741) and Hohenfriedberg (1745) Prussia held on to Silesia. Peace came in 1748. But it was no more than a truce, and in 1756 Prussia was again at war, subsidized by England but opposed by Austria, France, Russia and Saxony. This was the Seven Years' War (1756–63).

In this war Frederick was again his own commander-in-chief. In the formulation and execution of his strategy he had the immense asset of being absolute master of a highly efficient and militarily orientated government. Unlike his opponents he believed that the aim of strategy was the destruction of the forces of the enemy, not just the occupation or defence of a piece of territory. A resolute offensive on enemy soil would give Prussia the initiative and force the enemy commander to subordinate his movements to Frederick's. Besides, Frederick had so many enemies in this war that if he waited for them all to attack him in concert he was more likely than ever to be ruined. Having the advantages of interior lines his method was to move fast and strike hard at one enemy, and then move again quickly to face the next. Thus he opened the war himself by invading Saxony without a declaration, and then in 1757 he defeated the Austrians at Prague. But later in that year he was beaten by the Austrians with greatly superior numbers at Kolin, and then again by the Russians at Gross Jägersdorf. By the late autumn of 1757 the Prussians appeared to be doomed. But the quality of their government and army and the courage of their king kept them going. In November Frederick, still on the offensive, won a great victory over the combined Austrian and French army at Rossbach in Saxony, and in December he turned on the other Austrian force under Field-Marshal Daun and Charles of Lorraine and defeated them at Leuthen in Silesia.

Frederick's tactics as well as his strategy were always offensive because he believed that, given the initiative, his troops, being highly trained in the movements of battle and in the use of their weapons, could beat any number of the sluggish troops of his enemies. As a result of battle drill, he could write, 'a Prussian battalion is a moving battery . . . the rapidity in loading is such that it can triple the fire of all other troops. This gives to the Prussians a superiority of three to one.' Frederick used the 'oblique order' of battle a good deal, reminiscent of the method of Epaminondas. Its success depended on mobility, and he explained it as follows: 'You refuse one wing to the enemy and strengthen the one which is to attack. With the latter you do your utmost against one wing of the enemy which you take in flank. An army of 100,000 men taken in flank may be beaten by 30,000 in a very short time . . . The advantages of this arrangement are (1) a small force can engage one much stronger than itself; (2) it attacks an enemy at a decisive point; (3) if you are beaten, it is only part of your army, and you have the other three-fourths which are still fresh to cover your retreat.'

In practically all of his battles Frederick was outnumbered, and the odds at Leuthen were stacked heavily against Frederick's army. The Austrian army of Daun and Charles of Lorraine consisted of 84 battalions of infantry, 144 squadrons of cavalry and 210 guns: in all between 60,000 and 80,000 men. Frederick had only 36,000 men: 24,000 infantry in 48 battalions, 12,000 cavalry in 128 squadrons, and 167 guns. But when in early December he arrived in the enemy's vicinity in Silesia, country he knew well, he was determined to seek battle. On 4th December the Austrians took up a position in two lines in front of the Schweidnitz stream, on a five and a half mile front stretching from the bogs of Nippern in the north through the village of Leuthen, and thence south to Sagschütz. It was a strong defensive position, although somewhat long.

At 5 o'clock in the morning on 5th December 1757 Frederick advanced from the west straight along the Breslau road. His plan was to feint at the Austrian right but in fact to refuse his own left, and then march across the enemy's long front and hit him with great force on his left flank. The Prussian advance guard under his own command, 10 battalions and 60 squadrons, made contact with the enemy at the village of Borne in a dawn mist. The Prussians attacked straightaway, uncertain whether they were fighting the enemy's advance troops or his right wing. It turned out to be an advance formation of five regiments, which were rapidly scattered. Borne was captured, and from the village as the day dawned Frederick could see the

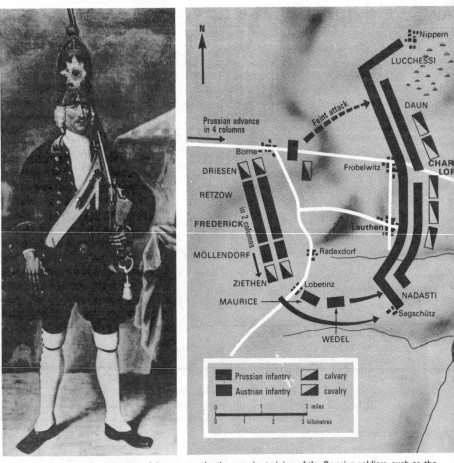

The battle of Leuthen *right* was won by the superior training of the Prussian soldiers, such as the famous regiment of exceptionally tall guardsmen *left*

whole line of the enemy's dispositions. The ground, sloping down behind Borne, concealed from the Austrians the advance of the four main Prussian columns.

As his main army came up, Frederick sent the advance guard to pursue the first Austrian fugitives and to feint at the enemy's right wing. The Austrian commander there, Lucchessi, thinking that he was about to receive a full attack, called urgently for help from his left. Daun sent him the reserve cavalry and some of the cavalry from the left. The preliminaries having been so successful, Frederick now put the main part of his plan into operation. Forming the four columns into two, he wheeled them away southward to the right, still covered from view by the lie of the ground. One who was present described this manoeuvre of the Prussian army: 'It was impossible to witness a more beautiful sight; all the heads of the columns were parallel to each other, and in exact distances to form line, and the divisions marched with such precision, that they seemed to be at a review.'

The Austrian commanders had expected a direct frontal assault, and when this did not happen they came to the conclusion that the Prussian army had decided not to attack. Suddenly they were disillusioned; the heads of the Prussian columns became visible, marching round towards their left flank, between Lobetinz and Sagschütz. Nadasti, the commander of the Austrian left, sent desperately for help when, soon after midday, the Prussian van under Wedel, supported by a battery of 6 guns and followed by Prince Maurice of Dessau and 6 infantry battalions, stormed the defences of Sagschütz. Nadasti charged the first of the Prussian cavalry, 43 squadrons led by Ziethen, but after a swaying fight the Austrian left was routed. The field between Sagschütz and Leuthen was covered with fugitives pursued by the Prussian hussars, the infantry and artillery following behind.

Charles of Lorraine in the Austrian centre, much dismayed, recalled the forces he had sent to the right, and sent forward his infantry battalion by battalion to defend Leuthen. The defenders of the village were overcrowded and their dispositions chaotic; nevertheless they resisted the Prussian attack with the courage of desperation. Frederick had to throw in more troops than he wished at this juncture, but a fine charge by Möllendorf's guards at last carried the village.

The next advance of the Prussians northwards was still harder, for during the defence of Leuthen the Austrian right had had time to establish a battery on the ridge above the village, and under its fire their infantry formed up in a suitable direction at right angles to their original front. Frederick ordered forward his left column, the infantry under Retzow and the cavalry under Driesen, but the artillery fire blocked them. His counteraction was to organize his own artillery fire, including ten extra heavy guns, from an eminence slightly to the west of Leuthen, called the Butterberg. This artillery fire, supported by the charge of the Prussian troops, forced back the Austrian right.

By 4 o'clock in the afternoon the Austrians were giving way, and Lucchessi made his last effort. Retzow's infantry had been temporarily checked and Lucchessi prepared to launch his cavalry at their right flank. But Driesen's forty squadrons of cavalry were hidden behind the village of Radaxdorf. At that moment, under cover from the Butterberg, they rode out, and Lucchessi's remaining troops taken simultaneously on three sides were routed. The rest of the Austrian infantry were then similarly attacked from all angles. By the time it was dark the Austrian army was in headlong flight. On 6th December Frederick rested his army, and then he mopped up the remnants of the enemy in the nearby countryside. On 19th December Breslau surrendered, and the possession of Silesia by Prussia was secured.

Napoleon described Leuthen as 'a masterpiece of movements, manoeuvres, and resolution'. 'Alone,' he said, 'it is sufficient to immortalize Frederick, and place him in the rank of the greatest generals.' The war, however, lasted another five years, during which Prussia fought alone against odds greater than ever. At one stage in

1759 the Russians actually occupied Berlin. But by his indomitable courage, and by the further victories of Zorndorf (1758), Liegnitz (1760) and Torgau (1760), Frederick staved off defeat. In 1762 Russia changed sides, and at the Peace of Hubertusburg the next year Prussia retained Silesia – one of the largest enduring conquests ever made in Europe.

After the Seven Years' War the Prussian army, exhausted but complacent, maintained its established methods and traditions. In France, on the other hand, many were shocked at the events of the war, and some important rethinking and reorganization began.

Frederick's use of horse artillery had been a highly important innovation; this reflected the technical improvements in heavy guns which had been made in recent years as well as the new concern for mobility. An Englishman, Benjamin Robins, had proved that a smaller charge and a lighter gun could still project shot the same distance. Gribeauval, Inspector-General of the French artillery after 1765, applied this lesson, aiming to make artillery more mobile. Gun-carriages were also made to run more smoothly, and horses replaced bullocks. Thus on the march artillery could now keep pace with infantry and it was now more manoeuvrable in battle. Numbers of guns also increased as the new process of coke-smelting made available improved and cheaper iron guns. There was no comparable technical development in small arms, but infantry firepower was increased by drill.

These developments and the experience of the War of American Independence suggested departures from traditional eighteenth-century tactical ideas. In 1778, in his pamphlet *Sur l'usage de l'artillerie nouvelle*, Du Teil proposed a system of mobile artillery and infantry working together. The artillery was to begin the battle, opening fire at a range of 1,000 yards, and, from a flank, bombarding the length of the enemy line. There was considerable discussion regarding the right point of compromise between mobility and firepower, and this raised the question of concentration of force. Folard suggested that the line should be abandoned for parallel columns, which by concentrated attacks would penetrate the enemy line at varying points – the spaces between the columns being filled with light infantry. Column formations required a new battle drill, and Guibert's *Essai général de tactique* in 1772 set forth a system of simple basic movements by which troops could form quickly and without confusion from line to column and *vice versa*.

The new tactical principles of offence and mobility suggested a strategy of seeking battle. With improved firepower, holding operations could be performed by smaller numbers of troops. A commander could thus divide his main forces into separate offensive columns, a converging net of detachments, which, if they could move fast enough, should be able to trap an enemy and force him into battle. Guibert suggested that the enterprising general should ignore the fortresses which had obsessed so many eighteenth-century commanders, and march straight on the enemy's capital. The idea of such a strategy was made more realistic by the great improvement in communications during the second half of the eighteenth century, particularly roads and canals. Agriculture and industrial productivity were also increasing, and armies could once again expect to live off the country and dispense with cumbrous baggage-trains. These more ambitious and complicated strategical concepts, on the other hand, demanded an ever improving administrative organization in peace time.

Until the French revolutionary war began in 1792 these new military ideas remained debatable and untried. The French revolution broke down conservatism in every way, and particularly in the armed forces by purging the officer corps. At least two-thirds of the officers in the French army before the revolution had been nobles, which was itself an important cause of revolutionary discontent. But by 1794 five-sixths of the noble officers had left the army, and the upper ranks were thus opened to the ablest of the soldiery. As the revolution fired the French nation with democratic enthusiasm, the character of the whole army changed. The voluntarily recruited new National Guard became its core, and in due course the majority of all recruits were volunteers. The new and special quality of this voluntary, national army was that the soldiers in it followed their officers rather than being driven by them. War broke out in April 1792 between France and Austria and Prussia. For the people's crusade against despotism the French would rise voluntarily to arms.

In the early stages of the war the French had few successes. Their politics were chaotic, inflation was rampant, and the army lacked leaders, discipline, training and supplies. The first force sent against the enemy at Tournai and Liège turned tail and fled. But the French had courage, enthusiasm and the right ideas, and they quickly improved. The thinking of Gribeauval, Guibert and Du Teil had largely passed into the official drill-book issued to the army in 1791. The test between the new and the old came when the French army of Dumouriez faced the Prussians and Austrians at Valmy in north-eastern France in September 1792.

The commander of the Prusso-Austrian army, the Duke of Brunswick, was widely considered by soldiers of the old school to be the best general of the day, on the strength of his bloodless and successful manoeuvring campaign in 1787 in Holland. For almost a month the enemies manoeuvred against each other. The operations of the French were marked by impetuosity, disagreement, inefficiency, and sudden brief panics. The Prussian movements were extremely slow, subordinated to a useless supply system, and Brunswick missed at least three opportunities to get past or destroy his enemy. By 20th September, however, Dumouriez achieved a battle situation at Valmy more or less as he desired. Both armies were in some disorder. The battle of Valmy was in fact no more than a tremendous cannonade. After a morning's artillery duel Brunswick ordered his infantry to advance, but he soon withdrew them from the fire of the French batteries and in the afternoon broke off the battle before the fighting had ever really begun.

Valmy, though not a major battle, was a French victory, for Brunswick decided not to attempt to push on to Paris. The revolution gained a vital respite, and the success in checking the enemy was a factor of enormous psychological importance for the French. A second victory shortly afterwards at Jemappes added to the new confidence. By 1793 almost all the significant powers of Europe were ranged against the French. Their response was the Law of August 23, 1793, the declaration which announced the era of total war:

The young men shall fight; the married men shall forge weapons and transport supplies; the women will make tents and clothes and will serve in the hospitals; the children will make up old linen into lint; the old men will have themselves carried in to the public squares and rouse the courage of the fighting men, to preach hatred against kings and the unity of the Republic.

The public buildings shall be turned into barracks, the public squares into munition factories. All firearms of suitable calibre shall be turned over to the troops: the interior shall be policed with shot-guns and cold steel. All saddle horses shall be seized for the cavalry; all draft horses not employed in cultivation will draw the artillery and supply wagons.

At the battle of Valmy the French revolutionary army halted the advancing Prussians with a tremendous cannonade

15 The Era of Nelson, Napoleon and Wellington

Not content with driving their enemies out of France, the French, motivated by desire for national security and aggrandisement as well as by revolutionary idealism, carried their war into all Europe. The war continued from 1792 till 1815. During that period there were pauses and shifts of alliance, but the basic disposition of the fighting was that four countries, Britain, Austria, Prussia and Russia, in combinations of two or three at a time, formed a league against the French – Britain being the chief. All the strategy of the French, under their political and military leader Napoleon, on land and sea was ultimately concerned to defeat Britain. The warfare was notable more for individual genius than for systems or technical factors. Many brilliant individuals appeared, but in our study we shall concentrate on three of them: Nelson, Napoleon and Wellington.

In the war against her enemy across the Channel, Britain's main effort naturally began at sea – particularly since her navy was in much better condition than her army. Indeed, the British navy has rarely been better prepared. There were 55 ships of the line in good fighting trim, and corruption and inefficiency in the administration had been greatly reduced. By contrast the French navy, which in the American war had been a stiff rival to the British, by 1793 had never been less fit for war. The revolutionary purge had deprived it of its best elements, and mere enthusiasm and numbers, which were enough to carry the army through the time of crisis, were no substitute in the navy for well-maintained ships and trained seamen. The French had only 42 ships of the line and lacked competent officers.

The French used their navy to damage British shipping and to threaten invasion. British naval strategy in the war had various aspects. Besides the usual functions of her seapower – the protection of British shipping and damage to the enemy's, and the protection of her shores from invasion – Britain also attempted to use seapower to confer mobility on her army. Several overseas operations were thus conducted, in Flanders, in the West Indies, and on the coast of France. But since they were unsuccessful this policy was abandoned for the time being and the British concentrated on blockading the coast of France, in order to stifle French trade and to force into battle any French fleet which dared to leave harbour.

Between 1794 and 1805 the British navy won six major victories. This period thus contrasted with the previous two hundred years since the defeat of the Armada, when full-scale and decisive naval engagements had been rare. The old warship remained technically much the same, but now at last British sailors discovered the most effective way to use it. One reason for this was the outstanding ability of some

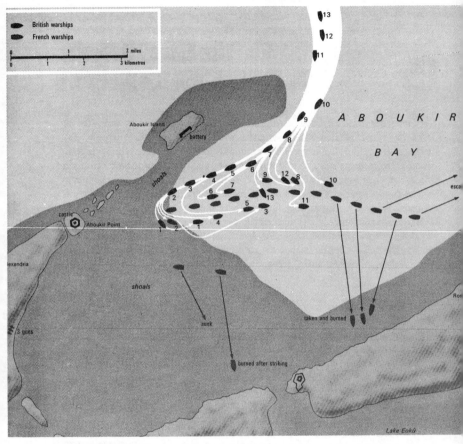

The battle of Aboukir Bay

of the British seamen, notably Howe and Nelson. A second reason was the introduction of a comprehensive signalling system, devised by Kempenfelt and Howe; this enabled commanders to progress from pre-set and rigid formations to more elaborate and flexible tactics. Once a commander's ships were locked in combat he could do no more; no signals could be seen through the smoke of battle and ships with broken spars and tattered sails could hardly respond even if a lull gave a glimpse of the flagship's masts. Howe or Nelson had a more difficult task than their successors; if their plans of approach had been faulty they could not remedy them by signal; we, in the days of oil fuel and wireless communications, are apt to forget how different conditions were in the days of sail.

The first British victory was won by Richard Howe on the 'Glorious First of June', 1794. Howe with 34 ships sighted the French with 25 far out in the Atlantic. He attacked on an entirely new principle – that of breaking the enemy line from windward. Having secured the windward position he was then able to choose his moment to bear down upon the enemy in an oblique formation, and cut their line at successive points; after this, each of the British ships engaged one of the enemy vessels at close quarters from leeward, the position which prevented the enemy escaping downwind. Howe's signalling system facilitated the perfect co-ordination of the fleet which his manoeuvre demanded. The battle of the First of June was a break-through in sailing tactics: Howe successfully combined the formal line approach with the ship-destroying *mêlée*. Six prizes were taken and one of the enemy ships was sunk. As a result of this action and of two lesser ones in 1795, the French conceded British dominance at sea and thereafter for the most part kept their fleets in port and on the defensive.

Nevertheless, by 1797 Britain's morale and war prospects were low. The French were completely successful on land in the Low Countries and Italy, and no British troops were left in Europe. Spain had joined France, and Britain was forced to evacuate the Mediterranean. In the winter of 1796–7 the French Brest fleet evaded the blockade, and was only prevented by storms from invading Ireland. Admiral Sir John Jervis retrieved the situation in February 1797 with his victory over the Spanish fleet off Cape St Vincent. But then came a moment of extreme danger for Britain, when mutiny broke out in the navy. The dissatisfaction among the seamen arose from injustices in recruitment, bad pay and savage discipline; their reasonable demands for better pay and treatment were met, though the press-gang and prisons continued to provide most naval conscripts. The mutinies were concealed from the enemy long enough for the blockade of the Texel not to be broken, and in October Admiral Duncan won the third major victory of the war off Camperdown repeating the new tactics of Howe.

Jervis, now Lord St Vincent, became First Lord of the Admiralty in 1801 and devoted himself to reforming the dockyards and making the administration simple and economical. He provided the essential basis of Britain's naval strength in this way until 1806. Jervis was a great naval officer, a fighter, strategist, leader and administrator. He was also a good judge of men, and it was he who first recognized and promoted Nelson.

Horatio Nelson was born in 1758 and joined the navy when he was thirteen; by 1793 he was a captain. In 1797 he took part in the Battle of Cape St Vincent. Jervis's plan in that battle was to cut through the enemy line and then turn about to attack before it could close again. Nelson's position in the British line was near the back, and he was able to see that the British van would be unable to tack back before the gap closed. Should he leave the line without orders, and attempt to prevent the junction? He decided to do so. He flung his ship alone into the gap, and the 74-gun *Captain* engaged seven of the enemy single-handed until the rest of the fleet came up. The result of Nelson's brilliant and brave decision was a complete victory.

Early in 1798 it was reported that Napoleon was preparing to launch an expedition from Toulon. After the successes of the previous year the British decided to return to the Mediterranean, and a squadron of 13 ships was sent there under the command of Nelson. Taking advantage of a storm, Napoleon with an army of about 35,000 and a fleet of 13 ships evaded Nelson and sailed to Egypt. Nelson discovered and bore down on the French fleet in Aboukir Bay late on the afternoon of 1st August.

Nelson decided to attack that very evening. All his captains were taken into his confidence; he could rely on their ability, and he wanted them to use their own initiative within his broad tactical scheme. The French line of 13 warships was anchored across the bay, its head so near the rocks and shoals off Aboukir Point that the admiral, Brueys, considered that nothing could pass between it and the shore. The British thought otherwise. As night was falling Captain Foley led four ships through the shoals to the French rear; Nelson remained outside with the rest of the fleet. The immobile French ships were simultaneously engaged from both sides; the French were completely confused in the darkness and could only wait to be attacked. At dawn only two French ships escaped: the enemy fleet had been sought out and destroyed. As a result of the victory a considerable number of French troops were trapped in the Levant and the Mediterranean became a British sea. The captures of Minorca (1798) and Malta (1800) reinforced this dominance.

Nelson's next action was at Copenhagen in 1801. Britain depended to a large extent for her naval stores and materials on Scandinavia. Realizing this and being dominant on land, Napoleon attempted to seal off Scandinavia to English shipping. An English expedition was sent to Copenhagen, with Sir Hyde Parker in command and Nelson his second. The enemy were caught ill-prepared, and Nelson persuaded Parker to let him lead a squadron of lighter-draught ships against the Danish fleet – which was lying at anchor and unrigged, but under the guns of the fort of Copenhagen. Finely judging tides and currents, Nelson sailed in and poured accurate gunfire into the enemy. At the height of the action Parker lost his nerve and signalled to Nelson to withdraw. Putting his telescope to his blind eye Nelson declared that he saw no signal, and coolly went on to take the surrender of the entire Danish fleet.

The military successes of the French on the Continent continued, but everything remained vitiated for them by the unsuppressed menace of British seapower. Between 1803 and 1805 Napoleon devised a succession of schemes for the invasion of England, and a large army was encamped at Boulogne. But he could not touch London unless he could be master of the Channel – for six hours, as he put it, though six days would have been more like the time required to conduct a full-scale invasion. By the summer of 1805 he had abandoned the hope of actually invading England, but he still saw the importance of breaking the British control of the seas, and he kept the naval part of his invasion plan. This was to try to break the blockades of both Toulon and Brest, and to converge the two fleets on the Channel fleet – a very unrealistic plan. The French Toulon fleet under Villeneuve did break out, and Nelson chased it and brought it to battle on 21st October at Trafalgar. The battle of Trafalgar was fought by the then established tactics of cutting the enemy line and turning on their ships in a *mêlée*. It was the most perfectly co-ordinated and

Nelson is shot down by a sharp-shooter in the French rigging at Trafalgar

thoroughly successful application of those tactics: 18 out of the enemy's 30 ships were captured or destroyed. In this type of fighting the sharp-shooting and broadsides of two ships engaged at the closest range inevitably caused a great deal of slaughter, and Nelson himself was killed in the battle. The secret of Nelson's strength was that he understood plain men and was, in turn, understood by them. He knew how to win the hearts of men. He seemed to have a magnetic influence over all who served with him; he led by love and example. There was nothing he would not do for those who served under him; there was nothing his captains and sailors would not dare for him. As an inspiring leader, a brilliant seaman, and a most original, intelligent and courageous fighter, Nelson's reputation is secure.

The consequence of Trafalgar was that Britain became totally dominant at sea, not only then but also for the rest of the nineteenth century, and her commerce was secured and increased. More immediately, with a sound backing of supplies and communication she was able at last to make a full contribution to the military effort of Europe against Napoleon, who was now confined to a land strategy: his final doom, in consequence, being certain.

In November 1792, two months after Valmy and Jemappes, the Convention of France declared that it would 'grant fraternity and aid to all peoples who wish to recover their liberty'. Thus the French declared war on Europe. The assets of France were a population of over 25 million (equal to the combined populations of Austria, Prussia and England), 730,000 muskets of the 1777 model, more than 2,000 pieces of artillery of Gribeauval's design, much confused mass enthusiasm, and a number of devoted and able leaders.

From 1792 to 1797 the most valuable of these leaders was Lazare Carnot, who saw that 'the popular frenzy must be organized'. An administrator of genius and willing to work sixteen hours a day, he tackled the major problems: the merging of the new citizen-soldiers with the old regulars into one national army; the training of officers, particularly in specialist arms; and the harnessing of industry and agriculture to war. The numbers under arms rose from 300,000 at the beginning of 1793 to over three quarters of a million in 1794. National Service was introduced in 1798 for all single men aged between twenty and twenty-five. The instruction of the army followed the new principles of Guibert and Du Teil, there were enough weapons, and the problem of supply was met by a system of living off the country. Carnot was also responsible for strategy in 1793–4, concerting the movements of twelve armies. It was his belief that 'it is the national characteristic of a Frenchman to attack all the time'. Full advantage was taken of French numbers and *élan*, and of the mobility which came from the absence of supply trains.

From March 1793 there was a continuous series of French victories. Relief turned to heroic exaltation. 'We marched', wrote Marmont long afterwards, 'surrounded by a kind of radiance whose warmth I can still feel as I did fifty years ago.' And a grenadier wrote: 'We suffered, but we were proud of our sufferings and tried to laugh at them. Our officers, with their packs on their backs, shared our meagre rations.' The tactics of this time were simple and costly of life, but well suited to numerically strong and enthusiastic troops commanded by young officers – of more energy and courage than experience or skill. A loose swarm of sharpshooters opened the attack; the artillery then prepared and covered the main advance; the infantry, formed in deep columns with their officers at their heads, dashed forward with fixed bayonets, shouting to keep up morale. A galaxy of brilliant commanders emerged, most of them in their twenties or thirties – Hoche, Jourdan, Augereau, Murat, Masséna, Napoleon and others. The career of Hoche is an epitome of these

Napoleon, at the height of his military career, receives the surrender of Ulm after an almost bloodless victory

times. Noticed early by Carnot, he won victories at Froeschwiller and Wissembourg following his maxim of 'prepare with caution, strike like lightning'. In 1797 he was commander of the famous Army of Sambre-et-Meuse, and pushed the Austrians back to Frankfurt. But in that year, aged twenty-nine, he died. The death of Hoche marked the end of the revolutionary era and the opening of the Napoleonic era.

Napoleon Bonaparte was born in Corsica in 1769. Between 1779 and 1785 he attended military colleges in France and after that he served as a lieutenant of artillery at Auxonne and Valence. He was a student of the writings of Du Teil, Gribeauval and Guibert. To the last named he was greatly indebted – for ideas on the military significance of nationalist feeling, on mobility, on column tactics, and many other matters. Napoleon was an enthusiastic student of military history, and a firm believer in the value of its study. He also supported the most radical party in the revolution. By 1796 he was in Paris, making the right friends and avoiding the wrong jobs.

In that year Napoleon was given command of the Army of Italy. He was then twenty-six. At the outset of his campaign he had 38,000 troops with which to face 47,000 Austrians and Sardinians; besides being inferior in numbers his army was also ill equipped, poorly clothed, hungry, unpaid and nearly mutinous. Within seven days sullen discontent was transformed into enthusiastic co-operation – Napoleon had given the army back its soul. Six weeks after the opening of hostilities the general could say to his soldiers without much exaggeration: 'You have won

Napoleon bolstered the morale of his troops by providing magnificent uniforms for the enthusiastic volunteers of the Revolutionary armies

Revolutionary infantryman   Revolutionary officer   Napoleonic grenadier

battles without guns, crossed rivers without bridges, made forced marches without boots, encamped often without food.'

A dozen victories in fact were to be won in twelve months, the most notable of which were Lodi, Castiglione, Bassano, Arcola and Rivoli. The Austrians were cleared out of central and northern Italy, and Napoleon marched within eighty miles of Vienna before peace negotiations began. The campaign was one of the most brilliant in all history. The elements in Napoleon's success were rapid marches, flexibility in manoeuvre, and the concentration of force at the enemy's weakest point. Unbroken victory raised French morale to fantastic heights, as well as turning Napoleon's head in no small way. At St Helena he recalled: 'It was only on the evening after Lodi that I realized I was a superior being and conceived the ambition of performing great things.'

The next phase in his career, the Egyptian expedition of 1798, fitted this mood. Strategically it made no sense, and any value in the victory of the Pyramids was offset by Nelson's victory of Aboukir Bay. In 1799 Napoleon deserted his army and hurried back to France, where by a political coup he was established as First Consul. This was to mean, in effect, that Napoleon Bonaparte was the military dictator of France. As Consul, he was in fact an extremely able and enlightened ruler. The defeat of the Austrians at Marengo and Hohenlinden in 1800 closed the war of the Second Coalition on the Continent, and in 1802 a truce was made with England.

Dragoon of the Imperial Guard   Officer of the Imperial Guard   Napoleonic hussar

Napoleon was a man of outstanding intellect, energy and willpower. He dominated all around him, and was totally self-centred. Caulaincourt, for ten years a close companion, said of him: 'He always applied all his means, all his faculties, all his attention to the action or discussion of the moment. Into everything he put passion.'

Napoleon was a master of strategy: the range, speed and co-ordination of his operations were unique. Since his armies lived off the country and roads were becoming good, he could move fast. He himself was a great builder of roads. He formulated his plans on the basis of information supplied by his staff, headed by Berthier. Information was kept up to date and immediately accessible on every relevant subject. Minute research preceded the organization of a campaign, and Napoleon himself issued the final orders on everything, even the length and route of the marches of each corps. Weapons, uniforms, supply, finances, and the administration of conquered territory all came under his scrutiny. He would dictate to several secretaries at a time, and go short of sleep for days on end. He regarded the long-term preparation and administration of a campaign as vitally important.

His strategy was always offensive. The campaigns of his early career in Italy were conducted in relatively small areas and with relatively small numbers. In Italy 35,000 men might be spread over a front of twenty miles, while Napoleon manoeuvred to concentrate superior strength at the weak point of the enemy's yet more extended front. Although continually outnumbered in the theatre of war, he seldom fought a battle without local superiority at the point of conflict. He always kept his eye on developments in neighbouring areas, and he planned his campaigns to unfold in such a way that the maximum political advantage could be seized immediately the actual fighting ended successfully – although his foreign minister Talleyrand felt that he exploited his victories too thoroughly to be diplomatic. After 1805 Napoleon developed a new strategical technique suitable for armies of 200,000 men and commensurate with the increased range of his political concerns. The army corps, a self-contained formation consisting of two or three divisions, had been introduced. Part of the secret of his success remained rapid and accurate movement. He would use a strong army corps as an advance-guard to pin down the enemy, while the other corps manoeuvred with precision to prise the enemy forces apart, outflank or encircle them, or deliver the final shattering blow.

Napoleon's tactics were also offensive, and long prepared. He did as much as possible in advance to determine the course of the battle, but he also had a perfect sense of timing in a fight. As he said, 'there is a moment in engagements when the least manoeuvre is decisive and gives victory; it is the one drop of water which makes the vessel run over'. His eye for ground was outstanding; Caulaincourt wrote that 'he seemed to extract men, horses and guns from the very bowels of the earth'.

Infantry was the chief arm of Napoleon's armies. In principle the infantry was deployed in *ordre mixte*, a formation of some battalions in line and some in column. The advantage of a line formation, which most other armies used exclusively, was that it produced the maximum firepower from the troops, whereas only the first two ranks or so of a column could use their muskets. But on the other hand inadequately trained troops would not fire steadily, and the psychological impact of massed troops in column was considerable. Columns had already proved their worth in the revolutionary wars. From the Italian campaigns onwards the French armies used the *ordre mixte* with great success, varying their tactical combinations according to the terrain and opposition. The basic pattern was that skirmishers harassed the enemy; then battalions in line formation contained them, weakening them to some extent and preventing them from concentrating; the column then broke through the disorganized and depleted enemy line.

The weapon of the infantry was the smooth-bored, muzzle-loading flint-lock of the eighteenth century. It was not very efficient since the flint had frequently to be replaced, the barrel became fouled by the coarse powder, and the powder itself was useless when damp. The most highly-trained soldiers could fire two rounds a minute. In fact, Napoleon bothered very little about developing the army's firepower by training. The ball would carry effectively not much more than 200 yards, at which range it was subject to an error of 9 feet. The more accurate rifle had been invented, but it was slow to operate and expensive, and therefore was little used.

Himself a gunner, Napoleon's most original contribution to tactics was in his use of artillery. He was fortunate in that now for the first time technological and industrial advance made it possible for a commander to use artillery lavishly. Hitherto artillery had merely been scattered along the front of a formation, to hamper the enemy troops as they formed up and to weaken their front before the real battle began. Napoleon reorganized the artillery into regiments, and exploited the mobility of Gribeauval's horse artillery. In battle he concentrated his guns – 200 of them at Borodino – and used them to blast holes in the ranks of the enemy before launching the infantry columns. As he continued on his career, and the quality of his troops began to decline, so Napoleon used ever more artillery and attached increasing importance to it. There was nothing new about the guns themselves. They were smooth-bored, muzzle-loading and fired by coarse powder, and their fire was neither very rapid nor accurate. Two rounds a minute was possible, and a 12-pounder could carry 3,500 yards.

Cavalry retained the functions of reconnaissance, providing cover in advance and retreat, and conducting minor operations at a distance from the main army. It took time to build up a strong cavalry force after the revolution, since it was expensive and the cavalry regiments had been *par excellence* the aristocratic ones. Napoleon changed the organization of the cavalry, and gave it an important function in battle. With the development of the division, an independent unit of all arms 6,000 to 9,000 strong, cavalry was needed in smaller units than in the past, and in a more intimate and flexible relation to infantry. The divisional cavalry were light cavalry, *chasseurs* and hussars. The number of heavy cavalry regiments was reduced by almost half; *cuirassiers*, armed with sabre, breast-plate and back-plate, were used in massed formations to deliver heavy charges at the appropriate moment in battle. The medium cavalry were the dragoons, who ceased to be just mounted infantry. They, and some of the light cavalry, formed the main cavalry reserve, the function of which was to follow up victory with an energetic pursuit to ensure that the defeated remnants of the enemy army were completely destroyed – as happened in the Ulm and Jena campaigns. Napoleon's greatest cavalry officer was Joachim Murat, his brother-in-law whom he was to make king of Naples. Murat was impetuous and temperamental, but he was an inspiring leader.

One of the principles of the revolution was *la carrière ouverte aux talents*, and Napoleon's own career shows how this could come true. Every man in the French army was said, if he was good enough, to carry a marshal's *bâton* in his knapsack. Of the twenty-six marshals created by Napoleon only two were of noble birth. However, while Napoleon was interested in talent rather than origin, he soon ceased to believe in *égalité*. The marshals were loaded with honours, from the new *Légion d'Honneur* to kingdoms. The military schools such as Saint-Cyr were for an *élite*. Crack regiments were formed, most notably the Imperial Guard. No one was eligible to be a guardsman who had not served in four campaigns, been wounded twice, or distinguished himself by some outstanding deed. But he was then paid more than the men of any other regiment, he had the best barracks and rations, and he escorted the emperor. Distinctions and ranks were multiplied in the army. There were gorgeous ceremonial uniforms. All this offended the pure principles of the revolution, but it was good for morale.

Some of the marshals were very able soldiers. Davout first fought with Napoleon in Egypt, where he became totally devoted to his master; his qualities were those of a regimental officer, a first-class organizer and disciplinarian, feared but also respected by his men. He was a tough fighter, and he understood Napoleon's mind to the full. In 1806 he won a valuable victory against heavy odds over the Prussians at Auerstedt, and he did outstandingly well in Russia. Masséna, according to Napoleon, possessed 'military qualities before which one should kneel'. He was a useful assistant to Napoleon in Italy in 1796, he checked the terrible Russian army of Suvorov in Switzerland in 1799, but he was beaten by Wellington in the Peninsula. Ney was another great cavalry leader, and when commanding the rearguard in the retreat from Moscow in 1812 he justified Napoleon's accolade of 'the bravest of the brave'. But Waterloo was to show up Ney's weakness; at the moment of crisis his judgment vanished. Soult was an able and reliable tactician and organizer. Others, such as Marmont, the artillery expert, and Augereau, a brave, dashing and brutal leader, deserve also to be mentioned. All these men, however, were under the shadow of Napoleon; without his mastery and inspiration they would have been lesser soldiers.

By 1805 Napoleon was set on building an empire, and in the summer of that year the Third Coalition – Britain, Austria and Russia – was formed against him. It was clear to him by then that he had no hope of invading England, and he therefore turned his attention eastwards. By August vast forces were assembling against him, but they were still scattered. The main axis of the conflict was to be the Danube valley, running through Austria and pointing to Russia. Eighty-four thousand Austrians in Italy could be barred off by 50,000 men under Masséna. Otherwise Napoleon had to deal with an Austrian army of 58,000 men on the Danube under Mack, and two Russian armies – one about to advance through Galicia under Kutusov and the other mobilizing in Poland. Further operations were threatening

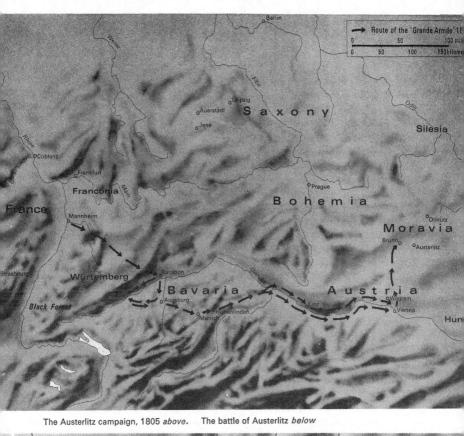

The Austerlitz campaign, 1805 *above*. The battle of Austerlitz *below*

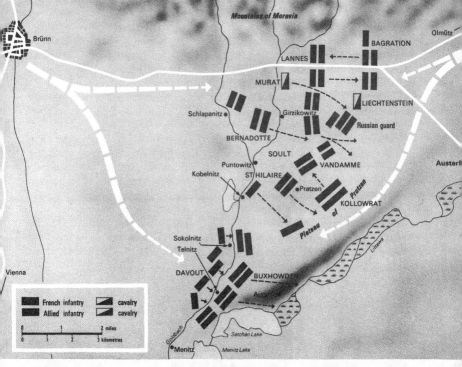

in the Low Countries and southern Italy. If Napoleon did not strike first his enemies were likely by the early winter to assemble 140,000 men at Ulm, at the head of the Danube, pointing into France. He calculated that he had less distance to travel from Boulogne, where his army was still massed, to Ulm, than the Russians had. He decided therefore to strike early and fast, and deal with his enemies singly, first wiping out the Austrian army at Ulm and then moving on down the Danube to deal with the Russians.

Napoleon's staff system served him at its best as he planned the march of 150,000 men from the English Channel to the Danube in the late summer of 1805. To conceal his strength and intentions from the Austrians he rejected the most direct route, instead striking the Danube beyond Ulm and taking the Austrians in rear. The *Grande Armée* marched dispersed in seven columns. The departures of the various forces were graduated so that in twenty-four marches all should converge along the Rhine, and then move north of the Black Forest, marching altogether on an 80-mile front. Supplies were laid on at scheduled halting places.

A diversion by the French in the Black Forest lured Mack up the Danube so that he could be cut off from behind. The *Grande Armée* followed its marching programme precisely, starting at dawn, doing between eight and twenty-five miles a day, and stopping in the middle of the day at a prepared camp. On 7th October the first four corps crossed the Danube. On the 9th Ulm was invested. Eighteen thousand Austrians who tried to break out were hounded down by the French cavalry, and after ten days Mack surrendered with his remaining 30,000 men. The first phase of Napoleon's strategy had culminated in a bloodless and complete victory.

It now seemed likely that the Prussians would also mobilize against the French. This reinforced Napoleon's view that bold and swift offensive action was the best plan, and on 26th October the army once more pressed down the Danube towards Vienna. But the men were tired, the weather was wintry, and Kutusov's 65,000 Russians were in front of them. The campaign was now a fight rather than a promenade. Napoleon wanted to encircle Kutusov, but the Russians, while slowing the advance of the French, kept dodging backwards out of reach. Vienna was entered on 14th November, and yielded valuable military stores. But Napoleon received the news of Trafalgar at about this time; his army was in the centre of a hostile Europe; it seemed that he would be unable to catch Kutusov before he should be reinforced by the second Russian army, and possibly by a Prussian army. It looked indeed as if Napoleon was trapped.

But he laid his counter-trap in Moravia. It was defensible country and he halted there to rest his army, while devising a way of provoking the enemy to attack him. He was aware that the Russo-Austrian army, now at Olmütz, was continually increasing in size. It already numbered 85,000, with the expectation of 60,000 more from Poland, and with the possibility of 80,000 Austrians breaking through the Alps to aid them. On the other hand the Prussians were hardly beginning to get under arms, and Napoleon had a month or so to play with. His plan was to lure the Russians to attack him by showing a weak front. Kutusov was allowed to see no more than 50,000 men at Brünn. But in fact more than 20,000 others under Bernadotte and

Davout were in reserve, scattered in corps forty or sixty miles back but ready to move up at twenty-four hours' notice. The enemy would think that they had a numerical advantage of two to one, whereas in fact the numbers were not far short of equal.

From about 21st November Napoleon was sure of his ground and had decided in his mind the general tactical approach to the battle which he was planning to bring about. Between Brünn and Olmütz was a quadrilateral. The north of this area was bounded by a straight line of wooded heights, known as the mountains of Moravia. Just south and parallel with the hills ran the main road, and a turning to the south-east ran off it to the village of Austerlitz three miles away. Two streams descending from the mountains converged a little south of the road, to form a marshy rivulet called the Goldbach, which flowed on southward until marshy lakes bounded the southern end of the area. There were seven villages along the Goldbach. The stream was not an obstacle, but it delimited the two halves of the terrain. West of it was a flat plain stretching to the well-fortified town of Brünn, which was in French hands. East of the Goldbach was a plateau called the Pratzen, rising gradually 350 feet from the stream and dropping more steeply the other side. Napoleon

Napoleon's army takes Ratisbon by storm

decided to station his forces, based on Brünn, on the eastern side of the Goldbach. The allies, concentrated at Olmütz, would hardly be able to resist the temptation to try and cut off the French from Vienna and from their retreat to the south-west by attacking their right. Napoleon deliberately exposed his communications with Vienna, and bunched his forces together on the road and at the foot of the mountains so as to increase the temptation for the allies to envelop his right with their larger forces. He was confident that if they would only swallow the bait he could defeat them overwhelmingly on ground of his own choosing.

There was much debate in the allied camp, where the tsar Alexander I had now taken supreme command, on the advisability of attack. Kutusov argued that everything was to be gained by delaying until they were reinforced and the French were further depleted. But Alexander, young, vainglorious and flattered by his courtiers, was persuaded that he really did have Napoleon in a trap. The Russian troops were in poor physical shape after months of continuous marching, but they were fine soldiers all the same – in 1799 under Suvorov's command the Russians had cleared northern Italy, fighting in masses like battering-rams. The detailed planning of the attack fell to Weirother, the Austrian chief of staff.

The allied advance began on 1st December, and in the evening Weirother outlined his tactical scheme. The allies had nearly 90,000 men, most of whom were Russians, and 278 cannon. The plan was to approach the French right from the north-east, the head of the army crossing the Goldbach between Telnitz and Sokolnitz and then wheeling round in three columns to attack the French in flank from the south. A fourth column was to engage the French front from the Pratzen, and further north another corps would hold the French on the line of the road. On the night of 1st December, Kutusov and several other senior Russian officers were drunk – hardly a good way to begin a battle.

By 1st December, when Napoleon was certain that the enemy were moving, Bernadotte's corps had already joined him and Davout was on his way. During the afternoon the emperor inspected his army, dressed in the green, white and red uniform of a colonel of the *chasseurs à cheval* of the Guard, his *redingote gris* blowing in the breeze. No doubt he was consciously the picture of his legend. He ignored the scruffy appearance of his men, but he repeatedly checked that weapons were in working order. The French forces numbered altogether 61,000 fit men, and 139 cannon. Although inferior in numbers Napoleon's forces were soundly positioned for the coming battle, and he had the great advantage of knowing the enemy plan, and knowing that it was bad – because he had forced it on them. Soult commanded the centre, opposite the Pratzen, with great strength in reserve. Lannes was on the left, together with Murat and most of the cavalry. Davout was on the right. That evening Napoleon published a proclamation to his army in which he revealed his scheme: 'The positions we occupy are strong, and as they advance to turn my right, they will expose their flank to me.' During the night, when it was reported that the Russians were still moving south, he moved some of his troops in the centre slightly to the right.

A curious incident took place after dark. Some straw caught fire, and a few French soldiers spread the fire – thinking it was a celebration of the anniversary of the emperor's coronation. For a few minutes the flames burned fiercely, and in a great surge of enthusiasm and devotion 30,000 men acclaimed Napoleon.

The battle on 2nd December went as Napoleon had willed. The allied attack was strong and persistent, but clumsily organized and lamentably controlled. With a minimal force, Davout held the right all day. A mist concealed the French centre until, in *ordre mixte* – skirmishers, artillery, line and column – Soult's men attacked the Russians in flank at the Pratzen, gaining complete surprise. During the morning the allies pressed the French right; but the French consolidated themselves better in the centre and cut the enemy army in two. The last area in which battle was joined was the north, and there an equal and hard struggle took place. Murat's cavalry, operating between the left and the centre, cut the allied right off from their centre by midday, and the Russians there began a slow withdrawal. Napoleon himself by this time was on the Pratzen, and two divisions of his centre were exerting a cross pressure on the defeated remnants of the Russian centre on the eastern slope. All that now remained was to relieve the French right, and ensure that the allies were thoroughly beaten at all points. A last desperate charge of the Russian Imperial Guard was repelled from the Pratzen. The French centre then turned to destroy the allied left. Some of the Russian infantry fought their way out to the south; others were drowned as the ice on the lakes broke beneath them; most were captured. Although the enemy left was caught, their right was not prevented from getting away in good order – Murat, having received no orders, hesitated to leave the centre altogether and encircle the enemy's wing. By 5 o'clock in the afternoon firing ceased. All told the allies had lost 27,000 men and 180 guns. The French losses were about 7,000.

The immediate consequence of Austerlitz was that Austria fell out of the Coalition. In 1806 Prussia attempted to prevent Napoleon finally dominating all Germany, and mobilized an army of 130,000, still complacent in the dated glory of Frederick the Great. In a three weeks' campaign the Prussians were crushed, by the double defeat of Jena and Auerstedt and by Napoleon's rapid pursuit and occupation of Berlin. The next year the French, fighting now in north-east Europe, snatched a narrow and bloody victory over the Russians at Eylau. In June 1807 Napoleon defeated them again at Friedland, inflicting a loss of 25,000 men, and the tsar thought it best to come to terms.

The victories of 1805–7 raised Napoleon to the pinnacle of his fortune. From then till 1812 he was master of a European empire stretching from Seville to Warsaw and from Naples to the Baltic – half a million square miles containing 44 million subjects. In much of that area valuable and enduring reforms were introduced: equality before the law, the abolition of serfdom, religious toleration, civil rights for Jews, secular education, unified systems of justice, road-building, single customs' areas, national armies.

The problem of Britain, however, still remained unsolved, and in November 1806 with Europe under his sway Napoleon opened a full-scale economic war against his arch-enemy. The Berlin Decree declared the British Isles to be 'in a state of blockade';

all commerce with them was forbidden and all goods in transit between Britain and her colonies were to be seized. If he could do it no other way Napoleon would 'conquer the sea by the power of the land'. As the English retaliated Napoleon extended the operation of this 'Continental System'. But so long as Britain ruled the sea there was no possibility, in fact, of Napoleon starving her into defeat by cutting off supplies of food and raw materials from her colonies.

The beginning of Napoleon's downfall can be sought at almost any stage of his career. It can perhaps be attributed to the fatal moment of excessive ambition on the evening after Lodi in 1796. The mistake may have been in 1801 when he imposed the humiliating Peace of Lunéville on Austria instead of coming to terms with her and joining forces to defeat England. Possibly, considering his genius, he did nothing unreasonable until his head was turned by the victories of Austerlitz and Jena, and he set out on the deluded path of mastering the world, and so to Spain and Moscow. He was driven back from Russia ignominiously in 1812, but by 1813 he had another army. In 1813 he suffered his first major personal defeat in battle at Leipzig, and in 1814 he had to defend the frontiers of France herself. By then the demands of conscription and the evident selfishness of his ambition had lost him the support of the French nation. But Austria still offered good terms, and even at that stage he was not ruined. His campaign of that year was one of his most brilliant: he repeatedly divided his enemies and defeated them in detail. Napoleon's military genius did not fail until 1815, and there is no clear path of political decline. But Napoleon himself attributed his ruin to the 'Spanish ulcer'.

One small flaw in the triumph of 1806 set in movement a train of events which sapped Napoleon's strength and gave encouragement to his enemies. In 1806 Portugal refused to accept the Continental System. Like most other countries of Europe she did not want to be dominated by France, and she wished to trade with England. Unlike most, she resisted. In 1807 Napoleon sent an army under Junot into the Peninsula and in the following year the king of Spain was treacherously deposed. The hatred of the Spanish and Portuguese peoples was aroused, and French armies from now on were harried by guerrillas; the Spanish irregulars killed about a hundred French soldiers daily. Europe was astounded when two French divisions surrendered to the Spaniards at Baylén. Such was the situation in the Peninsula in 1808 when the British expeditionary force landed there under Sir John Moore.

At first Napoleon took command in Spain, and almost succeeded in trapping Moore's contingent at Corunna. But events elsewhere in Europe called away from the Peninsula the man whose presence at the head of an army was estimated by Wellington to be worth 40,000 troops, and he never returned. So far the only effective contribution of England to the military efforts of her continental allies had been monetary subsidies. But now, with strong popular support against the French and backed by secure communications at sea, the British were at last able themselves to get a real foothold on the continent. In August 1808 Sir Arthur Wellesley, later Duke of Wellington, landed in Portugal with 13,000 men and defeated the French at Vimeiro – though by the stupidity of Wellington's seniors Junot was able to extricate his army by the Convention of Cintra.

Wellington was born of an aristocratic Irish family in 1769, the same year as Napoleon. He was educated at Eton where he showed some promise at mathematics and music. In 1787 he entered the army, not out of vocation or ambition, but because he had family interest and it was the normal career for less bright younger sons. He did little regular service in his regiment, but in 1796 he went to India. There he set about mastering his profession, studying all the best authorities on military science and on India. At this time he was said to be 'cheerful, free of speech and expansive among his particular friends but rather reserved in general society'. He always remained witty, but increasingly he was to conceal his sensitivity beneath a some-what crusty exterior. His natural lethargy and strong emotions were unfailingly controlled by the strongest self-discipline. Duty seems truly to have been a more powerful impulse in him than ambition.

In India he gained a sound military training and built up a considerable local reputation. No British commander had previously worked out a tactical technique for dealing with the hordes of Maratha horsemen, but Wellington found the answer with a line formation. His supply lines were well organized to give him a long line into the heart of the enemy country and mobility once he got there. His most notable engagements were the storming of Ahmednagar, one of the strongest fortresses in India, and his victory in the very bloody battle of Assaye in 1803.

In 1805, after nine years in India, he returned to England. Although the reputa-tion he had gained in India counted for nothing at home, he had accumulated very valuable experience – in pitched battles against heavy numerical odds, the organiza-tion of supply, forced marches, sieges, and the coaxing of difficult allies. Between 1805 and 1808 he occupied himself with politics, becoming Chief Secretary for Ireland. It was his political interest rather than his position in the army which secured him his next appointments. Following his success in the Peninsula in 1808, Wellington returned there in 1809 to command 21,000 men.

The British army of this period differed in many ways from the French. Most notably it was not a national army but an old-style small professional army, of the type which military theorists were then writing off as obsolete. The contrast between the careers of Wellington and Napoleon is characteristic. Officers' commissions in the British army were obtained by purchase and interest, and were normally avail-able only to men of gentle birth. Apart from six months' drill and the optional reading of a few pamphlets, most officers were untrained. It cannot be said that the soldiers were recruited from the criminal classes, but they were' not on the whole the best elements of the population. Yet the system worked, despite the element of amateurism and the social gulf. Discipline though sometimes savage was generally secured by good will, and the army was an efficient fighting force. This was an improvement on the situation in the past, but in 1803, in his camp at Shorncliffe, General Moore had revolutionized discipline and training, by relying on cooperation rather than coercion, and proving by the resultant high morale and efficiency that this was the better way. The administrative head of the army was the Duke of

York, an able man who founded a military academy and a staff college, and encouraged the rise of young officers of ability.

Wellington himself, in the Peninsula, attached great importance to the care and training of his troops. Finance, transport and supply were the domain of his able Commissary-General, Kennedy, who rarely failed to provide adequate supplies of clothing, food, cooking utensils, tents, blankets, boots and pay. Unlike the French, the British used a magazine system of supplies and paid for the products of the country; this was sound policy since it gained the support of the native populations of the areas of operation, even that of south-western France in 1814. Part of the purpose of Wellington's tough discipline was to prevent excesses among the soldiers, such as drunkenness, which might be harmful to their health. The Surgeon-General, McGrigor, could rely on his commander's full support (unlike Napoleon's Baron Larrey). Again, unlike Napoleon, Wellington thought it worth while to give his soldiers thorough training in the use of their weapons.

Before the Peninsular War the basic unit of the British army had normally been the brigade or regiment. Pride in long-standing regimental traditions was a most important factor in maintaining good morale – a problem since the army had achieved so little success in the field since the Seven Years' War. Wellington established the divisional system. The division was a formation of all arms and services, self-sufficient and detachable if necessary from the main force. To raise the numbers of his troops in the Peninsula, Wellington incorporated Portuguese troops into the British divisions, usually in a ratio of one Portuguese brigade, which included some British officers, to two British brigades. Eventually there were ten divisions; among the better known of his divisional commanders were Hill, Graham, Picton and Craufurd. Wellington was also responsible for the introduction of the first British corps of sappers and military police.

Wellington developed an efficient staff and intelligence system. He had a close understanding with his Quartermaster-General, Murray, who not only attended to the organization of encampments and troop movements, but was responsible for topographical intelligence and was an invaluable assistant in strategical and tactical planning. Other members of the staff whom Wellington probably saw daily were the Commissary-General, the Adjutant-General, the Inspector-General of Hospitals, the Commanding Officer of Artillery and the Commanding Royal Engineer. Wellington did not differ much from Napoleon in his attention to the important details of preparation, and in his capacity for getting through quantities of work. He was perhaps better at delegation, and his team was happier and more loyal than Napoleon's. But Wellington, unlike Napoleon and Blücher, had no chief of staff. The staff work, normally supervised and directed by one man, was shared amongst three officials – a Military Secretary, the Adjutant-General, and the Quartermaster-General.

Besides preparation behind the lines Wellington attached great importance to intelligence information about the enemy; later he said that he thought much of his success was due to his care in studying what was happening 'upon the other side of the hill'. Accordingly he built up a good intelligence organization. At the beginning of the Peninsular War no reliable maps of the area existed, but Murray's staff gradually remedied this situation in the areas that mattered. Efficient reconnaissance preceded the army's movements. Cavalry patrols and individual officers were sent forward every day; their function was to examine the ground and discover the enemy lay-out. News travelled fast in the native population, and good information could generally be had, at a price, from the guerrilla bands and in the villages. A network of 'confidential persons' was built up over the Peninsula. Most of the intelligence thus gathered was received personally by Wellington, who required the highest standards of accuracy.

Wellington's strategy in the Peninsula was conditioned by the numerical superiority of his enemies. He began with 21,000 men, and his army at no time exceeded 80,000. The French rarely had less than 250,000, commanded by Masséna, Marmont or Soult. Wellington depended on Portugal as his essential base of operations. Portugal must be held and then, if possible, he could advance from there. Moore had regarded Portugal as indefensible, but Wellington disagreed. There were five gaps in the mountain frontier of Portugal, but with the support of the Spaniards and Portuguese he reckoned a strong defensive area could be organized. The first necessity was to clear the French out of the country, at any rate for the time being, in order to give time to prepare the defences. Soult was attacked and beaten at Oporto, and Wellington advanced into Spain. His Spanish allies stupidly got themselves defeated and lost southern Spain, but at Talavera Wellington won a victory, and then retired back into Portugal.

By the winter of 1809–10 it was more than ever likely that the French, triumphant in Spain and Austria, would concentrate massive forces to finish off Wellington's army in Portugal. Some 10,000 reinforcements were sent out to him from England, but no more were available. He decided to make his stand in 1810 near the frontier, but he also prepared an immensely powerful defensive position to protect Lisbon – the Lines of Torres Vedras. Portuguese labourers supervised by English engineers constructed the defences: two lines of mutually supporting batteries and redoubts running for thirty miles through the hills between the Tagus and the sea.

In May 1810 Masséna took command of the French *Armée du Portugal* and began the advance to drive Wellington into the sea. Wellington resisted the temptation to try to save the Spanish frontier fortresses, and in September, as Masséna's 72,000 men advanced into Portugal along three routes, Wellington retired before him with his 49,000. At the Mondego river he decided to give battle, and there on the ridge of Busaco he defeated Masséna.

Wellington was as good at tactics as he was at other aspects of generalship. Napoleon and Wellington were both believers in firepower, and their troops used virtually the same musket and bayonet, which the British called the 'Brown Bess'. The difference was that Wellington's troops were well enough disciplined and trained to stand up in line against the French columns. That being the case it was an easy calculation that they would win, since they could bring to bear at least four times the firepower of their enemy. Wellington's normal tactics were to base his main strength on a double line of infantry, drawn up on the reverse slope of a ridge, since this screened his forces from the eyes and artillery of the enemy. In front of the line there were skirmishers, and the flanks were protected by cavalry and artillery. This was his lay-out at Busaco. He used no massed artillery in the Napoleonic style, though the mobility of the English horse artillery impressed the French. Since his cavalry was not numerous he did not generally follow up his victories by pursuit.

The impact that Wellington's army made on its enemy attacking was described by Bugeaud, later a French marshal:

The retreat from Moscow

The English generally occupied well chosen defensive positions having a certain command, and they showed only a portion of their forces. The usual artillery action first took place. Soon, in great haste, without studying the position, without taking time to examine if there were means to make a flank attack, we marched straight on, taking the bull by the horns. About 1,000 yards from the English line the men became excited, spoke to one another and hurried their march; the column began to be a little confused. The English remained quite silent with ordered arms, and from their steadiness appeared to be a long red wall. This steadiness invariably produced an effect on the young soldiers. Very soon we got nearer, shouting '*Vive l'Empereur! en avant! à la baionnette!*' Shakos were raised on the muzzles of the muskets; the column began to double, the ranks got into confusion, the agitation produced a tumult; shots were fired as we advanced. The English line remained silent, still and immovable, with ordered arms, even when we were only 300 yards distant, and it appeared to ignore the storm about to break. The contrast was striking; in our inmost thoughts each felt that the enemy was a long time in firing, and this fire reserved for so long, would be very unpleasant when it did come. Our ardour cooled. The moral power of steadiness, which nothing shakes (even if it be only appearance), over disorder which stupefies itself with noise, overcame our minds. At this moment of intense excitement, the English wall shouldered arms; an indescribable feeling rooted many of our men to the spot; they began to fire. The enemy's steady concentrated volleys swept our ranks; decimated, we turned round seeking to recover our equilibrium; then three deafening cheers broke the silence of our opponents; at the third they were on us, pushing our disorganized flight.

After the victory of Busaco, Wellington astonished his own army and the enemy by continuing to retreat. Masséna followed him up to the Lines of Torres Vedras; but there he was finally held. Through the winter of 1810–11 the armies faced each other. The British were secure and well supplied; the French were far from their bases and they could make no impression on the Lines. In March 1811 Masséna retreated, and Wellington began the long, slow advance which was to lead in three years to victory. The frontier area of Almeida, Ciudad Rodrigo and Badajoz was gained in 1811 and 1812, not without much manoeuvre, and with constant attention still to the preservation of the Portuguese base of operations. Disagreements among the French marshals in Spain and misguided instructions from Napoleon, sent from as far away as Moscow, assisted the British, but the success of the operations was the positive achievement of Wellington and his soldiers. His defensive genius and his skill in manoeuvre did not mean that he would not strike hard when the favourable moment for battle came. With two great victories, at Salamanca in 1812 and at Vittoria in 1813, he eventually cleared the Peninsula of its invaders.

The effect on Napoleon's fortunes of what he long tried to convince himself was a Spanish sideshow was profoundly damaging in various respects. It was a serious drain on his troops; for example, if he had not detached troops to the Peninsula in 1809 he might have avoided the repulse at Essling. It was also a training-ground for his marshals in disobedience and acceptance of defeat. The penetration of Wellington's army into south-west France by 1814 came at the same time that Napoleon was pressed back within his frontiers in the north-east. Furthermore the courage and success of the Spanish and Portuguese peoples gave courage to Europe. The Germans had been subjected by fear and force, but from 1808 a powerful surge of nationalism rose up against the alien French. Alexander also quarrelled with Napoleon, and in 1812 the Russians inflicted a defeat of the greatest magnitude on him in the Moscow campaign, destroying most of the original *Grande Armée*. (One of the basic rules of war is 'don't march on Moscow' – Hitler broke that rule and regretted it.) Leipzig followed in 1813. In 1814 came abdication, and in May of that year the fallen emperor arrived in Elba.

But for history it was not enough. In 1815 Napoleon came back. He suffered his final decisive defeat at the hands of allied armies under Wellington and Blücher at Waterloo. It was the first time the two great commanders had faced each other in battle, and neither was at his best in this campaign. It is a nice point as to who made the worse errors – Wellington or Napoleon. On the night of 15th June, Wellington was dancing at a ball in Brussels given by the Duchess of Richmond – his army not being deployed for battle and ready to fight effectively if surprised, although Napoleon and his army were within striking distance, having crossed the frontier that morning. Napoleon had gained complete surprise, and had placed his army between those of Wellington and Blücher – whose forces were too widely scattered to offer effective combined resistance if the initiative gained by Napoleon had been acted upon swiftly. But it wasn't. If ever victory was in the grasp of a commander, it lay on 15th June ready to be taken by Napoleon. Wellington had only himself to blame for allowing this situation to develop. Such neglect is almost unbelievable in a great soldier. And yet, in spite of all, three days later French success had been transformed into disaster, due to a series of blunders and omissions, the blame for which must be laid on Napoleon. I have read that he said later 'in spite of everything I should have won that battle'. And he might well have won if he had followed up the Prussians after Ligny with his whole army, and had hammered Blücher's army to such an extent that it could not have appeared again on the battlefield as an effective fighting force. The battle was a very equal affair, but the outcome was, as Wellington put it, that 'Napoleon . . . just moved forward in the old style, in columns, and was driven off in the old style'.

Peace came to Europe after twenty-three years, and Napoleon was exiled to St Helena where he died in 1821. Wellington continued his political career; he became prime minister from 1828 to 1830 and won civil rights for the Catholics. Like his vanquished and dead enemy, Wellington became more and more of a legend. He died in 1852.

An Anglo-French naval engagement. A detail from the painting of the action off San Domingo by Nicholas Pocock

16 The Beginngs of Modern War

In the nineteenth century whole societies organized themselves for war in a more complete way than ever before, and armies were equipped with weapons far more powerful. The new warfare developed in Europe and America, but it penetrated to all parts of the world. In fact the years between 1815 and 1848 were a period of relative peace in Europe. However, during that time general developments were taking place which had a direct bearing on the emergence of modern war. The ideas of imperialism and nationalism were hardening; revolutionary changes in armies and equipment were born with the growth of populations and new industrial techniques; new methods of communication increased the pace of life in general; and military theorists and politicians arose who rationalized and exploited these factors. Some trial was made of the new warfare in the fighting of the decade or so after 1848. Finally in the American Civil War (1861–5) and the Franco-Prussian War (1870–1), new techniques anticipated the twentieth century.

The most important background development was the rise in population – between 1830 and 1870 Europe's population increased by 30 per cent. Mass population meant mass production of armaments and mass armies. Vastly increased numbers created new problems in transport and supply as well as tactics. The increasing influence of public opinion was another new factor which had to be taken into account by commanders and politicians. Pressure of population gave an impulse to imperialism.

In the years after 1815 Britain was the strongest power, having emerged victorious from the Napoleonic Wars besides being the leader of the Industrial Revolution, and it suited her that the world should be at peace. The British navy, unchallengeable since Trafalgar, undertook to keep a *Pax Britannica*. Prince Albert, opening the Great Exhibition in Britain in 1851, declared his conviction that the 'unity of mankind' would shortly be realized, and disciples of the philosopher Saint-Simon hailed engineers and financiers as the pillars of a new and naturally pacific society.

Fighting was not, however, altogether avoided between 1815 and 1848; nationalism, allied with romanticism and liberalism, found outlets in numerous revolts. Most of these were suppressed by the great autocratic powers. However, the Greeks were supported in their struggle for independence from the Ottoman empire not only by Byron but also by a British fleet under the command of Sir Edward Codrington, the naval power of Turkey and Egypt being destroyed in Navarino Bay in 1827. The movement of the South American countries to free themselves from Spanish and Portuguese bonds was also tolerated. There were fifteen years of war in South America, during which the high plateaux of Peru and Bolivia were heavily

The battle of the Pyramids. A detail from the painting by General Lejeune, who served with distinction in Napoleon's armies

fought over. After more than two years of training and planning, San Martín invaded Chile from across the High Andes. The operation was carried out in the most arduous conditions and on a front of 500 miles. Concentrating his forces with precision he surprised his enemy at Chacabuco in February 1817. Peru was then liberated, with the aid of a fleet commanded by an intrepid and erratic British seaman, Thomas Cochrane. In the north at the same time Bolivar, with a mixed force of foreign legionaries, marched through the hot and flooded plains of the Orinoco, and over the bleak paramos of the Andes. The heroism of the 'Liberators' recalls that of the *conquistadores*. But the fighting was remote from that of modern war.

The same, on the whole, is true of the imperialist wars. The 'manifest destiny' of advancing the U.S. frontier westwards across North America was pursued throughout this period, and much fighting took place, chiefly against Red Indians and Mexicans. The defence of the Alamo (1836) and the stand of the U.S. 7th cavalry under Custer against the Sioux and Cheyenne at the Little Big Horn river (1876) are famous episodes. In southern Africa during the 1830's and 1840's the Boers were driven northwards from the Cape by the British, and became involved with a welter of warring Bantu tribes. The Zulus had been welded into a terrible military power by Chaka, but his successor Dingaan was eventually crushed at the Blood River by the Boers under Pretorius. Bloody fighting took place before the British were able to conquer the Maoris in New Zealand in the 1860's. British forces in India were constantly occupied and in 1837, with the First Afghan War, a new phase of war and conquest began which lasted for twenty years. The north-west frontier had to be secured; Sind was brought under control in 1843 when Charles Napier with 3,000 troops crushed 20,000 Baluchis at Meeanee, in possibly the most brilliant feat of arms in Indian history. The campaigns to suppress the mutiny of the native army of the East India Company in 1857–8 occasioned some notable military feats, particularly the clearing of central India by Sir Hugh Rose. The British also took the lead in the general competition of the European powers to exploit China, where the Opium War took place between 1839 and 1842. Russia was held up by the tenacious resistance of the Moslem guerrillas of the Caucasus under Kazimullah and Shamyl; but she too followed a manifest destiny of expansion into Turkestan and Siberia.

The clash between European and primitive warfare demonstrated that numbers and bravery could not prevail against superior weapons and discipline. The native peoples of the rest of the world therefore began to Europeanize their warfare – as in Li Hung-Chang's training of the Huai army to deal with the Taiping rebels. These wars were also opportunities for Europeans themselves to try out new techniques and ideas. But the mainstream of development was in Europe and in the old part of the United States.

In Europe after 1848 nationalism was once again in the ascendant. The diplomatic balance was upset as the powers looked jealously at the decaying Ottoman empire, and as the unification of Italy, and also of Germany, challenged the position of France. Four important wars took place within seventeen years: the Crimean War

The thin red line of the British infantry advances at the battle of the Alma in the Crimean War

(1853–6) between England, France and Turkey allied against Russia; the Italian war of 1859 in which the main contenders were France and Austria; the Prusso-Austrian war of 1866; and the Franco-Prussian War of 1870–1. European warfare was by now feeling the impact of the military theories of Jomini and Clausewitz, of the Industrial Revolution, and of the population explosion.

Military theory in the nineteenth century had to take account, as I have said, of new developments of fundamental importance: massive populations and nationalism, speedy communications, technical inventions and mass production. *Vom Krieg* by Clausewitz was published in 1832 and the *Précis de l'art de la guerre* by Jomini appeared in 1837. These two thinkers had both pondered upon what they had seen in the Napoleonic wars. Their views had a profound influence on military thinking in their times, and in the early years of the twentieth century.

Jomini's work is a technical analysis of the conduct of war, based on the study of Frederick and Napoleon. In fact he put military thought back into the eighteenth century – an approach which many professional soldiers of the nineteenth century found comfortable and safe. The emphasis of his book is too much on 'mathematics' to the exclusion of psychology. You cannot conduct war successfully like that – Jomini failed to allow for the factors of the unknown and the unexpected. In war only one thing is certain – that is, that everything will be uncertain.

Clausewitz, on the other hand realized that war could not be understood if isolated from its economic and social background, from the motives of politicians, and from the impulses of human beings. But some of his ideas were to have a tragic influence. He held that the destruction of the enemy's armed forces is the first aim of generalship, and that the best method of bringing this about is by direct attack. 'Let us not hear of generals who conquer without the shedding of blood.' Possibly because he was writing from the point of view of Germany Clausewitz overlooked the factor of seapower. Also, he failed to consider the movement of forces in terms of potential concentration rather than of actual mass. He wrote that 'there is no more imperative and no simpler law for strategy then to keep the forces concentrated'. On the eve of the mechanized age this observation, taken together with the remark that 'superiority in numbers becomes every day more decisive', pointed the disastrous way forward to the bulldozing methods of the 1914/18 war. Much of the blame should be laid on military leaders who misinterpreted Clausewitz's thinking, and took his startling sentences out of their context. But his language *is* exceedingly difficult to understand – personally I found it impossible.

With the Industrial Revolution there came a flood of inventions in weapons, armour and communications. At sea sail gave way to steam. The British resisted this transition because they had the most powerful fleet in the world and stood to lose by any change, and so the new trends were pioneered by lesser naval powers, France and the United States. John Ericsson, a Swede, tried unsuccessfully to interest the British Admiralty in the screw propeller, and in 1845 it was the U.S.A. that launched the first screw warship, the *Princeton*, with steam engines giving a speed of 13 knots. In the 1840's and 1850's, naval opinion in Britain and France was converted. With the development of ironclad ships more powerful engines were required, and in the 1850's compound engines of two or more cylinders came in. By 1870 horsepower had almost doubled, and in that year the British navy abandoned sail altogether. In the 1820's a Frenchman, Colonel Paixhans, had realized that the best way to render the British wooden fleet obsolete was to use shells instead of solid shot. The shell was like a mortar bomb, filled with gunpowder and detonated by means of a time-fuse; but it was fired more accurately on a flat trajectory by a cannon. In the 1830's it was adopted by the French navy, the British and American navies following suit. The counter to the introduction of shell-guns was to protect ships with armour, and in 1857 the French started to build their ironclad seagoing fleet. Britain followed their lead.

Since shell-guns had led to ironclads, gun fire had to be made more powerful. Ericsson designed a rotating gun-turret, and by 1870 a 7-inch cannon had been developed. The tactics of the days of sail were now obsolete, as was shown at the fight in Hampton Roads in the American Civil War in 1862 between the *Merrimac* and the *Monitor*. The result of a quarter of a century's evolution in fighting ships was the British *Devastation*, commissioned in 1875 – a ship described as 'an impregnable piece of Vauban fortification with bastions mounted on a fighting coal mine'. Her tonnage was 9,330, of which 27 per cent was armour; she had a prominent ram, carried four 35-ton guns in two turrets giving all-round fire, and had a speed of 15 knots. The *Devastation* presented a small target and was a very stable gun platform.

Three other inventions in naval warfare are worth mentioning. In 1855 Russia made the first serious use of floating mines. In 1863 Brun's submarine, *Le Plongeur*, was launched; and in 1864 in the American Civil War the small semi-submersibles of the South, called 'Davids', inflicted damage on Northern shipping. Americans also experimented with torpedoes, the earliest 'fish' torpedo being developed in 1866. While navies were being transformed, Britain kept her position as the strongest naval power. But the strategical circumstances of the wars of the nineteenth century did not allow the full implications of these technical naval developments to be revealed.

On top of all this, a military arms race took place. Advances in metallurgy, precision-engineering and ballistics made possible improvements in handguns. The muzzle-loading, flint-lock muskets of the Napoleonic era had been slow to load, were unreliable in wet weather, and inaccurate. The first improvement was the switch from the flint-lock to the percussion cap, which was weatherproof. Most countries had adopted it by 1842. At the same time the greater accuracy gained by rifled barrels was appreciated, and experiments were made everywhere to produce a conical bullet which could be fitted into a muzzle-loading handgun so that it gripped the rifling. In 1850 Captain Minié, a French officer, designed a bullet so that when the rifle was fired the bullet expanded to fill the rifling of the barrel; this was easy to load since it required no ramming. In 1853 the British army adopted a rifle firing a modified Minié bullet, which was used in the Crimean War. One of the provocations of the Indian Mutiny in 1857 was a rumour that the cartridges of the newly issued Enfield rifle were lubricated with the fat of cows, animals sacred to Hindus.

Rifles had by now been given increased range and accuracy, but so long as they were muzzle-loaders the rate of fire remained slow. The invention of a breech-loading system by Dreyse in 1839 was therefore a most important break-through. In 1842 the Prussians adopted a modified version of Dreyse's 'needle-gun', and tested it to their satisfaction in the war with Denmark over Schleswig-Holstein (1848–9). The virtue of the breech-loader was that it could be fired much more rapidly and be operated easily from a lying-down position. A further development was the addition of a magazine, pioneered in America in the 1860's. In 1866 the French adopted an improved breech-loader named after its inventor, Chassepot, which gained extra range from its smaller calibre and more gas-tight breech. Colonel Boxer, an Englishman, then invented a brass cartridge which expanded to seal the breech entirely. This was adopted by Britain for the Martini-Henry rifle in 1871, and within a short time it was used by most European countries. By the time of the Franco-Prussian War armies were normally equipped with rifles which were accurate to 600 yards, had ranges of up to 2,000 yards, and could be fired at a rapid rate by men lying down or from trenches.

Major advances in repeating weapons were also made during this period, mostly in America. In 1832 Samuel Colt patented his design for a revolver pistol, and its

Naval warfare saw many technical advances, some of which were developed during the American Civil War. The rotating gun turret of the *Monitor* (right) was pitted against the armour plate of the *Merrimac* (left)

advantages were demonstrated in 1835 in fighting against the Seminole Indians in Florida. Colt showed his various revolvers at the Great Exhibition in London in 1851, and sold some to the British navy for the Crimean War. A machine-gun, the Montigny *mitrailleuse*, was designed in Belgium about the same time. A better machine-gun was designed in America in 1862 by Richard Gatling, consisting of a number of barrels around a central axis. The magazine was a hopper above the gun which fed cartridges into the reloading and ejecting mechanism; the gunner turned a handle to rotate the barrels, and it could fire 600 rounds a minute. This was used in the American Civil War (1861–5).

Artillerymen were impressed by the improvement in handguns which resulted from percussion, rifling and breech-loading, but by 1850 no satisfactory way to incorporate these features in artillery had been made. Breech-loading mechanisms made artillery heavier and hence less mobile; it was difficult to devise a gas-tight breech; and a full-scale re-equipment in artillery was enormously expensive. In France Napoleon III retained his bronze muzzle-loading guns and modified them to Colonel de Beaulieu's system for large-grooved rifling and studded shot; they were used successfully at Magenta and Solferino in 1859. In England, William Armstrong at last discovered how to manufacture cannon of increased strength without adding weight, and this made breech-loading feasible. Armstrong's 9-pounders and 12-pounders were used in action in China in 1860. Prussia and Russia adopted breech-loading guns manufactured at the Krupp works in Essen. Prussia's artillery, weak in 1866, had been entirely re-equipped by 1870; but these Krupp guns did not prove reliable, and in the same year the British, after concluding that breech-loaders were too expensive and complicated, reverted to muzzle-loaders. However by 1900 the technical difficulties had been overcome and artillery by then was virtually the same as that used in the 1914/18 and 1939/45 wars.

The new inventions could be made available more readily than ever before. Mass production for mass markets was a basic feature of the new industrial age, and the output of coal, iron and steel was soaring. Samuel Colt was a good example of the new type of manufacturer; the North in the civil war in America bought from him 35,000 revolvers, 113,980 muskets, and 7,000 rifles.

Communications were also revolutionized in the nineteenth century. Roads improved and by the 1850's railways were being constructed apace; by 1855 in Germany, 5,410 miles had been built under strict state planning; and in America 30,000 miles of railroad were laid down between 1830 and 1860. The telegraph (1832) was taken up by the railway companies, and in the 1850's the cable networks in Europe and America were rapidly developed.

When a new era of war began in the middle of the nineteenth century practical answers thus had to be found to certain basic questions. With the great increases in numbers of men, what were to be the principles of recruitment and training? Should all these men be equipped with the new weapons, and if so, what was to be the tactical role of infantry armed with rifles, and of artillery? What was to be the role of cavalry? How should officers be trained? How should the new communications, particularly railways, affect strategic planning?

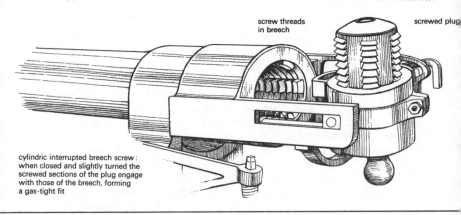

cylindric interrupted breech screw:
when closed and slightly turned the
screwed sections of the plug engage
with those of the breech, forming
a gas-tight fit

In artillery, breech-loading was gradually introduced

The military leaders of Europe moved into the modern age slowly and reluctantly. The years between 1830 and 1860 were, all the same, not barren of able soldiers, such as Radetzky, the octogenarian Austrian commander in the Italian war of 1848–9, and Garibaldi with his red-shirted Italian legion. The French army had the legend of Napoleon and a record of thirty years' success in Africa to convince itself that it was invincible. The first expeditionary force sent to Algeria in 1830, cumbrously organized in columns, had got into trouble against the nimble native forces led by Abd-el-Kader, emir of Mascara. But the tide turned in 1836, with Bugeaud's six weeks' campaign in western Algeria. His method was to make swift offensive thrusts with flying columns, lightly equipped and carrying their supplies on pack-animals. His thoughts on war provided a handbook for generations of French imperialist soldiers. New regiments were born in Africa – *zouaves*, *spahis* and others – and the soldiers of France kept their reputation for *élan*. The lively approach of commanders such as Bugeaud and Canrobert contrasted with the mentality of British and German generals of the day. In the Franco-Austrian war of 1859 in Italy the French infantry, in their skirmishing formations, showed impressive mobility and intelligence. Despite confused generalship at Solferino, the charging French infantry swept the Austrians away before they could bring their rifle-fire to bear.

Nonetheless the Crimean War and the Italian war revealed an unsatisfactory state of affairs in all armies – which could no longer be ignored. The Crimean War provided an object-lesson in how not to make war. The administrative organization on both sides was disastrous. The allies despatched a naval expedition to capture Sebastopol without discovering beforehand that the water on either side of the isthmus was too shallow for their ships to berth. The British brought no transport for their food and ammunition, and the troops lacked practically all the equipment necessary for a winter campaign. Tactical blundering led to one of the most famous military disasters of all time, the charge of the British Light Brigade at Balaclava, which brought the comment '*c'est magnifique mais ce n'est pas la guerre*'. The French under Napoleon III did not do much better in 1859, moving their troops into Italy with speed by rail but without arranging proper supplies. The first units were without blankets, cooking equipment or ammunition; shirts had to be torn up to bandage the wounded at Solferino while medical equipment was piled up in the docks at Genoa.

The appallingly high casualty rate in these wars provoked a revolution in medical services. In the Crimea, of 405,000 men sent out by the British and French armies, 25,600 were killed in action and 38,800 died of disease. Florence Nightingale with thirty-eight trained nurses went out to nurse the troops in the Crimea; it was not the least important consequence of this war that the emancipation of women was considerably advanced. Every war since then has seen a marked gain for women in social emancipation and public responsibility. Mainly as a result of the work of Henri Dunant, a Swiss banker and philanthropist, the International Red Cross Committee was set up and the first Geneva Convention was agreed by twelve powers in 1864. In the Franco-Prussian War the Red Cross was to care for over half a million sick and wounded.

The army which was most rapidly, efficiently and thoroughly reformed after 1859 was that of Germany. From 1858 Prince William brought to the government of Prussia a professionalism and single-minded enthusiasm for military matters to be compared with that of Frederick William I. Under William three men rose to eminence, who between them secured Prussia as an autocratic and militaristic state. Roon, minister of war after 1859; Moltke, chief of the general staff; and their political chief Bismarck, minister-president from 1862. The forces available to Prussia were professionalized by making long-term service compulsory and by spending more on equipment and training. 'Discipline, blind obedience, are things which can be inculcated and given permanence only by long familiarity', the regent considered. It took them some years to get their way with the public. Bismarck used war deliberately as a tool of policy. The outcome of his premeditated wars with Denmark (1864), Austria (1866) and France (1870) was the unification of Germany under Prussian leadership. She also became a major industrial power.

By 1868 the army of the North German Confederation had emerged. Universal obligation to military service was laid down, and the army was described as 'the training school of the entire nation for war'. Service with the colours was for three years from the age of twenty; conscripts then served with the reserve for a further four years; they then passed into the *Landwehr* or militia. Service with the *Landwehr* was for five years, and the force was supervised so closely by the regular army that it constituted in effect a second reserve. When the test came in 1870, Roon put into the field well over one million officers and men. The infantry were equipped with the Dreyse needle-gun, the effectiveness of which had been well demonstrated in 1866, when the Prussians firing six shots to every one fired by the Austrians swept the enemy from the field of Sadowa. The army was also equipped with up-to-date breech-loading Krupp artillery.

The most disastrous blunder of the Crimean War was the suicidal charge of the Light Brigade at Balaclava down a valley with Russian guns on three sides

Size would not however be an advantage without efficient organization. The training, mobilization and deployment of troops, and their supply, presented immense problems. The organization for command and control had now to take account of the increased areas over which operations would take place, due to the size of armies and to the strategic dispersal of forces made possible by railways, and to tactical dispersion made necessary in battle by rifled firearms. Greater responsibility and initiative had to be delegated to subordinate commanders, who must still be responsive to the ideas and methods of their seniors. But the Prussian army had, in its general staff, a body of skilled experts capable of dealing with these related problems of training, planning and communications.

Moltke was appointed chief of the Prussian general staff in 1857. He brought to his work personal dedication and a brilliant mind; his subordinates regarded him with the reverence of disciples. He was as Michael Howard puts it, 'the most exact and exacting of specialists', and he trained the staff officers of the German army in his own image. Twelve of the best graduates of the *Kriegsakademie* were selected each year for special training and to work under Moltke's personal supervision. Any who proved unsatisfactory were returned to regimental duty, and in any case all staff officers did a spell with their regiments before each step in promotion. The staff were thus kept in touch with the soldiery, and Moltke's ideas and standards permeated the army, which by 1870 was largely orientated as he had planned; most of the brigade and divisional commanders had been trained under him, and each corps and army commander had a chief of staff at his elbow.

Training the staff and the army command was Moltke's supreme contribution to the wars his country was to fight, and was of the greatest value when it came to drawing up war plans. These provided for the smooth and efficient mobilization of the army, and there were plans for deployment to meet any international crisis. By 1870 the machinery was perfect. The commanders of corps areas were briefed, and every unit had orders which needed only a code word and a date to be put into operation. Much of the German railway network had been constructed with strategic considerations in mind. In the campaign of 1866 there was some failure to co-ordinate the movement of troops and supplies by rail, but a 'Line of Communication Department' of the general staff was set up, and the mobilization by means of the railways in 1870 was highly successful. From 1858 to 1880 Moltke continually kept the mobilization plans up to date.

Military reform in France began later than in Prussia. After 1859 the French tried to persuade themselves for a while that all was well enough, though the weaknesses of the French army in that campaign were very apparent to German eyes beyond the Rhine. In due course disillusionment came when it was seen what the Prussians could do against Austria in 1866, and with the more ignominious aspects of the military intervention by France in Mexican affairs between 1861 and 1867. From 1866 Napoleon III and Marshal Niel, minister of war, worked to bring the French army more into line with Prussian standards. But in the comparatively liberal French state the reformers had to fight against strong opposition. The middle classes were interested above all in prosperity and peace, and the army was acceptable only if it cost no extra money and so long as those who wished could avoid military service. Since 1818 conscripts in France had been permitted to send substitutes; the result was that the army had developed as an element apart from the nation, and the officer corps was socially despised. In 1866 it was calculated that, while Prussia might be able to raise 1,200,000 trained men, the military strength of France could produce only 288,000 – from which contingents must be drawn to meet commitments in Algeria, Italy and Mexico. But when Niel proposed the adoption of universal military service on the Prussian model he was accused in the Legislature of wanting to make France a barracks. His reply was that if the French were not careful their country would be made a cemetery.

In 1868 a new law was passed. Under this, 172,000 men were to be called up annually, to do five years with the colours and four in the reserve – which by 1875 should provide a mobilized strength of 800,000 for the army. Another 500,000, drawn from those who escaped the call-up, were to be trained in the *Garde Mobile* – but the annual training period of two weeks could easily be evaded, and to avoid the taint of militarism it was laid down that the men were to be trained only for one day at a time, and in conditions which would enable them to get home by the evening; in 1869 the *Garde Mobile* was discarded altogether. By 1870 the professional army of France consisted of nearly half a million men, and it was well equipped. On the other hand, hardly a start had been made in those areas of staff work in which the Prussian army by now excelled: the training of officers, the organization of supply and railway communications, and machinery for mobilization and deployment. The French soldiers were courageous but indisciplined. Most French officers were

elderly, brave men who had risen in the colonial wars by their qualities of dash and
coup d'oeil, rather than for technical expertise in their profession. In 1870 the
French army was better prepared for war than it had been at any time since the
Napoleonic wars, but it was not prepared for modern war.

The outbreak of war between France and Prussia in 1870 was due ostensibly to
a dispute over the Spanish succession. But Napoleon III and Bismarck needed
only an excuse: Napoleon feared Prussia as the leader of a united Germany, while
Bismarck saw war with France as an opportunity to rally Germans to his programme.

Napoleon declared war on 19th July, and a week later he ordered the advance of
French forces across the Rhine near Strasbourg in order to prevent the junction
of the south and north German contingents. But the mobilization of the French did
not keep pace with their strategy, and a concentration of 300,000 men was achieved
only when it was too late. The Prussian mobilization had been brilliantly organized
by Moltke in advance, and in the opening phase each formation and unit followed
precise directives. The First Army, under General von Steinmetz, was pushed
forward on the right over the Rhine and towards the Moselle between Trier and
Wittlich. The Second Army, under Prince Frederick Charles, connected with the
left flank of the First around Homburg. The Third Army, commanded by the
Crown Prince of Prussia, assembled farther up the Rhine on the left wing. Two
additional corps were held in reserve for the Second Army. The three armies,
totalling 384,000 men, were mobilized and transported to the forward zone west
of the Rhine in eighteen days. Rail transport would be available in three weeks to
bring up three more army corps.

The detailed advance plans of Moltke ended at this point, with his troops facing
the enemy's capital and so deployed as to be able to attack the enemy in strength
as they appeared. His arrangements were simple and fluid. He had not lain down
precise plans too far ahead, since the situation beyond the first clash with the
enemy was bound to contain unknown factors. But he hoped to fight a decisive
battle in the area of the Saar, concentrating the weight of the three German armies
to crush the outnumbered French. His army commanders knew his broad plan and
had operational directives, but they were given latitude in their detailed operations
and were expected to show initiative.

The French had been foiled in their first plan, and now hesitated. But when they
had concentrated some 200,000 men in the forward area they opened the fighting –
a reconnaissance in force on 2nd August at Saarbrücken, which achieved little.
Moltke at this point thought that the French were about to launch a strong offensive.
He therefore closed the Second Army in the centre on to its advance posts; the
First Army on the right, the weakest and the farthest advanced, was ordered to halt;
and the Third Army, not quite completely assembled, was moved forward over the
frontier into northern Alsace at Wissembourg – where the first serious engagement
of the war took place on 4th August. Two days later the German Third Army,
pushing on forward to Wörth, enveloped part of the French right wing commanded
by MacMahon. The battle was fiercely contested, and included two gallant but

unavailing French cavalry charges. Eventually the superior handling of their artillery and the better fire-discipline of the Germans caused the French to retreat.

But at this stage matters ceased to go altogether as Moltke had ordained. On 6th August, the same day as the battle of Wörth, Steinmetz rashly engaged the First Army against French forces strongly entrenched at Spicheren, thirty-five miles to the north-west. The commanders of neighbouring German formations quickly came to the assistance of the leading attacking division, and by the evening the French were forced to withdraw. But the German losses in men at Spicheren were heavier than those of the French. The German reconnaissance now lost sight of MacMahon's movements, and Moltke supposed that the French right was moving north-westwards to join the forces of the French left under Bazaine near Metz – whereas in fact MacMahon was moving back south-westwards. Moltke also assumed that Bazaine was retreating from Metz, which was not the case. The German reconnaissance was not being well handled.

On 14th August a second unexpected battle took place at Colombey, which the Germans just won as before. By the evening of 15th August Bazaine was definitely retreating from Metz, but he had not gone as far towards Verdun as Moltke supposed when, on the 16th, the German Second Army pressed across the Moselle south of Metz to pursue Bazaine – whose forces were strongly concentrated less than ten miles to the west. The Second Army was strung out and isolated, and Bazaine had a golden opportunity to attack it in flank with superior forces – but he allowed events to drift. The first German corps collided with a stronger French force at Mars-la-Tour, and the same pattern unfolded as at Spicheren: the Germans fought desperately until additional forces came to their help, and by the end of the day they had gained some ground. Each side lost about 16,000 men.

Bazaine now decided to stand and fight, and he ordered his forces to entrench in a strong position just west of Metz – the ridge that runs for about seven miles between the villages of Gravelotte to the south and Saint-Privat to the north. The ridge sloped gently to the west and dropped steeply to the east. By 18th August the French defences were completed – fire and communication trenches had been dug, many of the batteries were protected by emplacements, and some farmhouses had been converted into small forts. In the battle which was about to take place both sides would actually face their own strategic rear. The German push since 6th August had brought their forces round on a wide south-westerly movement and, when the French did not retreat as expected, the German First and Second Armies found that they had completely enveloped the right flank of Bazaine's forces. On 18th August as dawn broke, Frederick Charles still imagined that Bazaine was retreating westwards, and he marched his army northwards in strong parallel columns west of the ridge – thereby exposing them to a situation of great potential danger. But Bazaine again failed to attack when the advantage was his. This time the Germans intended to fight when they should find the enemy, and for the first time the bulk of the forces of both sides were to be engaged in one battle. The Germans, having removed the original right of the French by the victory of Wörth, had 188,300 men and 732 guns to oppose 112,800 Frenchmen and 520 guns.

The leading corps of Frederick Charles's Second Army came into contact with the French at Amanvillers. The Germans at first supposed this to be the extreme right of the French position, and shortly before midday Manstein's IX Corps attacked the French positions commanded by Ladmirault beyond Verneville. By the time it was realized that the French were holding Saint-Privat in force, and might attack the German forces in flank, it was too late for Moltke to alter the orders for attack, which had been given on the assumption that the French position based on Gravelotte could be turned from the north. In the initial fighting around Amanvillers the Germans were checked by the fire of the French *chassepots* in the open fields, and they lost some artillery to a counter-attack. The battle in this area was then reduced to an artillery duel which the troops on both sides endured passively, while more troops of the German Second Army were brought up to support their left. By 3 o'clock Manstein had been reinforced and the Germans soon drove the French out of the village of Sainte-Marie-aux-Chênes. By 5 o'clock the French infantry was thickly bunched about Saint-Privat and their artillery did its best to protect them from the concentrated fire of 180 German guns.

Meanwhile around Gravelotte from the north and south 150 guns of the German VII and VIII Corps had at midday opened continuous fire on the French positions – the fire continuing until dark came, and causing considerable carnage and devastation. But neither artillery fire nor infantry attacks could move the French from the positions opposite Gravelotte, except at the outpost of Saint-Hubert. A little farther south, in the ravine of the Mance, Steinmetz made a series of flagrant mistakes. Assuming the fall of Saint-Hubert in the middle of the afternoon to be a sign of French disintegration, he ordered all the available infantry and artillery of VII Corps to attack along the axis of the narrow road into the ravine and, for a *coup de grâce*, sent with them the 1st cavalry division which was to chase the defeated French to Metz. A very few Germans fought their way through to Saint-Hubert, but the rest were blocked in bloody chaos in the ravine. By 5 o'clock it was clear that the First Army's attack had been a failure, and a withdrawal was beginning. Within an hour the German advantage at Saint-Privat was also to be prejudiced – when Prince Augustus of Würtemberg ordered the Guard Corps to advance on Saint-Privat before the Saxons could co-ordinate their attack farther to the north. When the skirmishing lines of the Guard advanced up the slope towards the French line of *chassepots* a massacre ensued: when the attack came to 600 yards from Saint-Privat it was halted – having suffered 8,000 casualties in twenty minutes.

By 6 o'clock the French had thus checked the Germans along the whole line from Gravelotte to Saint-Privat. The moment was now ripe for a French counter-attack. But Bazaine's will-power and energy appear to have been paralysed by the weight of responsibility. Refusing to come forward from his headquarters at Plappeville, he was aware only that the defence was succeeding – which seemed to him enough. When subordinate commanders asked for new orders he was hesitant and indecisive, and they themselves lacked the initiative necessary to complete the victory.

Even although the French did not launch a counter-attack, the German situation in the south had yet to deteriorate further. When Steinmetz's own troops had all

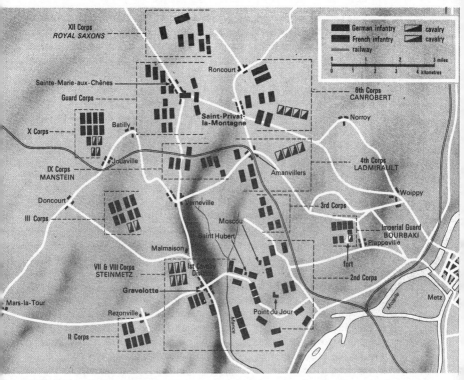

The battle of Gravelotte-Saint-Privat

been thrown into the chaos of the Mance ravine, he appealed to royal headquarters for permission to throw in fresh troops from II Corps, which was just arriving in the battle area. Since he reported untruthfully that he had all but carried the heights, permission was granted. The French could see the helmets of their enemies glinting in the evening sun, and they were ready. The assault was met with murderous fire at point-blank range, and the German infantry fell back in disorder. Then some of the horses began to bolt, and suddenly the tension broke in VII and VIII Corps. Cavalry and horse artillery careered in flight back through Gravelotte, and the German infantry ran back down the ravine – yet still the French did not counter-attack. II Corps resisted the tide of panic, but in the darkness the soldiers found themselves firing into disordered German troops; they did no more than hold the position and at 9.30 o'clock they ceased fire.

The king and his staff made their way to Rezonville, to contemplate the defeat of the First Army. Their gloom was not lightened until after midnight, when at last Moltke learned from Frederick Charles that the French right had collapsed. The tremendous pressure of the Guard Corps had in fact helped the German situation in no small way, for when the Saxons made their flank attack from the north the French were not ready to face them. At the same time artillery fire broke up all French attempts to move forward between Amanvillers and Saint-Privat, and Canrobert, commanding on the right, decided that he must fall back, requesting Bourbaki, commanding the Imperial Guard in reserve, to cover his retreat – which he was unable to do. A last charge by cavalry was quickly broken up by German rifle fire. Soon after 8 o'clock the Germans, 50,000 strong, had gained Saint-Privat at the point of the bayonet, and the French right withdrew down the Woippy road. Farther to the French left, at Amanvillers, Bourbaki in a rage refused to support Ladmirault in the centre, and there too the French started to retreat.

The retreat of the French right was an orderly affair compared to the rout of the Germans at Gravelotte, and the Germans were too disorganized to pursue. But it was enough to decide the verdict of the battle of Gravelotte-Saint-Privat in favour of the Germans. On 19th August the rest of Bazaine's Army of the Rhine retired into the defences of Metz. The Germans had suffered some 20,000 casualties, considerably more than the French, but they gained a decisive strategic advantage at the conclusion of the battle because they were able to bottle up Bazaine's army in Metz and eliminate it altogether from the rest of the war. The deplorable French command needs no discussion; the French troops had displayed a fighting quality which deserved better leadership. Moltke was lucky to have gained such a victory, for he had not really been in control of events at any time since 6th August. But his years of work in organization and training were triumphantly vindicated in the instinctive mutual understanding which German subordinate officers showed in this campaign; the blunders of Steinmetz and Frederick Charles were repaired repeatedly by the speed and intelligence with which the commanders of lesser German formations and units helped each other out, as well as by the discipline and courage of the troops – born of confidence in their officers.

The Germans next manoeuvred to surround a French relieving army at Sedan; there the French were penned into a cup of land, and the Germans used their artillery to defeat them from beyond the range of the *chassepot*. The next day the French surrendered, the Germans taking 104,000 prisoners, including Napoleon III – having lost only 9,000 men themselves. The Germans had effectively defeated the French in two months of operations, for France did not have another organized army. The war was, however, drawn out a further six months. A republic was declared in Paris, and Gambetta, minister of war, inspired the resistance. The sieges of Metz and Paris were prolonged. The French hurled themselves against the besieging Germans with ferocious courage, and in the countryside the *francs-tireurs* assailled them with guerrilla warfare. Gambetta escaped from Paris by balloon to organize an army of the Loire. Only in February 1871 did the last of the French surrender. William proclaimed himself German Emperor at Versailles, and the Germans marched in triumph through the streets of Paris. The French then fought and massacred each other in Paris during the Commune – watched by the Germans.

The defence of Châteaudun: an incident in the Franco-Prussian War. A detail from the painting by Felix Philippoteaux. *Overleaf* The Battle of the Alma by Felix Philippoteaux

Another great 'modern' war had taken place in North America. The origins of the American Civil War (1861–5) lay in the growing tension between two completely different types of society bound together under one government, and the issue of slavery sharpened hatreds during the 1850's. The North had a population of over 18 million to pit against the South's 9 million – one third of whom were negro slaves. The North possessed 90 per cent of the country's manufacturing capacity, two thirds of its railway mileage, control of the sea, and most of the mineral resources. The South was particularly badly off for weapons: of 135,000 handguns seized from government arsenals at secession, only 10,000 were rifles, the rest being old-fashioned smooth-bores and some of them flint-locks. In time Southerners were able to capture and improvize more modern weapons, but they remained at a grave disadvantage. But the South was fighting to protect its way of life and its homes from invaders, whereas the troops of the North were fighting only for an abstraction – the principle of the Union. For this reason the South found it easier to raise enthusiastic fighters. Moreover a much higher proportion of Southerners were countrymen – good horsemen and used to an open air life.

Let us consider the leadership on both sides. Lincoln considered that slavery was an issue which time and common sense would solve. But once the Union was split it would never be restored; North America would become like Europe, a continent torn with jealousy, economic rivalry and war. He fought to preserve the Union. Lincoln had no practical military experience, and his appointments were too often made on political grounds; when popular outcry demanded the recall of a defeated general, he generally yielded. Gradually the best men came to the top, but several good men disappeared. The general whom Lincoln eventually found, Ulysses Grant, was a soldier's general, thoughtful of his subordinates and fitting his orders to their experience and skill. Of all the generals on either side in the war, he alone demonstrated the capacity to command small forces as well as large ones in battle under a great variety of conditions – and finally to command and direct the operations of several armies. He did not believe in large staffs; in 1864 he commanded five armies operating in an area half the size of Europe, and his headquarters staff consisted of fourteen officers. Lincoln had at last found a general, but not until February 1864 – and then with a thankful heart he appointed Ulysses Grant to command the armies of the North. He and Sherman were the two best field commanders produced in the War between the States – both fighting for the North.

Davis in the South was well qualified to handle the material at his disposal; he was a graduate of West Point, had served several years in the regular army, and had been secretary for war in Washington. Not only did he select the right men, but he supported them in adversity and did not at once remove a general because he met with a reverse. Furthermore, he had in General Lee possibly the best American military thinker and organizer of those days, and during the first year of the war he retained Lee as his chief of staff in the capital, a decision which in my view had much to do with the initial success of the South. But as a commander in the field Lee was not sufficiently firm with his corps commanders, and he was not a good picker of men. His own judgment was generally sound, but he didn't like to give firm orders

The battle of Gettysburg. A detail from the Cyclorama by Paul Philippoteaux, depicting the climax of Pickett's Charge

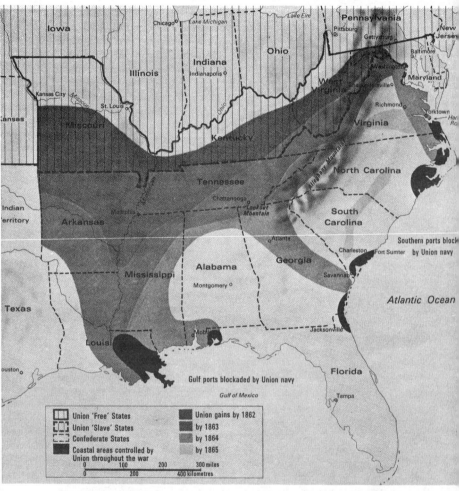

The American Civil War

to unwilling subordinates; this was brought out very clearly at Gettysburg, in which battle he was at his worst.

When the war began both sides had to create an army, and each was bound to be an army of volunteers. In 1860 the regular army of the United States totalled only some 16,000, mostly scattered in small detachments on the Indian frontier which could not be withdrawn. Both in the North and South there were many militia units, but these lacked training and discipline. It was a great advantage for the

South to be able to cut loose from the red tape of the War Department in Washington. Geography and the strategic use of railways played a large part in the war. In the western theatre the war was more fluid and mobile than in the east, being fought over vast areas. The control of rivers was a major strategic objective, particularly for the North as it had most of the steamboats, the trained river men, and organization for building and repair.

It was a major error for Davis to choose for the capital of the South Richmond, a city which was near the frontier and accessible from the sea – particularly since the North had the navy. The two capitals were within 100 miles of each other, and much of the effort of each side was directed to capturing the other's capital. If either had succeeded it would have been of great moral importance. If Washington had fallen at any time, the will to victory in the North might well have collapsed; Lincoln realized this; he also realized that the destruction of Lee's army would affect the South even more than the capture of Richmond. As events turned out, Washington was threatened more than once. But the North had in Lincoln a real man, of tremendous courage and singleness of mind.

The improvements in firearms which had taken place since Waterloo revolutionized tactics in this war. The solid infantry formations of earlier years disappeared; the old type of cavalry warfare, shock action against infantry, went out of business; the spade and the axe became necessary articles in battle; breastworks and rifle pits were used to give cover and protection. The civil war in America showed all this; yet most armies of Europe refused to take the lesson seriously.

The victory of the North in the American Civil War was a victory for nationalism, liberalism and industrialism. The Franco-Prussian War repeated many of the military experiences and lessons of the American Civil War. The effect of rifle fire at Saint-Privat as at Gettysburg indicated the new strength of the defensive. The fate of cavalry charging in the old style, as at Wörth, showed that it must devise different tactical functions; this was not appreciated in Europe so well as in America, where the Southern cavalry commander, Nathan B. Forrest, adapted his forces to use them mainly as mounted infantry. The defensive power of the machine-gun had yet to be gauged, but the paralysing and destructive power of modern artillery was felt. It was shown that railways could be an advantage or a disadvantage, depending on their use. The swift Prussian victory in 1870 was due to Moltke's efficient mobilization by means of railways as much as to any other factor. On the other hand one of the reasons why the North was unable to make any decisive breakthrough for so long was that it became tied too rigidly to fixed lines of supply; the North won quickly only when Sherman broke free of his dependence on railheads. The growing size of armies rendered mobility much more difficult, and gave increased importance to staffs, and to commanders of corps and divisions. It remained to see whether the lessons of those experiences would be drawn.

17 Learning the Hard Way

The years between 1870 and 1914 were years of armed peace within Europe, when the European powers furthered their interests and found outlets for their tensions in other areas of the world – notably East Asia, North Africa and the Balkans. Within this period, however, the emergence on the international scene outside Europe of two new industrial and mass powers indicated that imperialism might have to be curbed. In 1904–5 Japan defeated Russia in a war which involved more men then any previous war in history. Similarly, when the United States of America deprived Spain of Cuba in 1898, it was indicated that European powers would no longer be able to relieve their tensions by expressing them in a vast imperial arena; the world was beginning to be crowded with people and with industrial and military power.

It is remarkable that large-scale war was so successfully avoided in this period, considering how great were the strains set up in Europe by economic and social factors. The population of Europe rose by 10 per cent each decade, and industrialization continued to grow, with world production rising four times between 1870 and 1900. The cumulative interaction between population growth, industrial methods and pure science produced entirely new industries such as the electrical and chemical industries, and new sources of power such as the internal combustion engine. Aluminium, the pneumatic tyre and wireless made their appearance. The armaments industry entered a phase of fierce growth; the leading manufacturers of arms were the great firms of Armstrong, Krupp, and Creusot. No power would willingly allow another to grow stronger than itself and, with new inventions and the increase in productive capacity, the international arms race intensified, as did competition in strategic railway building and rivalry in the size of armies.

Universal service on the German pattern was adopted everywhere after 1870, except in Britain and the U.S.A. Altogether the number of men which the great powers of Europe could put into the field rose in twenty-five years by 10 million. The armed forces became the focus of violent patriotic emotions in all nations, as was evinced in France by the Dreyfus affair in the 1890's. A practical objection to mass armies was that they were not suitable for imperialist wars, and for this reason Britain preferred to maintain smaller long-service professional forces. But Britain was no less fiercely nationalistic than the other powers; her navy was as potent a national symbol to the British as their armies were to the continental peoples. The total expenditure of the European powers on defence increased between 1874 and 1896 by 50 per cent, and the pace of the arms race caused sufficient misgivings for a conference on disarmament to be held at The Hague in 1899 – but the American

The British army, adopting traditional tactics, was at first unable to cope with the guerrilla warfare and accurate marksmanship of the Boers representative stated that his government did not 'consider limitations in regard to the use of military inventions to be conducive to the peace of the world'.

As in numbers and equipment, so in organization European armies increasingly matched each other – the surviving differences being mostly small concessions to tradition and *esprit de corps*. The French infantry kept their red trousers, but most troops in the field now wore khaki, first used by the British in India. The need for efficient staffs was universally recognized. The German staff was the model; and the Nicholas General Staff Academy in St Petersburg and the Staff College at Camberley were counterparts of the Prussian War Academy. Standards in these institutions became far higher than before, with stiffer entrance requirements and a wider syllabus. Armies were increasingly professionalized, and drew more and more on the middle classes for their officers. In Britain the abolition of the purchase of commissions was one of many reforms which made the army more efficient during the time when Edward Cardwell was at the War Office.

In European armies the basic unit was the corps, a self-contained force of some 30,000 men organized to fight efficiently if detached from the parent army. The corps was usually linked to a particular territorial area, and its commander was responsible for organization, training, recruitment and supply. A typical corps might consist of two divisions, each containing two infantry brigades, one cavalry brigade and a regiment of field artillery. Under direct corps command were a regiment of heavy artillery, engineering and supply services, medical units, telegraph units, railway and balloon detachments, cyclists, bridge trains, and other administrative or ancillary services. Armament was by 1900 more or less uniform: infantry were armed with 8 or 9 mm. magazine-rifles, field artillery with 8 cm. steel guns, and siege and heavy artillery with guns, mortars and howitzers of 15 and 21 cm. calibre.

The arms race before 1914 ensured the continued development of military and naval technology. By 1900, rifles, pistols, carbines, and machine-guns were as they were to be during the 1914/18 war. The principal developments in the rifle were the magazine system of loading invented by James Lee, and smaller calibre bullets which, being lighter, travelled faster and on a flatter trajectory. Smokeless powder was adopted by the French in 1884 – a development which was literally to transform the face of battlefields. There were major developments in explosives, with the production of dynamite in 1867 by Alfred Nobel and cordite in 1890. In 1883 Hiram S. Maxim patented his machine-gun, with which the recoil was used to load, fire and eject continuously so long as the trigger was held back; the cartridges were stored in a flexible belt, and the barrel was cooled by a water jacket. In 1891 the British army adopted a special light model which weighed only 40 lb and fired 650 rounds a minute. With slight modifications Maxim's gun became the Vickers machine-gun, which was used in both world wars; more than any other weapon it was responsible for the character of trench warfare. In artillery, muzzle-loading gave way to breech-loading because long barrels gave velocity and range. The British field artillery adopted 12-pounder guns. By 1890 most European armies were equipped with the guns which they were to use, with only minor modifications, in the 1914/18 war.

Magazine-loaded rifles *below* and automatically re-loading machine guns
above enabled the rate of fire to be greatly increased

In this period war first took to the air. The value of observation from the air was recognized; balloons and airships were built in Britain, France and Germany, and the Army Balloon School was founded at Woolwich in 1878. The Germans developed the Zeppelin, and from 1909 the arms race was extended in earnest into the sphere of air warfare. Following the aeroplane flight by the Wright brothers in 1903, France was the first power to recognize the potential value of the aeroplane for military purposes. Progress in speed, range, and reliability was rapid, and by 1914 aeroplanes could fly at 75 m.p.h. and remain airborne for three hours. It was expected that they would be useful chiefly for reconnaissance. The British air force was divided in 1914 into the Royal Naval Air Service and an army component, the Royal Flying Corps.

During the 1870's as the penetrating power of shells increased so ships were protected with thicker iron armour, sometimes up to 24 inches. In the 1880's thin but adequate steel armour-plating became available and the demands of security and mobility ceased to be opposed. By 1900 battleships displaced some 15,000 tons, had a speed of 18 knots, and mounted 12- or 13-inch guns. Britain took alarm at the alliance of France and Russia, since their combined fleets were larger than her own, and by adopting a huge building programme in 1899 she intensified the naval race. The *Dreadnought* was laid down in 1904, and with her all-big-gun armament of ten 12-inch guns this ship out-moded all previous battleships, and remained the model for capital ships until the 1939/45 war. The introduction of the steam turbine and the change from coal to oil increased speeds to 25 knots, and made it possible for ships to remain at sea and run at high speeds for longer. In the years before 1914 Britain and Germany became the foremost rivals in the naval race. In one single year Britain laid down eight new ships. In 1877 the Russians used torpedoes effectively against stationary Turkish ships, and thereafter torpedo boats were generally commissioned. The real development of the submarine began with the invention in 1877 of the horizontal rudder, which made possible a controlled dive. The accumulator battery and the petrol engine finally made the submarine a weapon of great potential effectiveness. The French were the pioneers here: in 1901 France had twenty-three submarines built or under construction. Britain ordered five in that year, and by 1912 no major navy was without submarines. The powers had also to compete for bases in all parts of the world.

In the profusion of military literature which appeared during this period one outstanding work was Major-General Sir Charles Callwell's *Small Wars: Their Principles and Practice* (1896) – a consideration of the numerous campaigns of the imperialist powers. These were mostly irregular operations. Often the latest military equipment and the material resources of industrial societies were pitted against the forces of primitive peoples. Whatever the courage of the natives, the ultimate issue in such fighting could not be in doubt. But there were problems in this type of warfare arising from its irregularity; jungle, swamp and desert presented difficulties in supply and transport, and climate alone could be a formidable enemy. When the enemy avoided open fighting and relied on elusiveness and invisibility, ambushes, sniping and raiding, morale was liable to fall. It was often not easy to

The *Dreadnought* created a model for capital ships that was widely followed

find a worthwhile objective, with no main body of the enemy to seek out and destroy and no real capital to strike at. Regular troops were compelled to forget their formal tactical training for European war, and to adopt the methods of guerrilla and savage warfare.

One solution to the problem of the objective in this type of war was to strike at the enemy's sources of refuge and supply. Laying waste his crops and villages and impounding herds and stores were effective; on the other hand these methods made war savage and resentful, and military commanders with an eye to the future administration of the subjugated territory, such as Lyautey and Kitchener, were reluctant to resort to them. The enrolment of natives on the European side could be helpful, since they would know the country and the characteristics of the enemy – but they might be treacherous. Otherwise, in loose formations the tactical advantage lay with the side which had good horses, light field artillery and repeater rifles with a long range. Strategically an important rule was to maintain the offensive, because a bold bearing would gain the initiative and discourage the enemy. The ablest single commander of this period was the Russian conqueror of Turkestan, Mikhail Skobelev (1843–82). In 1880 he defeated the Tekke Turcomans with the numerical odds heavily against him and in country which was no more than a desert from the supply angle. He moved slowly and patiently, but never gave the enemy any respite. Similarly, in 1898 Kitchener never abandoned the strategic offensive against the Dervishes.

Tactically the offensive was not essential: when Kitchener reached Khartoum he adopted the defensive against the wild charges of the Dervishes, who were shattered by the fire of the Anglo-Egyptian troops. Against such brave fighters as the Maoris or the Dervishes or against the mountaineers of the Indian frontier a disaster was always possible. Rock-like defence which tempted the enemy forces to dash themselves to destruction, or resolute attack, would both be suitable – but indecision was fatal. At Maiwand in India in 1880 a British force moved forward from a defensive position but then failed to attack, and was annihilated. The Italian commander made every mistake against the Abyssinians at Adowa in 1896, underestimating the enemy's strength and allowing his own forces to straggle; the result was that his 15,000 men were routed. The Zulus were superb warriors, highly organized, drilled and disciplined; they had terrific mobility, moving on foot with their tireless lope almost as fast as cavalry and they had a wonderful sense of ground. Their battle horde, the *impi*, attacked with its centre moving relatively slowly to allow time for the horns to envelop the enemy. In 1879 a British force of some 6,000 men under Lord Chelmsford was all but wiped out at Isandlhwana by a much larger Zulu army, whose main body had completely concealed its presence. But later that same year at Ulundi, Chelmsford avenged his defeat: the rifle was too much for the *assegai*.

The Boer War of 1899–1902 was on a much larger scale, but it contained many of the features of the previous irregular imperialist wars. The Boers, hardy farmers and excellent marksmen with their Mauser rifles, were unhampered by traditional military methods and they resorted to guerrilla warfare on a large scale. They fought as a people-in-arms, determined to preserve their lands and way of life. 85,000 names were inscribed on the Boer Commando lists; they were first-class horsemen, with a natural sense of minor tactics; although nearly all were mounted, they fought on foot; they were unexpectedly strong in artillery. Their weakest feature was indiscipline: they disliked being organized and their officers could never count on all the men on the muster-roll being present to go into action. Fighting over their own country they had no problem about supply.

The British forces in South Africa in 1899 did not exceed 10,000 men; in small arms they were well equipped, but the Boers had the better artillery. The British soldiery were inadequately trained to deal with fighters so well armed and so capable as the Boers. As one staff officer wrote: 'We make the soldier in many cases a fool because we start with the assumption that he is a fool, and gradually teach him that he is thus to regard himself.'

The Boers adopted the offensive and by the autumn had met with quick success, driving the British troops to take refuge in the towns of Ladysmith, Kimberley and Mafeking. The British commander-in-chief, Buller, suffered reverses at the Tugela river and Colenso, and in January 1900 he was gravely defeated at Spion Kop. Cyril Falls calls that day 'the supreme day in the history of the rifle'. The Boers pushed home their attack to close quarters entirely by rifle fire, overwhelming the British troops without even having to make a final charge. They shot down their man if he exposed for a moment so much as a limb.

Early in 1900 reinforcements from Britain at last reached South Africa. Cardwell's organization of the army had been designed to supply fairly small contingents for imperial garrisons, and it had not been possible quickly to raise a substantial force suitable for this fighting. Britain's chief lesson from the war was to be the need for keeping a larger and better trained reserve, and by 1914 she was in a reasonable position to undertake a major war. Besides the reinforcements a new commander-in-chief arrived: Field-Marshal Roberts, the veteran commander of the north-west frontier of India. Roberts brought with him as chief-of-staff a first-class organizer, General Kitchener, and a brilliant railway engineer, Colonel Girouard. The transport was reorganized; Roberts manoeuvred skilfully; the besieged towns were relieved, and the Boers were defeated at Diamond Hill and Belfast. Kruger, the Boer president, fled to Europe; the war seemed virtually over and Kitchener was left to finish it off.

The war was in fact far from over. Under an outstanding guerrilla leader, Christian de Wet, the Boers carried on an irregular war for nearly two more years. Moving secretly and rapidly they executed highly skilful raids, sabotaging the railways, cutting off British detachments, and evading pursuit. Kitchener had repeatedly to call for reinforcements. To strike at the enemy lifeline Kitchener instituted the hated system of destroying the farms and interning the civilian population in camps, where inevitably the living conditions were terrible. Even that did not end the Boer resistance. Eventually Kitchener found the solution; he systematically partitioned the country into great areas enclosed by barbed wire. Slowly but thoroughly, British columns drove through each enclosure, and flushed out the enemy. At the peace of Vereeniging in 1902 generous terms were given – and kept.

As the Ottoman empire entered the last stages of decay, producing a vacuum of power, the Balkans became an increasingly dangerous flashpoint. Nationalism animated the Balkan peoples, and while Russia and Austria looked covetously at the decaying empire, Germany sought to extend her sphere of influence, and Britain was concerned to protect her interests in the Dardanelles and Suez Canal. Crisis exploded in 1876–8. The Bulgars revolted against the Turks, and the Russians crossed the Danube.

The Turkish troops, with the Martini-Peabody rifle and the Krupp breech-loading field gun, were better armed than their enemies and well entrenched, and the size of their forces soon increased considerably. The first Russian assault against Plevna in July was repelled with a loss of 35 per cent of the attacking force.

The second assault, though bravely carried out, was clumsy in conception, and the Turks coolly held their entrenchments. By September, Osman Pasha had 56,000 troops and had built eighteen redoubts. The Russians now had 84,000 men, and preceded their attack by a four-day bombardment. Only one section of the Russian assault, that commanded by Skobelev, was successful. He himself organized the reconnaissance. His losses in the assault were heavy, but he fed in reserves skilfully, and then at the crucial moment personally led his men to their objective. Plevna, however, did not fall yet. Only when still more Russian forces arrived and established a complete blockade did Osman consider he could do no more, and in December the Turks fell back.

This war presents interesting features. One was the skilful and inspiring leadership of Skobelev. Once before in Turkestan he had disguised himself as a Turcoman, and had fearlessly reconnoitred through hostile territory the route his men were to take. Now, following his achievement in the assaults on Plevna, in January he crossed the Balkan mountains in snowstorms, defeating the Turks at Senova and capturing 36,000 men and 90 guns. Dressed in white uniform and mounted on a white horse, and always in the thickest of the fighting, the 'White General' was adored by his soldiers. Skobelev died of heart disease in 1882 at the age of thirty-nine. Besides his leadership, the courage of the Russian soldiers must be praised; they returned again and again to the assault of the strongest entrenchments and would march all night over mountains under snow.

The success of the resistance put up by the Turks astonished contemporary Europe. Osman Pasha's field fortifications pointed to the character of future fighting between armies armed with rifles and the spade.

The diplomatic and military situation in the Far East in this period was transformed by the rapid emergence of modern Japan after 1853 (see Chapter 9). In the 1870's feudalism was abolished, two million *samurai* were pensioned off, and conscription of the whole male population was introduced. Equipment and training were provided for the Japanese army by Germany, and for the navy by Britain. Industrialization proceeded rapidly; and by 1903 Japan's population stood at 45 million. With the development of her capacities Japan's ambitions also grew. She first tried her strength with considerable success in the Sino-Japanese war of 1894-5, forcing China to lease the Liao-tung peninsula to her. Japan then found herself in direct competition with Russia; and eventually in February 1904 the Japanese opened war with the Russians – without a formal declaration.

It was astonishing that a fledgling power such as Japan should take on single-handed the most massive of all the old European powers. But the Japanese had calculated the odds well. A treaty of 1902 guaranteed that Britain would come to Japan's assistance if a third power intervened against her. The Japanese were fighting for a strictly limited aim: the security of a certain area of hegemony. The location

Breech-loaded guns with hydraulic buffers to check recoil were now standard equipment. Their range was greatly increased by firing from rifled barrels of the war was to Japan's advantage. The Russians of course possessed far greater resources of men and materials, but they had a huge problem in getting them to the theatre of war; when hostilities began the Trans-Siberian railway was not quite complete and it took a month to transport a battalion from Moscow to Port Arthur.

In 1904 Japan could put into the field immediately 300,000 troops in 13 divisions and 400,000 trained reserves, whereas Russia's available force was only 250,000 combatants at the end of that year. The equipment on each side was comparable, but the Japanese command, based on the German model, was better, and their troops had a higher morale. Seapower was a vital factor, for the Japanese communications with the mainland depended on their control of the seas. The Japanese fleet was slightly superior in size and quality to the Russian Far Eastern fleet based on Port Arthur with a detachment at Vladivostok. But the Russians had another fleet in the Baltic – though the long sea voyage to the theatre of operations would take time. The aim of the Japanese was to knock out Port Arthur, thus removing any threat to Japan herself and securing the free movement of her land forces – and then to win a major battle which would convince Russia that she must respect Japan in the Far East.

At the outset of war the Japanese fleet, commanded by Admiral Togo, took the initiative. On the night of 8th February his torpedo-boats surprised the Russian squadron in Port Arthur, seriously damaging two battleships and a cruiser; and on the same night in the Korean harbour of Chemulpo one Russian cruiser was sunk and another damaged. The Russian ships in Vladivostok were still icebound. Under testing winter conditions the Japanese established a tight blockade at Port Arthur and this allowed their forces to land unimpeded in Korea and drive back the Russians on the Yalu. In March a series of sorties by the Russian fleet caused Togo considerable anxiety. But in mid-April the Russian flagship was blown up by a mine, and Admiral Makarov was killed; his loss was a disaster for the Russians. The Japanese maintained their blockade during the year and held on to their vital advantage in keeping Russian seapower out of action.

By June 1904 enough Japanese troops had been transported for the siege of Port Arthur from the land to begin. The commander of the Japanese land forces, Oyama, was an able soldier; he was bold and encouraged his army commanders to use their initiative within the broad limits of his directives – one general, Nogi, being a gifted leader in battle. The Russian land commander, Kuropatkin, a former staff officer of Skobelev, was intelligent but lacking in confidence. The long siege of the fortress was a grim struggle. By means of dynamite and a loss of 52,000 men the Japanese at length prevailed, and on 1st January 1905 the Russians surrendered Port Arthur, losing 24,000 prisoners, 546 guns and what was left of their fleet.

The Japanese had already been seeking the great battle which was to make the Russians give up the struggle. After very heavy fighting in August and October Kuropatkin had decided to withdraw on Mukden. The battle of Mukden in March 1905 was the last of the war on land, and in the size of the operations it was the greatest battle which had ever been fought. The opposing forces were each some 310,000 strong extended on a strongly entrenched front of over forty miles. The

Japanese began the pressure. Their tactic was to open rifle fire at a distance of about half a mile from the position attacked; the soldiers would run forward in bursts, bodies bent low, then fall to the ground at a hand signal – maintaining strict discipline. At Mukden, Nogi succeeded in forcing back the Russian right; a powerful enemy counter-offensive failed and the Russians then conducted a well-controlled retreat.

Meanwhile the Russian Baltic fleet, under Admiral Rozhestvenski, was on its long and accident-ridden voyage half way round the world. On the fall of Port Arthur Togo had taken his ships back to Japan to refit. The Russian fleet was formidable on paper – 38 ships, including 7 battleships – and, although rumours of inefficiency and indiscipline had been heard, Togo was apprehensive. When the Russians approached the Straits of Tsushima on 27th May 1905 Togo's fleet awaited them; he had only 4 battleships, but this was offset by a superiority in cruisers. The Japanese ships had an advantage in quality, since some of the Russian ships were archaic and the fleet had to go at the pace of the slowest.

The Russian ships steamed into action with coal piled so high on their decks that they were low in the water and deprived of much of their manoeuvrability; all in all, the fleet was in some disorder. The fighting began with a cruiser action. Because of superior speed the Japanese line was able to steam across the head of the Russian line, in the tactic of 'crossing the T'. The leading Russian ships were enfiladed by each Japanese ship in turn while the Russian ships behind were not in a position to reply. The gunnery of the Japanese was skilled, and within forty minutes two Russian battleships and a cruiser were practically out of action. After a little over one hour the fleets became separated, but Togo again attacked in the evening, and three more Russian battleships and a cruiser were sunk. The enemy fleet was thus all but annihilated, and its remnants were beset by destroyers during the night and relentlessly pursued on the following day.

The battle of Tsushima was the first really major sea battle since Trafalgar, and Togo's 'crossing of the T' was an outstanding achievement in the history of naval tactics. It was this absolute defeat at sea rather than the situation on land after Mukden which persuaded the Russians to give up the war. By the Peace of Portsmouth (September 1905) Japan gained her precise aims in Korea, the Liao-tung peninsula and the southern half of Sakhalin. She had made her mark on the international scene.

In a book which received wide attention, *The Influence of Sea Power on History* (1890), the American naval historian A. T. Mahan made a profound analysis of the strategic role of seapower. The strength of the modern state depended on wealth which was to a large extent founded on trade and colonies; every part of the world was linked economically to Europe. For this reason every ambitious state must maintain a powerful modern navy and frame for itself a maritime strategy worldwide in its scope. European war in the future could only be world war.

The situation with regard to land warfare was not so well appreciated. The most significant characteristic of the wars of this time was the tactical power of the defensive. Rifle and artillery fire, machine-guns and hand grenades, all operated from the cover of entrenchments and earthworks protected by barbed wire, were making it difficult and costly for attacks to be brought to close quarters; the spade had now become an essential article of military equipment; the only defence against machine-guns and artillery fire was to dig in.

After 1870 military thinkers attempted to build theories on the basis of what had been experienced in the Franco-Prussian War. The tendency in France and Germany was to abandon the 'mathematics' of Jomini and think in Clausewitzian terms of force tempered by Moltke's more practical approach. In Germany the chief of the general staff from 1891 to 1906, Count von Schlieffen, produced the Schlieffen Plan for the invasion of France. But as technical change progressed and the experience of actual war in Europe receded, theory became less realistic. In France nationalistic pride caused the emphasis to be laid on the offensive, and when Foch wrote, 'Whatever the circumstances . . . it is the intention to advance with all forces to the attack', then, as Dr Luvaas puts it, 'indiscretion had become the better part of valour'. The best work in England was Callwell's book, but his subject was a marginal one. In the British army concern for vested interests produced an unrealistic approach to war: the *Cavalry Journal* was founded in 1906 by certain regiments of the British army, to propagate the idea that the shock action of cavalry was still the right tactical counter to infantry firepower.

Instead of noting the effect of entrenchments, barbed wire, and modern small arms, most European soldiers thus chose to ignore Plevna, to regard South Africa as irrelevant guerrilla war, and to congratulate themselves that the Japanese victory was a triumph for Moltke's system. Meanwhile south-eastern European countries were at war with each other again in 1885, 1897 and 1911–13. The industrial competition and the armaments race between the great powers intensified, and the strains on the diplomatic fabric increased.

I call to mind the words of Maeterlinck: 'The past is of use to me as the eve of tomorrow; my soul wrestles with the future.' In other words, to plan the future wisely nations must learn from the past. Neglect of this principle means that the path to success in the future has to be trodden the hard way – and the cost is then paid in men's lives. Only one man, I. S. Bloch, a Warsaw banker, in a work published in 1898 forecast the nature of total war. He knew that a great war could not be long delayed, and he argued that in the event of large-scale war in Europe a stalemate between the armed forces of the contending nations was inevitable – due to technical development of weapons, and to the harnessing of all the political and economic forces of powerful states to war. The only result would be the most fearful distress to civil populations, victor suffering as much as vanquished – with the ultimate collapse of social organization. Reading Bloch's book induced the Tsar to arrange the conference at the Hague in 1899, but nothing significant was achieved by it. Bloch's warnings were largely put aside by military commanders in Europe because he was not a professional soldier; they said much the same about the lessons of the civil war in America on the ground that it was fought between amateurs – a startling statement to make!

18   The 1914/18 War

The conflict which began in August 1914 in Europe developed into the bloodiest war in history. The only impressive results were the casualties – and these had a profound influence on my military thinking. A large number of those killed had no known grave; in some cases corpses formed part of trenches, and were devoured by rats. As the story unfolds we shall examine carefully the leadership, political and military, because when all is said and done it is there that the responsibility lies in war. The generalship on the western front was tragically dominated by the philosophy of the French general Foch that whatever the circumstances or conditions it was correct to attack. This was the answer of the generals to the great power of the defensive given by machine-guns, barbed wire, entrenchments, and artillery – to attack with infantry in close formations in a direct charge across no-man's-land, each soldier carrying almost half his own body weight. Of all this I was a witness: I suffered from it. I saw clearly that such tactics could not bring victory. The 1914/18 war presents a dismal canvas, with a very few bright spots.

I fought in the war side by side with splendid young men who offered their lives because we were all told by political leaders that it was to be 'a war to end war'. Let us first examine why the nations fought at all, and whether the tragedy could have been avoided.

On 28th June 1914 the Archduke Franz Ferdinand was assassinated in Bosnia. Austria, rightly supposing that pro-Serbian feeling in Bosnia accounted for the incident, delivered an ultimatum to Serbia on 25th July, and the following day declared war on her. Russia, the self-styled patron of the Slav peoples, mobilized against Austria on 30th July. Germany was an ally of Austria; France and Britain were allies of Russia, and so by early August Germany and Austria (the 'Central Powers') were aligned in war against France, Belgium, Britain, and Russia (the 'Entente Powers'). Turkey emerged from secret into open alliance with the Central Powers in September. Other countries entered the war later.

The 1914/18 war was caused by a murder in the Balkans. None of the statesmen or peoples of Europe positively desired war. Nobody consciously engineered it. A succession of diplomatic interchanges took place, in which the true object of national political leaders – Berchtold (Austria), Sazonov (Russia), Bethmann Hollweg (Germany), Viviani (Italy), and Asquith (Britain) – was to preserve the security of their countries. But they all miscalculated. Gestures intended to bluff and deter provoked violent reactions which were not anticipated: the politicians were playing with diplomacy in an atmosphere which was in fact highly inflammable.

First, rivalries existed between the various powers. Britain was acutely conscious of the challenge by Germany to her commercial and industrial power, and had been actively engaged in building up her naval and merchant fleets. In France there was resentment at the events of 1870–1 and at Germany's possession of Alsace and Lorraine. Germany and Russia were rivals for influence in the Balkans. The Ottoman empire in its ramshackle state had nothing conceivable to gain from being hostile to anybody; but the Germans had been wooing the Turks – who had a score to pay off against Britain and Russia, the two powers which had patronized or bullied them all the way through the nineteenth century. While these antagonisms were by no means enough to make war inevitable, they did mean that there was a highly charged atmosphere in which war might break out.

The situation was made still more dangerous by the fact that none of those responsible, and indeed few men in any nation, had any understanding of what war would mean. Nothing on a bigger scale than the recent small Balkan wars was imagined, and therefore the idea of war was generally taken lightly and irresponsibly. Maybe war could have been avoided; maybe not; but, as it seems to me, nobody *tried* to prevent it. The fatal step was the ordering of mobilization. From this point events got out of the control of individuals and became dictated by the war plans of the general staffs. These plans, because of the military doctrine of the time, were all offensive. Military escalation followed diplomatic insanity, and, as A. J. P. Taylor writes, the great armies which had been accumulated to provide security 'carried the nations to war by their own weight'.

The mobilization plans, once set in motion, removed the control of events from individuals. The German war plan was outstanding for its boldness and clarity of conception. Germany's intention was to gain the initiative; and in the event the German war plan did dictate the main course of events in the whole opening phase of the war during the autumn of 1914, and fixed the main theatres in which the remainder of the war was to be fought. The plan had originally been formed by Count von Schlieffen, chief of the general staff from 1891 to 1906, who in 1914 was dead. His idea was to attack France quickly with strong armies and knock her out in six weeks, before dealing with Russia. There was no question of a direct invasion of France, since the Franco-German border was barred by a line of fortresses, strongly manned. Schlieffen's own original plan was to draw the French forward and hold them with the German left wing in Lorraine, while the main force on the right was to carry out an enveloping offensive sweep through Belgium and then turn south-eastwards. But his plan had been modified by his successor who strengthened the German left.

I have discussed the plan at length with Liddell Hart. His description of the plan as a 'revolving door' conception is exactly right – 'the harder the French pushed on one side in their initial offensive, the more sharply would the other side swing round and strike them in the back'. 'It was a conception of Napoleonic boldness', he says, and he also points out that, while the plan was possibly suitable for Napoleonic times, the advent of the railway enabled the French to switch troops across the chord of the Schlieffen 'scythe-sweep', giving the plan small prospects of success in more modern times. In fact, the Schlieffen plan failed in 1914 for logistic reasons. The sweep of the marching German infantry and horse transport, their advance in any case slowed up by demolished bridges and rail tracks, was countered by more speedy French movements by rail.

None of the other powers which found themselves at war in 1914 had anything more than sketchy plans ready. Austria hoped to crush Serbia quickly and then advance against the Russians in the north-east. In France, Joffre said, 'There was never any plan of operations set down in writing. I adopted no preconceived idea other than a full determination to take the offensive with all my forces.' The French, unlike the Germans, intended to respect Belgian neutrality. Britain did not have a mass army; but she could carry out a naval blockade of the enemy, and a small British army would cover the French left. The Russian plan was to attack, sending two armies into East Prussia, and more troops farther south to envelop the Austrians north of the Carpathians.

Events began to unfold in the direction determined by the Schlieffen plan. The Germans were off the mark quickly: 350,000 troops moved into Lorraine and 400,000 into the Ardennes. On 4th August three German armies, totalling 750,000 men, were launched in the enveloping attack through Luxembourg and Belgium. The French launched their main offensives, just as their enemy had hoped, in north-eastern France: 450,000 men in Lorraine and 360,000 in the Ardennes. By 24th August the French had suffered very heavy losses in these areas, and were forced to retire behind the frontier. Meanwhile the Belgians had not been able to prevent the German advance through their territory. The Germans swung round through Brussels (20th August), and fell upon the French forces on the Franco-Belgian frontier commanded by Lanrezac. Outnumbered two to one in that area, the French fell back from the Sambre. On 21st August the British Expeditionary Force, some 100,000 strong under Sir John French, reached the Mons area and came under attack from German forces.

The Allies fought hard and retreated only slowly. The Germans were held up at Mons on the 23rd, at Le Cateau on the 26th, and at Guise on the 29th. The Germans were now behind on their programme, and were taken aback at the strength of the resistance they were meeting. The German advance, already slowed, wavered before Paris, and on 30th August von Kluck turned his First Army – the right-wing army of the German movement – south-eastwards, passing to the east of Paris instead of enveloping the city. The Allies now rallied, and French forces issued from Paris and struck the flank of von Kluck's army – which on 5th September began to withdraw north-eastwards. From that moment things definitely ceased to go according to the German plan. By this time Joffre had moved himself and considerable forces back from Lorraine, and he attacked Bülow's army on the Marne. The two armies held each other in deadlock, until the British army advanced into the gap which had been caused in the German front on Bülow's right by von Kluck's retreat, whereupon Bülow was also forced to withdraw. This fighting, which forced the Germans to retreat behind the Aisne, constituted the 'battle of the Marne'. It was one of the very few battles of the 1914/18 war to have a decisive strategical value. It had, in

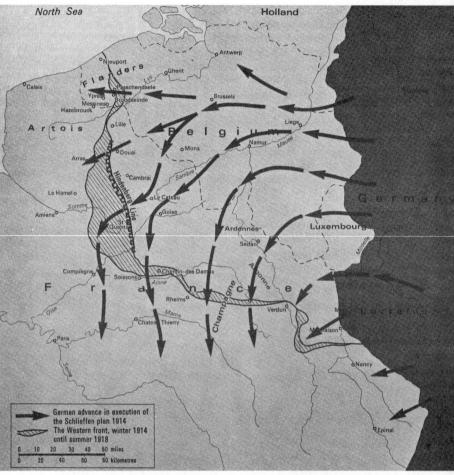

The Schlieffen Plan and the Western Front

fact, prevented the Germans from winning the war. But this, of course, was not then realized.

Behind the Aisne the Germans reorganized their front and dug in. The French assault was checked by 17th September. Both sides then raced to turn their opponents' open northern flank. The opposing lines were extended north from the Aisne, past Amiens and Arras, and were still neck and neck when they reached the sea at Nieuport in Flanders. There, in an attempt to roll up the Allied front, the Germans launched the first battle of Ypres. But heavy and repeated attacks by superior numbers could not move the Allies. The fighting to the south-east in the Nancy area reached a similar stalemate.

By the end of 1914 a deadlock existed on the western front in Europe. As winter descended on the tired soldiers, the western front congealed into trench warfare. Barbed wire and machine-guns dominated the battlefield. From now on generals on both sides would try to smash through the opposing front – but in vain: they did not know the answer and merely destroyed more lives.

A curious incident took place on Christmas Day, 1914. Soldiers of both sides fraternized in no-man's-land, exchanging cigarettes and playing football. But this was not approved and the friendly fraternization stopped – never to happen again.

The Germans had not defeated their enemies in the west in six weeks, which meant that the original plan for the eastern front could not be carried out. Things here had not begun as anticipated. The Austrians had actually been driven back from their invasion of Serbia, and the Russians had begun to move quickly. These first operations by the Russians exhibited two features which were to remain character-istic: loyalty to their allies, and inefficiency. In response to French pleas the Russian commander-in-chief, the Grand Duke Nicholas, pushed forward two armies towards East Prussia in August, although these were as yet quite unprepared. This theatre of operations was divided by the Masurian Lakes; one army under General Rennenkampf, which set out first, passed north of the Lakes, and the other, under General Samsonov, moved more or less parallel but south of them. When Rennen-kampf crossed the border the Germans had one army, under General Prittwitz, in East Prussia. Rennenkampf did not push forward vigorously, and his army was in a chaotic condition; for example, his staff had compasses but no maps. However, when he came in contact with a German corps on 20th August at Gumbinnen his advantage in numbers was very great and he gained a victory. There was no communication between the forces of Rennenkampf and Samsonov, due mainly to the mutual dislike between these two commanders. Samsonov concluded impet-uously that the whole German army had been routed and decided to push forward at top speed.

At this stage Prittwitz proposed that the Germans retire behind the Vistula. Thereupon he was dismissed from his command and was replaced by General Paul von Hindenburg, a veteran of 1866 and 1870. Hindenburg was a decent and conscientious officer, but in no way outstanding. In August 1914 he was recalled from retirement, at the age of sixty-seven, and given command of the German Eighth Army in East Prussia. He was given as his chief of staff one of the most brilliant officers in the army – General Erich von Ludendorff. Hindenburg at once saw in Ludendorff an officer of great intellectual powers and decided to give him a free hand and wide scope so as to get the utmost value from his military gifts. The two men stayed together for most of the war. Hindenburg was to become an idol to the German people – this could not have happened but for Ludendorff.

On their arrival at Marienburg on 23rd August Ludendorff found that the situation had been taken in hand by Prittwitz's staff, and preliminary moves were already under way in a scheme of operations which corresponded very closely with

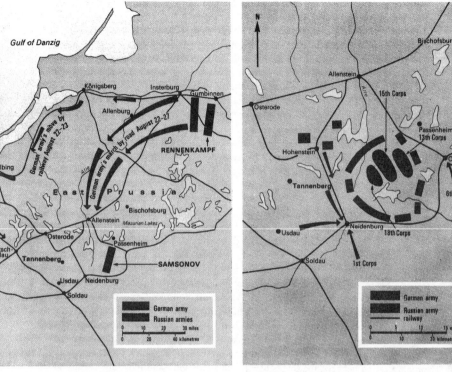

The battle of Tannenberg

his own ideas. Rennenkampf had done nothing to exploit his success at Gumbinnen and was hardly moving; on the other hand Samsonov was advancing dangerously. The Germans therefore decided to leave only a screen to bar Rennenkampf's northern army, and to move all possible strength southwards and fall upon Samsonov. It was a bold plan in that it was always possible that Rennenkampf would galvanize himself into activity. However, a copy of his orders had been found on a captured Russian officer, and these confirmed that he had no immediate plans which would endanger the German plan; and in any case the Masurian Lakes prevented him from going directly to help Samsonov. Samsonov's immediate intentions were also known to the Germans because of the Russian habit of sending wireless messages *en clair*. The speed of his advance was already widening the gap on his unprotected right. Ludendorff seized the opportunity.

The stealthy transference southwards of three corps facing Rennenkampf proceeded between 24th and 27th August. By the 27th only two German cavalry brigades were left to screen the whole of Rennenkampf's forces. Meanwhile, during the few days in which these movements were taking place, the German forces opposite Samsonov were critically placed, having to hold the Russian advance against odds of more than six to one.

On the 26th some of the reinforcements had arrived and Ludendorff could set in motion his tactical plan. His intention was to hold Samsonov's advance in the centre, and drive his wings right back in order to clear the way for the main envelopment of the centre. Some progress was made by hard fighting on the 26th. Samsonov was not unduly disturbed; he himself, exercising direct command in the centre, appears to have been ignorant of what was happening to his flanks. On the 27th the Russian right and left were both pressed back.

On 28th August the decisive movement of the battle began. The German right pressed on to Neidenburg, and the left turned inwards on Passenheim. A heavy attack was launched in the centre. On this day and the next two the Russian wings, after some ups and downs, were finally driven off the scene, and the Russian centre was hemmed in and surrounded. All the time, as Ludendorff wrote, 'Rennenkampf's formidable host hung like a threatening thunderclap to the north-east'. But his daring plan had been well judged and Rennenkampf did not move. The 31st was the day of 'harvesting', as Hindenburg called it, and he wrote in his dispatch to the Kaiser:

> The ring round the larger part of the Russian army was closed yesterday. The 13th, 15th and 18th Army Corps have been destroyed. We have already taken more than 60,000 prisoners . . . The guns are still in the forests and are now being brought in. The booty is immense . . . The Corps outside our ring, the 1st and 6th, have also suffered severely and are now retreating in hot haste.

Hindenburg and Ludendorff, now reinforced, crowned their brilliant victory by turning against Rennenkampf; the Russians were driven back in the battle of the Masurian Lakes and 30,000 prisoners were taken. Thus the Germans recovered their position in East Prussia which had been in danger. But elsewhere the Russians were doing well: Galicia was taken from the Austrians, and far to the south the Turks were being driven back from the Caucasus. Had Hindenburg been beaten in East Prussia it would have been a total disaster for Germany. As it was, the Russians had received a heavy blow.

By the winter of 1914–15 the impetus of the German war plan had run out. Its legacy remained in the position of the battle fronts, which were now more or less settled. The political leaders and military chiefs on both sides sought to get a grip on events. Let us outline the overall strategical picture of the 1914/18 war after the initial clashes of the mighty forces.

The Germans had gained considerable advantages in the 1914 phase. In the west they were in possession of enemy soil, which included important industrial regions of France. In the east they had dealt a heavy blow at the Russians. On the other hand it had always been the nightmare of the general staff that Germany might have to fight a war on two fronts. Now she had to do so. Furthermore, so did Austria and Turkey; these two allies could fight well, but it was already clear that the Germans would have to stiffen the effort of each with economic assistance, military ideas and manpower.

The chief of the German general staff, Falkenhayn, adopted for 1915 a defensive strategy in the west, holding the German gains, while making a major effort to settle the issue in the east. The Germans would then be able to concentrate all their strength in the west to finish off the war victoriously. Having interior lines between the western and the eastern fronts, and a good railway system, so long as their resources lasted it was possible for the Germans to switch pressure from point to point at will and quickly meet new threats. To counter the blockade by the British fleet, Germany embarked on a policy of submarine warfare.

There was little co-ordination in strategy between the Allied powers – the first military conference of all the Allies not being held until December 1915. The only way for the Allies to win the war was to defeat Germany decisively on one of her own main fronts. The Russians were unlikely to achieve this, so the Allies must seek to win on the western front. The French, much of whose soil had been occupied by the Germans, naturally accepted this as the main task, and viewed all other ideas with suspicion. The Russians were, on the whole, willing to co-ordinate their operations with those of the Allies in the west, so that the maximum pressure could be brought to bear on both fronts of the Central Powers at the same time; but this ideal of synchronization rarely operated satisfactorily in practice.

Britain, the great naval power, considered her major task to be the strangling of Germany by a blockade of her commerce and supplies from the sea. Regarding the war on land, Britain recognized that the key theatre must be the western front; but the implications of this fact were not generally agreed among those who had to formulate British policy. Asquith, the prime minister, and Sir William Robertson, who became C.I.G.S. at the end of 1915, were in favour of doing as the French wished: concentrating on building up the British forces on the western front. But this approach, whose advocates included most of the military experts, was opposed by another group. The second school considered that the Germans could be defeated on the western front only by a force as large as theirs; but Britain had only a small army, and she did not want to raise and commit such vast numbers of men. Would it not be better to leave the western front to the French, while Britain made her contribution to the war on land by an indirect strategy which would be more economical in manpower? These two schools of thought became known as the 'Easterners' and the 'Westerners'. The Easterners considered the war could be won by 'knocking away the props' – in other words, by defeating Germany's allies. The Westerners considered the war could be won only by defeating Germany decisively on the western front.

The chief Easterners, the politicians Churchill and Lloyd George, wanted to see Allied strategy developed in south-eastern Europe. If the Allies could achieve domination in that theatre valuable results would follow – Turkey would be knocked out; Russia would be strengthened for her effort on the eastern front by being free of having to fight the Turks, and also by receiving supplies from the west; Austria would be forced to fight on two fronts, and the Germans would have to divert yet more troops to bolster her up; and if Austria could be knocked out, Germany herself would have to fight on a third front. All these ideas were attractive. Accordingly in 1915 the British sent an expedition to the Dardanelles. In this and the next year the Central and Entente Powers competed in bidding for the favour of the various countries of south and south-eastern Europe. Italy entered the war on the side of the Allies in 1915, and Rumania in 1916. Serbia was already fighting against Austria. Bulgaria on the other hand joined the Central Powers in 1915.

The strategy of the Allies in south-eastern Europe had much to commend it. While it was wishful thinking to suppose that the war could actually be won by any 'side shows', nonetheless it was true that extremely valuable advantages would accrue if the Allies could definitely gain the upper hand in this theatre. But, as we shall see, this was not in fact achieved quickly. And the longer it took, the greater was the drain of troops that might have been used elsewhere. In the end a great army did have to be raised in Britain, and most of the troops were sent to the western front.

The British also opened up another separate theatre of war: the Middle East. The intention behind the operations in Egypt, which were extended into Arabia, Palestine and Syria, was to safeguard British economic interests, particularly in the Suez Canal, and to deliver a blow from behind at the Turkish empire. The armed intervention in Mesopotamia was justified by the need to protect oil supplies from the Persian Gulf.

To complete the strategical picture we must mention the war in other parts of the world. In 1914 the Japanese moved into the German territory of Shantung, and between 1914 and 1918 they succeeded in extending their influence in China very considerably. Where colonies of the belligerents were neighbours, as in parts of Africa and the south Pacific, they took the opportunity to 'have a go' at each other. However, all in all, it can be said that the war in theatres outside Europe was of minor strategical importance. The 1914/18 war was essentially a European war. It came later to be called a 'world war' because contingents from many parts of the British empire served in Europe, and because the United States joined the Entente Powers in 1917.

Having glanced at the picture of the war as a whole, I will now look more closely at certain parts of the canvas.

The war on the western front had congealed into immobility at the first battle of Ypres. The German line ran between Flanders and Switzerland, bulging in a broad salient with its blunt apex at Compiègne. The fighting in this theatre in 1915 consisted mainly of two big Allied offensives in Artois and two in Champagne. The casualties in the autumn offensives alone were 190,000 French, 50,000 British and 140,000 Germans. The achievement of this carnage was that the German positions were slightly dented.

The great battles of 1916 were Verdun and the Somme. The battle for Verdun lasted in all nearly ten months; a French estimate placed the total losses on the two sides as 420,000 dead, and 800,000 gassed or wounded; at the end the front was

almost exactly where it had been when the battle began. Alistair Horne wrote of Verdun: 'It was the indecisive battle in an indecisive war; the unnecessary battle in an unnecessary war; the battle that had no victors in a war that had no victors.' The battle of the Somme, from 1st July to 18th November, cost each side about 500,000 men killed, wounded or taken prisoner; the Allies gained thereby a wedge of muddy ground, at no point more than about nine miles deep on a front of some twenty miles or so – and of no strategic value.

The man responsible for the conduct of operations on the German side during these two years was Falkenhayn. He took over control in September 1914 and prevented the failure of the Schlieffen plan from becoming a disaster. He recognized that on the whole the defensive was now best for the Germans in the west; and the only major offensive by the Germans between 1914 and 1918 was the attack at Verdun – a frontier fortress which became a symbol to the French, who allowed their manhood to be bled almost white in its defence. Falkenhayn was replaced by Hindenburg and Ludendorff in August 1916. He was the only prominent strategist on either side to urge that it would be wise to aim ultimately for something less than total victory.

There was no one supreme commander of the Allied forces on the western front before 1918. In 1915 and 1916 the French commander-in-chief, General Joffre, was the guiding force for all. The British commanders – French was superseded by Sir Douglas Haig in December 1915 – although theoretically independent did not yet have enough troops of their own to be in a position to dictate a strategy themselves, and on the whole they fell in with that of the French. Joffre was tough and brutal. He would not give in, no matter what the suffering. He was also stupid. He won the battle of the Marne by pure luck; as Liddell Hart observes, he had launched a million Frenchmen against a million and a half Germans in the wrong place, and it was only because he failed in Lorraine that he was able to halt the Germans at the last moment after they had marched almost round to the back of his forces. Since the German front in 1915 offered no exposed flank to turn, Joffre set about hammering frontally at either end of it – the offensives in Artois and Champagne – in an attempt to cut off the salient. In a life which has seen much fighting I have learnt that what is strategically desirable must be tactically possible with the resources at one's disposal. Joffre did not seem to understand this fundamental truth.

It was beyond question that the Allies did have to operate offensively; the Germans were on French and Belgian soil and public opinion demanded that they be removed. Furthermore, if the Germans were left undisturbed on their western front they would be all the stronger to deal with the Russians in the east. But the method of the offensive to be adopted was open to question, and several possibilities existed. One was to entice the enemy forward into a 'sack' which could then be closed by an envelopment from both flanks, as was almost to happen by accident in 1918. Alternatively, the German front might have been turned by the use of British seapower in full combination with an assault on land on the Flanders flank. But the method chosen was simple frontal bludgeoning in repeated assaults. It was a basic miscalculation to suppose that such a method could prevail: all commanders

The 1914/18 war developed into a deadlock of trench warfare, with appalling casualties from gunfire and poison gas. French troops in gas masks stand ready to repel an attack

German machine-gunners take advantage of a shell hole after a heavy bombardment

underestimated the power of the tactical defensive. The Allied commanders should have realized at least by the end of 1915 that such frontal assaults were not going to achieve positive results. But they decided to continue the same policy on a more massive scale for the next year – which was not generalship as I understand it.

The strength of the defensive consisted essentially in men firing rifles and machine-guns from the security of entrenchments and supported by artillery. How could assailants even reach close quarters ? Trench warfare was in fact siege fighting rather than open battle. That was the problem; it had been clearly indicated, not only in the Russo-Japanese and recent Balkan wars, but also in the engagements at Mons and Guise where a very few troops had seriously checked the great German sweep forward. At one time in the initial clashes in the Mons-Le Cateau area two British divisions had held off two German army corps. Quite apart from logistical factors, the tactical strength of the defensive alone made it practically certain that the Schlieffen plan would fall behind in its timing and would therefore fail.

A rifleman in a stationary position could fire fifteen rounds per minute accurately

British infantry go forward from their trench to an attack across no-man's-land

across the normal no-man's-land. The machine-gun fired a continuous stream of
bullets. The number of machine-guns was soon stepped up; Haig at first considered
two per battalion enough, but by the end of the war there were machine-gun
battalions each of forty-eight guns. Barbed wire entanglements made another
obstacle to approach. As time went on refinements were added to defence. The
Germans introduced gas of various types: asphyxiating, lachrymatory and blister-
ing. Mustard gas, in the last mentioned category, was the worst, because it was
the most unpleasant and disabling and took a long time to clear. The trench
systems consisted of several lines in depth, so that if the first line should be
penetrated the assailants were little better off. With rail and motor transport, fresh
defenders could always be brought up from behind to fill a gap faster than the
attackers could keep pushing forward. For example at one point in the first battle
of Ypres the Germans penetrated right through the British fighting lines into the
back area of administrative services, but they did not succeed in using the advantage.
During the winter of 1916–17 the Germans prepared a reserve trench system, the

'Hindenburg line', to which they fell back in the early part of 1917. The site was chosen for its natural and strategic advantages. The trenches contained deep dug-outs in which men would be secure from practically all forms of artillery fire; concrete emplacements were built for machine-guns; and a network of light railways could carry men and materials up to the forward area.

The fact was that, with the weapons available, the advantages in battle were heavily stacked on the side of the defensive. But a theory at odds with this had been formulated before the war – summed up in the words of Foch that 'to make war means always attacking'. It was supposed that modern artillery and small arms fire would give such power in attack that the enemy could be attacked successfully at his strongest point. Foch wrote: 'A battle cannot be lost physically . . . it can only be lost morally . . . A battle won is a battle in which one will not confess oneself beaten.' I would agree that determination is vital – but so is a well-balanced judgment; although a commander will always aim to force his will on his opponent, he must know when discretion is the better part of valour; his desire to dominate his opponent must not outweigh his judgment of the actual possibilities of the situation. Furthermore, the good general wins his battles with the least possible loss of life. A blind offensive at all times is not the way to do this. The defensive is often advis-able while a favourable tactical objective is sought; when that is found, then is the time for boldness: everything having been done to ensure success which reason can dictate. Foch did not understand this.

The normal pattern of an attack was a preliminary bombardment by artillery, followed by assaulting waves of men armed with rifle and bayonet. Machine-guns and gas were less useful in assault than in defence.

Attacks on the western front were preceded by an artillery bombardment lasting several days, the main purpose being to cut lanes in the barbed wire and put located enemy machine-guns out of action before the infantry assault began. The German artillery was at first superior both in quantity and in quality, but later the types of artillery became much the same in all armies. During the war the proportion of medium and heavy artillery greatly increased. The British guns most used were the 18- and 60-pounders and 4.5-inch, 6-inch, and 9.2-inch howitzers, with ranges rising to over 10,000 yards. Motor transport came to be used to some extent, but guns were mostly moved by horses; larger weapons were often on railway mountings. Some very large guns, such as the famous 17-inch 'Big Berthas', were used for long-range bombardment, mostly by the Germans. Mortars, which had long been dis-carded, reappeared for this siege type of warfare; high explosive shells gradually replaced shrapnel; smoke and gas shells were also used. The bombardments which took place were on a tremendous scale and required a high degree of organization. The command of artillery along wide stretches of front came to be more and more centralized, so that the bombardment could be co-ordinated and fire concentrated at the right time and place. This was assisted by improved methods of communica-tion – telephone, wireless and observation aircraft – and by means such as sound-ranging and flash spotting. By 1916 and 1917 these techniques were well developed.

The disadvantage of such artillery bombardments was that they removed all possibility of tactical surprise. Moreover, in wet weather they churned up the ground to such an extent that movement became very difficult for soldiers who had to advance on foot carrying equipment which weighed some 66 lbs. When the bombardment was finished, sometimes with a smoke screen to conceal movement, waves of attacking infantry left the trenches, threaded their way through the wire on their own side, formed up and advanced at a walking pace behind a creeping barrage.

The process of a fairly characteristic assault and its fate is described by an officer of the German 180 Regiment facing the British 8th Division in the Battle of the Somme:

The intense bombardment was realized by all to be the prelude to an infantry assault sooner or later. The men in the dugouts therefore waited, belts full of hand-grenades, gripping their rifles and listening for the bombardment to lift from the front defence zone on to the rear defences. It was of vital importance to lose not a second in taking up positions to meet the British infantry which would advance immediately behind the artillery barrage. Looking towards the British trenches through the long trench periscopes held up out of the dugout entrances there could be seen a mass of steel helmets above the parapet showing that the storm troops were ready for the assault. At 7.30 a.m. the hurricane of shells ceased as suddenly as it had begun. Our men at once clambered up the steep shafts leading from the dugouts and ran singly or in groups to the nearest shell craters. The machine-guns were pulled out of the dugouts and hurriedly placed in position, their crews dragging the heavy ammunition boxes up the steps and out to the guns. A rough firing line was thus rapidly established.

As soon as the men were in position, a series of extended lines of infantry were seen moving forward from the British trenches. The first line appeared to continue without end to right and left. It was quickly followed by a second line, then a third and fourth. They came on at a steady easy pace as if expecting to find nothing alive in our front trenches. The front line, preceded by a thin line of skirmishers and bombers, was now half way across No Man's Land. 'Get ready' was passed along our front from crater to crater, and heads appeared over the crater edges as final positions were taken up for the best view, and machine-guns mounted in place. A few moments later, when the leading British line was within a hundred yards, the rattle of machine-gun and rifle broke out along the whole line of shell holes. Some fired kneeling so as to get a better target over the broken ground, whilst others, in the excitement of the moment, stood up regardless of their own safety, to fire into the crowd of men in front of them. Red rockets sped up as a signal to the artillery, and immediately afterwards a mass of shells from the German batteries in rear tore through the air and burst among the advancing lines. Whole sections seemed to fall, and the rear formations, moving in close order, quickly scattered. The advance rapidly crumpled under this hail of shells and bullets. All along the line men could be seen throwing up their arms and collapsing, never to move again. Badly wounded rolled about in their agony, and others, less severely injured, crawled to the nearest shell hole for shelter.

The British soldier, however, has no lack of courage. The extended lines, though badly shaken and with many gaps, now came on all the faster. Instead of a leisurely walk they covered the ground in short rushes at the double. Within a few minutes the leading troops had advanced to within a stone's throw of our front trench, and whilst some of us continued to fire at point-blank range, others threw hand grenades among them. The British bombers answered back, whilst the infantry rushed forward with fixed bayonets. The shouting of orders and the shrill cheer as the British charged forward could be heard above the violent and intense fusillade of machine-guns and rifles and bursting bombs, and above the deep thunderings of the artillery and shell explosions. With all this were mingled the moans and groans of the wounded, the cries for help and the last screams of death. Again and again the extended lines of British infantry broke against the German defence like waves against a cliff, only to be beaten back.

Such was the general pattern of war on the western front in Europe. With the weapons available, and within the existing strategical situation, there was little opportunity in trench fighting for variation of the set pattern and the exercise of tactical skill.

Nonetheless there were periods of fighting a little better managed than the normal. The Germans in their tactics at Verdun continually sought to achieve surprise and to attack the enemy in force at his weakest rather than his strongest point. Reconnaissance parties, daringly and intelligently led under cover of darkness, would probe the enemy front for weak spots. If they found the French at some point especially alert and strong, they would switch their attack elsewhere, or postpone it while continuing further artillery preparation. In their minor attacks they reinforced success rather than failure, demonstrating that it was possible to penetrate an enemy line; and they exploited the loops of the Meuse and the suitability of the ground in searching for possibilities of envelopment. Detailed co-operation between artillery and infantry was achieved by signals with yellow, red and green rockets, in a way which the Allied troops had not achieved. The German soldiers were also very hard working and thorough in their entrenching techniques. On the whole, and particularly at Verdun, the Germans made better use than their enemies of such scanty tactical opportunities as existed. But in the end they were unable to break the French resistance at Verdun: trench warfare as it had to be fought could yield no decisive results.

The scene on the front, in the Passchendaele area during the third battle of Ypres in 1917, is described in the British Official History: 'The shelled areas near the front became a barrier of swamp. The margins of the overflowing streams were transformed into long stretches of bog, passable only by a few well-defined tracks which became targets for the enemy's artillery; and to leave the tracks was to risk death by drowning.' If in these filthy and dangerous conditions ardour gradually lessened, courage and self-sacrifice, however, remained constant. Comradeship was sustaining above all. Sidney Rogerson wrote: 'Life in the trenches was not all ghastliness. It was a compound of many things: fright and boredom, humour, comradeship, tragedy, weariness, courage and despair.'

A remarkable, and disgraceful, fact is that a high proportion of senior officers were ignorant of the conditions in which the soldiers were fighting. It was normal for orders to be given that attacks were to be delivered *'regardless of loss'* – often for several days in succession. A. J. P. Taylor justly observes: 'The unknown soldier was the hero of the First World War.' The soldiers were worthy of better generalship.

If both sides persisted in fighting by this method of frontal attack, then the war on the western front must become a war of attrition – a trial of each side's endurance and resources.

But amazingly, the soldiers on both sides did not flag. The Germans were succeeding in fighting a war on two fronts; everywhere they were holding their ground and killing greater numbers of their enemies than they were losing themselves. Because of their pre-war territorial system of recruitment with its long training period, the fronts could still be supplied with high-grade troops. The French also were holding out, their morale actually heightened by the saving of Verdun; their losses had been the worst so far, both in numbers and the quality of the men killed; the best of their regular soldiers had gone, but the French spirit was not broken. The British were just coming in to their own on the western front. After the 100,000 or so of the original B.E.F., 500,000 civilians had volunteered for the 'New Army' in the first month of the recruiting drive launched by Kitchener, secretary of state for war. They were rather haphazardly trained and equipment was in short supply, but by 1916 the British felt ready to take an equal share of the burden with the French. The Allied forces at the Somme in 1916 were nearly all British. During the experiences of 1916 the original cheerfulness of the volunteers only changed to a grim determination.

Both sides in the war could draw on immense resources of population and materials. In 1910 the populations were: Germany 65 million, France 39 million, Britain 45 million. Britain also drew, much more than the other powers, on the population of her overseas empire. Britain and Germany were, apart from the U.S.A., the two greatest industrial and commercial powers of the world. The German economy was run during the war by a businessman, Walter Rathenau, who kept it going remarkably. The Germans could draw on the agricultural lands of central Europe for food; the French relied on their own farming; the British could import. The mobilization of millions of men inevitably affected the nature of society in the countries involved, making the conflict 'total war', and giving the 'home front' an importance it had never had before. David Lloyd George emerged as a great war leader in Britain, rallying enthusiasm with his oratory. He persuaded trade union leaders and businessmen alike to give support in the reorientation of manufacture to meet war needs. To fill the places of the men who were away fighting he encouraged women to work in factories and offices. In this way the war left a permanent mark on home life, as it did in many smaller ways, such as the institution of British summer time and set closing hours for public houses – the purpose of both being to make people do more work. Careful censorship and propaganda in all countries kept the public unaware of what was really happening at the front, and generally speaking people were enthusiastic for the war. Bombing raids made no serious impact on national life; that was to come in Hitler's war.

The Central Powers and the Entente were thus well matched in manpower and well supplied materially; morale on the home fronts was reasonable; and as things stood in 1916 a war of attrition could continue for some time. At the end of 1916 Ludendorff told the Germans that there was no question of a compromise peace: the war must be won. Lloyd George became prime minister in Britain in December of that year, and declared the same. In France a new figure came into prominence, General Nivelle, promoted commander-in-chief in place of Joffre. Nivelle had achieved at Verdun what was regarded as a spectacular success, actually gaining an extent of ground with relatively few casualties, and he now proclaimed that he knew 'the secret of victory'.

Lloyd George was an excellent leader of the British people on the home front, but his intervention in the military conduct of the war was less satisfactory. He disliked the war on the western front and had a poor opinion of Haig. His first scheme was for a major effort in 1917 on the Italian front, but the Allies would not have it. Then he became impressed by Nivelle. He decided to commit the British effort in support of Nivelle, and intrigued to ensure that Haig would be subordinated to the French high command.

Nivelle never divulged in so many words what his 'secret' was, but his actions when in command soon revealed that he had no new formula. Once again in 1917 the Allies hurled an even greater weight of men and metal against the Germans than in the previous year. In two offensives in the spring of 1917 – the battles at Arras and on the Aisne – the French losses were heavy. Then in May the French army began to crack up. Nivelle was removed from his command and replaced by Pétain, the real hero of Verdun. It was a black time for the Allies: Russia was in the throes of revolution, and German submarines were devastating Allied shipping.

At this point Haig took the lead in the planning of Allied operations on the western front. His idea was to make a heavy frontal assault against the Germans in Flanders. Here the British might draw off pressure from the French and, more importantly in his view, avoid being entangled with them; furthermore a victory could turn the flank of the German front, and assist British seapower to prevent enemy submarines from operating from ports bordering on the North Sea. The Messines Ridge was taken in June 1917. A pause followed, and then the third battle of Ypres took place from 11th July to 10th November. The rainfall in August happened to be double the normal average, and from 3rd October onwards the rain came down almost ceaselessly. Men fought and died in the mud, and were drowned in shell holes. This offensive culminated in the capture of the Passchendaele ridge and no more, the British having lost 240,000 men and the Germans the same number.

Farther to the south-east Pétain launched an offensive in October at Malmaison, which merely removed a few ragged edges on the battle front. The Allied strategy of 1917 had proved to be completely sterile. Through all the futility and horribleness of this trench warfare, however, the fighting spirit of the men was still bearing up.

The 1917 season of slogging in 'mud and blood' all but broke the French, who had been dashing themselves in suicidal attacks against entrenchments for so long, and mutinies occurred after Nivelle's offensives. But Pétain weeded out the bad elements and nursed the rest back into condition, so that by the autumn of 1917 the French army had achieved a good recovery. The British were still hopeful and were glad to be reinforced by contingents from the dominions and by the first Americans. The endurance of the German soldiers was the most remarkable, for they bore the burden on their side of the western front for four years without any outside assistance.

In the third battle of Ypres the rain, the mud, and the cold earned a terrible reputation for 'Passchendaele', which was one part of the whole battle; yet it was here, as John Terraine observes, that the science of the persistent application of sheer weight in order to breach the enemy front was brought to its highest level. The man who achieved this was General Herbert Plumer, under whom I was then serving. Plumer was one of the very few commanders in the war who was a high-class professional and a soldier's soldier, held in trust and respect by his men. He planned and prepared for two years the mining operation which gained the Messines Ridge in June 1917. Nineteen deep mines had been dug more than 100 feet below the surface and filled with a million pounds of explosive. They were all set off together at dawn on the morning of 7th June, and the British troops merely had to walk in and take possession of the ridge. When after the end of August his Second Army became the spearhead of the battle, Plumer conducted its operations with the same thoroughness. Terraine writes:

> Plumer's method was the carefully prepared, limited advance, step-by-step, approximately 1,500 yards at a time, of which 1,000 yards would be saturated by the initial barrage. He was a firm believer in guns. He asked for three weeks to prepare his first attack, and for over 1,300 guns and howitzers to carry it out. These, with 240 machine-guns, laid down five belts of fire along the whole front of attack. When Plumer's first attack came, it was a model of forethought and precision.

At the Menin Road Ridge in September enemy positions on a 4,000-yard frontage were taken with little struggle. Twice more, by the same technique of delivering a massive and concentrated artillery preparation beforehand, Plumer's men gained ground on a limited front, at Polygon Wood and Broodseinde: the casualty rate being far lower than at the Somme, or, for that matter, at Waterloo.

Ground could be gained. But at the rate of 1,500 yards in three weeks it would take a long time to drive the Germans back to their own country. But then at last there came an indication of how the war might really be made to move again. On 20th November 1917 the British used tanks in an offensive at Cambrai. Without any preliminary bombardment over 300 tanks went forward in massed formations. That day they made a hole in the Hindenburg Line four miles wide, and for a loss of 1,500 men took 10,000 German prisoners and 200 guns. The tanks penetrated altogether five miles – a distance which it had taken four months and 300,000 lives to gain at Ypres. The impact of their immediate onset in the battle is described by Captain D. G. Browne: 'The triple belts of wire were crossed as if they had been beds of nettles, and 350 pathways were sheared through them for the infantry. The defenders of the front trench, scrambling out of dug-outs and shelters to meet the crash and flame of the barrage, saw the leading tanks almost upon them, their appearance grotesque and terrifying.'

The advantage gained was in fact then lost by the inefficiency of the high command; the only reserves available to exploit success were horse cavalry, whose tactical effectiveness in the face of modern weapons had long disappeared. On 30th November the Germans staged a surprise counter stroke on the flank and rear of the British penetration, and wiped out the British gains. Nonetheless the use of tanks in the battle of Cambrai was a major technical landmark. Churchill wrote in *World Crisis 1911–1918*:

> Accusing as I do without exception all the great ally offensives of 1915, 1916, and 1917, as needless and wrongly conceived operations of infinite cost, I am bound to reply to the question, What else could be done? And I answer it, pointing to the Battle of Cambrai, '*This* could have been done'. This in many variants, this in larger and better forms ought to have been done, and would have been done if only the Generals had not been content to fight machine-gun bullets with the breasts of gallant men, and think that that was waging war.

In the strategy of the Allies at sea the main role was taken by the British navy, while the French played a useful part in the Mediterranean and Russian fleets operated in the Baltic and the Black Sea. As usual, Britain's naval policy was to secure the lines of sea communication upon which she and her allies depended for survival, and to damage those of the enemy. In 1914, thanks to Admiral Fisher's pre-war *Dreadnought* programme, British naval strength was 20 battleships and 7 battle-cruisers as opposed to Germany's 13 battleships and 3 battle-cruisers. The British set about sweeping the seas clear of the enemy. A German squadron under Admiral von Spee was on the loose and ran into an inferior British force under Cradock off Coronel on 1st November, sinking two cruisers. But when von Spee met the British a second time – by accident – at the Falkland Islands in December, four out of the five German ships were sunk. The German High Command then made the decision not to risk its High Seas Fleet against the British navy, but, instead, to keep it in operational order in the Baltic – where it would be a perpetual threat and possibly a bargaining factor in later armistice negotiations. The British were thus left to carry out their traditional policy of blockade – to confine the enemy fleet to its harbours and destroy it should it venture out.

The blockade was not, however, to be by the old method of cruising outside enemy harbours, since mines and submarines made this too dangerous. Instead, an invisible blockade was established, the operations of the Grand Fleet being based on Scapa Flow in the Orkneys, facing the Baltic at a distance. The main activity of British ships was in arresting German merchant shipping, in checking neutral shipping, and in waging war against submarines. Various actions were fought in the North Sea between battle-cruisers, but there was only one full-scale confrontation of the two fleets – off Jutland in 1916. The German admiral, Scheer, had ventured out, but with no intention of engaging in full battle. Jellicoe, the British admiral, was aware of the danger from torpedoes, and considered that as things

Tanks represented the only means of breaking the stalemate

were Britain had little to gain from a naval victory and everything to lose in a defeat. The fleets were slightly engaged during the night of 31st May–1st June. But then both sides were content to draw off. Thereafter the German fleet remained almost entirely inactive, and in 1918 the sailors mutinied partly from sheer boredom.

Germany accepted more or less without challenge that Britannia ruled the waves. But the sea beneath the surface waves was a different matter. The British blockade would be countered by submarine warfare.

Research and experiment had recently developed the submarine into a weapon of great effectiveness. Its striking power lay in torpedoes, launched by compressed air from tubes in the bows. The biggest submarines had four tubes and carried two torpedoes for each tube; 500 lbs of T.N.T. could be launched at 36 m.p.h. for 7,000 to 8,000 yards. While cruising at a depth of some 25 feet the whole horizon could be observed through a periscope. In 1914 Britain actually had more submarines than Germany: 36 to 28. But when the Germans committed themselves at the end of 1914 to large-scale submarine warfare they rapidly built a large number of U-boats (as they were called) of increased size, striking power and endurance.

The Germans opened their submarine campaign early in 1915. They hoped at first to strike at the Grand Fleet, but, despite alarms, no U-boat ever succeeded in penetrating Scapa Flow. They did however become devastatingly effective in their attacks on merchant shipping. The German policy in 1915 was 'unrestricted submarine warfare': striking at sight and without warning at all merchant shipping of enemies and neutrals. This was contrary to international law, and strong protests from neutral America caused the Germans to limit their U-boat campaign. Nevertheless immense quantities of Allied shipping continued to be sunk in the North Sea, in the Western Approaches between Ireland and Ushant, and in the Mediterranean. By the spring of 1917 it seemed as if the operations of U-boats might almost win the war for Germany. In April alone more than a million tons of British and neutral ships were destroyed. One ship in every four sailing from British ports failed to get home, and crews of foreign ships were refusing to sail to England. The Germans at that point resumed unrestricted submarine warfare in the hope of finishing things off.

It took a long time to discover the best anti-submarine measures. Mines were laid extensively; ships could sail in zig-zags and drop depth charges; and towards the end of the war 'asdic' was invented, a device which detected nearby submarines by sending out high frequency sound waves. But none of these methods was really effective. The answer was discovered only in the nick of time: against the advice of the Admiralty, Lloyd George ordered the institution of the convoy system at the end of April 1917. Although the number of U-boats in operation rose to 140 by October, the rate of loss in Allied shipping had by that time fallen sharply and the rate of destruction of enemy submarines increased. A convoy was harder for the U-boats to attack than isolated ships, since the herd of merchant ships could be defended by ships of the navy with all the means available. The success of the convoy system against submarines was a gleam of light for the Allies in 1917. Further hope was given to the Allied cause by the decision of the United States of America to enter the war on the side of the Allies in April – the U.S. being provoked by the renewal of unrestricted submarine warfare by the Germans.

The contribution of British seapower to the whole war effort of the Allies was of crucial importance, since command of the seas made it possible to transport troops to the various theatres; it also ensured the continual flow of supplies; and in this respect her seapower complemented another role of Britain, that of banker to the Entente Powers. Furthermore, although the Central Powers possessed immense domestic resources of food and materials, eventually the blockade seriously weakened them. For more than two years the U-boats were a serious menace, but they were dealt with in the end, and the entry of the Americans was a heavy blow to Germany.

Air power was never of more than minor importance during the 1914/18 war. Aeroplanes were used as adjuncts to army and naval operations. They were most useful for reconnaissance and attacking supply lines, but until the last year of the war they played only a minor part in the tactics of land warfare. The exploits of some of the air aces, such as Immelmann, became celebrated, but really they hardly mattered. Nor did bombing make any real material impact, although the raids by Zeppelin airships over British cities caused a flurry of alarm. The R.A.F. was, however, developing into a considerable force by 1918.

The eastern front was another area where victory by one or other of the belligerents might influence the war decisively. The tactics were the same as those on the western front, but more movement took place – the front moving backward or forward often fifty miles, and sometimes more. In those vast spaces the troops were relatively thin on the ground; furthermore, many of the Austrian and Russian troops were inadequately equipped and trained; thus it was often possible for attackers to send the defence reeling back. The quality of command in this theatre ranged, more

U-boats nearly brought Britain's overseas supplies to a halt *above*, but their attacks on merchant shipping were eventually countered by the convoy system *below*

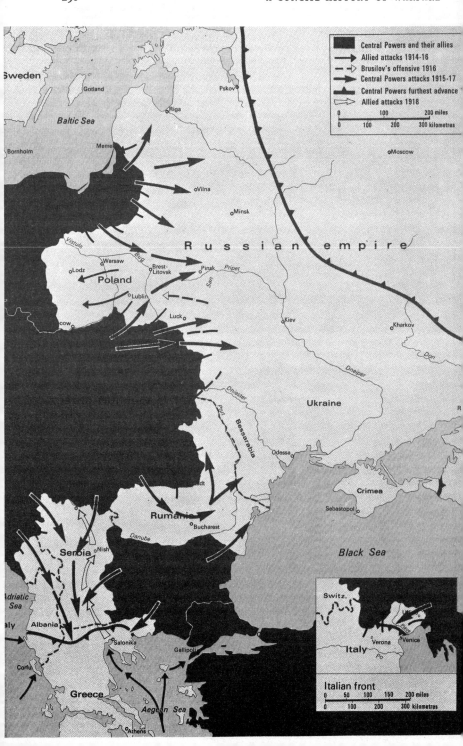

extremely than in the west, from abysmal to brilliant. The war on the eastern front was even more murderous than the war in the west: Russia alone is said to have lost two million men in 1915, and a further million in 1916.

Instead of following up their victory at Tannenberg by an advance into Poland, the Germans had to go to the relief of the Austrians in Galicia. There the Russians resumed the offensive in the spring of 1915. Undeterred by Joffre's offensives in the west, Falkenhayn switched large numbers of German troops eastwards by rail for a great effort against the Russians. The German campaign of 1915 succeeded as far as it was possible to succeed against that particular enemy. In May combined German and Austrian forces commanded by Mackensen attacked on a 28-mile front at Gorlice. Many of the Russian soldiers did not even have rifles. For the only time in the war a front was broken through so widely and deeply that the defenders were unable to seal off the gap. The Russians were driven out of Galicia and then forced to abandon most of Poland. Ten million civilian refugees trailed along in the retreat. Yet the defeat was not decisive, because the Russians were falling back on to their home territory, with its infinite reserves of population; furthermore their production of armaments was actually increasing. In September a new front was established 300 miles farther east; this was easier to defend, being shorter and with no vulnerable flanks. The Germans made overtures for a compromise peace, but the tsar, Nicholas II, in personal command of his armies, refused to contemplate the idea of sacrificing Russian territory and abandoning his western allies.

Yet, for all his goodwill, Nicholas proved a thoroughly bad commander. Under him the Russian forces were given no coherent strategy. Morale was still reasonably good and the supply situation continued to improve, but the chaos in the staff system became even worse than before. In March 1916 masses of men were thrown against the strongest parts of the German front in the north: the Russian losses were five to every one German. Shortly after this failure Italy appealed to Russia to relieve her by attacking Austria. The commander of the south-western group of Russian armies, Brusilov, responded.

General Alexei Brusilov was one of the few exceptional fighting commanders whose ability shone out in the murk of the military misconduct of most of the 1914/18 war. He had a remarkable record of success in command before 1916. In the early months of the war his army had swept into Galicia and made possible the taking of Lemberg in thirty days. Later he was penetrating into the plain of Hungary, causing panic among the enemy, when the destruction of the neighbouring army on his right necessitated a general retreat; with his right flank exposed to attacks by greatly superior numbers of Germans and short of ammunition, Brusilov withdrew his army through difficult country in good order, and was actually able to deliver a check to the Germans on the San. He was a man of humour and humanity, qualities which contributed to his military ability. His first act after taking over command in 1916 was to visit his troops at the front, thereby getting to know them and thus

The fronts in eastern and south-eastern Europe

being able to judge what to expect from his soldiers. He always made a careful study of ground, built up an efficient staff, and studied the ways of his enemy. He was, in fact, a good professional soldier.

Brusilov's 1916 offensive against the Austro-Hungarians was pushed high into the Carpathians before it finally halted in October, when German reinforcements made the resistance stronger at the same time as the Russian communications were becoming strained to breaking point. The Russians had captured 400,000 prisoners and 500 guns. When Nicholas refused to launch a balancing offensive in the north, Brusilov had to retreat. Two years later Brusilov was serving another master – Trotsky.

The Russian effort in 1916 was of very great value to France and Britain, since it forced Germany to keep large forces on the eastern front. It was a calamity for the Austro-Hungarian empire, where utter demoralization set in among the people as well as in the army. But it was also the ruin of Russia. The million casualties in 1916, the strain on production, and the rottenness of the government were cumulatively having their effect. During the winter the shortage of food caused riots in the cities, and in March 1917 the tsar was forced to abdicate. Ludendorff took the opportunity to put the cat among the pigeons by allowing Lenin to travel through Germany in a sealed train on his way to Russia. Russia had still not quite dropped out of the war, but discipline in the army was crumbling when, in July, Kerensky launched it once more against the Germans. This last offensive destroyed the Russian army and opened the way to the Bolshevik revolution. On 8th November Lenin read out a 'Decree on Peace'. The Bolsheviks hoped for a peace which would be 'fair for all nationalities without exception', but the Germans were not so obliging. In effect the terms they dictated at Brest-Litovsk in March 1918 removed from the former Russian empire a quarter of its population and of its arable land, three-quarters of its iron and coal resources, and half its industrial plant.

The general strategical purpose of the operations in south-eastern Europe has already been outlined. But the best known of these, the British expedition to the Dardanelles in 1915, is worth examining in some detail.

After the fighting of December 1914 the Russians asked their western allies to give them some relief by carrying out operations against the Turks, and in Britain the idea was enthusiastically received by Kitchener, Fisher and Churchill. There were many strategical advantages to be gained by the Entente Powers from domination in south-eastern Europe, and success of any kind was desirable at that stage. The Turks, it was attractive to suppose, were the least formidable of the Central Powers.

A German military mission, headed by Liman von Sanders, had recently effected a considerable improvement in the training and organization of the Turkish army, and its soldiers were notably brave and disciplined. But they were poorly equipped, only the crack troops being armed with the modern Mauser rifle. What is more, in the winter fighting against the Russians in the Caucasus the Turks had lost 53,600 men out of 66,000; and they still had to keep troops on the Russian front and garrison the extensive Ottoman empire. So at the beginning of 1915 the approach to Constantinople through the Dardanelles was guarded only by two divisions and a few dilapidated forts.

After some hesitation the British War Council decided in January 1915 that the expedition against Constantinople should be purely naval. But by 19th February, when ships of the British navy bombarded the outer forts of the Dardanelles, the plan had been changed; orders had been given that an army should be formed in Egypt, and under General Sir Ian Hamilton take part in an amphibious operation to open a passage through the Dardanelles. Hamilton's army should have been ready to start operations by 18th March, but it was held up when the transport vessels were wrongly loaded – certain essential equipment being loaded at the bottom of the holds. Nonetheless the warships entered the narrow straits a second time – though when three were sunk by mines Admiral de Robeck would take no further risk and withdrew. In fact the Turks had practically run out of ammunition and the squadron could have steamed up to Constantinople. But the opportunity was lost. Instead, the two uncoordinated naval operations merely sacrificed surprise and gave the Turks warning to strengthen their defences guarding the straits.

During March and April the German mission increased the Turkish forces on the Gallipoli peninsula to 6 divisions, and the Turks worked hard at digging trenches and preparing the beaches for defence. The Allies built up their force to 84 ships and 5 divisions; but there was only one regular division in the force, the rest being inexperienced dominion troops and territorials – none of whom had ever studied or rehearsed the operation of an opposed landing on a hostile coast. Hamilton had left London without a staff, without proper maps, and with no information about the Turkish defences more recent than 1906.

At any rate the initial landing on 25th April went relatively well, taking the Turks by surprise. But the first impetus quickly ran down, and the operation degenerated into the stagnation of trench warfare. One Turkish commander, Mustapha Kemal, later to be known as Ataturk, distinguished himself in repelling the Australians and New Zealanders north of Gaba Tepe. Repeated frontal assaults were made against Turkish defensive positions. These attacks were as hopeless and costly as those on the western front – and the physical conditions were possibly worse, since the men had no secure rear and no shade from the hot sun. The Turks continued to bring up reinforcements and supplies. They had 15 divisions in July by the time the Allies had increased their strength to 12.

On 6th August Hamilton launched a double assault. In a thrust from Anzac Cove to Sari Bair Ridge the troops made a difficult advance by night over mountainous country, only to be shelled on the last stretch by their own ships which mistook them for the enemy. The other thrust, at Suvla Bay, was commanded by General Stopford, who had previously commanded the Tower of London but no forces in war. His 20,000 men landed almost without loss, whereupon they were congratulated and told to relax. Stopford himself did not go ashore, but settled down for his afternoon nap. Hamilton woke him up and remonstrated politely. But when the advance tried to move again the Turkish defence had been alerted and was too strong.

All through the autumn the British forces remained frustrated on the Gallipoli peninsula. The politicians at home pondered the question of withdrawal, but were worried that Britain might lose prestige. Meanwhile men at Gallipoli went on dying. At Joffre's demand more British troops were thrown into the autumn offensive on the western front. Eventually the expedition was evacuated at the turn of the year. A brilliant strategic idea had been thrown away because of every conceivable mistake in its execution by the commanders.

In 1915 the Allies opened a second area of operations in the Balkans, from Salonika. The Germans were preparing to deal with Serbia and give effective aid to Turkey, and had drawn Bulgaria in on their side. In October an Allied force landed at Salonika with the object of going to the help of the Serbians, but it was driven back by the Bulgarians. Although few believed it could have any further value, the force was kept at Salonika for the rest of the war. It grew to nearly 500,000 men – who were serving no useful function; music-hall comedians in London in 1917 used to sing 'if you want a holiday go to Salonika'; the Germans called Salonika 'their largest internment camp'. Only in September 1918 did this force launch a serious offensive; the whole war in Macedonia was misconceived.

One other country entered the war in south-eastern Europe: Italy. The Allies reckoned the Italians might usefully attack Austria-Hungary by the 'back door', and the Italians thought they should play the part of a great power. As it turned out the Italians were not of much use to the Allies, being a considerable economic burden to the British who were already giving supplies to France. The Italian navy co-operated in the Mediterranean; but the army was short of equipment after the Libyan War of 1911–12. The 'back door' of Austria was in fact a barricade of mountains, and the Austrians easily held it against the Italians, who in repeated battles of the Isonzo failed to drive the Austrians from their mountain positions. In October 1917 the Germans intervened, and a strong counter-attack was launched at Caporetto. The Italians were driven back seventy miles, losing 200,000 men; many more deserted before a new front could be stabilized. Caporetto was one more dismal episode for the Allies at the end of 1917.

The war in theatres outside Europe was of minor strategical importance, but it did produce some good generalship – notably in the Middle East.

By 1916 the British had 250,000 men in Egypt, the original purpose of the force being to keep the Turks away from the Suez Canal. In the winter of 1916, in order to gain elbow room, General Murray advanced into the Sinai Desert. Meanwhile plans had been made with Hussein, Sherif of Mecca, that he should start an Arab rising in the Hejaz which would draw the attention of the Turks away from the British force. The Arab revolt broke out in Mecca in June 1916. When the Turks with their superior weapons drove southwards from Medina towards Mecca the Arab forces scattered. However the atrocities perpetrated by the Turks caused the revolt to spread, and late in 1916 the British sent Captain T. E. Lawrence, an Arab expert aged 29, to assist the revolt.

The Arab forces were primitively armed and indisciplined, their military virtue lying in their mobility. Lawrence saw how to use them as an independent irregular

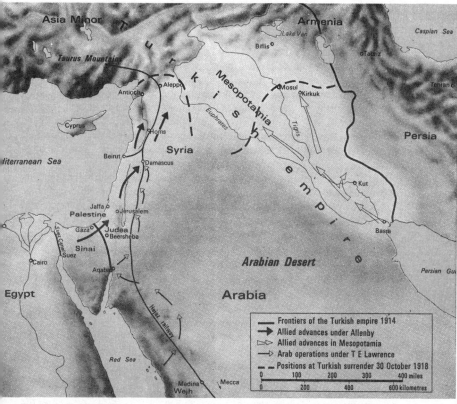

The war in the Middle East

force. His strategy was to make tip and run raids on the long communication lines of the Turks, particularly the Hejaz railway, and to spread the revolt northwards to Damascus by propaganda. His first operation with Feisal, Hussein's son, in January 1917 was a striking success. Skirting 250 miles round the flank of the Turkish force which was advancing on Mecca, he threatened their communications from Wejh. He then moved on to Aqaba, again riding round in a great loop to enlist tribesmen and avoid the Turks. Aqaba was not fortified against an attack by land, and Lawrence captured the town in July.

Meanwhile the British force had twice been repulsed by the Turks at Gaza. The new British commander, Allenby, saw that the Arabs might play an important part in another offensive at Gaza which he was preparing; so arms, ammunition and aircraft were sent to their new base at Aqaba. Lawrence and the Arabs then pushed northwards, raiding the Hejaz railway and threatening the Turkish rear. They succeeded in diverting considerable Turkish forces from the front at Gaza, and at the same time protected Allenby's flank. Lawrence's military skill and personal endurance in these operations made him a hero among the Arabs, and earned him a place among the great guerrilla leaders.

The British force now planned to progress northwards into Palestine. When General Allenby took command in June 1917 the force was halted in front of the Gaza-Beersheba line. The troops – British, Australians, New Zealanders, Indians and French, many of them survivors of Gallipoli – were dispirited by heat, dust and lack of progress. Allenby immediately went to the front himself to raise the morale of his troops. He reorganized the force into three corps. The Turks were commanded by the German General Kressenstein; their line was well fortified with entrenchments, barbed wire entanglements and machine-guns.

The plan which Allenby made for breaking the Gaza Line embodied the principles of deception and surprise. Blows were to be delivered alternately at either end of the line, so as to confuse the Turks as to where the main thrust would come. A final feint at Gaza would precede the real break-through at Beersheba. At Beersheba were the water wells which were necessary for the further advance to Jerusalem. The offensive was well prepared. False papers were allowed to fall into Turkish hands to mislead them, and to reinforce the deception elaborate movements of troops and supplies were staged at Gaza. Meanwhile the army was thoroughly equipped and thousands of water-carrying camels assembled. The offensive opened in the last week of October with a massive artillery bombardment at Gaza from land and sea. The Turks, concentrated as Allenby had intended at that end of the line, sat under the storm while XX Corps and the Desert Mounted Corps moved by night on Beersheba. The infantry delivered a direct surprise attack on the town at daybreak, while the cavalry drove in on the flank. The Turks were thrown into confusion and two days later Gaza fell.

This breaking of the Turkish line was immediately followed by a tremendous push of the Mounted Corps towards Jerusalem. On the coast XXI Corps drove the Turks back relentlessly, and by the second week in November an advance of forty miles had been made. Despite fatigue and casualties the offensive was pressed on continuously so that the Turks should never have time to settle into new defensive positions. Jaffa was taken on the 16th. Then Allenby drew his forces together in the foothills of Judea. The assault of Jerusalem was rendered difficult by bad weather and the undesirability of harming the city. But an encircling movement broke the Turkish defences, and Jerusalem was occupied on 9th December 1917.

Allenby did not resume his advance into Syria until September 1918. Some of his troops were removed to the western front, and the new troops in his army needed training. His plan for breaking the new Turkish front was similar to his previous one; the Turks were taken off balance, one army was pushed back, and the other two encircled and destroyed. This was one of the best and virtually the last horsed cavalry operation in history. Lawrence and Allenby raced for Damascus, which Lawrence reached first on 1st October; on 30th October Turkey signed an armistice of surrender.

There is one other notable individual commander in the war outside Europe – Colonel von Lettow-Vorbeck, who conducted German operations in East Africa for four years, causing a nuisance to the Allies out of all proportion to the size of his force. Through his understanding of the nature of war in a tropical climate and in the vast hinterland of East Africa without roads and railways, he defied all attempts to put an end to his activities and did not surrender until after the armistice in November 1918. A large scale combined operation was conducted by General Smuts in 1916, but Lettow-Vorbeck still eluded his enemies. He never had more than 3,500 Europeans and 12,000 natives under his command, and there was no question of his defeating the British forces in Africa. His achievement lay in having diverted, by the end, 130,000 enemy troops from the war elsewhere at a cost to Britain of £72 million. For his military skill, presence of mind, determination and leadership, Lettow-Vorbeck deserves to be remembered as a master of irregular warfare.

The more sober and pessimistic school of strategists were right: whatever happened elsewhere, the ultimate resolution of the war could be reached only on the western front. Ludendorff decided that Germany must go all out for victory in the west in 1918. Russia was out of the war and there was no danger from Italy; at last Germany could concentrate her whole strength on a single front. But it was important to strike quickly. Austria was tottering; American troops were beginning to pour into Europe; and although Germany had a supply of food in the newly gained territories of the Eastern front, British mastery of the seas was causing her to run dangerously short of industrial materials. Finally, Ludendorff hated the idea of a compromise peace. Between 21st March and 15th July 1918 a major German offensive in several phases was launched on the western front.

The Germans had no particular advantages for the offensive. The opposing forces were more or less equal, even after the Germans had moved fifty-two divisions from the eastern front. Nor did they have a new weapon, since the general staff had not recognized the value of tanks. Ludendorff intended to rely on the principles of deception and surprise which had been practically forgotten in the tactics of trench warfare. The enemy was to be misled as far as possible by continual movements of troop-trains behind the lines, and attacking forces were to take up their battle dispositions by night. There was to be no heavy preliminary bombardment. The infantry were to probe to find the weakest spots in the enemy line, instead of just hurling themselves *en masse* against the front. Ludendorff's strategy was to feint in the south, in some force in the Somme area, where the British and French lines joined. The real breakthrough would be sought just south of Ypres, with the object of turning the Allied front from the north.

The Germans achieved a considerable measure of success in this ambitious strategical programme. They opened the offensive with an attack against the British on the Somme on 21st March, using their new tactics, and helped by a dense fog. The British defence crumbled and was driven back some distance before the German onslaught. Pétain made ready to cover Paris while Haig was concerned for the Channel ports, and there was a brief danger that the French and British might themselves open a gap in their front. The alarm at this development caused the appointment at last, on 14th April, of a 'Commander-in-Chief of the Allied Armies in France': Marshal Foch. Even then Foch was not empowered to give orders to the commanders of the fighting forces – Haig, Pétain and Pershing (the American) – who continued to fight without full co-ordination to the end. However he did control the reserves.

The impetus of the German advance on the Somme ran down, as the defenders brought up reserves by train faster than the attacking troops could fight their way forward on foot. But Ludendorff broke his own rule of not attacking the enemy where they were strong, and ordered the offensive to be continued, expanding it on 28th March northwards towards Arras, where it met strong resistance and suffered heavy losses. The German blow in the north was then not delivered until 9th April on the Lys, by which time they had only 11 fresh divisions instead of the 35 originally envisaged. However the attack broke into the front at Hazebrouck, which was held only by one Portuguese division, and Ludendorff threw in all the reserves he could find. Haig abandoned Passchendaele and moved back on to the ports, requesting reserves from Foch, who sent 4 divisions – and the defenders held firm. The Germans had not discovered the secret of how to crown initial success in an offensive – the secret which had also eluded the Allies.

The Allies now tried out some new methods: enemy troops were bombarded with propaganda urging them to desert, and the Czechs were encouraged to break away as an independent nation from the Austro-Hungarian Empire. Meanwhile Ludendorff was developing new plans. During May well concealed preparations were made for a second diversionary offensive against the French in the south. On 27th May the Allies were surprised by an attack in the Chemin des Dames area on the Aisne, and by 3rd June the Germans had reached the Marne – bombarding Paris with long-range artillery. But for the second time Ludendorff was tempted by success to neglect the main part of his plan elsewhere; again all available reinforcements were thrown in, and again the Germans were halted. Foch used his reserves skilfully, ensuring that adequate troops should be available if needed elsewhere. Nerves were on edge in Paris, but Foch knew what he was doing and the French prime minister, Clemenceau, supported him. In June Ludendorff again rejected the idea of a compromise peace, and on 15th July he launched an offensive astride Rheims – which brought the Germans nearer to Paris than they had been before. But Foch had foreseen the attacks and the enemy was halted. Ludendorff's strategy had been thwarted.

Then the tide turned. On 18th July the French attacked the Germans with tanks west of Rheims. Ludendorff called off his projected blow in the north and ordered his forces to retreat to a front behind the Marne. On 24th July Foch concerted plans with the Allied commanders for a general offensive. Joffre's old idea of cutting off the salient was adopted, but with better tactics. The British were to attack in the north and the Americans in the south, while the French held the centre. On 8th August the British took the offensive at Amiens, using tanks in considerable numbers.

After November 1917 a number of senior officers at last realized that the problem of deadlock in trench warfare could be resolved. Sir John Monash, the Australian Corps Commander, formed the theory that, 'The true role of the infantry was not to expend itself upon heroic physical effort, not to wither away under merciless machine-gun fire nor to impale itself on hostile bayonets, but on the contrary, to advance under the maximum possible protection of the maximum possible array of mechanical resources, in the form of guns, machine-guns, tanks, mortars and aeroplanes.' Based on this view, it was decided to go in for tank production in a big way.

Tanks were used in a number of minor operations in the first part of 1918. Monash tested his ideas in a small operation at Le Hamel on 4th July. There was no preliminary artillery bombardment; instead infantry and tanks advanced in co-operation. Four carrier-tanks were used, which took forward loads that would have needed 1,250 men to carry, and aircraft were also used for the first time on the western front to lift supplies on the battlefield. Monash insisted that his master plan for the battle, carefully worked out with his commanders and staff in advance, was not to be departed from during the fighting. The operation at Le Hamel was a success, and the same principles were applied in the planning of the battle of Amiens on 8th August, in which Monash advised General Rawlinson – another convert to tanks. Rawlinson had 13 infantry divisions and 3 cavalry divisions, 2,070 guns, 800 aircraft and 540 tanks, consisting of 324 heavy Mark V's, 96 lighter 'Whippets', and 120 supply tanks. The forces were well supplied, thanks to a great effort to boost production in Britain during 1918. Every precaution was taken to conceal from the enemy the dispositions of the troops, and to confuse them as to British intentions.

The mist on the morning of 8th August assisted surprise. There was a brief artillery bombardment, then the long lines of tanks and infantry swept forward. The dovetailed plan unfolded as intended, except on the left where the Germans had been alert during the night and the ground was steep. By 11 o'clock there was more noise of movement than of firing, and a little over two hours later the main fighting was finished, the Australians having gained almost all their objectives and the Canadians having advanced over seven miles. It was the use of tanks which had achieved these results. They had passed with ease through the barriers of barbed wire, trenches, machine-gun and rifle fire; the enemy artillery knocked out a considerable number, but those which got right through went on to cause havoc.

The battle of Amiens did not yield the full promise of its opening; the infantry fell behind and the attempt to co-ordinate cavalry with tanks did not work. Nonetheless Ludendorff called 8th August 'the black day'. The Allies pressed forward their offensives. As September went on the German resistance stiffened. The British reached their former Flanders battle area, where mud, the old enemy, again bogged them down. On 26th September the Americans launched an attack in the Argonne, in the old style of trench warfare, suffering very heavy casualties for an advance of eight miles in one week. Then on 4th October Germany requested an armistice. During the negotiations fighting still continued, the Germans being driven from western Belgium and almost out of France. The fighting on the western front ceased on 11th November 1918.

The war came to an end about the same time in all the theatres, but there was hardly any strategical connection in this. The collapse of the Turks and the Bulgarians made no difference to the Germans and Austrians beyond discouraging them. The fact was that the Austrians and the Italians had had enough, and so had the Germans. The war was lost for Germany in Ludendorff's 1918 offensive rather than in the Allied counter-offensive or in the blockade. The spirit of the German soldiers at long last broke as they smashed themselves against defensive positions which they had not the means to overcome – in the manner of the Allied forces in previous years. When the Germans asked for an armistice their front was still intact on the old ground of the war, and although they lost ground during the month after they admitted defeat the Allies even then did not succeed in breaking up their armies. The deadlock, which was the accidental product of the technology of the time, remained the prime factor in the warfare of 1914 to 1918. Even the use of tanks did not resolve the deadlock enough to make decisive tactical victory possible. The 1914/18 war could not be won; it could only be lost in a final failure of endurance by the men of one or other side. The men on both sides fought with tenacity and courage, but in the end the Germans broke.

The war defied the attempts of the generals to master it, but the generalship was by no means all poor. If the war produced no soldier of genius, Falkenhayn, Ludendorff, Mustapha Kemal, Plumer, Monash, Allenby and Brusilov were all outstanding fighting commanders. Lawrence and Lettow-Vorbeck had their special abilities. I consider Monash to have been the best general on the western front; he had creative originality, and the war might well have been over sooner, and certainly with fewer casualties, had he been appointed to command the British armies in place of Haig. Maybe Haig was competent according to his lights, but these were dim; confidence of divine approval appeared to satisfy him. Nothing can excuse the casualties of the Somme and Passchendaele. Furthermore, he intrigued against his commander-in-chief and his political masters.

In the realm of strategy the Entente Powers dissipated too much strength in minor theatres, and conducted the war in the main theatres crudely and without imagination. The Russians were admirably loyal to their allies, but they handled most of the war on the eastern front inefficiently. Joffre began the crude strategy in the west. Foch, because of his theory of tactics, must bear much responsibility for the carnage of the war, although his handling of the reserves and the counter-offensive in 1918 indicate that latterly he had begun to see the light.

On the German side, the two chiefs of the general staff, Falkenhayn and Ludendorff, deployed their forces wisely to meet requirements on the various fronts, and were right to maintain a defensive strategy in the west for most of the war. But Ludendorff threw everything away in the end by refusing a compromise peace, and by going over in 1918 to the type of offensive which had all but lost the war for the Allies in previous years.

The powers found it no easier to make a satisfactory peace than it had been to win the war. As a last manoeuvre against France and Britain the Germans sent their request for an armistice to President Wilson of the United States. But France and Britain would not be done down. Peace was *dictated* from Versailles on 28th June. Alsace and Lorraine were returned to France; the British empire and France acquired considerable territories under the guise of 'mandates'; a new Poland was created. The former Austro-Hungarian and Ottoman empires were abolished by the recognition of new national states. Germany lost comparatively little territory in Europe, but was disarmed and ordered to pay reparations. Russia, after the Bolshevik revolution, was not accepted in the comity of civilized nations, and the territorial settlement of Brest-Litovsk was left in effect to stand. A League of Nations was set up, but Germany was not allowed to join for some years, and the United States chose not to. The lasting and dangerous effects of the 1914/18 war were a humiliated and resentful Germany and an outlawed and mistrustful Russia. The economic stability of the pre-1914 world was never quite restored. The conditions of the peace of Versailles were to prove profoundly unsatisfactory.

19 Twenty Years After:1939/45

When Foch heard of the signing of the Peace Treaty of Versailles he observed: 'This is not peace; it is an armistice for 20 years.' He was right: a peace which had been dictated to humiliate and avenge could not last. Hitler made it clear that peace was merely a period of preparation for total war, and the Nazi state became a war machine tuned for action. The principles held by the new German leaders – total war and *blitzkrieg* tactics – were in utter contrast to the defensive attitudes of the western democracies, where it was believed that war would be avoided. I had many discussions about Hitler's war with Sir Winston Churchill when it was all over; he was of the opinion that the tragedy could have been prevented: 'the malice of the wicked was reinforced by the weakness of the virtuous'. 'Thrice armed is he who hath his quarrel just'; but Hitler knew well that he is four times armed who gets his blow in first. The *blitzkrieg* burst on Poland in September 1939, and then on the west in May 1940.

The war which thus engulfed the world was totally different from the conflict of 1914/18; trench systems, barbed wire, siege warfare, all disappeared; I who fought in both can bear witness to this. During the war, crimes were committed by the Germans and Japanese which have no parallel in scale and wickedness in history. Moreover, the mighty weapon of air power brought destruction and misery to non-combatants on the home fronts by the hideous process of bombarding open cities and industrial centres from the air – begun by the Germans, but well and truly repaid by the Allies as the war progressed. The 1939/45 war was, I suppose, the greatest tragedy in the history of mankind. It has been estimated that the total number of people killed from all causes was nearly 40 million – of whom at least 17 to 18 million were civilians. The amount of human suffering was beyond all belief.

Adolf Hitler became Führer in 1934, and was thereafter in practice dictator. He used the Spanish Civil War which began in 1936 to try out new weapons and tactics. In 1936 he marched into the Rhineland, and in 1938 annexed Austria and the Sudetenland. Chamberlain and Daladier, the leaders of Britain and France, thought that these German gains must be accepted as the price of a secure and lasting peace, and in a meeting with Hitler at Munich they condoned what he had done. How could Germany be denied her legitimate revival? How could politicians start a second major war for the sake of a scrap of territory? Gauging her chances, Germany got away with one coup after another. Hitler was no fool in those early days, whatever he became later. It has been said that Hitler did not seek the war which began in 1939; that, in so many words, may be true. But I find it impossible

The 1939/45 war was total war — for civilians as much as for fighting men.
Allied troops advance through the ruins of a German town

to believe that he thought he could trouble the nations of Europe in the way he was doing without it ending in a fight. Britain and France guaranteed the integrity of Poland in March 1939, yet six months later Hitler invaded Poland, deliberately unleashing the hounds of war. The Nazi regime was based on the emotional appeal to the German people of militarism, racialism, and a nationalism which was embittered and arrogant.

The guarantee by Britain and France to preserve the integrity of Poland was a strategical objective impossible to implement without the armed assistance of Russia, which was not forthcoming because in August 1939 Hitler had obtained a non-aggression pact with Russia – a very cunning move. But Britain and France sought to honour their word and both declared war on Germany on 3rd September – the nations of the British empire rallying to the support of the mother country. The United States of America decided to avoid commitment. Other European countries remained neutral (though most of them were totally unprepared to defend their neutrality).

Neither Britain nor France was satisfactorily prepared for war in 1939. How about Germany ? In numbers of trained men she was better off, since Hitler had introduced conscription early in 1935, and in the theory of warfare the Germans had moved far ahead of the victors of the 1914/18 conflict. It was realized in Germany that a new warfare of vastly increased mobility and striking power was possible with the use of the tank and the aeroplane. The German army had developed a new tactical doctrine, the *blitzkrieg* – the essence of which was to achieve a break-through and deep penetration by an armoured force, supported from the air. Aircraft would create havoc among the enemy communications and installations, would assist the field artillery during the advance by attacking ground targets, and would keep the attacking force supplied with men and materials. Tanks, supported by infantry, would achieve the break-through on the ground. The tactical principles in the *blitzkrieg* were concentration, surprise and speed – the enemy being overwhelmed and shattered with ruthless thoroughness.

Except in aircraft there had been little technical inventiveness between 1918 and 1939. The weapons of the 1914/18 war had been further developed, though without urgency. The speed, armour and armament of tanks improved; anti-tank guns emerged; mortars were adapted for use in the field, and a sub-machine-gun was developed which could be carried by hand; gas-masks, camouflage and dispersion techniques were improved; and transport was mechanized.

Since 1918 the only other power apart from Germany to have adopted new ideas on the conduct of war was Russia, where tanks and airborne troops were highly esteemed. The victorious powers of 1914/18 hardly altered their ideas at all; the complacency of having won the last war and the expectation of future peace stultified military development. The writings of a few soldiers, such as Liddell Hart and Fuller, who argued that the fighting of the future would not be dominated by the defensive, were ignored by those in authority in Britain and France; in both countries equipment and training were at a very low ebb in 1939. The French built

the Maginot Line to protect their frontier with Germany, a defensive line of fortification which would have been impregnable in the 1914/18 war but had no place in
the new tactical conceptions. Only in Germany were the ideas of Liddell Hart
carefully studied and applied by those in authority.

The German invasion of Poland gave a first and most convincing demonstration
of the power of *blitzkrieg* tactics. The initiative was gained by striking without a
declaration of war. First the German air force, the Luftwaffe, destroyed the Polish
air force within two days – much of it never even getting off the ground to meet the
enemy. The undefended railways were paralyzed by attacks from the air so that the
Polish army could not properly mobilize. To add to the chaos and demoralization,
towns, villages and columns of refugees were bombed and strafed from the air. The
Poles brought up what forces they could to resist the ground invasion, but Marshal
Smigly-Rydz handled them in the 1914/18 manner – deploying them all along the
frontier so that they were weak everywhere and strong nowhere. The German
forces advanced in three massed columns from north, north-west and south, and
armoured spearheads penetrated the Polish front with ease. By 7th September the
two northern armies under Bock were converging near Lodz; and large Polish forces
were enveloped in the triangle Lodz-Warsaw-Torun. Farther south, forces from
the Carpathians under Rundstedt crossed the San, and on the 17th Stalin moved
Russian forces in behind the Polish army from the east. Poland was again partitioned.
The conquest of Poland, a country of 33 million people, had been carried out by
the Germans in eighteen days for a loss of 10,500 men killed and 30,000 wounded.

Britain and France, having embarked on war for the purpose of preserving
Poland, could no nothing for her. Britain sent her expeditionary force to France in
September; it consisted of four infantry divisions, one tank brigade (and we were
the nation which had first used the tank in battle in 1916) and an air force component;
it occupied its time extending the defences of the Maginot Line northwards along
the Belgian frontier. Possessed by the theory of the defensive, the British and French
forces did not even attack Germany on her western front when her armies were
engaged in eastern Europe. Instead, they bombed her with propaganda leaflets!
The inactivity on the western front lasted from September 1939 to May 1940, a
period which became known as the 'phoney war'. During that time the Russians
conquered Finland for themselves, and German forces gained control of Denmark
and Norway.

The phoney war finally ended on 10th May 1940 with the German invasion
of the Low Countries and France. The French had mobilized eighty divisions. The
British had ten in France by May 1940, but some of the Territorial divisions were
seriously lacking in equipment and training. Hitler adopted a plan made by General
von Manstein. This was to overrun neutral Belgium and Holland, thus outflanking
the Maginot Line and securing North Sea ports and air bases. France was then to
be attacked immediately. Anticipating that the British and French would have
directed their forces to meet an invasion through Belgium, the Germans decided to
deliver their main armoured thrust through the Ardennes towards the Meuse at
Sedan, on the hinge of the Allied wheel towards and into Belgium. All went as

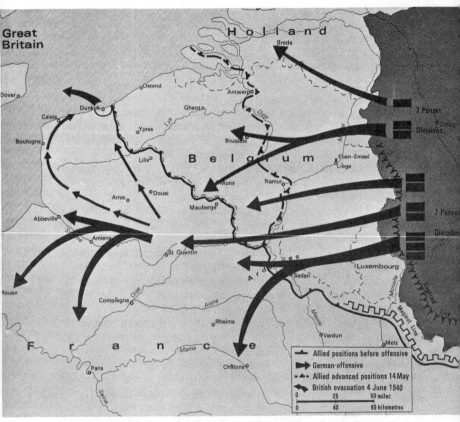

The German campaign in north-western Europe, 1940

planned. The *blitzkrieg* offensive overwhelmed Holland in five days. A combat team of parachutists and assault engineers captured the supposedly impregnable Belgian fortress of Eben-Emael in thirty-six hours. The thrust to the Meuse went faster even than the Germans had expected, as the French artillerymen were demoralized by the attacks of Stuka dive-bombers. A breach fifty miles wide was torn in the Allied front, and then General Guderian thrust on westwards towards Saint-Quentin with his armoured group – motorized divisions moving up to form 'hedges' on either side of the passage blasted by the armour. The German command of the air was virtually absolute – and the Allied commanders, Gamelin and Gort, were bewildered.

By 23rd May the Germans reached Boulogne. At midnight on 27th May the Belgians capitulated. This was awkward for me and my division, because by that time we had become the left division of the Franco-British forces, with a Belgian army prolonging our left to the sea. At dawn on 28th May I learned that the king of the Belgians had surrendered the whole of his army to the Germans. I decided in my own mind that it is not suitable in the mid-twentieth century for kings to command their national armies in battle. There was little which could be done for the British forces. By 4th June the British troops and 120,000 French soldiers had been evacuated from Dunkirk with their personal weapons, all vehicles and other equipment being left behind.

The evacuation of the British forces from the Dunkirk beaches lasted nine days, and saved 338,000 men. This was a remarkable achievement by the British navy which assembled 887 vessels of all sizes, and by the R.A.F. which in one period of four days shot down 179 enemy aircraft for the loss of 29. The relief in Britain at the extrication of the troops countered the shock, but the truth was that the British army had been thoroughly defeated in battle. So much of its equipment had been abandoned in France that in the summer of 1940 only one division in England was respectably equipped.

The German armour had not pursued the British up to Dunkirk; this was on the orders of Hitler, who decided to turn south and finish off the French. French morale cracked, and on 16th June the French government under Pétain surrendered. The Germans occupied northern and western France. At this stage Italy declared war on Germany's side.

In the following years the French resistance movement and agents of the British Special Operations Executive harassed the German forces of occupation, and organized escape routes for soldiers who had escaped from prisoner-of-war camps and for airmen shot down over France. Commando raids were a nuisance to the Germans, and Free French units served in Britain and Africa. But the fact had to be faced that in June 1940 Britain and her empire stood alone against the Axis powers, Germany and Italy.

The German conquest of the Low Countries and France was due to superior tactical methods and leadership; the Allies actually had a slight superiority in numbers and equipment: 146 to 126 divisions. Manstein's overall plan and the panzer tactics by which it was carried out, particularly Guderian's strong westward thrust, altogether constituted a remarkable military achievement.

The British people prepared for invasion; for nearly 900 years no foreign invading force had set foot on the soil of Britain, and although nobody in the country knew how the Germans were to be beaten, nobody thought of giving in. Even Winston Churchill did not see at that time how it was to be done, as he told me in June 1940; but he was in no doubt about the final result; nor was I, because I saw in him the leader we needed, the man who could rally a defeated nation, and would lead it through further troubles.

Churchill had been Prime Minister since May, and after the disaster of Dunkirk he called forth the spirit of the British people by his courage and oratory:

> We shall not flag or fail. We shall go on to the end. We shall fight in France, we shall fight in the seas and oceans, we shall fight with growing confidence and growing

strength in the air; we shall defend our island whatever the cost may be. We shall fight on the beaches, we shall fight on the landing-grounds, we shall fight in the fields and in the streets, we shall fight in the hills; we shall never surrender.

A Home Guard sprang into being. Britain's productive capacity was turned over to the war effort, and much material aid came from neutral America. The re-equipment and enlargement of the army, and the adaptation of training to up-to-date methods got under way. Great things from now on were achieved in the organization of the British army by Sir Alan Brooke, C-in-C Home Forces and later C.I.G.S. But there was much to be done, and I myself, commanding a corps on the south coast of England, was not sure how long we had before Hitler would strike. The armed forces of Germany were in occupation of the whole of western Europe from Norway to France; Churchill told us that Hitler knew he must conquer Britain or else lose the war.

We will now examine the war in the air in Europe between the summer of 1940 and May 1941. To prevent the Germans in 1940 from crossing the Channel, Britain had to rely on her strength in the air and at sea. The essential preliminary for a German invasion against the island shores of an enemy who was immensely superior at sea was command of the air.

Since 1918 aircraft had developed enormously. During the 1939/45 war air power became a mighty weapon which transformed the conception of war at sea, as well as ground tactics, enabling land battles to be won in less time and with fewer casualties than would otherwise have been the case. Strategic bombing played a large part in warfare and Allied air power was a decisive factor in the war in Europe. Before embarking on the land or sea battle, it was necessary to gain, so far as possible, mastery in the air over the area of operations.

The task of the Luftwaffe in the summer of 1940 was to gain that air mastery over England and the Channel as a prelude to invasion. The man responsible for German airpower was Hermann Göring. By August he had concentrated two *luftflotten* between the Netherlands and Brittany, one commanded by Kesselring at Brussels and the other by Sperrle at Paris. A third, small *luftflotte* commanded by Stumpff was based in Norway. The two main *luftflotten* had a first line strength of about 2,000 serviceable aircraft. These consisted of Junker 88 bombers, the fastest and best yet made, Junker 87 dive-bombers, Messerschmitt 109 fighters and Messerschmitt 110's. To oppose this force, the British Fighter Command under Air Chief Marshal Dowding had 50 squadrons of Hurricanes and Spitfires – a first-line strength of about 900 aircraft. There were also 1,700 anti-aircraft guns. With a numerically inferior force the British had to defend a whole coastline, whereas the Germans could choose the areas in which to concentrate their forces for a massive attack.

There was little to choose between the British and German fighters. The Spitfire and Hurricane, armed with eight machine-guns, were slightly slower than the Messerschmitt 109 (358 m.p.h.) but made up for it with greater manoeuvrability. The German bombers were slow and vulnerable, and consequently had to be escorted by fighters – which limited the activities of both. Furthermore Fighter

The Battle of Britain was Hitler's first check. Fighter pilots of the R.A.F. run to take off

Command was well organized, the system having been set up under Dowding in 1936; the essence of it was the centralization of an early warning complex and the decentralization of tactical control to subordinate Groups throughout the country. Information of the approach of enemy aircraft was collected from twenty or so radar stations on the coast. (Radar was a recently discovered device which detected objects at a distance by bouncing radio waves against them.) The information was then passed on to the relevant Group Headquarters whose responsibility it was to engage the enemy, bringing into operation its fighters, searchlights and anti-aircraft guns.

On 2nd July Hitler ordered his armed forces to prepare for the invasion of Britain and Göring launched the Battle of Britain in the air with a limited preliminary offensive against shipping in the straits of Dover. Dowding refused to be drawn. The first main phase began in mid-August. The R.A.F. was to be smashed by the destruction of aircraft in the air, while at the same time the offensive against shipping was to continue. Kesselring and Sperrle concentrated their Groups on south-eastern England, and Stumpff on the Midlands. During the first big battle, 13th August, British fighters in the south-east Group commanded by Park destroyed 45 German planes for the loss of 13 of their own. In the next major clash Stumpff lost one sixth of his force, and thereafter could only play a minor part in operations. Between 16th and 18th August the Germans again suffered heavy losses: 236 for 95 British planes. The R.A.F. had the advantage that the pilots of their destroyed planes were not necessarily lost to them, but might parachute to safety. Also, aircraft production in Britain was proceeding rapidly.

Göring now saw that he had made a mistake in not first concentrating his whole force on defeating the R.A.F. in the air. From 19th August to 6th September – the second phase – this was his main object; Kesselring's fighters came over by day, and Sperle's bombers by night. Park would not be drawn to risk all his strength against the fighters, but continued to pick off the German bombers.

The third phase began early in September, when the whole German attack was concentrated on London. Hitler spoke, characteristically, of 'extermination'. On 7th September Kesselring attacked London with 300 bombers and 600 fighters. Most of the bombs were dropped, causing heavy damage and casualties in the docks. But 21 fighter squadrons of the R.A.F. engaged the enemy, and again the Germans suffered many more losses in aircraft then they inflicted. The German raids continued, culminating in the fighting of 15th September. On that day Kesselring threw in all his strength, making one raid in the morning and another in the afternoon. Park, reinforced by neighbouring Groups, committed practically his whole force. Kesselring's bombers were decimated and the German fighters decisively repulsed.

The Luftwaffe admitted defeat by Fighter Command, and on 12th October Hitler cancelled his invasion plan. Churchill's tribute to the men of the R.A.F. who won the Battle of Britain was: 'Never in the field of human conflict was so much owed by so many to so few.' The Luftwaffe continued night bombing through the following winter and spring, not now to clear the way for invasion but with the object of dislocating production and breaking civilian morale. Most of the main cities of Britain suffered greatly, Coventry in particular, yet the Germans did not achieve these strategic objects. In mid-May 1941 the Luftwaffe began to look towards Russia.

The Battle of Britain had been a rebuff to Germany, but, despite that, the Axis powers thereafter widened their strategy. The roots of British strength were attacked. Manufacturing centres and bases were bombed, and British maritime communications everywhere attacked by air and sea. In September 1940 the Italians started an offensive in North Africa, and in October they invaded Greece. The Germans quickly had to support them in both these areas. Mussolini's motive was probably envy of German success, but the war in the Mediterranean theatre had a true strategic value for the Axis in that it was a further blow to the communica-

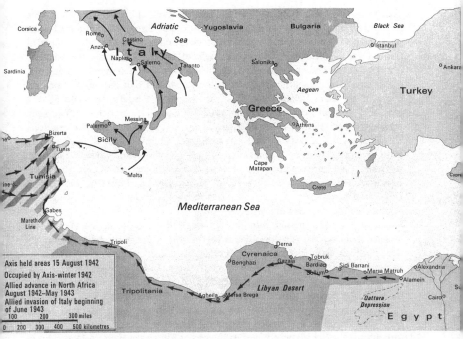

The war in the Mediterranean

tions of Britain's empire. Axis strategy thus far was bold and, temporarily, realistic and successful.

Then on 22nd June 1941 Germany attacked Russia – a major strategic error. On 11th December 1941 she declared war on the United States of America. Hitler's motive in thus pitting Germany against the two most powerful states in the world simultaneously is unfathomable. As it turned out, the war in the west and the war which began in the Far East when Japan attacked the United States at Pearl Harbour on 7th December 1941 were little related. Germany and Japan had a pact, but in practice they did not concert operations as allies. Since they had common enemies, each did to some extent divert the other's opponents, although Russia and Japan never fought each other. Hitler now had to fight not only the British empire but also Russia and the U.S.A.; his service chiefs could hardly view the problem with any great hope, particularly since one of the Axis powers, Italy, was already proving a broken reed.

The Italians had strong naval forces and an air force in the Mediterranean, as well as a large army in Libya. On 13th September 1940 the Italian forces began an advance from Cyrenaica towards Egypt and moved as far as Sidi Barrani, where they halted.

The British C-in-C, General Wavell, decided, even although his forces were greatly inferior to those of the Italians, that the enemy threat to Egypt must be met with boldness. The Western Desert Force took the offensive under the command of Major-General O'Connor. During the night of 8th–9th December the offensive cut through the line of Italian forts, capturing them one after the other, and two nights later had cut across the desert to the sea west of Sidi Barrani to block the retreat of the main Italian force. What had begun as a raid was pushed on as a campaign. Tobruk was captured on 22nd January 1941, and the British again pushed forward boldly; on 8th February Mersa Brega and Agheila were captured. The British force of two divisions had destroyed the Italian force of ten divisions, taking 130,000 prisoners, 380 tanks and 845 guns for the loss of 500 dead and 1,400 wounded. Boldness, mobility, the command of O'Connor and Wavell and inter-service cooperation were the elements in this success. The Italians in East Africa, Eritrea and Abyssinia were also defeated by virtue of the mobility and driving force of much smaller British armies.

During the same period Admiral Cunningham's fleet, based on Alexandria, inflicted serious damage on the Italian navy. On 15th October three Italian destroyers were sunk; on 11th November the Fleet Air Arm torpedoed and sank three battle-ships in Taranto harbour; on 9th February the docks of Genoa were bombarded; and on 19th March in an engagement off Cape Matapan Cunningham destroyed three cruisers and two destroyers for the loss of only two aircraft.

These were heartening successes. But on 12th February 1941 General Rommel arrived in Tripoli with advanced elements of his Afrika Korps and events began to turn against the British once more. At the end of March the Western Desert Force was attacked at Mersa Brega by Rommel's armoured force and had to retire, having been weakened by the withdrawal of troops for operations in Greece. During the withdrawal O'Connor was taken prisoner. By 13th April Rommel had encircled Tobruk, which was besieged but held out, and by 28th April he had crossed the Egyptian frontier and occupied Halfaya Pass and Sollum. Wavell launched various offensives but to no avail, and Rommel continued to dominate the desert scene. On 1st July 1941, Wavell having been appointed C-in-C India, Auchinleck took over as C-in-C Middle East.

In October 1940 the Italians had invaded Greece, but failed there too; so the Germans had to intervene – overrunning Yugoslavia and Greece in the spring of 1941. On 20th May the Germans invaded Crete. After bombing out the anti-aircraft installations they dropped paratroops and followed them by glider-borne troops. It was a bold and skilful though costly operation, and Crete fell to them. The Greek and Cretan operations had diverted troops from the desert, and also air power. The British intervention in Greece was a strategic error; it weakened the British front south of Benghazi; and in the end the British forces were driven out of Greece, Crete and Cyrenaica.

We must now examine the attack by the Germans on Russia, called 'Barbarossa' and launched on 22nd June 1941, in which they soon made great advances. This was

The war in eastern Europe, 1942–4

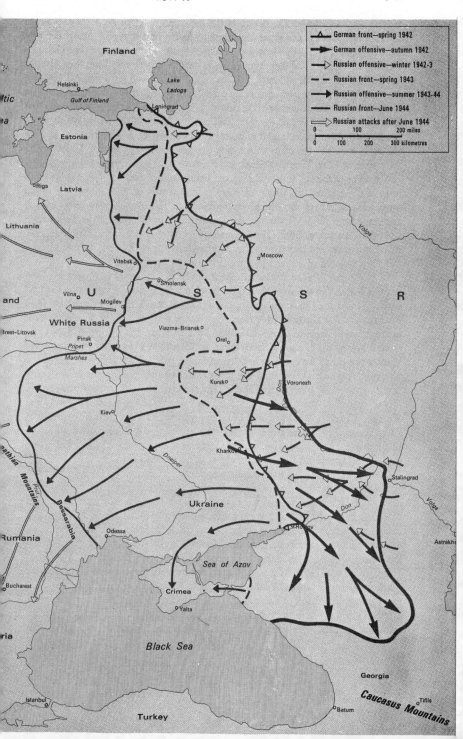

△△△	German front—spring 1942
➤	German offensive—autumn 1942
←	Russian offensive—winter 1942-3
----	Russian front—spring 1943
➤	Russian offensive—summer 1943-44
—	Russian front—June 1944
▷	Russian attacks after June 1944

0   100   200 miles
0   100   200   300 kilometres

war on a colossal scale. The design of the operation was that the Germans should envelop the Russians in a series of pockets by means of convergent thrusts made by columns, and not be drawn into the great open spaces of the country. The Germans had 145 divisions, 20 of them armoured, as well as some forces from their satellite countries, with which to attack 158 Russian divisions and 55 armoured brigades near the frontier. The convergent thrust method was highly successful, and Russian troops were captured during 1941 in enormous numbers. Guderian with his armoured divisions conducted one of the most brilliant operations of the war in his thrust to Smolensk and the encirclement of enemy forces in that area. The Russians had not the equipment nor the ideas with which to oppose *blitzkrieg* tactics. Major battles took place at Kiev, Viazma-Briansk and the Azov Sea. But after covering 700 miles and getting within 15 miles of Moscow before winter fell, the German generals were not permitted by Hitler to make a final thrust on the centre of Russian communications and the capital of communism. Hitler took over direct overall command from Field-Marshal von Brauchitsch, and the Germans fell back somewhat and fortified a winter front. The German troops were not equipped for the terrible Russian winter, and they also suffered considerably from Russian counter-attacks. But they endured great hardships with remarkable fortitude.

In the spring of 1942 the eastern front ran from Leningrad to Rostov-on-Don, some of Russia's best corn lands and her chief industrial areas being thus in German hands. At first the Russian people rather welcomed the Germans as liberators from Stalin's rule. But Hitler failed to take advantage of this; instead, he decided that the best method of pacification was cruelty and destruction – mass depopulations being carried out by the 'Security Service' run by Himmler. From then on torture and murder became all too common in German dealings with those they conquered or imprisoned. A murderous partisan warfare was the natural consequence of this policy in the occupied areas of eastern Europe – and the Germans suffered severely from it.

They resumed the offensive in 1942, confining it to the southern front from Kursk to Kharkov. Some fifty-one German divisions, with complete air superiority, swept forward to Voronezh on the left and to Stalingrad in the centre – bracing themselves for a decisive drive into the Caucasus to capture the oilfields. But before that could happen the Russians counter-attacked at Stalingrad.

Offering fierce resistance the Russians had held out against the German offensive at Stalingrad. At this time they were being rapidly strengthened by increased production in factories behind the fighting area, and by American and British aid delivered via Persia and by the sea route round the North Cape of Norway. The ablest men were now coming to the top in the Red Army. In November 1942, heavily reinforced, the Russians under Marshal Zhukov went over to the offensive, the pincers closing in on eighteen German and Rumanian divisions at Stalingrad. Hitler would not allow retreat, and on 31st January 1943 the remnants of the German Sixth Army under General Paulus surrendered. Simultaneously the Russians broke through the investment of Leningrad. Field-Marshal von List had to withdraw the German army group in the Caucasus to prevent it being trapped, and to repair the front on the Don; this retreat, through Rostov, was conducted with great skill.

The Russians now advanced in strides, reaching Kharkov, 350 miles west of Stalingrad, by mid-February 1943. The advance was checked for a while, as Manstein stabilized the front in that area and the spring thaw rendered movement difficult. In July the Germans launched the most powerful armoured assault of the war at Kursk. But the Russians held firm.

During this time the Russian army was gradually growing stronger in equipment and numbers, under able new commanders – notably Koniev and Rokossovsky. The Germans were not the force they had been in 1941. In September the Russians reached Smolensk in the north, and, by the end of 1943, Kiev in the south.

Hitler's fatal mistake was to attack Russia. It was doubly stupid of him to do so before the Germans had successfully finished off the war against the British in the Mediterranean and northern Africa. Had a proportion of the troops and equipment used against the Russians been sent to Africa, and particularly armoured divisions, it is reasonable to presume that the Germans would have gained Egypt, the Suez Canal and possibly established a stronghold in the Middle East. As it was, the turn of the tide on the Russian front was matched elsewhere. In the six months from October 1942 (the battle of Alamein) the Germans were driven out of North Africa, and the Allies followed up that victory by conquering Sicily and invading Italy.

German troops stumble through the snows of Russia to a disastrous defeat

The Americans were now making headway in building up their great strength, which was badly needed. The Allied bombing attack on Germany was stepped up during the winter of 1942–3 and in the summer of 1943 the war in the Atlantic turned decisively in favour of the British and Americans.

Confident of victory, Churchill met Roosevelt at Casablanca in January 1943 to formulate strategy. Together they declared that the policy of the Allies was to force the 'unconditional surrender' of Germany, Italy and Japan. I have always considered this decision to have been a tragic mistake. What it led to was well summarized by Lord Hankey:

> It embittered the war, rendered inevitable a fight to the finish, banged the door on any possibility of either side offering terms or opening up negotiations, gave the Germans and Japanese the courage of despair, strengthened Hitler's position as Germany's 'only hope', aided Goebbels' propaganda, and made inevitable the Normandy landing and the subsequent terribly exhausting and destructive advance through North France, Belgium, Luxemburg, Holland and Germany. The lengthening of the war enabled Stalin to occupy the whole of eastern Europe, to ring down the iron curtain. By disposing of all the more competent administrators in Germany and Japan this policy retarded recovery and reconstruction. Unfortunately also, these policies, so contrary to the spirit of the Sermon on the Mount, did nothing to strengthen the moral position of the Allies.

But from the time the war turned in favour of the Allies the unconditional surrender of all their enemies was their strategic objective.

Success in the war in the African desert depended to a more than usual extent on the factors of equipment and supply. Important changes in the balance of these two factors were the chief reason for the shuttling of the two sides backwards and forwards across the desert. With smaller numbers but better equipment Wavell defeated the Italians in 1940. Then Rommel arrived with his Afrika Korps and the balance switched back in favour of the Axis. In 1941 and until autumn 1942 the Germans had superior equipment. Their tanks had a better armament than the British ones, which were under-gunned. The British 2-pounder anti-tank gun, and even the 6-pounder, were less powerful for example than the German 88-mm. gun, which could pierce thick tank armour at 2,000 yards; this was, in fact, an anti-aircraft gun, but Rommel found it to be a very effective anti-tank gun and often used it as such. The Germans also had better petrol cans and tank-transporters which saved wear of tracks. Equipment which gave any superiority in mobility and fire-power counted for much in war in the open desert, with its independence of fixed defences. Rapid and wide manoeuvre, and superiority in gun-power and armour, were the best means to win battles. Wavell compared the tactics of war in the desert to war at sea; minefields were laid in the desert very much as they were at sea.

The Germans had the advantage in equipment but not always in supply – which also counted for much. The British retention of Tobruk after the reverse of March 1941 deprived Rommel of an important base. Malta was also a crucial supply point for the British, as well as being a base whence submarines and aircraft could attack the enemy supply lines. The Germans did not pay enough attention to Malta in 1941, and in August of that year 35 per cent of German and Italian supplies and reinforcements were lost when trying to cross the Mediterranean; in the autumn the figure rose towards 75 per cent. When Rommel was relatively short of supplies between October 1941 and early January 1942, Auchinleck was able to drive him back to Agheila – causing him many casualties in men and armoured vehicles. The Germans then realized how essential was the supply factor. In the winter of 1941, twenty-five U-boats were diverted from the Atlantic to the Mediterranean, and in December the Axis began an intense air attack on Malta, the result being that in January 1942 they did not lose a single ton of supplies in the Mediterranean, while British naval losses in that period were severe.

It was then the turn of the British to be short of supplies. Auchinleck had advanced a long way and his army was at the end of communications stretching back to Egypt. In the first half of 1942 Rommel hit back; Tobruk fell on 21st June, and Malta became in great danger. Rommel pressed on with brilliant and daring rapidity. The British were bounced out of Mersa Matruh before they could collect themselves, and by the end of June 1942 they were back at the Alamein position. Here, between the sea and the impassable Qattara Depression, a position was established – some thirty miles in a straight line. During the winter of 1941–2 Auchinleck had had to send away some of his forces for the war against Japan, and this did not help in his efforts to deal with Rommel. But the Alamein position held against Rommel's assaults; it had no open flanks.

Again, with the Germans only sixty miles from Alexandria, the supply pendulum swung. It was now Rommel's army which found itself at the end of a long supply line. Auchinleck and the air C-in-C, Tedder, took advantage of this fact and bombed the German supply points along the coast, leaving Rommel with no proper base nearer than Benghazi – 680 miles to the west. Furthermore, Hitler deferred the final reduction of Malta, which staged a recovery, and the British supply situation began to improve. Additional troops arrived, and the Americans sent 300 Sherman tanks and 100 self-propelled guns – equipment at last to match that of the Germans. Such was the situation in mid-August, when General Alexander replaced Auchinleck as C-in-C Middle East, and I took over command of the Eighth Army.

My determination to deal firmly with Rommel and his army once and for all was clearly expressed to the Eighth Army: to hit the Axis forces right out of Africa. But I was equally determined not to begin the attempt until we were fully prepared, and I said as much to officers and men. We must have enough supplies not only to defeat Rommel at Alamein but also to pursue him westwards until we could open up the ports of Tobruk and Benghazi. Accordingly I spent two months building up the army and its morale. I instituted a system of command which was efficient and novel, whereby the detail of staff work was handled by a chief of staff, I myself being free to concentrate on the main problem of defeating my famous opponent.

On 30th August Rommel attacked the Eighth Army – a gambler's last throw to get to Cairo and Alexandria. His objective was the Alam Halfa ridge, the real key to the Alamein position. I was expecting such an attack. I had pondered over Rommel's previous successes in the desert, and had observed that his favourite tactic was to induce the British tanks to attack his armour which he protected by a screen of anti-tank guns; he thus knocked out most of the British armour – having done which he launched his own armour and won the *mêlée*. I decided to play this tactic with him, and did so in the Alam Halfa battle; his forces had a good hammering from my anti-tank guns and tanks in dug-in positions, and he gave up the contest and withdrew. So I won my first battle with Rommel, a defensive one.

After Alam Halfa I continued with my own preparations for a large scale offensive which I was determined would be the beginning of the end for Rommel in Africa. We had a considerable superiority in troops and tanks, and air superiority of three to one. The Germans were desperately short of petrol. Strategical surprise was not possible; I therefore planned for tactical surprise.

By an elaborate cover plan, with dummy installations and diversionary operations, we conveyed the impression that our main attack would be launched in the south. Actually, the essence of the plan was to punch two corridors through the enemy front *in the north*. Engineers would clear the corridors through the mines with detectors, assisted by flail tanks. The infantry divisions were to lead through the corridors, followed by armoured divisions. I then reckoned that Rommel's armoured divisions would have to attack mine in position, and while this conflict was going on my infantry divisions would defeat the enemy infantry by what I described as 'crumbling' operations on their flanks and rear.

So it worked out. But the battle of Alamein, which began on 23rd October 1942, was a stern fight; our offensive met desperate resistance and the counter-attacks of the enemy armour were formidable. Since the German resistance was particularly strong in the north, where our break-in had originally been made, I decided to put in the final break-out thrust a little to the south – on the Italian part of the enemy front. This knock-out blow was launched on 2nd November – 'Operation Supercharge'. By 4th November the battle was definitely won, and insofar as the British were concerned it was the turning-point of the war. It had lasted twelve days; we took 30,000 prisoners, including nine generals; our casualties (all kinds) were just over 13,000. The pursuit then began.

Rommel had often before been forced to break off a battle and withdraw, generally for administrative reasons; he had never before at any time during the war in the desert been smashed in battle. That had now been done. The driving of him and his forces out of Africa remained. He was so short of petrol that he would be unable to carry out any major manoeuvre for the time being; but he was a very good general and had several times hit back when it was least expected. I was determined not to have any more set-backs in the desert war, and was not prepared to run undue risks during the long march to Tripoli and then on to Tunis. Moreover, I wanted as few casualties as possible.

Such was the state of confusion in the break-in area after the battle, and the delay caused by rain, that it took time to develop the pursuit. But when the Eighth Army got going it moved fast, with its eye always on the essential supply points of Tobruk, Benghazi and Tripoli. Tripoli was reached on 23rd January 1943, and once we had opened the port there was no further danger of our losing the advantage for lack of supplies. Meanwhile in November an Anglo-American force under General Eisenhower had landed in French North Africa, and Rommel, in Tunisia, was thus caught between two fires. In February he dealt some stinging blows to the Americans in the region of the Kasserine Pass. But on 30th March the Eighth Army attacked him at the Mareth Line, turning the German right flank and forcing a withdrawal. This was the beginning of the end. On 13th May 1943 the Axis forces in Tunisia laid down their arms.

The clearing of the Mediterranean for Allied shipping was completed by the conquest of Sicily, which was overrun between 10th July and 16th August. The invasion cf Italy began on 3rd September. The Italians quickly capitulated, but the German forces in Italy resisted strongly. The progress of the Americans on the west coast and of the British on the Adriatic side slowed as the Italian winter set in.

The reader should now know something of the bombing of Germany. The purpose of it was later defined at the Casablanca Conference in January 1943 as being 'the progressive destruction and dislocation of the German military, industrial and economic system and the undermining of the morale of the German people to a point where their capacity for armed resistance is fatally weakened'. Bombing was intended to complement the naval blockade, in striking at the basis of Germany's economic strength. Bombing, as much as concentration camps, made the 1939/45 conflict 'total war'. The first raid took place on the night of 15th May 1940, when a British force of ninety-nine bombers attacked oil and railway targets in the Ruhr. The offensive was kept up all through 1940 and 1941, but the results were not what had been hoped. Daytime bombing was out of the question because of German anti-aircraft guns and fighters. So the raids had to be launched at night, but even then the Germans made it very dangerous, with the aid of radar, and accuracy could not be achieved on selected targets. All in all, the bombing had little effect on full production in Germany at that time.

Then in 1942 the bombing offensive was intensified, the Americans now being in the war. In March the first Lancaster bombers came into use – strong and reliable four-engined aircraft. In February, Air Marshal Harris took command of the whole British bombing offensive, and by his energy and drive he improved the system. The training of navigators and bomb-aimers was stepped up; and in August the 'Pathfinder' force was introduced: a force of light, fast, manoeuvrable Mosquito bombers which went ahead of the Lancasters, Stirlings and Halifaxes to mark the target accurately. In 1943 several radar devices were introduced to assist navigation and aiming. Large-scale destruction was caused in the Ruhr, and the breaching of the Möhne and Eder dams in May 1943 by Gibson's 617 Squadron was a spectacular feat. Nine thousand tons of bombs were dropped in four major attacks on Hamburg, and then attention was switched to Berlin. The British raids by night were complemented by the Americans who insisted on making their raids in daylight.

By 1944 the Allies had gained command of the air over Germany. But even in 1943 and 1944 the achievement of the bombing offensive fell very far short of the paralysis of the enemy which had been hoped for. It did at any rate cause the Germans to concentrate on the production of fighter aircraft, and to give up almost all bombing themselves.

We will now turn to the war at sea. On 17th August 1940 Hitler declared a total blockade of Britain. The war at sea was of crucial importance, since Britain was not able to supply herself adequately with food or arms except by imports. Hitler had, however, neglected to build up sufficient seapower before he began to implement his intentions. In 1940 German naval strength was not enough to maintain an effective blockade, and the Germans had no hope of dominating the Channel by seapower for the projected invasion of Britain. The German strategy at sea was threefold: submarines went out in packs, surface vessels in sorties, and bombers attacked shipping within reasonable range of land. The British navy was employed in defending convoys and seeking out the German surface raiders; but it was handicapped by the fact that many of its ships were out of date, and by a shortage of submarines and aircraft.

From the start the struggle on the surface of the seas was evenly matched. In

German cities were reduced to rubble by Allied bombing. The centre of Stuttgart

January 1941 Admiral Lütjens left Kiel with *Scharnhorst* and *Gneisenau* for a two-month cruise during which he sank or took twenty-two ships (115,600 tons). Similar destructive forays were successfully made by the pocket-battleship *Scheer* and the heavy cruiser *Hipper*. But the British also struck. In December 1939 the German pocket-battleship *Graf Spee*, which had sunk nine British ships, was brought to battle outside the River Plate by three cruisers under Commodore Harwood and so damaged that she was scuttled by her captain. Cunningham overwhelmed the Italian fleet in the Mediterranean. Later *Bismarck* and *Scharnhorst* were sunk – to mention two notable incidents. German commerce was very hard hit from the beginning.

The operations of the German U-boats were extremely effective, and serious for Britain. In 1942 the Allies lost 1,664 ships (7,790,697 tons), of which 1,160 were sunk by U-boats. For a while in 1942 Britain ran perilously short of oil. Most of the submarine operations took place on the trans-Atlantic routes, but there were other vital areas: the Indian Ocean, the convoy route to Malta, and the route to Archangel – a terrible sea route for the sailors.

The whole war at sea began to move in favour of the Allies in the autumn of 1942. The key factor in this development was air power. Coastal Command had hitherto been kept short of aircraft, priority being given to the bombing offensive against Germany. But that bombing had not been particularly fruitful, and even when it was concentrated on the U-boat yards and bases between January and May 1943 it did little good. But from the autumn of 1942 Coastal Command had more aircraft at its disposal, capable of patrolling 800 miles out to sea; aircraft were also used from convoy escort carriers. Further factors in the Allied recovery were short-wave radar to detect nearby submarines and heavier depth charges. In late 1942 the Arctic convoy PQ.18 lost 13 out of 43 ships, but the convoy fought its way through. The struggle remained desperate throughout the winter, and Admiral Doenitz kept 100 U-boats on patrol. Some 108 Allied ships were lost in March 1943. But then the new system began to yield results. In May, convoy SC.130 from Canada, supported by Liberators from Iceland, got through unscathed in a battle which cost the enemy 5 U-boats. During that month Allied losses in merchant shipping fell greatly, while the Germans lost 41 U-boats.

The U-boats however did not give up their operations and no reliable way of destroying them was ever discovered; but at least patrolling aircraft forced them to stay submerged, thus reducing their mobility and preventing them from getting at convoys. Germany's grip on Britain's lifeline now progressively weakened, and although there was often fierce fighting at sea the strategic danger was practically removed. Altogether by the end of the war the Germans lost 785 out of 1,162 U-boats. The U-boats had sunk 14,687,230 tons of Allied shipping. Air power gained the final mastery for Britain over Germany's surface fleet as well. On 19th November 1944 thirty-two Lancasters bombed and wrecked the battleship *Tirpitz*. German maritime trade had ceased to exist, while Britain's survived.

By the beginning of 1944 success in the Mediterranean, in the Atlantic and on the eastern front was clearly in sight. Some twenty-three German divisions were being contained in Italy – though Kesselring's able generalship, for example at Anzio and Cassino, prevented the Allies from progressing before mid-1944 as well as had been hoped. Tito's partisans in Yugoslavia were diverting other German troops. In the east the Russians began the year by bursting out from the salient west of Kiev, and in the south by May 1944 they had passed the upper Prut. The next task of the Allied strategists was clearly the recovery of France, followed by the invasion of Germany itself from the west. The Russians were pressing for the opening of a second major front in Europe in order to take some of the German pressure off them.

Stalin, unlike some other statesmen of the Alliance, seeing that victory was certain, had a far-sighted political strategy. He was determined to confine the operations of the British and Americans to western Europe, so that he could conquer eastern Europe for communism. At a conference between Stalin, Roosevelt and Churchill, held at Teheran in November 1943, Stalin agreed with the Americans that divisions from the Italian front should be used to land in southern France and develop an offensive up the Rhône valley and thence towards the Vosges and the upper reaches of the Rhine. Churchill disagreed with this strategy, and I consider rightly; it removed ten divisions from Italy and thus made it impossible for an offensive from that country to be developed northwards through the Ljubljana Gap towards Vienna. The war in Italy then became senseless; as Fuller wrote, it became 'a campaign with inadequate means, with no strategic goal and with no political bottom'. The invasion of southern France was, of course, exactly right for Stalin: it would keep the British and Americans well away from the Balkans and eastern Europe. I argued fiercely against it with Eisenhower when we were preparing the invasion of Normandy, but to no avail – the Americans were set on it. In my view it was one of the great strategic mistakes of the war. What it made clear to me was that Russia was now fighting not only to defeat Germany, but also to win the peace from her allies. It was impossible to make the American leaders understand this.

It was further agreed at the Teheran conference that the main task of the British and Americans in 1944 should be the invasion of north-west Europe. The experience of the raid on Dieppe in August 1942 by Canadian troops not adequately supported from air and sea had taught the Allies the absolute necessity of making an opposed landing on a hostile coast – one of the most difficult operations in all warfare – a fully combined operation by all three services. The supreme commander was an American general, Eisenhower; his deputy was a British airman, Tedder. The air forces were commanded by Leigh-Mallory, and the naval forces by Ramsay – both British. I had been appointed by the British government to command the British armies to take part in the invasion – the 21st Army Group. But Eisenhower ordered me to take operational direction of the American armies as well, so as to have all the land forces under one commander for the landing and subsequent break-out from the lodgment area.

The area selected for the landing of the Allied forces was the part of Normandy between Cabourg and Valognes. This plan was disguised from the Germans by full scale dummy preparations for an invasion of the Pas de Calais area. During some months before D-day railways, bridges, and other means of communication were intensely bombed; the object was, first, to dislocate the German supply organization, and secondly to isolate the battle area and make it difficult for divisions from other parts of France to intervene quickly in the bridgehead battle – and this second object was maintained once we were ashore in Normandy, so much so that the first arrivals of reinforcing German divisions generally appeared on bicycles!

The Germans, having lost hope of winning on the eastern front, put a great deal of what they had into the west. Field-Marshal von Rundstedt, C-in-C West, had under his command 60 divisions, 11 of them armoured, organized in two army groups. These were stretched from Holland via Antwerp, Normandy, and the Biscay coast to the Mediterranean; and a proportion of them were poorly equipped. My opponent of the desert days, Rommel, commanded Army Group B, in the area from Holland to Normandy. The Germans were very weak in air power, having only 90 bombers and 70 fighters fit for action. They were also, ironically, somewhat as the French in 1939 – strung out along a line of defences uncertain when or where to expect the

The battle of Normandy

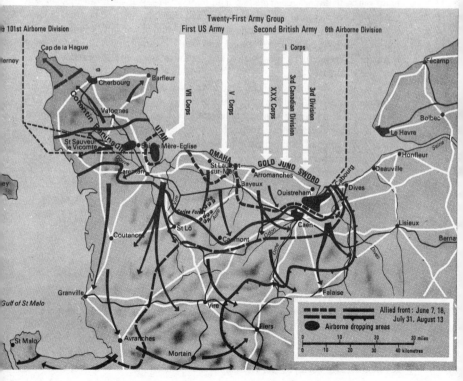

enemy to strike. Furthermore there was disagreement between Rundstedt and Rommel as to the tactics of opposing the invasion. Rundstedt favoured holding the forces slightly inland, and then counter-attacking before the Allies could consolidate a beach-head; Rommel wanted to position his-forces well forward to prevent any landing on the beaches – although he did not know where the attempt might be made. Hitler agreed with Rommel, and a compromise was adopted, with most of the infantry well forward and most of the armour back. Hitler had frequently intervened to bad effect in the conduct of the war in the east; he was to do the same in France.

The forces I proposed to use for the first wave of the landing were 5 seaborne divisions and 3 airborne (150,000 men in all), and I planned to have 18 divisions on shore in Normandy by the end of the first week or so. We also had 5,300 ships and craft, 12,000 planes and 1,500 tanks. For the actual invasion we had the advantages of surprise and concentration of effort; the Allied armies were a balanced force of all arms; finally we had complete air superiority, thus ensuring that the enemy concentration and subsequent movements would be greatly hindered. A number of tanks, called 'funnies', had been specially converted for invasion purposes: amphibious tanks, flail tanks for exploding land mines, mat-laying tanks for crossing soft patches on beaches, and several other varieties. Old ships were to be sunk to make breakwaters; there were two artificial harbours built of concrete caissons; and a cross-Channel pipe-line, called 'Pluto', was ready to supply petrol to the shore of Normandy. Preparations for invasion had begun in 1943, and the expedition was very well equipped.

D-day was 6th June 1944. The Americans were on the right and the British and Canadians on the left. In the early hours of 6th June three airborne divisions were dropped to secure the flanks of the lodgment area, engaging the Germans to prevent them attacking the seaborne troops as they were landing on the beaches. Gliders brought in anti-tank equipment. The landings on the beaches were preceded by bombardment from ships, and by intensive air bombing on radar stations, airfields, gun positions and beach defences generally. The hardest resistance was met by the Americans on Omaha beach; the exits from the beach were steep, and the Americans had declined to use any of the British 'funnies'. Also, they made the mistake of transferring to their landing-craft too far off shore, and the troops were exposed to rough seas and gunfire for a considerable time. Nevertheless, fighting with great gallantry, the Americans gained their bridge-head. The British landings were very well supported by the Royal Navy, with accurate navigation and bombardment; the run-in in the landing-craft was quite short; and the specialized tanks proved their worth.

The Allies were assisted by a certain dislocation in the German command – Rommel and two other commanders were absent; certain armoured units were not to be used without Hitler's personal order; and, it has been said, the Führer was in bed at Berchtesgaden and it was not permitted to awaken him. Rundstedt wondered for some time whether the landings might not be just a feint for a real invasion farther north, so the German counter-attacks got off to a slow start and, thanks largely to Allied air action, were badly co-ordinated. The Allies secured bridge-heads at all landing points on 6th June, with 9,000 casualties. The counter-attacks built up during the next week, but they were fought off, and by 11th June the beach-heads had all been linked and some elbow-room gained. By 12th June, 326,547 men had been landed, with 54,186 vehicles and 104,428 tons of stores. More delay was caused to the Allied landing programme by bad weather than by the Germans.

My plan, after establishing a firm lodgment area, was so to conduct the land battle that the British would draw the main German strength, and particularly the enemy armoured divisions, on to our left flank in the Caen area, to fight it and keep it there, so that the Americans might the more easily gain territory on our right or western flank – and then to make the ultimate break-out on that flank. So, more or less, the battle developed. With total air superiority our attacks on the ground were more effective than ever before, and the army and air co-operation became highly developed. General Arnold describes the advance of American troops towards St Lô: 'Fighters and fighter-bombers in closest communication and under common direction ranged ahead of them destroying military targets. Fighters in direct communication with tanks by radio flew constant alert over our armored columns. Ground officers called on the fighters to bomb or strafe artillery or armour in their path. Pilots warned tank commanders of traps.'

In spite of the vital part played in battle by aircraft, artillery and tanks, to my mind in modern war it is, however, the infantry soldier who in the end plays the decisive part in the land battle. The infantry is the most versatile of all the arms; it can operate in any weather, in any type of ground. The infantry soldier remains in the battle day and night, with little rest and without adequate sleep. He can use very expressive language about the way he has to bear the main burden in battle, but he does it! I salute him.

The German soldiers, with no air support, fought hard against the Allies in Normandy. The disorganization in the German High Command added to their disadvantages, and the crisis came (on 20th July) when a number of generals made an unsuccessful attempt to assassinate Hitler. In my view they were wrong; it is not the job of generals to 'bump off' political leaders; if it ought to be done it is best done by the politicians themselves! Hitler replaced Rundstedt by Kluge as commander in France, and later Kluge by Model; Rommel's car was strafed by fighters on 15th July and he was so badly wounded that his part in the battle in Normandy was ended. Hitler then intervened, and, being ignorant of the fact that the Germans had lost the battle in Normandy, or may be not wanting to believe it, he ordered on 7th August an armoured thrust from Mortain westwards to the coast at Avranches in the hope of cutting the American armies in two. Such a thrust could achieve nothing; without air support it was madness; and in any case the battle was already lost. The only imaginable hope for the Germans was to withdraw quickly over the Seine and try to form a new front behind that obstacle. But Hitler refused to allow any withdrawal, and even if he had, in fact by 7th August it was too late. In the event, the armoured thrust to Mortain was penned into a pocket, known as the 'Falaise

Pocket', by the American, British and Canadian armies, and was there pounded for several days. The carnage was terrible.

Allied bridge-heads over the Seine were soon established, and on 25th August Paris was liberated by French forces. Normandy and Brittany had been conquered, and the Germans had lost half a million men. I issued orders for further operations designed to push home the advantage we had gained, and to end the German war by Christmas. But on 1st September Eisenhower assumed direct command of the land armies himself, in addition to his responsibilities as supreme commander of all the Allied forces in western Europe; he had different ideas, and fresh orders were issued.

The precise details of German losses in Normandy were not known. But General Bradley considered that by 'the first of September the enemy's June strength on the western front had been cut down to a disorganized corporal's guard. The total of all German remnants north of the Ardennes equalled only 11 divisions'. Clearly the Germans had been severely beaten, and the task of the supreme commander of the Allied forces then was to drive the enemy back into Germany and end the war as quickly as possible. The right military action could yet have averted some of the political implications of the Teheran agreement. I therefore urged that the Allied forces should be concentrated for a thrust in overwhelming strength, first to seize the Ruhr and then to move on Berlin: the political heart of Germany. German military opinion, according to Liddell Hart, admitted after the war that 'such a break-through, coupled with air domination, would have torn in pieces the weak German front and ended the war in the winter of 1944'. But the Americans considered such a policy to be militarily risky and politically unnecessary. Roosevelt was not alarmed at the idea of Russian forces overrunning eastern Europe. The Americans now provided far more strength than the British, and they had to have their way. The American method was to form up on the Rhine from Switzerland to the North Sea, and then to decide what should be done. All the armies were to advance simultaneously on a broad front. I pointed out the three main disadvantages of a 'broad front' strategy: our administration was becoming very stretched, and could not support an advance of all the armies; nowhere would we be strong enough to get decisive results quickly, and this was necessary if we were to finish the war by the end of the year; the advance would gradually peter out and the Germans would be given time to recover. To get decisive results we must concentrate somewhere – left, centre, or right, whichever the supreme commander considered most suitable. It was as simple as that, and the British chiefs of staff supported my view. But the American generals did not agree. The Germans recovered.

In mid-September, the Germans, having been given breathing space to recover, delivered a repulse to airborne forces at Arnhem who were fighting for a bridge-head over the Neder Rhine. Later, in December they gathered enough armour for a strong offensive, thrusting through the Ardennes towards Antwerp. This started

American troops go ashore on the Normandy beaches for the invasion of Europe

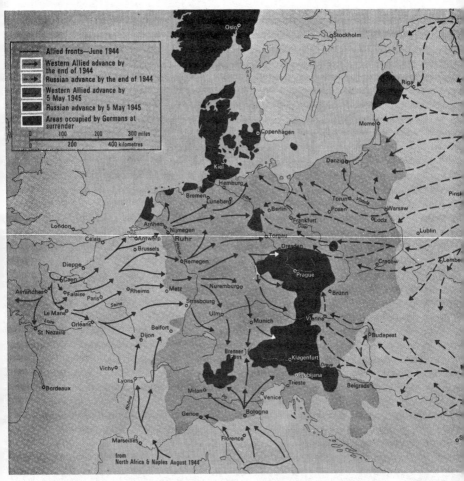

The defeat of Germany, 1944–5

successfully, but broke down under attacks on the flanks and from the air. The German 'secret weapons' for the second half of 1944, the V1 and V2 'flying bombs' or missiles, caused some terror but insignificant damage in Britain. After the Ardennes battle the Germans gave no serious resistance. The Rhine was crossed at various points in March 1945, and the Allied armies advanced as far as the Elbe.

Meanwhile on the eastern front the Russians wasted no time. At about the time of the Allied break-out in Normandy they had launched a massive offensive from Vitebsk to the Pripet Marshes, and by early August 1944 the Red Army had reached

Memel and Warsaw. The German S.S. had time to wreak savage punishment on a Polish rising in Warsaw. Then the Russians pressed on to shatter German Army Group North and reach the Baltic. From the point of view of defeating the Germans they might then have continued their offensive into Germany in 1944 – but that could come later: Stalin's first concern was to overrun the countries of south-eastern Europe. The Russians were in Rumania in August, Yugoslavia in October, and Hungary in December. Only in January 1945 did the armies of Koniev, Zhukov, Rokossovsky and Cherniakovsky sweep into Germany. On 4th February Stalin, Roosevelt and Churchill met again, at Yalta in the Crimea.

The leaders of the democratic nations behaved to the communist dictator at Yalta much as their despised predecessors had to the Nazi dictator at Munich. They persuaded themselves that Stalin was a gentleman, and agreed to the partition of Germany. But by that time there was nothing else they could do. Stalin had outwitted his allies; he had won the peace for Russia at Teheran; Yalta crowned his victory.

Events now moved rapidly. On 30th April Hitler committed suicide in Berlin. On 4th May a delegation from Admiral Doenitz, the new German leader, arrived at my headquarters on Lüneburg Heath and signed a declaration of unconditional surrender of all German armed forces from Holland to Denmark – a total of nearly two million fighting men. On 7th May Germany's unconditional surrender of all her armed forces on all fronts was signed at Eisenhower's headquarters in Rheims. The German war thus ended, with the Russians in possession of the great political centres of mid-Europe – Berlin, Prague, Vienna, Belgrade – and all capital cities east of that general line. The Japanese war remained, and we will now look at that.

Japan was a more natural enemy to the United States than was Germany. After her mushroom growth to economic maturity Japan had become ambitious, and planned to weld the area of eastern Asia and the Pacific into one sphere under her economic and political domination. In March 1933 she formally announced her withdrawal from the League of Nations, thereafter invading Manchuria and making substantial progress towards her goal. Taking advantage of the fall of France, the Japanese had called up over a million conscripts and in July 1941 announced a protectorate over Indo-China. General Tojo, who had been war minister, became premier of Japan in October 1941, and the country came under the grip of a military autocracy. The progress of Japanese ambitions and particularly the aggressive declarations of the new regime alarmed America, with her established interests in the Pacific. When in 1941 the American government applied oil sanctions to Japan, and warned that nation to cease aggression, war became inevitable. Japan resolved to strike when the moment was favourable.

Late 1941 was, all in all, an opportune time for Japan to make war against the imperial powers of the Far East. Her leaders certainly made a miscalculation in supposing that the Germans had as good as won the war in the west, but nonetheless at that time the Dutch were powerless, and the British had no strength they could afford to spare. The best troops of the British imperial possessions, Australia, New Zealand and India, were engaged in the Middle East. The British navy was strained to its utmost, and the R.A.F. in Asia was equipped with obsolete aircraft. America had greater armed force than Japan, but the Americans at this time were looking westwards and had transferred ships from the Pacific to the Atlantic.

Between 1936 and 1941 Japan had doubled the tonnage of her navy, and modernized her older ships. She had 10 battleships, 10 aircraft-carriers, 38 cruisers, 112 destroyers and 65 submarines. Japanese warships were not basically different in design from those of the western powers. Their aircraft-carriers could each carry some 63 fighters, torpedo-bombers, and bombers. The Japanese army in 1941 totalled 750,000 men, in 51 divisions. There was no independent Japanese air force, but five air divisions, comprising some 1,500 aircraft, were attached to the army, and the navy had an operational strength of about 3,300 aircraft. Since the invasion of China the Japanese had gained valuable experience in modern warfare, and their equipment was highly developed. The Japanese people fought with a ferocity and a fanatical courage alien to the peoples of the West.

The Japanese plan was to strike fast and hard. The American fleet in the Pacific was to be destroyed, and the Philippines, Borneo, Malaya, the Dutch East Indies and Burma overrun. Beyond the southward advance an impregnable ring of ocean fortresses was to be established, running through Wake, the Marshall Islands and the archipelago north of Australia. On 7th December 1941, without a declaration of war, simultaneous attacks were launched on Pearl Harbour, the Philippines and Malaya.

The Americans were taken completely by surprise by the attack on their Pacific Fleet in Pearl Harbour, Hawaii. The Japanese naval striking force of six carriers, with a total of 450 planes, under Vice-Admiral Nagumo, launched its aircraft at daylight on 7th December. The main Japanese targets were 7 battleships at their moorings. All were hit; only one escaped serious damage and 2 were lost completely. Very heavy damage was also inflicted on other ships and on installations, and 200 of a total of 400 American aircraft parked close together were destroyed. The Japanese lost 30 aircraft. The success of the raid was due to complete surprise and to the skill of the Japanese air arm, particularly in shallow-run torpedo attacks.

Simultaneously with Pearl Harbour the Japanese launched air attacks against the Americans in the Philippines, destroying a third of their fighters and half their bombers, and on 10th December the naval base of Cavite was smashed. By these quick, devastating air blows at Pearl Harbour and the Philippines the Japanese gained that period of complete superiority at sea and in the air which they needed to give security to their invasion operations. They confirmed the advantage in December by overrunning the enemy bases of Guam, Wake, and Hong Kong. The Philippines were not finally overrun until the following May – because of the resistance organized by General MacArthur, who finally left in March 1942 for Australia in order to take command of the American offensive against Japan to be launched from that country.

The invasion of the Malay Peninsula, under General Yamashita, also began on 7th December, with Japanese forces landing in Siam and crossing the frontier. On 10th December shore-based Japanese aircraft sank the British *Prince of Wales* and

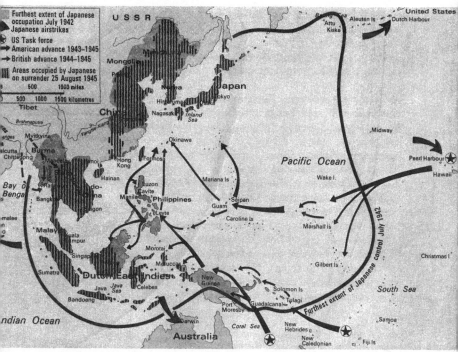

The Japanese war, 1941–5

Repulse off the east coast of Malaya. Using captured British shipping the Japanese advanced down the coast by means of combined operations against the flanks of the defence. Their numerical superiority was not great, but the Japanese troops were more enterprising and more highly trained in jungle fighting than the defending British, Australian and Indian troops. British air power was quickly written off and then unopposed bombing of towns destroyed the will to resist. On 11th January 1942 the Japanese were in Kuala Lumpur, and on 15th February Britain's foremost commercial and naval centre in the Far East, Singapore, with its garrison of over 70,000 troops, surrendered to Yamashita.

The Dutch East Indies now lay exposed. Since January the Japanese had gained footings in Borneo and Celebes, and they were now ready to strike at Java. On 27th February the Dutch Allied commander, Admiral Doorman, learned that a Japanese convoy of 30 troop-transports escorted by 3 cruisers and 7 destroyers was heading for Java. Doorman mustered a force of 5 cruisers and 10 destroyers and engaged the Japanese under Vice-Admiral Kondo off the north coast of Java. A complex battle took place, largely in darkness; it ended with the Japanese sinking half the Allied ships without losing any of their own. In gunpower the Allies were superior, but the battle was won by superior Japanese tactics, communications, torpedoes and air power. On 8th March some 90,000 European and Indonesian troops surrendered at Bandoeng. The remaining islands were quickly conquered, and isolated pockets of guerrilla resistance made no strategic difference. All remaining Allied shipping in the area was sunk.

We now move to Burma. Simultaneously with their campaign against the Dutch East Indies and even before the fall of Singapore, the Japanese had turned westwards against Burma. They aimed ultimately to cut the Burma Road, the route by which assistance was reaching Chiang Kai-shek in China, and with the help of Indian nationalism to remove the hold of the British on India. Bangkok provided the advanced base for the invasion, and their first objective was Rangoon. The defence of Burma was weak, since Wavell, in command, had only two incomplete divisions – later reinforced by a similar Chinese force, commanded by Lieutenant-General Stilwell, chief of staff to Chiang Kai-Shek. There were not enough resources in Burma to nourish a campaign and supplies had to come from India – but communications were extremely difficult. The Japanese controlled the normal sea routes from India and there were no roads across the mountains; communication and supply had therefore to be by air. The communication routes inside Burma were the valleys of the Chindwin, Irrawaddy and Sittang rivers, and a single railway track which ran northwards from Rangoon through Meiktila and Mandalay.

Naval warfare in the Pacific. Japanese aircraft attack the U.S. fleet

The Japanese, commanded by Lieutenant-General Kawabe, opened the attack on Burma by bombing Rangoon in January 1942. Then they moved in from Malaya and Siam, and on 7th March Rangoon was abandoned. The new British commander, Alexander, decided he must get his troops back to India before the monsoon broke and establish a defensive front on the Assam frontier.

In the retreat the British and Indian troops suffered severely; but the Japanese never seemed to tire. There had never before been war between modern armies in that type of country; but the Japanese had trained in similar country and had become really first-class fighters. They fought in small, lightly equipped detachments, armed principally with light machine-guns and mortars. They made skilful and daring manoeuvres to infiltrate, envelop, and cut communications – fighting their way up the parallel valleys of the Irrawaddy and Sittang and continually outflanking resistance.

As the British withdrew, the weight of the Japanese attack was transferred to the Chinese front in the north-east, where resistance soon petered out. They then pushed rapidly towards the Burma Road at Lashio, reached it at the end of April, and operated up that axis – crossing the Chinese frontier on 15th May. The British, accompanied and hampered by many thousand native refugees, struggled through jungle and over mountains to reach Imphal just inside the Indian frontier. By the end of May 1942 Alexander had succeeded in extricating most of his men, but much equipment was lost.

By mid-1942 the Japanese, travelling as fast and fighting as efficiently and ruthlessly as any of the Mongol hordes of history, had gained all their immediate objectives, not only in Burma but also in Indonesia and in the Pacific. After conquering Burma they did not penetrate into India, but established themselves in strong defensible country. From the Dutch East Indies they extended their conquests east to New Guinea and to the Gilbert and Solomon Islands. In April a Japanese squadron under Nagumo had entered the Indian Ocean, and was able to roam at will, inflicting immense damage on British merchant shipping and bases on the Indian coast. Without seapower the Allies could not begin to assail the ring of Japanese positions.

The war at sea in the Pacific is a story of tremendous interest. The problem for the Japanese now lay in the air and naval power of her enemies. The raid on Pearl Harbour in December 1941 had crippled the Americans in the Pacific, but only temporarily; it did not prove, in fact, to be the decisive success for Japan which she had hoped. The Americans had lost their battleships – but with the advent of the aircraft-carrier the era of the large battleship was really over. The American Pacific Fleet had four carriers, capable of operating between them 350 aircraft. This was what mattered. The damage to installations at Pearl Harbour was repaired and, with ten times the industrial capacity of Japan, America was able to build up her relative strength rapidly. The Americans reckoned they could be ready to launch a counter-offensive by 1943. The Japanese saw the weakness in their situation and realized they must destroy the enemy naval strength in the Pacific during 1942. Admiral

Yamamoto, head of the Japanese navy, considered that Pearl Harbour was too distant for the Japanese to be able to strike there immediately in sufficient strength; he therefore evolved a double plan to bring the American carrier fleet within striking range. First, he planned to gain command of the Coral Sea and mount a threat to Australia – which would entice the Americans to the rescue. Secondly, he would capture the American base at Midway, a small atoll half way between California and China.

The advance of the Japanese into the Coral Sea began in late April 1942. They aimed to seize two points. Tulagi was captured as planned on 3rd May, and a second naval group moved on Port Moresby. But Japanese security measures were poor, and Admiral Nimitz, in command at Pearl Harbour, learned what was afoot. The carriers *Lexington* and *Yorktown*, commanded by Admiral Fletcher, had been positioned near Samoa to prevent the enemy capture of Port Moresby.

On 7th May the Japanese covering force, the light carrier *Shoho* and a screen of light cruisers, was located by Fletcher. A swarm of 193 bombers from *Lexington* and *Yorktown* attacked *Shoho* and sank her in half an hour. The main striking force under Admiral Takagi still continued steaming westwards through the Coral Sea. On the next day, when the opposing forces were 200 miles apart, their scouts sighted each other. American bombers attacked the Japanese carriers, and *Shokaku* was left blazing and *Zuikaku* damaged. Japanese torpedo-bombers scored six hits on *Lexington*, which blew up during the night.

Strategically the battle of the Coral Sea was an American victory, since it thwarted the Japanese plans both against Australia and against the American Pacific Fleet. Tactically the battle is of great interest, marking a revolution in naval warfare. Both sides had a considerable force of conventional warships, but these were not engaged. The battle was fought out between aircraft-carriers, and the fleets never even sighted each other. Aircraft-carriers were not battleships but *mobile bases of air power*, and their strength was offensive – carrying torpedo-planes, dive-bombers and fighters.

At this stage, the Japanese aircraft were rather more powerful than the American. But later the Americans introduced the Avenger torpedo-plane and the Hellcat fighter with greatly improved performances; furthermore, American carriers carried more aircraft than the Japanese. An aircraft-carrier itself was not thickly armoured and constituted a huge target of oil and explosives. It relied for defence on its fighters, and on the firepower of a protective screen of light warships. Aircraft-carriers proved, in fact, to be extremely vulnerable to attack from the air.

The setback in the Coral Sea did not cause the Japanese to put off the second part of their programme, the attack on Midway. In May, Yamamoto assembled almost the entire Japanese navy, some ninety ships, in the Inland Sea and the Mariana Islands. But the Americans had broken the Japanese code (Japanese security and reconnaissance were often bad) and by mid-May Nimitz knew that an attack on Midway from the north-west was due in early June. Midway was reinforced, and the Americans formed two task forces under Admirals Fletcher and Spruance. There were no battleships; the nuclei of aircraft-carriers were screened by cruisers and destroyers. In late May the two task forces left Pearl Harbour for a point in the Pacific 300 miles north-east of Midway, where they were to cruise in ambush. As the Japanese approached the Americans had an enormous advantage: the Japanese did not have radar and they did not know that the American fleet was at sea. In the battle between the opposed forces of carrier-based aircraft, between 4th and 6th June, the Americans inflicted a major defeat on the Japanese.

Strategically Midway in June 1942 was an immensely important battle. Had the American carrier fleet been destroyed the United States would have had no chance of defeating the Japanese in the Pacific for a considerable time. In the following years of the war seapower in terms of carriers was to be vital. The conquest of the island-studded western Pacific was impossible without air cover. The Japanese, having lost four carriers at Midway, were from now on at a serious disadvantage. They built only one more reliable carrier before the end of the war; otherwise they had to use converted battleships which were no proper substitute.

The Americans were now in a position to take the offensive. Their long campaign began with the struggle for Guadalcanal, lasting from August 1942 to January 1943. Guadalcanal, an island in the Solomon group on which the Japanese were building an airstrip, was an important strategic point. On 7th August an American fleet entered the area, and nearly 20,000 marines were successfully landed. But two days later a Japanese naval squadron came on the scene, and in a night action four American cruisers were sunk – half the American force. The ensuing struggle for Guadalcanal was very fierce. Besides numerous small actions and constant air attacks by both sides, six more naval battles were fought. But eventually the Americans were successful, thus finally stopping the southern advance of the Japanese, and providing a launching pad for the American counter-offensive.

By early 1943 heavy losses among Japanese ships and aircraft were limiting the support they could give to their outlying garrisons, and the Americans began to develop their campaign of reconquest. Their strategy brought the art of combined service operations to a high level. The advances on Japan had to be made along the various island chains in a series of hops, gaining one Japanese-held island before moving on to the next. From an advanced air base or carrier, air power was used in a preparatory strike against the enemy base; then a forward bound was made by sea-borne and airborne troops to seize the point; a 'mobile base', composed of craft carrying all stores and equipment, was then established in preparation for the next bound. General Douglas MacArthur was in command of the line of progress along the north coast of New Guinea, the Moluccas and on to the Philippines. Simultaneously Admiral Nimitz advanced from Hawaii to the Gilbert and Marshall Islands and on to the Marianas. Admiral Halsey mopped up the area south-east of New Guinea.

The fighting was hard throughout these campaigns, but by the time the Marianas were attacked in June 1944 Japanese production of war material was failing badly, whereas the Americans were introducing new aircraft in large numbers, and their carrier superiority was vast. The Japanese used their submarines to attack American warships; American submarines more profitably concentrated on enemy freighters and tankers. The Japanese were rarely able to reinforce the islands, and the Americans bombed them very thoroughly before attempting to land. But the fighting was always fierce, with no quarter given by either side. The Japanese waited in the jungle and attacked the marines on the steeply sloping beaches. After several weeks of fighting, however, the Marianas were captured. Next, in the battle of the Philippine Sea, on 19th and 20th June, Spruance's fleet sank two of the best Japanese carriers and damaged another, while over 400 Japanese planes were destroyed by Hellcats.

MacArthur and Nimitz fought brilliant campaigns in their war against the Japanese in the Far East. They fought a novel war by novel means and saw it through to complete success. MacArthur had no inconvenient ally to suggest alternatives to him! A most profound impact was made on naval warfare in the 1939/45 war by the Americans. They developed new strategy, tactics and techniques suited to war at sea in the new age of air power, and in those four years of war rose to become the strongest naval power in the world.

We must now return to Burma, where General Slim was fighting brilliant battles with his Fourteenth Army. While the tide was turning against the Japanese in the Pacific, the Allies took up the offensive in Burma. Stagnation had for a while followed the retreat of Alexander's forces in 1942; the British carried out a major retraining programme in India, and the Japanese reinforced their positions in Burma. But in January 1943 the British reopened operations – somewhat experimentally. A drive was made down the west coast belt of Arakan. The Japanese withdrew to a prepared position in the Mayu Peninsula, defended with a maze of bunkers. Here against odds of two to one they repulsed repeated attacks and the British eventually withdrew, having suffered heavy casualties and a further loss of morale. Meanwhile Brigadier Orde Wingate carried out an operation of his own conception approved by Wavell; his theory was that a small and highly trained force could operate in the interior of Burma, waging guerrilla warfare against the Japanese communications while avoiding their main forces – without ground communications but supplied by air. In February 1943 Wingate crossed the Chindwin river with 3,000 men and penetrated deep into Japanese-occupied territory. In March he cut the railway from Mandalay to Myitkyina in numerous places and killed hundreds of the enemy. Some 2,000 of his men survived to return to India in May. Materially Wingate's expedition was not of great value, and the necessity of abandoning his sick and wounded to the brutal Japanese made its value seem even more doubtful. But useful experience had been gained regarding air supply.

A new Allied command organization was set up in 1943, Admiral Mountbatten becoming supreme commander responsible for co-ordinating forces in south-east Asia. His deputy was Stilwell, who was in command of the American-Chinese force in the northern area, amounting to three Chinese divisions, three American battalions and a small irregular force. The other main force was the British Fourteenth Army, consisting of about ten divisions of British, Indian, Gurkha and West African troops with two brigades of tanks. Late in 1943 General Slim took

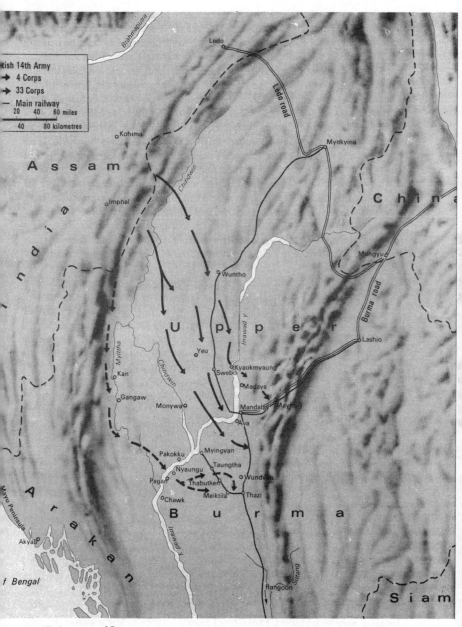

The Allied recovery of Burma

command of the Fourteenth Army. The Japanese forces in Burma, under General Kawabe, totalled about nine complete divisions, divided into three armies: the 28th responsible for the Arakan front, the 15th for the central front and particularly the railway corridor, and the 33rd which held the north-eastern front.

The Americans considered the first priority to be the clearing of the route through northern Burma into China, and Allied strategy for the winter offensive of 1943–4 was framed around this principle. The offensive was to be renewed in Arakan, while Stilwell's force moved south on Myitkyina to cover the Ledo road. A second 'Wingate offensive' would cooperate with Stilwell's northern force. An essential feature of the campaign was the new use of air support. Communications were entirely by air; a division advancing rapidly through difficult country was supplied throughout from the air. The campaign went well. In Arakan the Japanese, attempting to envelop the British, were themselves enveloped when Slim flew in additional forces. This first British victory over the Japanese brought a great rise in morale. Stilwell's forces were opposed by only one division, and gained their objectives. Two brigades of Wingate's 'Chindits' landed by glider at different points while one brigade marched, and by attacking communications these succeeded in drawing Japanese forces away from Stilwell before they joined up with him. Wingate himself was killed.

The Japanese launched, in March 1944, a major offensive against Assam. A three-month struggle took place in the area of Imphal and Kohima. Again Slim fed in troops by air, until the British had six divisions against the Japanese three. After a desperate assault on Imphal in June the Japanese broke and withdrew across the Chindwin. They had fought ferociously, losing over 53,000 men. Many extra casualties were caused by disease, particularly malaria. It says a great deal for the medical services that campaigns could be conducted at all in that type of country.

Following the crushing defeat of the Japanese in Assam, Slim's task was to occupy central Burma as far south as Mandalay. The total strength of the Japanese was now ten infantry divisions, two 'Indian National Army' divisions, one tank regiment, and numerous troops on the communication lines. Of this total, two divisions might be drawn off by the Allied northern force, now commanded by General Sultan, and three by the force in Arakan and the threat of amphibious landings. Thus an offensive into central Burma by the Fourteenth Army of six divisions could expect to face five enemy divisions. The Japanese had a new C-in-C, General Kimura. Slim divided his army into two corps; the 5th Division was held in reserve. Air transport was to be the means of supply to forward positions.

The Fourteenth Army offensive began on 3rd December 1944. Slim's six divisions crossed the Chindwin with the intention of bringing the Japanese to battle and defeating them in the Shwebo plain. However, after the battering at Imphal, Kimura decided not to risk battle in an open plain, and gradually withdraw his forces behind the Irrawaddy – where he prepared for a 'battle of the Irrawaddy shore'. He hoped to cripple the Fourteenth Army as it attempted to cross the river, and then destroy it as it limped back to the Chindwin. But when it became clear that the Japanese were withdrawing, Slim formed a new plan for the destruction of the main

Japanese forces beyond the Irrawaddy. 33 Corps (Stopford) was to force the crossing of the river north and west of Mandalay, drawing on to itself the greatest possible concentration of Japanese forces. Meanwhile 4 Corps (Messervy) would steal along the Gangaw valley and cross the Irrawaddy near Pakokku, and then without pausing would strike violently with armoured and airborne forces at Meiktila – the main administrative centre of the Japanese armies. In this area were their chief supply bases, ammunition dumps, hospitals, and several airfields; road and rail routes from the south-east and west converged there before spreading out again to the north. If Meiktila was taken the communications of the Japanese armies in an arc from the Salween to the Irrawaddy would be cut, and Kimura would be compelled to fight a battle off-balance to recover them. The British could follow up the victory by a dash to Rangoon.

By the second week in January 1945 Slim's army was approaching the Irrawaddy on a front of over 200 miles from Wuntho to Pakokku. The Japanese did not attempt to hold the entire river line, but concentrated defences at the likely crossing places – with reserves mobile and held well back until the British intentions became clear. On the night of 14th January 33 Corps began to execute its part of Slim's strategy. The 19th Division started the crossing of the Irrawaddy north of Mandalay at Kyaukmyaung, and a bridge-head was established. By the 17th the enemy had decided that this was the main British crossing operation, and Japanese forces were concentrated to make a heavy attack there. In the next three weeks heavy fighting built up. Kimura brought in more and more troops, including reinforcements from Meiktila, to beat back the British from the Irrawaddy. But the British bridge-head was steadily expanded, and another crossing was made west of Mandalay.

Meanwhile 4 Corps was driving southwards beyond the Chindwin towards the Irrawaddy at Pakokku. The deadline for crossing was 15th February. To forestall a hold-up by the Japanese rearguards, the advance was made beyond the Kan area on a wide front so as to outflank the enemy. On 28th January 4 Corps reached the Irrawaddy valley. Every man was set to work building airstrips and improving roads so that tanks and transport vehicles could be moved forward, together with material for the crossing. Messervy decided that the crossing was to be made near Nyaungu where the river was narrowest. To divert the enemy two demonstrations were mounted at other points of the river. Just before dawn on 14th February the first troops crossed by boat in complete silence about a mile north of Nyaungu, and established a defensible position on the far bank. A larger force followed in daylight with artillery, tanks and air support to expand the bridge-head for the remaining troops. Nyaungu was captured on the 16th. The Japanese had been taken completely by surprise, having formed no idea that a major force was in the area. Such an operation was possible only with the cover afforded to troop movements by the jungle and air superiority.

Kimura was completely deceived by Slim's plan. He still thought that practically the whole of the Fourteenth Army was in the loop north and west of Mandalay. Expecting that the British would made a major attempt to break out towards Mandalay, he continued to withdraw forces from all other sectors to concentrate

Japanese snipers put up an obstinate resistance to the British troops as they worked their way towards Mandalay

them for the battle of the Irrawaddy shore. Towards the end of February reinforcements had brought Kimura's strength up to nine divisions as against the British five at Mandalay. The local odds against 33 Corps were thus heavy. Both corps were making heavy demands on a long supply line. It was necessary for 4 Corps to achieve a quick success in its attack on Meiktila, and one which would force Kimura to turn to its relief, thus exposing his forces to a double assault.

On 21st February the 17th Division and the Tank Brigade of 4 Corps began the advance of Meiktila. On the 25th they occupied the Thabutkon airstrip only ten miles from the town. Next day more troops were flown in. Attempts by the Japanese to block the road were quickly overrun by frontal assaults of massed tanks. Then five miles from the town 4 Corps stopped to regroup. The Japanese at Meiktila, under Major-General Kasuya, had spent several days digging defences. Kasuya disposed of a fighting strength of about 3,200 men, and large numbers of guns; all his available men, even hospital patients, were armed and established in strong

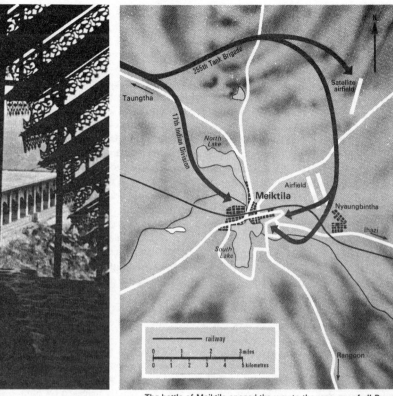

The battle of Meiktila opened the way to the recovery of all Burma

points; anti-aircraft guns from the nearby airfields were set up as anti-tank guns and for perimeter defence. In any case Meiktila was a most difficult place to attack; on the north and south of the town were lakes which made the roads easily defended causeways, and the surrounding country was cut up by irrigation channels and ditches.

The first step in the attack was to seize the airfield on the eastern outskirts of the town, in order to fly in reinforcements and supplies. On 28th February, while an attack on the western defences held the attention of the Japanese, 255 Tank Brigade made a 10-mile sweep round Meiktila from the north and regrouped on the east. Then, with artillery and air support, a heavy armoured assault was launched and the British penetrated into the town – where the resistance of the Japanese was fanatical, pockets of survivors fighting desperately in the overrun area. March 1st was the day of bitterest fighting. As the advance was pressed in the east, further attacks were launched at western and south-easterly points. Savage in-fighting took place as the

British pressed in from the outskirts towards the centre of the town, Japanese snipers and machine-gun nests being concealed in every house, water channel and heap of rubble. The Japanese never surrendered, but died where they fought. But by 3rd March 1945 the garrison was almost entirely wiped out, and Meiktila was in British hands.

Kimura was astonished at the fall of the town. He duly abandoned his projected offensive against 33 Corps at Mandalay, and diverted troops to recover Meiktila. The Japanese had large forces available for this operation, but they had to be assembled from different directions, and it was difficult to co-ordinate the movements. The Allies now had complete control of the air. As the Japanese forces began to converge on Meiktila from north and south 4 Corps struck out in all directions in a bold offensive. Infantry and tanks made daily sorties to a 20-mile radius to hunt and attack approaching Japanese forces. The first objective of the Japanese was the airstrip, the occupation of which would cut off British supplies. After a savage and continuous struggle, during which the Japanese reached its very edge, they were gradually beaten back. By the last week in March Meiktila was secure.

Meanwhile, at the moment Kimura turned to recover Meiktila, 33 Corps launched an all-out offensive from its bridge-head on to Mandalay. When the drive began on 26th February, the Japanese were swept back, leaving only pockets of resistance which could be dealt with later. But as the British moved nearer to Mandalay fanatical resistance was met. The Japanese used human mines – a soldier crouching in a fox-hole with a 100-kilo aircraft bomb between his knees; though in fact the human mines did little damage. The last Japanese stronghold at Mandalay did not fall until 20th March.

By the end of March 1945 the Allies held both banks of the Irrawaddy from Mandalay to Chawk and the main road and railway to Rangoon as far south as Wundwin. From the firm position of Meiktila the Allied hold on the country could now be expanded. The subsequent campaign was as brilliantly managed by Slim as had been the Mandalay-Meiktila phase. An advance in Arakan opened up new airfields and sea supply routes. Rangoon was recovered on 3rd May. The Japanese fled eastwards across the Sittang river, though tough fighting was necessary to round them up. Preparations then began for the invasion of Malaya. But this never had to take place.

By September 1944 MacArthur's and Nimitz's forces were poised for the attack on the Philippines and Japan. On 20th October the 6th Army, supported by battleships, cruisers, destroyers and eighteen escort carriers, started to land on the island of Leyte. The Japanese decided that the Philippines must be saved, and all available naval forces converged from various bases. The struggle for Leyte Gulf was a series of battles, separated by hundreds of miles, over a period of four days, and was the largest-scale naval engagement of the war. The Japanese fought with desperation. Japanese pilots used *kamikaze* tactics, whereby they dived their bomb-laden planes directly into the decks of American carriers and other unarmoured vessels. This tactic accounted for thirty-three American ships. But, thanks principally to the

American air superiority, the Japanese suffered a serious defeat, losing four carriers, two escort carriers, three battleships and much else.

By May 1945 the entire Philippines had been recovered by the Allies. The next main objective was the island of Okinawa, an important advance air base. The fighting on Okinawa was the most savage of the war; it lasted until 21st June, when the Americans finally secured the island. Over 100,000 Japanese were killed, the American casualties (all types) being 39,000.

Aircraft operating from Okinawa now joined in the bombing offensive against Japan herself, in preparation for invasion. Previously carrier-borne aircraft had done most of the bombing, but now B.29 Superfortresses took over the main work. From Okinawa attacks were concentrated on Nagasaki, destroying the docks and aircraft production area. From bases in China and the Marianas planes bombed industrial centres, Tokyo and Osaka suffering immense devastation.

The bombing offensive reached its culmination in August. On 6th August the Americans dropped the first atomic bomb on Hiroshima, killing 80,000 people. On 9th August the second atomic bomb was dropped on Nagasaki, killing 40,000 people – more than the total killed in all the air raids of the war on London. The Americans felt justified in using this new weapon. The Japanese still had 250,000 troops in the Pacific Islands, with more established in the Dutch East Indies, Malaya and China. The nation which treated their prisoners as atrociously as the Japanese had done, which violated all conventions of war, which used human mines and suicide pilots – received no pity. On 10th August 1945 the Japanese government surrendered unconditionally, and the 1939/45 war was over.

I would like to conclude this chapter with a few reflections on certain general issues of this war.

National leadership was needless to say immensely important. Hitler was, indeed, an evil man, but he was a leader. He had no use for 'declaring' war and giving the victim time to prepare for the blow; he reckoned that was not the way to fight, and that view is logical if it is accepted that a nation fights only to win militarily. But that should not be the ultimate object in war. He imparted his evilness to others.

Who made the worst mistakes in the conduct of war? I think Hitler. It was a fatal error to attack Russia in 1941; one of the first rules of war is: don't march on Moscow. He probably could not prevent the Japanese from attacking America, after which he declared war on the United States because of his pact with Japan. He then found himself fighting the British empire, Russia and America – and could not hope to win. Subsequently on the western front he made three major mistakes – to try to fight the battle of France south of the Seine after his defeat in Normandy in 1944, to launch a counter-offensive in the Ardennes in December 1944, and to stand and fight west of the Rhine in the hope of saving the Ruhr. He began well. From the viewpoint of sheer tactical efficiency one cannot but admire the cold-blooded assault of the Wehrmacht on western Europe in the spring of 1940; it upset the world balance of military power, and made Germany the dominant nation-in-arms. But in the end Hitler brought destruction on his country.

Now consider Stalin. Ruthless maybe he was, and no kind of gentleman; but if it hadn't been for him the Russians might well have left the war early in 1942. Only Churchill realized that he would use the war to fasten his grip on eastern Europe and that this political strategy was uppermost in his mind before the conflict ever began. Indeed, he began to implement it the moment the ink was dry on his non-aggression pact with Germany in August 1939. Stalin made almost no mistakes; he had a clear-cut political strategy and he pursued it relentlessly with the military and political means at his disposal. When I stayed as his guest in Moscow in 1947 I was highly impressed by his discussion of strategical matters.

Roosevelt never seemed to me to be clear about what he was fighting for. He tried to woo Stalin, but the latter won the peace for Russia at the Teheran conference, and Yalta crowned his victory. Stalin had no difficulty in fooling Roosevelt, and so the six years of war from 1939 to 1945 did not end with the just and lasting peace for which the Western nations fought.

Churchill was a great leader of the British people in a crisis. I got to know him really well and he became chief among all my friends. One thing is clear – by standing firm against Hitler when all seemed lost, he saved not only Britain but Western civilization from destruction. For a time he was the sole leader of the Western world against the Nazi tyranny. Churchill had the quality of vision – a quality which entitles him to a foremost place among strategists. (As a commander-in-chief in the field, it must be admitted, I often wished Churchill had not himself once been a soldier; he was so interested in the tactical conduct of a battle that he would occasionally try to interfere – though he never pressed his point and would always accept my explanation.) Never has any nation found any leader who so matched the hour as did the British in Winston Churchill during Hitler's war.

The scientific and technological developments that affected this war were vast and complex. Put very simply, war before 1918 can be said to have been concerned with fighting in two dimensions (land and sea) over short visual ranges, with weapons of small area coverage and a low degree of deadliness. Tremendous changes came during the 1939/45 war – extensions into a third dimension (the air), extension of the ability to 'see' the enemy (radar), extensions in the range at which battles are fought, increases in the effect of weapons. To these must be added counter-measures of all kinds. The most important impact on battle during the 1939/45 war was made by air power. It revolutionized the strategy and tactics of war on land 'and at sea. The United States became the strongest naval power in the world by recognizing the impact of air power on war at sea.

One last point. In my view it was unnecessary to drop two atomic bombs on Japan in August 1945, and I cannot think it was right to do so. According to President Truman it was done to save 'hundreds of thousands of lives, both American and Japanese'. But the removal of the obstacle of unconditional surrender would of itself have saved those lives, because, I consider, Japan would then have surrendered earlier. The Japanese had already been defeated by conventional weapons. The dropping of the bombs was a prime example of our failure in the modern world to match technological progress with moral progress.

20   The Present and the Future

The Hague Convention of 1907 agreed certain resolutions for the 'humane conduct of war'. But we should get out of our heads once and for all that war can ever be anything but cruel. Total war in the twentieth century has brought about a decline in moral standards far beyond anything known before; mankind would seem merely to have progressed in hypocrisy since Blaise de Montluc, Marshal of France, wrote in the sixteenth century: 'Towards an Enemy all advantages are good, and for my part (God forgive me) if I could call all the devils in Hell to beat out the brains of an Enemy that would beat out mine, I would do it with all my heart.'

Liddell Hart wrote: 'If you want peace, understand war.' If we do understand war perhaps we shall be prompted to avoid its inhumanity. And if we cannot avoid war let us remember that Clausewitz called war 'a continuation of political transactions intermingled with other means'. I read these words as a statement for the supremacy of political over narrow military policies, and for the exercise of moderation once victory has been ensured. The ultimate responsibility lies with politicians. The higher direction of war is in their hands and unless they understand that the object of Grand Strategy must be a peace in which true values may be preserved, and unless they direct all military effort in war to the attainment of a favourable controlling position at the end of it, they will throw away the fruits of tremendous sacrifices and all the slaughter will have been useless – more than ever in a nuclear age. In the 1939/45 war this principle was ignored in certain quarters, and the most humane intentions and sentiments cannot cover up the mischief that was wrought.

I propose to devote the last pages of this book to a discussion of certain problems which are not yet part of history, but which our study of history may help us to understand. This is a realm in which decision and moral courage to face up to practical realities is sadly lacking, as an uneasy peace broods over our world. It seems to me that a soldier with considerable practical experience of war, and of working with political leaders in many countries in peace, has a right to state our current problems as he sees them. 'The Iron Curtain' is an expression which owes its wide currency to Winston Churchill. Churchill was disturbed at the victory Stalin had gained at the Yalta conference, and on 12th May 1945 he sent President Truman a telegram beginning with the words: 'I am profoundly concerned about the European situation.' He then analysed the position of the Western Allies *vis-à-vis* Russia, and went on: 'An iron curtain is drawn down upon their front. We do not know what is going on behind.' After I had been appointed commander-in-chief and military governor of the British Zone of Germany in 1945, I became very conscious of the truth of his words.

Insofar as I am aware the expression the 'Cold War' came into common use a few months after the end of Hitler's war, being used to describe the state of tension which then began to develop between the Western nations and the Soviet bloc. In the past when tension became unbearable the nations concerned resolved it by declaring war. But in the mid-twentieth century the destructive power of nuclear weapons and the perfection of delivery systems have made open war between powerful states an utterly self-negating method of trying to enforce political ends. No nation wants to commit suicide. In the mid-twentieth century we live in a split world: as well as hostility between communist and democratic peoples, there is hostility between white and coloured peoples. Conflict between differing societies has come to be regarded as inevitable, but aggressors have resorted in so-called peacetime to lesser forms of war – subversion, colonial rebellion, satellite aggression; they become experts at combining and operating non-military forms of war – political, economic, psychological; they incite small countries to armed aggression and support such activities financially and by providing weapons. All this activity, falling short of total war, is part of what has come to be called the 'cold war'.

Why are things in the world today in such a mess ? I hold that it has been due in large measure to the decline of the white man in Oriental and African countries. The former submissiveness of Asiatics and coloured peoples to white European rule disappeared in the winter of 1941–2 when Japan entered the Second World War and her armed forces overran south-east Asia. The Japanese conquerors appeared at first as liberators to the peoples in that part of the world, in spite of their imperialistic intentions and their brutal and barbarous methods. When Japanese overlordship ended in 1945, as suddenly as it had begun, the peoples in that part of the world did not want to take their old masters back – who, in truth, had not on the whole done very much for the mass of the people but rather had used the natural resources of the countries to increase their own national wealth. Inevitably, movements of independence began; as it was in India, so it has been in south-east Asia and among the dark masses of Africa. Everywhere the white man has been forced on to the defensive; and, of course, the process was hastened by Stalin's Russia promising freedom to all backward peoples and denouncing imperialism, colonialism and capitalism. Perhaps most important of all, the peoples of the West were unsure of any ideals themselves. Since 1945 politics have been no better than a struggle for power by ambitious men. Nowhere is that struggle more evident today than in Asia and Africa, where government can be defined as subjugation of the masses.

In this close-knit world there is always a danger that war in one place may spread and involve the whole world, and become total. Proposals are put forward for disarmament. But all such proposals depend on a degree of confidence and trust between nations which does not exist. Nothing has happened since the end of the 1939/45 war to suggest that an enemy would refrain from taking advantage of a nation's military weakness – as enemies have always done throughout recorded history. Therefore military planning must continue, being directed to *preventing* war. One has a feeling today that there is a lack of long-term strategy; responsible leaders, and their officials, are pre-occupied in coping with the complexity of day-to-day affairs with the result that too often short-term improvizations masquerade as policy.

Political leaders must face up to practical realities. The greatest danger is to be a slave to preconceived ideas and slogans of the past. It is an illusion, for example, to think that a united Germany is possible in any future we can foresee. The Russians will never allow a nation of 70 million Germans in the middle of Europe, with nuclear launching sites on the Polish border. It is no use supposing that the true government of China is in Formosa, or that we can move towards a more peaceful world without bringing the biggest nation in the world to the conference table. Equally, it is no use supposing that the Americans can gain their strategic objectives in south-east Asia on the battlefield.

The two sides have got into a log-jam and cannot get clear. Some have the hope that one day a stage will be reached in the cold war when one side will surrender and peace can be agreed – but such a hope is a delusion. The present confrontation between the ideologies of the free world and the communist is a continuing struggle, sometimes diffuse and unobtrusive and at other times very much in focus, which will go on for a generation or longer and it is not likely to be solved in a conclusive way. It is inseparable from other equally pressing international problems – such as economic viability and the demand for equality. We must reject any solution to our problems of today which is based exclusively on *winning* the cold war. I do not believe that total victory in that sense is possible. But by the patient exercise of diplomacy, and by the determination to break down suspicion, fear and hatred, the mutual relationships between different social systems and ideologies can be made less liable to erupt into war and more consistent with a true meaning of peaceful co-existence. There has been a tendency in recent years in this direction, but not enough sincerity was behind it, no determination to end the conflict. All will agree on one point: a permanent state of *peaceless* co-existence will merely bring misery to millions of decent people.

But let us examine more closely the nuclear deterrent which is what has prevented all-out war between the great powers since 1945. The first live test of an atomic bomb was made by the Allies in New Mexico on the morning of 16th July 1945 and was completely successful. The war against Japan still remained, and it was agreed by the British and American delegations at the Potsdam conference that the bomb should be used against the Japanese. Churchill wrote in *The Second World War*: 'We seemed suddenly to have become possessed of a merciful abridgement of the slaughter in the East and of a far happier prospect in Europe. There was unanimous, automatic, unquestioned agreement around our table; nor did I hear the slightest suggestion that we should do otherwise.'

Many people, in fact, including myself, considered it was unnecessary to use the bomb against Japan. However the first atomic bomb was dropped on Hiroshima on 6th August 1945, and the second on Nagasaki on 8th August. Six days later the 1939/45 war was over.

But the scientists continued their work to develop an even more powerful bomb; the first H-bomb explosion took place in the Pacific in 1952. Russia was not far behind the United States in developing nuclear weapons; Russian scientists had exploded their first atomic bomb in 1949, and had the H-bomb in 1953. In September 1954, a Japanese fisherman died from jaundice brought on by radiation sickness caused by exposure to 'fall-out' – and public opinion throughout the world became alarmed, demanding a suspension of testing in the atmosphere – and this was agreed in 1958. But then came a characteristic development. In 1962 President Kennedy announced that the United States would resume nuclear testing in the atmosphere because Russia had broken the then existing moratorium. The president's statement contained the following paragraph:

> We must test in the atmosphere to permit the development of those more advanced concepts and more effective, efficient weapons which, in the light of Soviet tests, are deemed essential to our security. Nuclear weapon technology is still a constantly changing field. If our weapons are to be more secure, more flexible in their use and more selective in their impact – if we are to be alert to new break-throughs, to experiment with new designs – if we are to maintain our scientific momentum and leadership – then our weapons progress must not be limited to theory or to the confines of laboratories or caves.

The statement is valid. What then is the way out of the race? Both France and China now have a nuclear strike potential.

The H-bomb is not merely another weapon with greater destructive power. There are today in existence delivery systems which can take a bomb at ever increasing speeds to any target in the world; this amazing combination of firepower and mobility has revolutionized warfare. In bygone days offensive action to capture or destroy a military objective took many weeks or months; today, one single H-bomb could do the job in moments. The total weight of bombs dropped by the Allies during the 1939/45 war both in the European and Pacific theatres was about 3½ million tons; expressed in nuclear parlance this figure would be 3.5 megatons – which is less than the yield of one medium-sized H-bomb or missile warhead. To get an idea of the explosive power of a single multi-megaton H-bomb let us assume that the weapon has struck the centre of a city. The explosion produces a crater about 350 feet deep, and 3,700 feet in diameter. Beyond this crater a 'lip' of radio-active debris extends outwards for approximately 1,800 feet, and to a height of nearly 100 feet. The resulting fireball is 2 to 4 miles in diameter and temperatures within it may reach millions of degrees. All matter within that area, living and inanimate, has been pulverized, and lingering radio-activity will make it impossible to rebuild this area within very many years. In addition to the blast effects which have caused this damage, the heat has started fires; widespread devastation, raging fires, electrical short circuits, and millions of casualties extend to some 18 miles from the centre of the city. Heavy radio-active fall-out starts raining down on this area within 20 minutes after detonation of the bomb, and will last up to half-an-hour before subsiding. And for 48 hours after the time of burst, a lethal fall-out pattern some 18 miles wide will extend downwind for about 130 miles – resulting in further heavy casualties. All this can be caused by one single H-bomb.

This, then, is the weapon the fear of which has prevented all-out war for a quarter of a century. No matter how successful a surprise attack might be, an aggressor could not escape a terrible degree of retaliation. The stakes in all-out nuclear war are too high to warrant a gamble in the matter. The outcome of the Cuban crisis of 1962 was reassuring. Yet it is possible that the principle of deterrence could fail, if a political leader should lose his sense or nerve. For example, the crunch might come when a nuclear power waging a conventional war against another nuclear power found itself likely to lose. Would it then, as a last resort, try to snatch victory by using a nuclear weapon at a decisive moment? Probably not, but there is no absolute certainty.

Unfortunately, we are faced with the ironical fact that while nuclear war seems capable of destroying society, the means to avert it consist in building up the means to wage it. What we must hope for is some measure of arms control; pending agreement on this problem, prevention of nuclear war will depend on the maintenance of a balance of political and military forces between East and West. But such a balance can easily be upset – a new weapon, a new defence system, a new method of attack, any striking innovation could disrupt the balance and give an advantage to one side. And there is no certainty that world leaders will always be men of such statesman-like courage as President Kennedy.

Some have said that the chances of preventing nuclear war lie in the creation of some supranational authority or world government to control relations between states. The difficulties in any such solution to the problem are insuperable. The United Nations is merely a mirror of a divided world, a battleground of the cold war rather than a resolver of it. The most which might be possible at present is to prevent the proliferation of nuclear weapons beyond the existing nuclear powers.

So long as peaceful partnership between the nations of East and West is not possible, the only sound strategy for national security on the part of major powers is the maintenance of both nuclear deterrent and conventional forces. This, of course, makes the respite unstable and uncertain. And meanwhile scientists on both sides pursue their investigations to produce even more powerful weapons, while service chiefs wrestle with the problem of designing a strategy for their deployment in the nuclear age. The prospects for nuclear disarmament are dim; the destruction of all nuclear weapons would not destroy the knowledge of how to make them. As one writer has put it: 'Pandora's box, having once been opened, can hardly be closed.'

We must not, however, rely on diplomatic relations standing still in the nuclear age. Equally, in any military organization there is no surer way to disaster than to take what has been done for many years, and to go on doing it – *the problem having changed*. Seapower, for example, will in the future be operated differently from in the past, because of the impact of science on warfare. Navies will go increasingly under the sea, their main armament being the submarine. Strike aircraft will give way to missiles. Until suitable V.T.O.L. aircraft capable of being operated from small ships can be produced, aircraft carriers will be required; by the 1980's the large carrier may well disappear from the navies of world powers. The control of all available air power, land and sea based, will have to be centralized, with command of all arms exercised through one channel.

The more I consider the problem of defence the more I reach the conclusion that the answer lies basically in the ability to be able to use sea and air power freely, and to confine the enemy to a land strategy. Only in this way will the maximum flexibility be possible. The Western Alliance, to which my nation belongs, must plan to be so well and flexibly deployed that it can deal quickly and effectively with all situations, including the unlikely and the unexpected – an elastic deployment based on a maritime strategy. This demands unity and leadership. When planning defence, and deciding the best organization for armed forces, a *long-term* strategy is essential. I am doubtful whether the West is best served by a multitude of fixed land bases. They may in a crisis suddenly be found to be facing in the wrong direction. They tend to cramp force-mobility. They are hostages to fortune. Those which are considered essential must not be in territory where the local inhabitants are none too friendly, or may not be friendly for long – in fact such bases make good propaganda for enemies of the West. Armies must go to sea.

These points are merely the outline of a very big problem. But when all is said and done, it is essential to remember that the true and ultimate strength of a nation does not lie in its armed forces, nor in its gold and dollar reserves. It lies in the national character, in its people – in their virility, in their willingness to work, in their understanding of the truth that if they want prosperity and economic strength they must get it for themselves or else go without it.

This brings me to the end of my thoughts on war. The Epilogue – the Ideal of Peace – remains.

21 Epilogue · The Ideal of Peace

When reading my Bible one night I came across the following in Jeremiah:

> From the prophet even unto the priest every one dealeth falsely saying, Peace, peace – when there is no peace.

These words were probably written nearly 3,000 years ago; they apply equally today. Many who read this book will have had their fill of war, and know how tempting it is to paper over the cracks in the concord of the world.

Notwithstanding the progress in civilization, and the longing for peace in the minds of all decent people over the past 2,000 years or more, mankind has not been able to prevent the twentieth century from being the bloodiest and most turbulent period in recorded history. During the years of the Nazi regime in Germany things happened which could not find a parallel in the most debased days of the Roman or Mongol empires, crimes were committed which most people could not imagine – unless they had seen a place like Belsen, which I entered on the day of its liberation by my troops in April 1945. The wholesale liquidation of civilians was unprecedented. A study of the German assault on Russia which began in 1941 reveals scenes where 'the septic violence of German Nazism festered openly'. Mass murder, deportations, deliberate starvation in prisoner-of-war cages, the burning alive of school children, target practice on civilian hospitals – such atrocities were common under the warlike passions of German brutality in the Russian-German conflict.

All these things were the responsibility of one evil man – Hitler. Millions starved and died while he and his followers feasted. He parted the wife from her husband, the maid from her lover, the child from its parents. If he had lived he could never have given back what he had taken from those he had so cruelly wronged – years of life and health and happiness, wives and children, loved ones and friends. If he had had ten thousand lives they could not atone, even though each was dragged out to the bitter end in the misery which he meted out to others. The harnessing of the whole German national life to war ended in the complete destruction of the vanquished state; and the problem then arose of feeding a starving nation, as I know very well because that problem became my responsibility in the British zone of 20 million Germans. Things were much the same in the Far East with the Japanese – whose brutality equalled that of the Germans.

Is it possible that such things could happen again? Can others such as Hitler arise? These questions have to be faced by responsible political leaders. A study of warfare over the ages, with the many interlocking political and economic elements which erupt in armed conflict, should help to show us what to do to prevent it and find the answer we have not yet got.

We know that on the physical and material plane the keys of peace are in the hands of strength; the strong man armed keeps his goods in peace. But on the spiritual plane there is a stronger than he. The big battalions do not always win. Great occupying armies cannot for ever hold in check that which moves in the minds of people. The study of warfare brings to light spiritual values significant for the future.

What of the future? This is in the hands of youth, and these hands are at present unsteady. Youth is saying: 'Our fathers have made such a mess of things, we must break away and go on our own and do better.' But what better to do, they do not know. They tend to move towards materialism and pleasure – 'Gather ye rose-buds while ye may' – and think that devotion to peace as the condition of a pleasant, happy life was what their fathers lacked. But their peace-loving fathers fought for freedom and justice, without which the peace of cowed and enslaved peoples would have been hell on earth. The peace we now enjoy is the peace of victory over the beast in men, and this victory will not survive if the virtues which gained and sustain it are lost. What worth is peace without freedom, or freedom without justice between one man and another? The ideal of peace must not walk too closely with the temptress to a slack and easy life. We must marry the ideal of peace to the practice of virtue.

A nation must stand for something of spiritual and not only material value, and the key to the true life of the spirit is in religion. There is always a choice to be made, and I believe the Kingdom of God to be the right choice, and that those who choose it will never lack support. I wrote this in my *Memoirs*: 'I do not believe that today a commander can inspire great armies, or single units, or even individual men, unless he has a proper sense of religious truth. All leadership is based on the spiritual quality, the power to inspire others to follow.' But this lead will be of no avail unless others are inspired to accept it.

Peace is what we pray for – but if there must be war, let it be recognized that much good as well as much evil is released in war. When men are inspired to offer themselves to a high and noble cause, the hardships of war draw out of them their best qualities – comradeship, endurance, courage, self-sacrifice, willingness to die. This was expressed in a poem found in the Western Desert during the onward march of the Eighth Army after Alamein:

> Help me, O God, when Death is near
> To mock the haggard face of fear,
> That when I fall – if fall I must –
> My soul may triumph in the Dust.

To that spirit I have unveiled many memorials. When I unveiled the Alamein Memorial in the Western Desert of Egypt in October 1954 and gazed over the scene, the crosses standing row after row, each one a life dear to someone at home, I could not but think that there is no merit in needless loss of life – indeed, nothing but shame and folly. The lives of men should be precious; they are not to be risked without cause, nor used when other means will serve.

But there are times in war when men must do a hazardous job, when a position must be held or taken whatever the cost, and when a nation's fate depends on the courage, determination and tenacity of officers and men. Then those who set duty before self give their lives to see the task committed to them through to its completion; they win the day and, in our Christian faith, a higher honour than mortal man can give. And for the immortal virtue of that choice, the crosses stand – whatever the religion, faith, or form of worship.

Through the mists of years, through the gulfs of twilight, could we but listen hard enough, we might catch some message of hope and encouragement from those who gave their lives – a message which would help us to create a better world than that in which they lived:

> We are the Dead . . .
> To you from failing hands we throw
> The torch; be yours to hold it high.
> If ye break faith with us who die,
> We shall not sleep . . .

There must be no broken faith with the torch of Justice and Freedom which they threw to us.

The true soldier is the enemy of the beast in man and of none other; and it is a soldier's prayer that one day will come a golden sunset when the Last Post will be sounded over enmity and strife, and a glorious sunrise when Reveille will waken the nations of the world to an era of goodwill and peace.

Acknowledgments for Illustrations

The producers wish to express their thanks to the trustees and staffs of the libraries, galleries and museums, and to the individuals, who have allowed objects from their collections to be reproduced in this book, and to the photographers who have supplied copyright illustrations, as listed below.

Index

The symbol ✕ indicates battles.